Critical
Issues in
Qualitative
Research
Methods

edited by
Janice M. Morse

SAGE Publications
International Educational and Professional Publisher
Thousand Oaks   London   New Delhi

For information address:

 SAGE Publications, Inc.
2455 Teller Road
Thousand Oaks, California 91320

SAGE Publications Ltd.
6 Bonhill Street
London EC2A 4PU
United Kingdom

SAGE Publications India Pvt. Ltd.
M-32 Market
Greater Kailash I
New Delhi 110 048 India

Printed in the United States of America

Library of Congress Cataloging-in-Publication Data

Main entry under title:

Critical issues in qualitative research methods/editor, Janice M.
   Morse.
      p. cm.
   Based on a two day "think tank" symposium held in Nov. 1992 at
Samuel Merritt College, Oakland, Calif.
   Companion v. to: Qualitative nursing research/edited by Janice
M. Morse. ©1991.
   Includes bibliographical references and index.
   ISBN 0-8039-5042-X (cl).–ISBN 0-8039-5043-8 (pb)
   1. Nursing–Research–Methodology. 2. Sociology–Methodology.
I. Morse, Janice M. II. Qualitative nursing research.
   [DNLM: 1. Nursing Research–methods–congresses. W Y 20.5 C9345
1994]
RT81.5.C75   1994
610.73'072–dc20
DNLM/DLC   93-34535

94 95 96 97 10 9 8 7 6 5 4 3

Sage Production Editor: Diane S. Foster

Contents

Preface   x

Dialogue: On Origins   xii
1. Qualitative Research: Fact or Fantasy?   1
   JANICE M. MORSE

Dialogue: On Learning Qualitative Methods   8
2. Abstract Knowing:
   The Case for Magic in Method   10
   KATHARYN A. MAY

Dialogue: More on Theory   22
3. "Emerging From the Data":
   The Cognitive Processes of
   Analysis in Qualitative Inquiry   23
   JANICE M. MORSE

Dialogue: The Democracy of Interpretation   44
4. The Proof Is in the Pottery:
   Toward a Poetic for Qualitative Inquiry   46
   MARGARETE SANDELOWSKI

Dialogue: On Qualitatively Derived Intervention   64

5. Inside the Black Box: Theoretical and
   Methodological Issues in Conducting
   Evaluation Research Using
   a Qualitative Approach   66
   JANICE M. SWANSON and LINDA CHAPMAN

Dialogue: Basic Versus Applied Ethnography   94

6. Evaluation Criteria and Critique of Qualitative
   Research Studies   95
   MADELEINE LEININGER

Dialogue: Good Phenomenology Is . . .   116

7. The Richness of Phenomenology:
   Philosophic, Theoretic, and
   Methodologic Concerns   117
   MARILYN A. RAY

Dialogue: Clarifying Phenomenological Methods   134

8. Schools of Phenomenology:
   Implications for Research   136
   MARLENE ZICHI COHEN and ANNA OMERY

Dialogue: On Emic and Etic   158

9. Styles of Ethnography   159
   JOYCEEN S. BOYLE

Dialogue: Sorting Out the Styles . . .   186

10. On the Evaluation of Ethnographies   187
    MARJORIE A. MUECKE

Dialogue: More on Muddling Methods   210

11. Eroding Grounded Theory   212
    PHYLLIS NOERAGER STERN

Dialogue: Questions About Focus Groups   224

12. The Group Effect in Focus Groups:
Planning, Implementing, and
Interpreting Focus Group Research   225
MARTHA ANN CAREY

Dialogue: Using Videotaped Data   242

13. Using Videotaped Recordings in Qualitative
Research   244
JOAN L. BOTTORFF

Dialogue: On Mentoring   262

14. Secondary Analysis in Qualitative Research:
Issues and Implications   263
SALLY THORNE

Dialogue: On Writing It Up   280

15. Qualitative Research Methods From the
Reviewer's Perspective   281
MELANIE DREHER

Dialogue: Researcher-Participant Relationships   298

16. Research and Therapeutic Interviews:
A Poststructuralist Perspective   300
SALLY HUTCHINSON and HOLLY WILSON

Dialogue: On Being a Stranger in the Field   316

17. Research Teams: Possibilities and Pitfalls in
Collaborative Qualitative Research   318
*TONI TRIPP-REIMER, BERNARD SOROFMAN,
JENNIFER PETERS, and JAMES E. WATERMAN*

Dialogue: The Politics of Writing   332

18. Ethical Issues in Ethnography   333
JULIENE G. LIPSON

Dialogue: Sloppy Science   356

19. Promoting Academic Integrity in
        Qualitative Research   357
    KATHLEEN A. KNAFL

    Author Index   375

    Subject Index   383

    About the Authors   388

To those who participate in our projects

We are trying to find ways
to communicate what you know
so that others may understand

Preface

This book is intended to supplement and complement *Qualitative Nursing Research: A Contemporary Dialogue* (Morse, 1991). The dialogues between the chapters are portions of the discussion at the 2-day symposium. They are intended to stimulate and permit the reader to consider important issues facing qualitative research in the 1990s. Often there are no real answers to the questions, and such struggles are revealed in these discussions. Each chapter has an introduction by the author—a summary or a short statement that highlights the unresolved issues in the writing.

Whereas the first book addressed a variety of unresolved issues in qualitative methodology, this book is more focused, targeting issues in the quality of qualitative research. It addresses lesser known or explicated qualitative research methods (e.g., ethology, focus groups), the mysterious processes of insight when developing theory from data, the essential concepts of rigor and evaluation, dilemmas in data collection, and issues of scientific misconduct.

Similar to the first book, the chapters are a result of a 2-day "think tank," this time held in November 1992 at Samuel Merritt College, Oakland, California. Participants prepared and circulated chapters beforehand. During the meeting the papers were discussed, debated, and generally sorted out. Authors then retreated to various parts of the country to revise their chapters.

The final drafts were reviewed by selected participants and were returned to the authors for "polishing." Thus, as in the previous volume, the chapters are the sum of the group's thinking, the product of their debates, and are a reflection of the status quo of qualitative research.

Present at the symposium were Joan Bottorff, University of British Columbia; Joyceen Boyle, Medical College of Georgia; Martha Ann Carey, National Institute for Nursing Research, NIH; Marlene Cohen, University of Southern California; Melanie Dreher, University of Massachusetts; Mary Duffy, University of Utah; Jill Hoggard-Green, University of Utah; Sally Hutchinson, University of Florida Health Sciences Center; Katharyn May, Vanderbilt University; Kathy Knafl, University of Illinois, Chicago; Jan Morse, Pennsylvania State University; Marjorie Muecke, University of Washington; Madeleine Leininger, Wayne State University; Juliene Lipson, University of California, San Francisco; Marilyn Ray, Florida Atlantic University; Christine Smedley, Sage Publications; Margarete Sandelowski, University of North Carolina, Chapel Hill; Phyllis Stern, Indiana University; Janice Swanson, Samuel Merritt College; Sally Thorne, University of British Columbia; and Holly Wilson, University of California, San Francisco.

I am most appreciative of Anna Lombard, State College, Pennsylvania, for her organizational abilities in the preparation of the manuscripts. I thank those who contributed to this volume; deadlines were tight, work was demanding, yet you gave of your time and your expertise freely and with laughter. Thank you. We are indebted to Janice Swanson and Abby Heydan, Dean, Samuel Merritt College, for their hospitality during the two meeting days. Finally we are indebted to Christine Smedley, Senior Nursing Editor, Sage Publications, for her support and encouragement of nursing scholarship.

References

Morse, J. M. (1991). *Qualitative nursing research: A contemporary dialogue* (rev. ed.). Newbury Park, CA: Sage.

JANICE M. MORSE
The Pennsylvania State University

Dialogue

On Origins

BOYLE Can you do phenomenology by just looking at recently published phenomenology? Or do you need to go back and look at
Heidegger and Husserl?

MAY Oh, that's a good question—

BOYLE Because that affects all of us. Do you need to go back to the
originals?

MAY I'm mind-reading here [for those who choose not to do it]—but by
dragging the great ones with us you sometimes obfuscate the
method and make it unclear.

COHEN One of the difficulties of phenomenology [is that] phenomenologists are not noted for their clear language, and it is very
difficult material to understand, but it's material we need to try to
understand.

MAY Yes—I know that I am on dangerous turf here when I suggest that
the language be simplified because the language is the essence,
the words are on purpose. And I would imagine that it is difficult
to communicate the complexity of meaning when you try to strip
the language down enough. So leave the learned language, but
translate it.

1

Qualitative Research: Fact or Fantasy?

JANICE M. MORSE

> If I go out into nature, into the unknown, to the fringes of knowledge, everything seems mixed up and contradictory, illogical and incoherent. This is what research does; it smoothes out contradiction and makes things simple, logical and coherent. (Szent-Györgyi, 1980)

Obviously, those who like to "do" science in order to discover and live on the fringes of knowledge should be qualitative researchers. In Szent-Györgyi's (1980) terms, the reality that qualitative researchers address is "contradictory, illogical and incoherent." Qualitative methods "smooth out" those contradictions and are in themselves a mysterious combination of strategies for collecting images of reality. The process of doing qualitative research presents a challenge because procedures for organizing images are ill-defined and rely on processes of inference, insight, logic, and luck, and eventually, with creativity and hard work, the results emerge as a coherent whole. The laboratory of the qualitative researcher is everyday life and cannot be contained in a test tube, started, stopped, manipulated, or washed down the sink. Variables are not controlled, and until qualitative researchers get close to the end of a study, they may not even be able to determine what those variables are. Therefore, theory development, description, and operationalization are often the outcomes. They are the products of the research process, rather than the means, and the tools used while conducting research.

There is no doubt that important work is conducted using qualitative inquiry. Science begins with observations, and these observations lay the theoretical foundation and determine the conceptual parameters of the discipline. It is on this foundation that the more clearly defined quantitative methods test and refine a growing body of knowledge.

Qualitative work is thus essential to the knowledge development of the health care disciplines, yet this foundation has been established most unevenly. In clinical medicine, for example, the large compendium of signs and symptoms used in diagnoses was developed informally over several centuries by thoughtful physicians carefully observing the sick and noting and teaching the characteristic patterns that accompanied patients' illnesses. However, one exception was obstetrics. Until the last century, male physicians interested in obstetrics had limited access to pregnant and laboring women. Thus present day obstetrical texts are relatively devoid of descriptions of the normal behavioral signs of the progress of labor, with physicians relying on monitors and pelvic examination to determine the stage of labor.

Because of this long (albeit informal) history of qualitative inquiry, current research in medicine may be grouped broadly as the precise measurement of competing therapies (as in clinical drug trials), or research identifying illness causation and innovative therapies at the cellular or organ system level. Both of these research agendas require an enormous amount of basic research that contributes the knowledge base that forms the foundation of their research agendas.

In comparison, the discipline of nursing has only several decades of research forming its foundation. As nursing is a relative newcomer to the research arena, the foundation of knowledge that is relevant to and developed from the clinical area is thin and has been borrowed carte blanche from other disciplines. Elsewhere I have argued that this uncritical adoption and application of concepts and theories from other disciplines is a compromise solution for nursing science (Morse et al., 1982). There is now an urgent need to reexamine this acquired theoretical base and to develop concepts and theories relevant to nursing's own clinical reality. Until this step is completed, there will be a poor fit between the practitioner's clinical reality and nursing's actual knowledge base.

Nursing is beginning to address this weighty problem. As qualitative research is considered to be "soft" and less sophisticated than quantitative research, qualitative research may receive lower priority ratings in the review committee meetings; should this occur, nursing as a discipline will be handicapped in the rush to obtain research funds. Furthermore, disciplines with long histories of supporting a cadre of researchers have a well-developed theoretical base. They have operationalized variables and have established procedures and means for measurement that are reliable and valid, so they will continue to be perceived as more rigorous and more scientific. Qualitative research methods are, in comparison, poorly described and lack prescriptive procedures, so that often individual investigators tend to adapt techniques, rather than adhere to the recommended protocols. Because the goals of qualitative research are generally the development of theory, description, explanation, and understanding, rather than precise testing of hypotheses to the fourth decimal place, social science—and, in particular, qualitative methods—appear to the quantitative researcher as so crude that they may not even be classified as science (see Diamond, 1987). Therefore, it is time to "get our act together" and move qualitative research from the accusations of "fantasy" phase to the more concrete phase of accepted reality. Working outside the mainstream of science is challenging and difficult, but as Szent-Györgyi (1971) noted, it is the curious, creative, and committed scientists who are willing to take risks and investigate ambiguous, difficult problems where the outcome cannot be predicted—or publication guaranteed—who will make the most important contribution to their discipline.

In all fairness, the stigma and accusations that have followed qualitative researchers are not entirely unwarranted. Qualitative researchers have been slow to explain exactly what they do and how conclusions are reached (see, e.g., the criticism by Downs, 1983). Few attempts have been made to untangle the methodological ambiguities, the disagreements among methodologists about the best way to proceed, and which protocols are right. There is even disagreement about the terminology used to refer to relatively common procedures. And the findings oft~ ~~~ ~~ insight or intuition, so the processes for arriving at c(are difficult to document. New investigators become as they are told that the only way to learn to do "good" work is to find a mentor who will teach them to *think qualitatively*. Although finding a mentor is difficult, it is just not possible to become a qualitative researcher by following written directions, and although mentors are necessary, they are scarce.

This book is an attempt to begin to correct some of these problems. More specifically, it is an attempt to address the issue of "soundness" of qualitative research. Some of these topics have been addressed previously in the literature. Other topics have been approached, but not directly, or have been addressed in other fields, in other contexts, and the special problems inherent in conducting qualitative clinical research have not yet been discussed. Other chapters break new ground, with those authors plunging into unexplored territory.

The soundness of qualitative methodology is the most urgent challenge for those researchers interested in the growth of qualitative inquiry. *Soundness* has to do with the certainty of the qualitative results. It also has to do with the acceptability of the qualitative approach and the "softness" of the method.

The question Are you sure? has ramifications for the entire field. It is more than an issue of methodological protocol (How do you *do it?*) and more than demonstrating reliability and validity (How do you *know?*). The issue of certainty permeates the entire research process—from the selection of the topic to publication, implementation, and beyond. The confidence that one has in qualitative inquiry affects what is studied and why, for inquiry is limited by our tools or methods, and what we cannot study remains beyond our reach. Some would argue that what we study is also limited by our perception, for perception limits what we may see as a research problem.

How do you do it? is an interesting question. Until a decade ago, methods books were relatively rare for some qualitative methods, ethnography perhaps being the exception. In the case of phenomenology, this rarity is still probably true.

The question on how closely one adheres to the original "masters" was discussed and is introduced in the dialogue preceding this chapter. In addition to the question raised in this dialogue, many others emerge as the researcher moves through the process of "doing" qualitative research. For example, if the researcher deviates from the developer's protocol, is the researcher still using the original method? What are the ramifications of such deviations? If researchers cannot "deviate," how will the method be modified so that the field may advance? Furthermore, if qualitative methods are revised or new ones are developed, who will undertake the task, and how will this work be funded?

Already researcher funding is diminished for all research; qualitative methods are no exception. But funding becomes an extraordinary problem when granting agencies also are required to have faith in a product, to "buy" a product, before even the researcher is certain that the product will be useful and important.

How we do research has implications for the choice of research method, of what we consider as "legitimate data," and for the quantity of data collected before the data set "saturates." The issue includes our choice for method of analysis, the role of insight, and to what level of abstraction we choose to push the findings. These issues direct the researcher, and the onus is on the qualitative researcher to become more versatile and expert in the use of qualitative methods.

When the "finished" qualitative results are submitted to a journal for publication, the editor and the reviewers must share our standards of rigor, for they will inspect—and perhaps approve—the work for soundness, uniqueness, and significance. It is important to ask, "How much of the methods must be described so that the reviewers and the readers understand exactly what was done and how the results were derived?" As editor of *Qualitative Health Research,* I read many detailed but remarkably similar descriptions of ethnography or grounded theory methods in submitted manuscripts. Will qualitative research ever get confidence enough to move to the point where our quantitative colleagues state what method was used, provide a reference, and move on?

How do you know? or issues of reliability are addressed in this issue by Leininger (Chapter 6), who points out that addressing reliability and validity in qualitative research is such a different process that quantitative labels should not be used. Many qualitative researchers are struggling with this issue. Quantitative labels may or may not be obscuring the process. It is clear that the jury is still out.

The interface between "reliability and validity" issues and methodological issues is important, especially in the analysis process. In this volume, Dreher (Chapter 15) eloquently labels problems of this nature as problems with "the democracy of interpretation." Although standards of rigor in qualitative research ensure that alternative explanations are discounted or accounted for in the emerging model, the possible range of explanations produced are under the control of the conscientious care and creativity of the researcher. Therefore, as with all research, the product is only as good as the investigator.

This book is an attempt to address comprehensively the issues of soundness of qualitative research. Some topics previously addressed in *Qualitative Nursing Research: A Contemporary Dialogue* are addressed differently in this volume. Other topics, although covered elsewhere, are discussed more directly or are brought to new fields, new contexts, and cover the special problems inherent in conducting clinical research. Finally, some chapters break new ground, with those authors plunging into unexplored territory.

In brief, the first two chapters address the issue of theory development. May (Chapter 2) examines the role of insight, of how students learn to acquire the conceptual skills necessary to conduct qualitative inquiry. Morse (Chapter 3), on the other hand, tackles the issue of how theory "emerges" from data. The approach of these two authors is different: May, in arguing for insight, is more inclined to make a plea for magic (with the post hoc ability to trace the clues that resulted in the insight), and Morse for hard labor, persistence, data preparation, and a lot of earnest thinking and discussion.

Swanson and Chapman (Chapter 5) address qualitative evaluation research, which is employed to determine exactly what happens when an intervention is used. These two authors have written a pragmatic chapter addressing this lesser known application of qualitative methods. In a subsequent chapter, Bottorff (Chapter 13) describes an observational method using videotaped data. She notes that with the increasing use of video systems in clinical areas, videotaped data will be more commonly available and more easily used in the future. The use of focus groups research methods are becoming popular and provide a relatively fast and efficient method of collecting data. Carey (Chapter 12) addresses the paradoxical, yet unanswered, questions regarding this method of data collection and discusses the management of the group effect when conducting group interviews.

The various schools of phenomenological tradition are explicated by Cohen and Omery (Chapter 8). They provide a very nice signpost to a confusing field. Then the major characteristics of excellence in phenomenology are described by Ray (Chapter 7). Two parallel chapters are provided for ethnography, with Boyle (Chapter 9) addressing types of ethnographic research and Muecke (Chapter 10) presenting evaluation criteria. Stern (Chapter 11) examines the present divergence between Glaserian and Straussian methods. A long-neglected topic—the secondary analysis of qualitative data sets—is addressed by Thorne (Chapter 14).

In the final chapters, Dreher (Chapter 15) offers invaluable advice for preparing qualitative proposals: the essence is being clear. Lipson (Chapter 18) also discusses being clear about what one is doing and what one has done regarding ethical issues in qualitative research, while Knafl (Chapter 19) discusses being clear about issues regarding scientific integrity.

Although, in this book, we cannot possibly address all of the critical issues facing qualitative researchers, we do hope this book will make a contribution to advancing qualitative research. In the field of scientific inquiry, we do know that if a problem is not resolved, at least the questions can be better understood. We therefore are trying to strengthen qualitative methods, to pave the way for the next generation of qualitative researchers, and to show that qualitative research is not a process of creating fantasy, but fact.

References

Diamond, J. (1987). Soft sciences are often harder than hard sciences. *Discover, 8*(8), 34-39.

Downs, F. (1983). "One dark and stormy night." *Nursing Research, 32*(5), 259.

Morse, J. M., Anderson, G., Bottorff, J. L., Yonge, O., O'Brien, B., Solberg, S. M., & McIlveen, K. H. (1982). Exploring empathy: A conceptual fit for nursing practice? *Image: Journal of Nursing Scholarship, 24*(4), 273-280.

Szent-Györgyi, A. (1971). Looking back. *Perspectives in Biology and Medicine, 15,* 1-5.

Szent-Györgyi, A. (1980). Dionysians and Apollonians. In M. R. Key (Ed.), *The relationship of verbal and non-verbal communication* (pp. 317-318). New York: Mouton.

Dialogue

On Learning Qualitative Methods

MAY You can describe methods and technique to a point—and it's like that cartoon—"and then a miracle occurs!" And I can't tell you that this is good work and this is bad work. I can only tell you that this is good work and this is thin. It doesn't matter if you audit my trail till hell comes home—while I'm in the process, there is a semantic shift. I feel a shift and I know it's right! I can justify the conclusion backwards, but I can't tell you what you must do to get there.

THORNE If we say it is magic, then are we contributing to the problem of people thinking it is magic and mixing methods?

MAY You are right! [To evaluate methods] I would want to know your academic pedigree. I want to know who you studied with, and for how long, and what you read, and if I agree with that, then I'll buy your magic. You know, that's a really stupid way to make a decision, but that's what I work with.

STERN Yeah. But I've stopped looking to see if I'm on the reference list—[laughter].

MAY I facetiously talk about pedigrees. But if you accept for a moment that there is a level of technique here that is not teachable, then how you learn and from whom you learn becomes critical. There is an account that describes how lasers were invented. And the scientists who were working at a geographical distance from each other could not move forward. It was only when the scientists were brought together that they could communicate the uncommunicatable knowledge, and it was only at that point that they invented this thing they had known for years was theoretically possible. I think teaching grounded theory method is the same. You have to watch the fire in the eye when the expert analyst gets it. That's how I learned from Anselm [Strauss]. I would watch for the fire and then try to figure out how he got there. And then after a while I sort of knew. Now, I can't tell you how I know, but I know.

BOTTORFF But if you call it magic, it sounds as if you just sit there long enough this magic will happen. And it doesn't! It comes with hard work and working with someone who has done it before.

STERN Well, I can elaborate on that somewhat. The student who said
    that [it was magic] did not actually collect data and do the analysis.
    She audited the class. She did not understand what happened. We
    would sit there in the seminar and somebody would say something
    and it would start playing back and forth, and whoever was chief
    analyst for that day would say "This is ____ ." That's what makes it
    seem like magic.
HUTCHINSON I see now the problems that my students have that have
    to do with the magic. It's the idea of mental immersion—like when
    you are driving, you have to constantly think about it. It's constant
    questioning. They don't understand that you have to think, think,
    think, think over and over again to have the magic happen. It just
    doesn't happen in class.
SWANSON It's passion, too!
ALL Right—Magic and passion!

2

Abstract Knowing:
The Case for Magic in Method

KATHARYN A. MAY

I tried to take this from a very pragmatic level, and back up and ask: What is the analytic experience of knowing—the day-to-day lived work of the research?—and bounce this off the very sparse methodological literature. How does the scientist decide what is known, in the context of the scientist's own work? Those of us in qualitative work have dodged the issue—the process of moving to insight is "out there" somewhere, and it is not accessible to me in the phenomenological literature, largely because of the language. Grounded theorists are no better. We talk about "emerging from the data"—which is garbage. We DRAG it out of the data! [BOYLE: We suspected that!] So I decided to take a straightforward route to creativity, reasoned decision making, and the nursing literature on personal knowing. Then I realized that the description in my head of how I move through data is related to Benner's work (not Benner's method, but Benner's product). So I extrapolated from Benner's description of expert judgment to expert practice in the world of qualitative research.

> In the long, narrow office on Speichergasse, the room full of practical ideas, the young patent clerk sprawls in his chair, head down on his desk. For the past several months, since the middle of April, he has dreamed many dreams about time. His dreams have taken hold of his research. His dreams have worn him out, exhausted him so that he sometimes cannot tell whether he is awake or asleep. But the dreaming is finished. Out of many possible natures of time, imagined in as many nights, one seems compelling. Not that the others are impossible. The others might exist in other worlds. (Lightman, 1993, pp. 6-7

Describing and defining the process of "knowing" is a central concern to those who write about and do science. The question *How does the scientist decide what is known (in the context of his or her own work)?* or, perhaps more precisely, *When does the scientist know?* is a question that has concerned philosophers and scientists for decades. The question becomes more complex if one accepts the premise that knowledge comes to the scientist in various forms and in various ways and when it is framed from the perspective of a practice discipline. As Schultz and Meleis (1988) noted:

> If we agree that there are different ways of knowing, different unknowns to be known, different propensities of knowers for knowing and different aspects to be known about the same phenomenon, then perhaps we can develop appropriate criteria for knowing from what we do know, and then, for knowing what we want to know. (p. 221)

Contemporary dialogue in nursing suggests that the discipline is prepared to acknowledge the complexity of knowledge building in all of its forms and to wrestle with the notion of "tacit" or "practitioner" knowledge as distinct from "scientific" knowledge (Meerabeau, 1992). However, even within the realm of scientific work are multiple levels of discussion and concern regarding the nature of abstract knowledge.

At one level, debate about the nature of abstract knowledge is the central concern of epistemology, and scholars typically approach this question from lofty conceptual heights (Chisholm, 1982). This debate, however, lacks the specificity demanded by those who seek to argue for the validity of their intellectual work and to convince others that "knowledge" is the result of their efforts. Thus, at another level, methodological experts approach more closely; they outline processes of data collection and analysis and speak in general terms about how the analyst will "know." At the most practical level, individual investigators argue the truth value of their findings-based methodologic rigor. They present evidence that appropriate methods have been applied appropriately, that the logical processes in the analysis can be discerned; thus they assert that the result of their work is "knowledge" and therefore distinguished from "opinion" or "conjecture."

Those who work primarily in the qualitative paradigm come to grips with the question When does the scientist know? on a rather fundamental and pragmatic level. Because qualitative work is not yet considered to be mainstream science, its proponents continually face challenges based on the truth value of their work. It is not that mainstream scientists are completely unconcerned with epistemological questions, it is simply that they have relegated those questions to the lofty domain of the philosophers of science.

The accepted conventions of mainstream science provide a structure in which replicability of procedures and verifiability of findings are the standards of "good science." The answer to the question *When?* is provided by an agreed-upon reliance on the probabilistic model and the ubiquitous statement "$p \leq .05$." At that very point in time, the scientist in the positivist paradigm "knows." To be slightly facetious, one might say that knowing depends on where the p-value is set and how comfortable the scientist is with being wrong. Although it is certainly not that simple, the example does point out that the rules regarding knowledge are clearer in the positivist paradigm. Because findings are seen to be a direct product of the observable processes of science and therefore can be verified and replicated, they are judged to be knowledge. The internal ("between the ears") processes whereby the mainstream scientist arrived at knowledge are ignored, and only the external ("observable and describable") processes are considered to be important.

However, the question of *when* the scientist knows is somewhat more complicated for those engaged in qualitative research. The very nature of the work itself requires the scientist to create a structure that fits observations, rather than to fit observations into an a priori agreed-upon structure. As in Lightman's (1993) fantasy about Einstein's dreams, qualitative analysts must select paths through complex and voluminous data sets, because not all paths can be explored, and must decide which is the most compelling direction, because there are many possible directions to pursue.

Although the method's analytic processes provide considerable guidance in making these decisions, it is also true that the qualitative analyst, at times, has to go with a "gut feeling." Seasoned investigators acknowledge the importance of the hunch or the feeling. Critics of qualitative research, however, are quick to point out that, although intuition and creativity may lead to insight, the journey is not predictable and replicable. Thus, to the extent that qualitative methods rely on such nonobservable and nonmeasurable processes, they are vulnerable to the criticism that they are, inherently, nonscientific.

I argue that rigorous implementation and explication of method alone never explains the process of abstract knowing, regardless of which paradigm the scientist espouses and which method is chosen. Method does not produce insight or understanding or the creative leap that the agile mind makes in the struggle to comprehend observations and to link them together. Regardless of the paradigmatic perspective held by the scientist, the process of knowing itself cannot be observed and measured directly, but only indirectly by its product. What the scientist thinks, does, records, and analyzes can be described and accounted for, but the specific internal process whereby the scientist "knows" cannot be laid out for inspection.

The scientist can backtrack to explain lines of thought, patterns of introspection, and mental conditions at the time of the insight. Nevertheless, these preexisting conditions do not explain how knowing was achieved. Knowing, in both paradigms, is to a certain extent a "black box" phenomenon: We can identify input and output, but what happens between the two is sometimes unknown.

An interesting difference, however, occurs between the positivist and qualitative paradigms in when knowing occurs. Work in the positivist paradigm is usually linear and is seen to proceed logically from previously established knowledge. The starting point is a highly structured view of the phenomenon of interest. The conduct of research serves to verify or refute previous knowledge that was held to be provisional in nature. How the scientist comes to this highly differentiated view is preamble to, rather than the substance of, research.

How well the scientist selects and relates the various components of this highly differentiated view is virtually always the element that distinguishes powerful explanation from predictable and uninspiring description. In the positivist paradigm, the important intellectual work is finished long before the first datum is collected and begins again only when the numbers, having been crunched and printed out, must now be explained. Despite the verifiable measurements and reproducible procedures, the knowing cannot be explained by method alone; it can be understood only by retracing the scientist's intellectual journey through juxtaposition of concepts to examine, generation of hypotheses to test, and explanation of what the numbers mean.

In the qualitative paradigm, the knowing occurs at a different point in the process. In this case the starting point for investigation is typically a somewhat undifferentiated view. The conduct of the research serves to move the analyst to a simultaneously more differentiated and abstract view of the phenomenon (which is the product and may be called "understanding," "rich description," or "theory"). How the scientist comes to this more abstract view is the process as well as the substance of the research. However, how well the scientist chooses which hunch to play out and which of the many possible explanations is the one to work on is virtually always the element that distinguishes powerful explanation from predictable and uninspired description.

Thus, from the perspective of understanding how the scientist knows in the qualitative paradigm, one must recognize that important but unexplained intellectual work is embedded deep in the analytic processes themselves. Expert qualitative analysts can always explain their analytic processes and can recount the sequence of cognitive operations they carried out that preceded discovery, as Morse describes in Chapter 3. Technique and rigor, however, cannot entirely explain what moved the analyst from confusion to insight, from chaos to order, and from simple description to understanding. The product (knowledge) is shaped *but not completely defined* by the process through which it was created.

Thus I conclude that the question, *When does the scientist in the qualitative paradigm know?* requires us to consider elements that transcend method. In all realms of science, and perhaps most specifically in qualitative research, is a point past which knowing cannot be explained. Past this point, we must attribute insight to immeasurables and unobservables such as intuition and creativity—what I call only for the purposes of this chapter, "magic." I choose the word quite carefully, not unmindful of the controversy I create by doing so. I hope that, in inviting controversy, I also invite discussion and debate.

Let me be quick to point out that giving credence to creativity and intuition does not give permission for methodologic or intellectual sloppiness. In fact, the two are often not compatible bedfellows. Intuition, creativity, and intellectual agility are most often found operating within the context of careful and rigorous attention to method (Perkins, 1981). Care and precision are necessary in qualitative work, just as they are in any other kinds of inquiry. Insight achieved through intuition and creativity must be evaluated through the use of appropriate analytic techniques, just as it is in hypothetico-deductive research. In both cases the scientist must turn to systematic data collection and analysis for evidence to substantiate or refute the tentative conclusion.

To rely solely on the compelling feeling about the scientific problem is inappropriate in either paradigm; the scientist then must proceed to use accepted procedures for verification and refutation. However, ignoring the role of creativity and intuition in qualitative work is also inappropriate because there is a growing consensus in the scientific community that "method is not enough." The magic in qualitative work has been avoided in the past, perhaps because it raised questions about methodologic precision and rigor that we were unprepared to answer. I suggest it is time to begin discussing this element in science and to understand that although qualitative researchers have a particular perspective to offer, we have no corner on the market. Creativity and intuition operate in all fields of intellectual endeavor.

The Case for "Magic" in Science

One has only to browse recent books on science and discovery to understand that seemingly entrenched views on the nature of knowledge are changing. Interestingly enough, this change is most visible in the "hardest" of all sciences, physics (Bohm, 1993). Quantum theory implies that, at the most elemental level, the universe is an indivisible whole. At the quantum level, the observing instrument and the observed object are thought to be in mutual and irreducible interaction. In this contemporary quantum understanding of the universe, theorists describe perception and action as inseparable. This scientific revolution in views on objectivity and subjectivity has been apparent in the social sciences and humanities for some time (Casti, 1989; Lincoln & Guba, 1985; Minnich, 1990).

This revolution also has underscored the importance of creativity in scientific thought. Once the principle of scientific objectivity was brought into question, the issue of scientific subjectivity and the reflexive nature of knowledge construction became topics of broader intellectual interest. Increasingly the work of science came to be seen, not as the accumulation of knowledge from which the scientist is distanced, but rather as the creation of cognitive maps that shape and are shaped by the scientist's perceptions and actions (Bohm, 1987).

At the same time that this new view of science was being forged, a new view of scientists also was being constructed. Biographies and autobiographies began to describe the day-to-day work of science and, in many cases, outlined the contribution made by intuition and creativity in scientific discovery (Crick, 1988; Hawking, 1988; Keller, 1983; Watson, 1980). Philosophers of science, theoreticians, and working scientists began to cross over their respective disciplinary lines and began a dialogue about the nature of intuition and creativity and their relationship to research and scholarship (Bohm, 1987; Lamb, 1991; Minnich, 1990).

At the same time, the scientific community was focusing new attention on the power of dialogue and collaboration in scientific work. Collins (1974) described how personal contact between investigators was required before teams could successfully construct the first lasers. Although they knew "theoretically" how it should be done, essential yet unformalized (or tacit) knowledge could only be communicated through interaction. I would argue that a significant element of this tacit knowledge could be described as insight fostered by creative leap and gut feeling. Science writers began to describe the collective nature of knowledge and how dialogue allows individuals to observe their own thinking, thus taking "a more creative, less reactive stance" toward their own thought (Singe, 1990).

Thus intuition and creativity are acknowledged increasingly as important, if not essential, ingredients for scientific discovery. "Hard" scientists are writing and talking about it, but there is relatively less discussion underway in the social or health sciences. This discussion would be a useful addition to the ongoing deliberation and dialogue about qualitative methods. My review of current methodologic references in grounded theory, phenomenology, and ethnomethodology yielded little evidence that elements of creativity and intuition are considered to be important, or even acknowledged. Whereas methodologic references remain silent on the matter, "reality" suggests there is something here. I know from my own experience and from talking with other experienced analysts that occasionally magic happens in this work—that insight comes, and I "backtrack" to verify or refute it from the data, rather than get to the insight "through" the data. Thus I began to speculate on the relationship between experience, expertise, and magic in qualitative research.

Expert Practice in Qualitative Research: An Acquired Aptitude for "Magic"?

In collecting information with which to consider the question *When does the qualitative analyst know?* I read in a variety of areas: nursing epistemology, philosophy of science, science journalism, psychology, gender studies, even a little science fiction. After reading much, I still understood little. Although it was clear to me that intuition and creativity are as much a part of scientific work as are careful observation and description, I still was left with a sense that there was something about the role of magic in qualitative research I had not yet grasped.

As an experienced field-worker, I concluded that I needed to return to the source to complete this exploration—to the "real world" where analysts collect, analyze, struggle with, and write up qualitative work. I began talking to colleagues about their experiences, and I heard the same words I myself have used: "It just felt right," "It occurred to me that," "I wondered whether," and "It suddenly made sense."

I soon realized that I had read the words somewhere but in a very different context, and I discovered virtually those same sentiments expressed by expert nurses in Benner's (1984) description of expert clinical judgment. Benner noted that experts view situations holistically and draw on a vast data set of past experiences. They move beyond method as they confront information that must be understood, whereas those less expert must consciously use skills or techniques to move to insight. The expert tends to use specific techniques or skills consciously only in situations where previous experience is not helpful in achieving insight or when initial suppositions collapse under closer scrutiny. This practice parallels closely my experience and the experiences of my seasoned colleagues as we use grounded theory and phenomenologic and ethnomethodologic techniques for analyzing data and underscores the interaction between magic and experience.

The factor of experience is an interesting one to consider when discussing the product of qualitative research. We would not expect novice researchers to successfully manage complex theory-testing studies early in their careers, yet we appear to expect novice qualitative analysts to produce high-quality work immediately and at a steady initial rate—that is, without a learning curve. From what we know about novice and expert reasoning, this seems to be a rather unrealistic expectation. Perkins (1981) noted that although the basic processes of creative intellectual work are the same in the novice and the expert, the expert will notice more, remember more, and exercise better judgment.

I would argue that an attribute of expert practice in qualitative research is an exquisitely tuned capacity for pattern acquisition and recognition. Pattern acquisition is the ability to know where to look; in this area, the expert analyst may be informed substantially by intuition and creative reasoning. Pattern recognition is the ability to know similarities and differences, based on previous experience. Again these processes cannot be observed or understood directly; they can only be understood by the product. Expert analysts cannot tell you how a pattern was seen; they can tell you how their procedures set up the conditions in which pattern was discerned, what attracted their attention, and, after the fact, how the pattern is evidenced in the data. Pattern recognition is instantaneous and can be substantiated in retrospect but cannot be predicted.

Scientists become primed for specialized pattern recognition through the process of disciplinary socialization; sociologists are interested preferentially in social patterns, anthropologists in cultural patterns, and so on. Methodologic traditions also inculcate the capacity for pattern recognition, and specific methodologies direct the analyst to see some kinds of patterns more readily than others. Disciplinary and methodologic socialization probably also contributes to the capacity for pattern acquisition (knowing where to look), but it is also possible that, in this area, the expert analyst relies as much on intuition and creative reasoning as on past experience.

Another potentially important difference between how novice and expert analysts know involves the interaction between pattern recognition skill and knowledge of the substantive area related to the phenomenon being studied. A still-prevalent myth is that qualitative work is atheoretical in nature and that the researcher can accomplish such work without having mastered the relevant extant knowledge. The problem appears to be confusion between the different operations of "being atheoretical" and "objectifying the received view."

Let me state clearly that qualitative work is rarely, if ever, launched from an atheoretical stance. Morse's argument (Chapter 3) is compelling, and I cannot improve it. Striving for an atheoretical stance ("suspending belief in the received view") is far more likely to be used by the expert analyst as a technique to help move analysis forward and freshen up the analyst's perspective on the data, rather than the starting point of investigation. Although, in principle, it is possible for a skilled analyst to launch a project and achieve insight in a field where previous experience and knowledge are limited, in practical terms, the product will be far less valuable than it would be if the analyst were well-informed. Thus expert analysts are virtually always informed by extant knowledge and use this knowledge as if it were another informant. Because all qualitative methods have procedures for avoiding overreliance on the "received view," the potential validity threat can be minimized.

The intellectual risks, however, are significantly greater for the novice analyst who begins research in the absence of an adequate grounding in extant knowledge. Without that knowledge, pattern recognition will be limited to the obvious and superficial, and pattern acquisition is likely to be a considerable challenge. In grounded theory terms, the analyst will have little conceptual leverage from which to begin theorizing. Theorizing without experiential and substantive knowledge in the area is a bit like "trying to push the bus you are riding on"—a problem of leverage and position.

I suspect that excellent qualitative work is done most often by experienced analysts. This may seem to be stating the obvious, but the matter of experience, expertise, and substantive grounding in qualitative work is a topic addressed only in discussions among methodologists and has not been considered in any depth in the literature. I suggest that experience develops an aptitude for moving to insight as readily through creative leaps and intuition as through systematic analysis. The expert analyst is more likely to have such insight, is more efficient at using techniques to test the truth value of the insight achieved, and is more likely to have acquired some depth and breadth of pattern "exposure."

In conclusion, I propose that the magic of creativity and intuition is a manifest expression of substantive and methodologic expertise. The saying "Chance favors the prepared mind" applies, at least in part, to the question of "abstract knowing" in qualitative research. Moving from intuition to insight, from an interesting but quirky question to an important revelation—these processes are not governed by chance. Rather they may be governed by a readiness to see the possibilities when they are "there" and to bring them to the surface when they are not. We probably will continue to be slightly uncomfortable with this vaguely unscientific element in our work because we do not yet have the means to explain creativity and intuition. However, the fact that we cannot explain the magic in qualitative method does not mean we ought not to think about it, to discuss it, and to argue about it. Out of many possible paths to abstract knowledge, this one seems compelling.

References

Benner, P. (1984). *From novice to expert.* Menlo Park, CA: Addison-Wesley.
Bohm, D. (1987). *Science, order, and creativity.* New York: Bantam.
Bohm, D. (1993). *The undivided universe.* London: Routledge.
Casti, J. (1989). *Paradigms lost: Images of man in the mirror of science.* New York: William Morrow.
Chisholm, R. (1982). *The foundations of knowing.* Minneapolis: University of Minnesota Press.
Collins, H. (1974). The TEA set: Tacit knowledge and scientific networks. *Science Studies, 4,* 165-185.

Crick, F. (1988). *What mad pursuit: A personal view of scientific discovery.* New York: Basic Books.

Hawking, S. (1988). *A brief history of time: From the big bang to black holes.* New York: Bantam.

Keller, E. (1983). *A feeling for the organism: The life and work of Barbara McClintock.* San Francisco: Freeman.

Lamb, D. (1991). *Discovery, creativity, and problem-solving.* Brookfield, CT: Avebury.

Lightman, A. (1993). *Einstein's dreams: A novel.* New York: Pantheon.

Lincoln, Y., & Guba, E. (1985). *Naturalistic inquiry.* Beverly Hills, CA: Sage.

Meerabeau, L. (1992). Tacit nursing knowledge: An untapped resource or methodological headache. *Journal of Advanced Nursing, 17,* 108-112.

Minnich, E. (1990). *Transforming knowledge.* Philadelphia: Temple University Press.

Perkins, D. (1981). *The mind's best work.* Cambridge, MA: Harvard University Press.

Schultz, P., & Meleis, A. (1988). Nursing epistemology: Traditions, insights, questions. *Image: Journal of Nursing Scholarship, 20*(4), 217-221.

Singe, P. (1990). *The fifth discipline.* Garden City, NY: Doubleday.

Watson, J. (1980). *The double helix: A personal account of the discovery of the structure of DNA.* New York: Norton.

Dialogue

More on Theory

MAY I think your concern about people doing this work without sufficient grounding in a discipline is legitimate, so that they are theorizing with nothing—as opposed to being atheoretical, which is different. Occasionally we may approach a problem atheoretically, because we are good enough at doing it theoretically.

LEININGER I think what you are saying is very important. From a nursing viewpoint, you are really asking *How do nurses get insight?* It may not be from phenomenology method; it may not be from ethnology; it may not be from any of these. What you are beginning to look at is the methodology of the insight that nurses have discovered and are using. I like your idea of the methodological patterns of connectedness. You can create some new methods by connecting selected features for new methods. This will help us in nursing, but I question that we need to be dependent upon the other past methodologies. Go fresh! Go bold!

3

"Emerging From the Data": The Cognitive Processes of Analysis in Qualitative Inquiry

JANICE M. MORSE

I have been struggling with teaching analysis of qualitative data for a long time and am aware the we have to make these analysis processes explicit. I don't really believe that something magical happens. But I think you have to set the stage, organize your data, and organize your brain, so that you set the stage for having the insight. And I think that the other critical part is the knowledge base of the investigator. You have to be fantastically wise in social science theory, and I cringe when I see people from nutrition and other areas doing qualitative research when they haven't had that base. The problem that we have in qualitative analysis is that investigators are not pushing their analyses far enough—sometimes not even past content analysis. And I hope this chapter will challenge people to take more risks in theory development, for I believe that is where the real contribution of qualitative research lies.

Despite the proliferation of qualitative research methodology texts detailing techniques for conducting a qualitative project, the actual process of data analysis remains poorly described. Qualitative researchers primarily still learn process of model and theory development by doing qualitative research, ideally under the sponsorship of an experienced mentor. The actual cognitive processes inherent in analysis, processes of synthesization that lead to the aggregation of categories, strategies for linking categories, and decisions and processes of falsification and confirmation in theory development remain mysterious to all but the qualitative researcher. Despite the development of the notion of the "audit trail" (Halpern, 1983, cited in Lincoln & Guba, 1985)—a technique that permits research validation by allowing another investigator to follow the cognitive development of a project as it developed—the only other guidance that researchers may find is examples of data analysis in methods books. For example, texts by Chenitz and Swanson (1986) and Strauss (1987) list passages of interview data with the researchers' summaries and memos to show how data abstraction and reduction are conducted. Because processes of data analysis are poorly understood even by experienced quantitative researchers, Tripp-Reimer and Cohen (1991) recommended that examples be placed in the body of proposals so that reviewers may see what data may be expected to look like and how they will be analyzed, and thus may be assured that the researcher actually knows how to conduct the analysis. However, much to the frustration of the uninitiated and to the chagrin of the qualitative researcher, the process of theory development remains cursorily summarized as "emerging from the data."

The neglect or inability of qualitative researchers to make explicit the cognitive struggle of model or theory construction has led to the belief that qualitative research is "easy" and to the criticism that it is subjective and "unscientific." Further, the belief is that "untested" theory is interpreted as "not to be applied in the clinical setting" and results in a lack of appreciation of the generalizability of the findings. These shortcomings undoubtedly have increased the difficulty of getting qualitative research funded, of having articles accepted into major research journals, and of getting the "real" scholars interested in quantitative inquiry to take qualitative research seriously. Interesting and important qualitative research is frequently dismissed with, "But that's only a qualitative study."

This overt denunciation of qualitative methods has been exacerbated by internal conflicts among qualitative researchers themselves. Conflicting advice about the application of a priori knowledge and disagreements about threats to the process of induction (e.g., the use of the literature when planning a project) have led to the accusation that qualitative inquiry is "atheoretical."

Fear of violating the inductive process has resulted in qualitative researchers ignoring the findings of others, which, paradoxically, subsequently has impeded the development of their own work.

Qualitative research has reached a crisis point at which these challenges can no longer be ignored. In this chapter I attempt to fill this void by discussing the cognitive processes that researchers use in developing theory from data. I argue that although these processes are common to all qualitative methods (and possibly similar to those used in the conceptual phases of quantitative inquiry), it is how these methods are focused, sequenced, targeted, and employed that differentiates the various qualitative methods. Examples from four qualitative methods—phenomenology, ethnography, ethnoscience, and grounded theory—are used to illustrate the various processes of cognitive development, and, finally, the ramifications of not developing theory from qualitative research in the health sciences is discussed.

The Cognitive Processes Inherent in Data Analysis

Doing qualitative research is not a passive endeavor. Despite current perceptions and students' prayers, theory does not magically emerge from data. Nor is it true that, if only one is patient enough, insight wondrously enlightens the researcher. Rather, data analysis is a process that requires astute questioning, a relentless search for answers, active observation, and accurate recall. It is a process of piecing together data, of making the invisible obvious, of recognizing the significant from the insignificant, of linking seemingly unrelated facts logically, of fitting categories one with another, and of attributing consequences to antecedents. It is a process of conjecture and verification, of correction and modification, of suggestion and defense. It is a creative process of organizing data so that the analytic scheme will appear obvious.

Four cognitive processes appear integral to all qualitative methods: *comprehending, synthesizing, theorizing,* and *recontextualizing.* Although the nature of the research topic, the purpose of the research investigation, the type of research question, the constraints derived from the setting and the participants, and even the disciplinary background of the researcher have some bearing, at a broader level it is the qualitative methods chosen that provide the epistemological basis for the method. The research method provides the lens by dictating how the four cognitive processes of comprehending, synthesizing, theorizing and recontextualizing are weighted, targeted, and sequenced. It also restricts the intensity to which they are used and the level of abstraction attained, and ultimately it dictates how the findings are presented.

These four cognitive processes occur more or less sequentially because the researcher must reach a reasonable level of comprehension before being able to synthesize (to make generalized statements about the participants), and until the researcher is able to synthesize, theorizing is not possible. Recontextualization cannot occur until the concepts or models in the investigation are developed fully. Experienced researchers are able to set up the database so that they make the transitions from one type of thinking to another with ease. In addition, some looping back and forward is inevitable as, for instance, some gaps in comprehension may be noted if some areas of the database seem uneven and more data are needed for saturation. In such cases data collection may be resumed. As the inquiry progresses, it is possible to work on several problems at several levels simultaneously.

Comprehending

The debate about how much the researcher should learn about the setting before beginning the study is not difficult to resolve: The researcher should learn everything possible if he or she is to avoid reinventing the wheel. Search for and learn everything there is to know about the setting, the culture, and the study topic. Read both the classic and the lesser known research, as well as the most recent; critique identified relevant concepts to understand the underlying perspectives, beliefs, and values of other researchers and then use this information to justify your investigation in the proposal and to provide a theoretical context for your study (Field & Morse, 1985). However, it is crucial that the researcher keep the literature "in abeyance" and at all times separate from the data to prevent this information from contaminating the data or the researcher's perspective. The theory obtained from the literature is a template for comparison so that the researcher may recognize what is new and exciting when something new and exciting is discovered and may recognize instantly when he or she views something that is known. The goal is to become a wise and smart researcher, not a directed researcher. The goal is to gain maximal awareness and to recognize leads without being led. Thus when entering the setting, the researcher relies on the ability to view the experience from the participant's perspective—the key to good qualitative research. To do this, the researcher must enter the setting as a "stranger," earn the trust of the participants, and establish a level of intimacy with the participants so that they will be willing to share information freely with the researcher (Agar, 1980). *Comprehension* is reached when the researcher has enough data to be able to write a complete, detailed, coherent, and rich description.

Several conditions are essential for attaining optimal comprehension. First, the researcher should enter the setting as a "stranger." If the researcher is already familiar with the setting in a nonresearch capacity, then special precautions must be taken to avoid threats to validity (e.g., bias), and political and social problems associated with the role change.[1] Familiarity with the setting or previous acquaintance with the participants dulls the researcher's ability to view the setting with the sensitivity one would have when seeing it for the first time. If the researcher has a previously established work role in the setting, negative events may become difficult to handle. Thus, if the researcher has a previously established work role in the setting, then qualitative work is handicapped. One cannot observe or interview while at the same time working; such competing agendas are distracting for the researcher, and the process of observing and recording notes interferes with doing work. Observing and not "getting on" with one's work assignment causes resentment among the staff, and, even if the researcher makes it clear that he or she is no longer "working," at busy times the changed role from employee to researcher requires continual renegotiation. Of greatest concern is that information provided to the researcher may clash with the workers' responsibility to deal with such information.

Comprehending—learning everything about a setting or the experiences of participants—is exhausting and time-consuming. The second condition for obtaining optimal comprehension is that the researcher must be capable of passively learning—of absorbing nonjudgmentally and with concentrated effort—everything remotely relevant to the topic of interest. It takes time and patience to gain the trust of the participants and to become a part of the setting.

The third essential condition is that the participants must be willing to tolerate intrusion and to share their world with the researcher. They must be willing to be observed, to respond to the researcher's questions, and to take time to be interviewed. They perhaps also take a risk, for they must trust that the researcher will maintain their anonymity and that the report will not have any untoward ramifications for them personally.

The process of comprehension may be hastened during data collection by the adherence to several techniques. The first technique is to adopt a stance of active inquiry. When observing, consciously note what is happening and commit these events to memory. Actively ask informants questions about the data and seek answers: "What kinds of _____?" "When?" "Where?" "Why?" "Tell me about _____ ." The investigator must be able to distinguish the usual from the unusual, the norm from the exception. The researcher must be able to describe the norm and most types of exceptions that occur. Ask participants: "Do all _____?" "Do others _____?" Those in the setting usually can help sort the usual from the exceptions and describe exceptions. When some sense of the exception is developed, ask "Why?" or "How come?" The investigator must act like a sponge, absorbing and drawing in information, maintaining a spirit of inquisitiveness, rather than a judgmental or evaluative manner.

The second technique is to make notes frequently and as completely as possible. These notes should be descriptive, and any reflection or conjecture should be noted elsewhere, separate from the example. As the process of coding begins, thoughtfully ask questions of these data. Cluster and sort similar events together, but move them around freely and in different combinations. If categories are labeled, keep these "working" labels close to the terms used in the data. Later in the study, as the researcher compares the findings with the literature, if that label for a concept is appropriate, the working label should be replaced with the published term at that time.

The third technique is to keep the literature and "nondata knowledge" of the setting or topic separate from the data. The language of science may not have the same meaning as everyday language (Diesing, 1971). For instance, if participants describe a concept, such as *coping,* do not assume that their use of the term is the same as that used in the literature. Examine its use again in the interview data and observe coping behaviors. It cannot be assumed that categories that develop are identical to well-established concepts described in the literature. Therefore the labels must be selected cautiously. Furthermore, good researchers do not explain their informants' behavior with such phrases as "They *deny* . . . " without much trepidation, exploration, and confirmation that the behavior being labeled as denial is actually denial as described in the psychological literature or as used in lay terminology. If, eventually, the researcher chooses to use the same label to describe the behavior, the description of the "denial" is complete and includes a comparative analysis of how it resembles or is dissimilar from the ways other authors use the term.

As the processes of data collection facilitate comprehension, so do the processes of data analysis. Coding, as a central process, helps the researcher sort the data and uncover underlying meanings in the text and metaphorical references, and brings both the central and peripheral referents to the researcher's attention. Intraparticipant microanalysis, or line-by-line (and sometimes word-by-word) analysis, of an interview transcript from one participant is the primary mechanism by which understanding is achieved. When coding line by line (Peirce, 1931, cited in Atkinson, 1990, p. 84), look for and note signs that may reveal implied meanings, cultural values, and linkages to other concepts or contexts. *Signs* (an icon, index, and symbol) distinguish the relations between the sign and what it signifies, as follows: An *icon* is dependent on the relationship of the sign and what is signified, with an iconic relationship based on qualities between the two; an *index* is a sign that points to something else, indicating causality; and a *symbol* represents an arbitrary relationship between the sign and its representation. Thus established theory is used as a "backdrop" to sensitize and illuminate the data or to enlighten the researcher.

The process of comprehending is often a painful process of maturing, from examining piles of seemingly unrelated bits of knowledge to identifying something that is patterned, is predictable, and that "flows." This strategy involves tagging and labeling the text so that when cohesive pieces of text from the transcriptions are physically separated from the body of the transcript, they can be traced to their sources. These excerpts then are compiled into categories according to common themes, and the categories are labeled. This process of analysis, of aggregating similar data, is most useful in assisting the researcher because it allows the researcher to determine whether there are holes in the data (areas where scant information is available). If this is the case, additional data can be collected so that rich descriptions of each category may be developed. Careful analysis of a saturated category enables the researcher to identify the characteristics of a concept, and continued sorting of a saturated category enables the researcher to identify the characteristics of phenomena and to develop complex taxonomies that reveal the components of phenomena.

When comprehension is reached, the researcher is able to identify stories that are a part of the topic, identify patterns of experience, and predict their outcome. When little new is being learned, when the interviewer has heard "everything" and becomes bored, then saturation is reached and comprehending is complete.

Synthesizing

Synthesizing is the merging of several stories, experiences, or cases to describe a typical, composite pattern of behavior or response. It is the ability of the researcher to merge several stories or cases to describe the typical patterns or behaviors or responses of the group. Synthesizing is the "sifting" part of the analysis—of weeding the significant from the insignificant—and it begins when the investigator is "getting a feel" for the setting. At this stage the investigator can describe the norms eloquently (as "these folk do this and that") and have some notion about the range and variation of behaviors. Researchers have reached this level in the data collection when they can describe "aggregate" stories of "how these people do ____." Tripp-Reimer and Cohen

(1991) described synthesizing as rather like "taking an average." Indications that the stage of synthesis has been reached are, for example, (a) the ability to provide, with confidence and without referring to notes, composite descriptions of how people act or relate or respond when suffering and (b) the ability to provide specific stories as examples to illustrate the generalization (e.g., saying, "These people do this and that . . . ").

These aggregate stories may be composite longitudinal stories of an experience. In a process of learning, of actively seeking information, stories are collected first from one informant and then the next until the story becomes patterned and the patterns of alternate stories (variations) are evident. When synthesizing, the researcher becomes aware of certain points of juncture, or critical factors, as significant and then is able to explain variation in the data. It is important that these factors *earn* their way into the data set and that they are not placed there inappropriately, such as by the researcher's overreliance on demographics. For this reason, critical factors are usually nontraditional variables and are difficult to identify at the outset. They may be such things as a significant or transient event, a belief, or an attitude.

Diesing (1971) noted that the trick in developing theory is to move from the particular to the general in small steps, rather than in one sweep. Potential generalizations first are discovered in one case, and then this case is compared with another similar case, and another, and this process is repeated until the phenomena identified can be tested against all similar cases. If the generalization survives, it then can be tested against cases that differ by certain characteristics.

This process "decontextualizes" (Atkinson, 1992) as data are removed from the individual, from a specific instance, from the particular, and are abstracted to a more generalized mode of description. *Sifting* is the process that shakes off the insignificant "noise" from the aggregate stories, leaving only the common but important features. In essence, sifting occurs when conducting factor analysis or exploratory data analysis in quantitative analysis. In qualitative inquiry, whether the researcher uses a computer program for qualitative analysis or "cuts and pastes" by hand, the process of sifting during analysis facilitates synthesizing. Data analysis usually assumes two mechanical forms: (a) interparticipant analysis, or the comparison of transcripts from several participants, and (b) the analysis of categories, sorted by commonalties, consisting of segments of transcripts or notes compiled from transcripts of several participants. Each form of analysis facilitates cognitive processes that enable the researcher to synthesize and, as the research process continues, to interpret, to link (both with data and with other concepts), to see relationships, to conjecture, and to verify findings.

Theorizing

> Cultural analysis is (or should be) guessing at meanings, assessing the guesses, and drawing explanatory conclusions from the better guesses, not discovering the Continent of Meaning and mapping out its bodiless landscape. (Geertz, 1973, p. 20)

Elsewhere I have argued that the greatest trap in research is to mistake conjecture for fact by treating theory as fact and forgetting that a theory was created as nothing more than a "best guess" (Morse, 1992). Recognizing that theory is merely a tool to guide investigation is critical in all methods of inquiry, including qualitative research. But in qualitative investigation, the theory is developed from comprehending and synthesizing data, not as a structure or frame within which to sort data. Theory gives qualitative data structure. Theory gives qualitative findings application. Without theory, qualitative results would be disconnected from the greater body of knowledge.

Unfortunately theory is not acquired passively in moments of blinding insight. It is earned through an active, continuous, and rigorous process of viewing data as a puzzle as large as life: a puzzle that is life, a board game of wits. *Theorizing* is the constant development and manipulation of malleable theoretical schemes until the "best" theoretical scheme is developed. It is a process of speculation and conjecture, of falsification and verification, of selecting, revising, and discarding. If one ever finishes, the final "solution" is the theory that provides the best comprehensive, coherent, and simplest model for linking diverse and unrelated facts in a useful, pragmatic way. It is a way of revealing the obvious, the implicit, the unrecognized, and the unknown. It is a way of discovering the insignificance of the significant and the significance of the insignificant.

Theorizing may be considered as the sorting phase of the analysis. Briefly it is the systematic selection and "fitting" of alternative models to the data. Theorizing is the process of constructing alternative explanations and of holding these against the data until a best fit that explains the data most simply is obtained.

The process of data collection and analysis should not be forced and cannot be rushed (Glaser, 1979). Until processes of comprehension "mature" the data and the researcher is able to synthesize, the researcher must remain open to alternative modes of sorting, to alternative explanations, and to alternative theories. The researcher must be wary of being wed to one explanation too early, as this leads to "premature closure." If premature closure occurs, the resulting theory may have gaps, be thin, be weak, and may even be wrong. Additionally, if the preceding stages have been rushed and inadequate data have been collected, it may be difficult or impossible for categories to emerge that meaningfully link to form the theory. Thus, although theorizing is the real work of qualitative inquiry, it cannot take place without the first two phases. Theorizing without the foundation of data—without in-depth and systematic inquiry that results in comprehension of everyday life—is prone to error, and this is the much debated weakness of philosophical methods in conceptual inquiry (see Diesing, 1971, pp. 316-318).

The first step in theorizing is to ask questions of the data that will create links to established theory. Several strategies may be used. The first method is to identify the beliefs and values in the data. This strategy may, for example, establish emic-etic or micro-macro linkages from the data to theory, from the informant's perspective to a described worldview. If correct, such linkages greatly speed the analysis. The second method is to use lateral thinking by examining similar concepts in other settings or by seeking other complementary data sources in other contexts. The third method is the systematic and inductive incremental development of substantive or formal theory from the data. A fourth method may use conjecture and falsification by systematically hypothesizing causal links or the sequencing of characteristics attributed to certain behaviors or experiences. Key to this process is the technique of theoretical sampling. The patterns developing in the analysis are "checked out" in interviews with selected informants, who may verify or refute the hunch.

Recontextualizing

Recontextualizing is the real power of qualitative research. *Recontextualization* is the development of the emerging theory so that the theory is applicable to other settings and to other populations to whom the research may be applied. In qualitative research, the theory is the most important product. It is, therefore, the theory that is generalized and recontextualized into different settings. In addition, it is the theoretical elegance that makes qualitative inquiry generalizable, that gives it power in the process of recontextualization.

In the process of recontextualization, the work of other researchers and established theory plays a critical role. Established theory may provide the context in which a researcher's model links the new findings with established knowledge. Established theory recontextualizes the new findings by providing a context in which to fit the new findings, and thus the discipline advances. Finally, established theory provides a mechanism with which to demonstrate the usefulness and implications of the findings. The goal is to be able to place the results in the context of established knowledge, to identify clearly findings that support established knowledge/theory, and to claim clearly new contributions.

On Technique and Method

In the first part of this chapter, I argued that the cognitive processes used in qualitative data analysis are common to all qualitative methods. However, it is the way each process is applied, targeted, sequenced, weighted, or used that distinguishes one qualitative method from another and gives each method its unique perspective. In the next sections, the differences in the use of the cognitive process are outlined for phenomenology, ethnography, ethnoscience, and grounded theory (see Table 3.1).

TABLE 3.1 The Identification of the Four Cognitive Processes in Selected Qualitative Methods

Method	Conceptual Basis	Comprehending	Synthesizing	Theorizing	Recontextualizing
Phenomenology	Based on reflections of the lived experience and the four existentials	Conversations/ Dialogues	Linking to descriptions of experience in other sources	By doing phenomenological writing and rewriting	Recognition of the lived experience in self and others
Ethnography	Based on theories of culture	Observations Interviews Use of other documents	Content analysis Saturation of categories	Emic-etic linkages Lateral linkages Comparative method	Theory-based generalizations Cultural universals and comparisons
Ethnoscience	Culture and cognitions theory	Interviews Observations	Sentence frames Card sorts Q-sorts	Taxonomy	Abstract statements
Grounded theory	Symbolic interationism	Interviews	Coding (1st & 2nd level) Memoing Analyzing negative cases Theoretical sampling	Development of typologies Model/ theory development	Development of substantive theory Development of formal theory

35

Phenomenology. In phenomenology, comprehending (or having in-depth knowledge of a phenomenon or setting) is attained by first reflecting on one's own experiences; these experiences are often the first source of "data" in a phenomenological study. Next researchers may dialogue on the topic with others to obtain experiential descriptions from others and may tape-record these dialogues. They then examine the transcript and inspect the dialogue, highlighting descriptive words, tracing etymological sources, and searching transcripts for idiomatic phrases that will add to the understanding of the experience (see van Manen, 1990, pp. 53-63).

Phenomenologists also may observe everyday life and seek experiential descriptions in the literature. Data from these sources complement the "conversations" with participants about their experience. These sources provide the researcher with understanding, with insight, and with comprehension about the meaning of the lived experience.

The principal means for *synthesizing,* or "merging," data is the process of conducting thematic analyses. These analyses are conducted primarily by identifying common structures of the particular experience, and these provide the researcher with "our understanding of the world" (van Manen, 1990, p. 79).

Although phenomenologists would not label themselves "theorists" in the strict sense of the term, in phenomenology the linkages from data to theoretical knowledge are achieved through reflection by using the phenomenological literature—by using what van Manen refers to as "the four existentials" (lived space [spatiality], lived body [corporeality], lived time [temporality], and lived human relations [relationality]) as guidelines for reflection (van Manen, 1990, p. 101).

Refinement of the phenomenological reflection is attained also through writing and rewriting. This process sensitizes the investigator by providing new insights, increasing the level of abstraction, and moving the descriptions away from the particular to a more universal sphere. It is this process that develops the experiential themes, moving the phenomenology away from a lived body, lived relations, lived time, and lived space and recontextualizing the lived experience to one that we, as humans, can identify.

Ethnography. Comprehension in ethnography increases as data collection progresses. Initially observation is unfocused and the collection of meaningful data proceeds slowly, with the researcher first learning about the setting in general and then focusing on the more specific research problem (Field & Morse, 1985). As comprehension increases and participant observation data become more meaningful, the researcher may use unstructured interviews to supplement the observational data. Data from various sources provide additional knowledge about the setting. Such sources of data may be maps or floor plans, minutes from meetings, and other institutional records.

Over time, processes of comprehension become efficient as the participants in the setting become used to the researcher and understand what he or she actually is needing to know and understand. Data collection becomes more focused, and events extraneous to the topic no longer distract the researcher. With continued observation, however, the researcher gradually loses the sensitivity that is dependent on unfamiliarity, and his or her attention drifts with boredom of repetition. Of even more concern, the researcher's allegiance to the method and his or her determinedly neutral position changes as the researcher becomes a part of the group, "goes native," and adopts the value and belief systems inherent in the setting. When this happens, the researcher no longer can observe neutrally and should withdraw from the setting. Comprehension is complete when the researcher has conducted enough participant observation to describe fully the behaviors and actions of the participants and to describe the events, incidents, and exceptions from an emic perspective.

The processes of data collection inherent in interpretative ethnography are different. Here the focus is not on the patterned behavior and action of participants, but rather on the *experience* of participants (Bruner, 1986). In this case, data are tape-recorded interactive interviews, and line-by-line textual analyses are performed (Atkinson, 1990).

Synthesis is facilitated by the processes of coding and content analysis.[2] By pooling data from all transcriptions and notes, categories are constructed and data are linked both from transcripts from one participant and between participants. Synthesis has occurred when data are saturated—that is, when no new categories emerge. Often ethnographic work is not developed beyond the level of description, but is presented as "thick description." Such research is punctuated with informants' stories and with case studies that illuminate and illustrate each point in the presentation of the data. Marcus (1986) noted that often, in ethnography, theorizing is embedded in the data synthesis as reflections within the contextual data. The "analysis" phase of theorizing rarely is separated in its own section as a separate level of discourse with a distinct purpose, such as embedding the analysis in critical theory, political discourse, and so forth.

Ethnography is embedded in cultural theory, explicating that beliefs and values are shared among participants, that cultural beliefs and values are learned, and that behavior is patterned. It is from this foundation that theorizing develops. First, cultural norms are identified within the study setting. *Theorizing* begins by establishing macro-micro linkages (or etic-emic distinctions), by identifying beliefs and values in the data, and by linking these with established theory.[3] Concepts are identified, analyzed, and compared and contrasted with those in the literature. In addition, the comparative method is used to compare the differences and identify the similarities in the data with those for another cultural group. New explanatory models and theories may be derived in the course of analysis. *Retextualization* is achieved by forcing the theory to a level of abstraction. The degree of abstractness attained, in turn, determines the generalizability of the theory.

Ethnoscience. Superficially the process of comprehension for ethnoscience resembles that used in ethnography. It consists of fieldwork, participant observation, and interviews. However, after the first few unstructured interviews that provide context for the topic of study, the interviews take a very different form. Ethnoscientists have developed techniques to elicit the cognitive structure of a domain: Their interview techniques are designed to determine the boundaries, to elicit the characteristics, to compare and contrast, and to determine the relationships within the cultural domain (see Werner & Schoepfle, 1987). *Synthesis* is attained through the use of such techniques as card sorts, q-sorts, sentence frames, and even games, such as Twenty Questions (Spradley, 1979).

Theorizing consists of determining linkages and relationships between categories and displaying them by developing taxonomic diagrams and models. *Recontextualization* is reached by forming explanatory, hypothetical, abstract statements derived from the taxonomic analysis and from the developing models.

Grounded Theory. Comprehension is achieved in grounded theory by using tape-recorded, unstructured interviews and by observing participants in their daily lives. However, the assumptions of symbolic interactionism that underlie grounded theory set the stage for examining process, for identifying stages and phases in the participants' experience. Symbolic interaction purports that meaning is socially constructed, negotiated, and changes over time. Therefore the interview process seeks to elicit a participant's story, and this story is told sequentially as the events being reported unfolded. Comprehension is reached when the researcher has interviewed enough participants to gain in-depth understanding.

Synthesis is facilitated by adequacy of the data and the processes of analysis (Morse, 1986). During this phase the researcher is able to create a generalized story and to determine points of departure, of variation in this story. The process of analysis begins with line-by-line analysis to identify first-level codes. Second-level codes are used to identify significant portions of text and to compile these excerpts into categories. Writing memos is key to recording insight and facilitates, at an early stage, the development of theory.

As *synthesis* is gained and the variation in the data becomes evident, grounded theorists sample according to the theoretical needs of the study. If a negative case is identified, the researcher, theoretically, must sample for more negative cases until saturation is reached when synthesis is attained.

Theorizing follows from the processes of theoretically sampling. Typologies are constructed by determining two significant characteristics and sorting participants against each characteristic on a 2 × 2 matrix. Diagramming is used to enhance understanding and identifying the basic social process (BSP) that accounts for most of the variation in the data.

As with the methods previously discussed, *recontextualization* is determined by the level of abstraction attained in the model development. Whereas substantive theory is context bound, formal theory is more abstract and may be applicable to many settings or other experiences.

The Next Challenge

The outside lack of appreciation of qualitative inquiry and the devaluation of the processes implicit in qualitative inquiry have resulted in the stigmatization of qualitative research. The ramifications of this stigmatization include a stunting of qualitative studies so that findings seldom are developed beyond the descriptive level, and overly timid attempts at theory building have delayed advances within the health care disciplines. In 1983, Landy described medical anthropology as being "long on data and short on theory" (p. 186). And Singer (1992) noted that medical anthropologists are just beginning to become "impatient with the failure to move from example to explanation, from case to cause, from issue to interpretation" (p. 2) and are at last beginning to develop a "new appreciation for both the nature and the role of theory in the subdiscipline" (p. 2).

Hammersley and Atkinson (1983) and Silverman (1989b) placed some responsibility for the lack of theory use and development on the recent push for naturalism. They argued that the dichotomy between "natural" and "artificial" research settings is false—data are simply data; that the tendency in naturalism to avoid theory and not to see beyond the data—"to tell it like it is"—denies the strength of qualitative work that must be derived from theoretical linkages and from theoretical elegance; and finally, that naturalism tends to ignore comparative methods and to adhere to cultural description. Such descriptions are endless, limited in scope, and restricted in their usefulness.

In nursing, the lack of strong qualitative studies has been a particularly serious handicap to the profession. The immense interest in nursing theory and nursing models in the 1970s culminated in the development of several high-level (or grand) theories. Because the theorists viewed the defining and operationalization of their variables as the researcher's task (rather than the theoretician's), and because of the abstract nature of these theories, pragmatic application of their work could not occur. This lack, combined with the conservative tendency of qualitative researchers to resist going "beyond their data," resulted in a gap between theory and practice that impeded the development of the profession as a whole. Practitioners still tended to view nursing theory as an impractical nuisance, to consider researchers as folks who are "out of touch with the clinical reality," and to consider research as an impedance to "getting the work done."

This tendency is the crisis in health care research today. We must no longer tolerate the handicap inherent in importing concepts and theories from other social science disciplines and expecting these concepts to fit clinical phenomena, to provide satisfactory explanations for the experiences of our clients, and to predict the outcome of health care. If nursing is an independent discipline and provides a unique service, then it is absurd to expect concepts developed in psychology or sociology, such as *coping* or *support,* to be useful in the nurse-patient relationship.

Given such diversity in nursing's unique roles, we also must become impatient with the habit of borrowing concepts to "explain" nursing practice. It is clear that the present poor fit of nursing theory impedes the advance of nursing practice and is stifling to our profession. Qualitative researchers have an important contribution to make in developing the theoretical foundations of health care. We are reluctant to assume this task: We can no longer afford timid researchers.

Notes

1. "Familiarity with the setting" implies familiarity and a work role established in that particular setting. This problem is easily avoided; for instance, if a nurse normally is employed in an emergency department, his or her study should be conducted at an emergency department in another hospital where the staff are strangers and have no expectations of the researcher to assist with work.

2. This fragmentation process of "detextualization and recontextualizing" (Atkinson, 1992) has been criticized by Lincoln (1992), who noted that such treatment of data may violate assumptions inherent in the holistic approach and tends to be used by researchers who are attracted to the richness that qualitative methods provide but are unwilling to relinquish their positivistic stance. She argued that the process also lends itself to data reduction and all that that entails.

Despite this warning, content analysis is useful—and often necessary—for organizing qualitative data. It greatly facilitates concept analysis and concept identification and is a commonly used qualitative analysis technique. The important point is to continue data collection and analysis until saturation is reached—that is, until no new data emerge and until data appear repetitious.

3. Elsewhere Silverman (1989a) argued forcefully that accepting informants' stories without such reflection and linkages simplifies and invalidates qualitative inquiry to the level of post-Romanticism.

References

Agar, M. A. (1980). *The professional stranger.* New York: Academic Press.

Agar, M. A. (1983). Inference and schema: An ethnographic view. *Human Studies, 6,* 53-66.

Atkinson, P. (1990). *The ethnographic imagination: Textual constructions of reality.* New York: Routledge.

Atkinson, P. (1992). The ethnography of a medical setting: Reading, writing, and rhetoric. *Qualitative Health Research, 2,* 451-474.

Bailyn, L. (1977). Research as a cognitive process: Implications for data analysis. *Quality and Quantity, 11,* 97-117.

Bruner, E. M. (1986). Experience and its expression. In V. W. Turner & E. M. Bruner (Eds.), *The anthropology of experience* (pp. 3-30). Urbana: University of Illinois Press.

Chenitz, W. C., & Swanson, J. M. (1986). *From practice to grounded theory.* Menlo Park, CA: Addison-Wesley.

Corbin, J. (1986). Coding, writing memos, and diagramming. In W. C. Chenitz & J. M. Swanson (Eds.), *From practice to grounded theory* (pp. 102-129). Menlo Park, CA: Addison-Wesley.

Diesing, P. (1971). *Patterns of discovery in the social sciences.* Hawthorne, NY: Aldine.

Field, P. A., & Morse, J. M. (1985). *Qualitative approaches to nursing research.* Edinburgh: Chapman & Hall.

Geertz, C. (1973). *The interpretation of cultures.* New York: Basic Books.

Glaser, B. G. (1978). *Theoretical sensitivity.* Mill Valley, CA: Sociology Press.

Hammersley, M., & Atkinson, P. (1983). *Ethnography: Principles and practice.* New York: Tavistock.

Landy, D. (1983). Medical anthropology. In J. Ruffini (Ed.), *Advances in medical social sciences* (Vol. 1, pp. 185-314). New York: Gordon & Breach.

Lincoln, Y. S. (1992). Sympathetic connections between qualitative connections and health research. *Qualitative Health Research, 2,* 375-391.

Lincoln, Y. S., & Guba, E. G. (1985). *Naturalistic inquiry.* Beverly Hills, CA: Sage.

Marcus, G. E. (1986). Contemporary problems of ethnography in the modern world system. In J. Clifford & C. E. Marcus (Eds.), *Writing culture: The poetics and politics of ethnography* (pp. 165-193). Berkeley: University of California Press.

Morse, J. M. (1986). Qualitative research: Issues in sampling. In P. L. Chinn (Ed.), *Nursing research methodology: Issues and implementation* (pp. 181-193). Rockville, MD: Aspen.

Morse, J. M. (1992). "If you believe in theories. . ." (Editorial). *Qualitative Health Research, 2*(4), 259-262.

Silverman, D. (1989a). Six rules of qualitative research: A post romantic argument. *Symbolic Interaction, 12*(2), 215-230.

Silverman, D. (1989b). Telling convincing stories: A plea for cautious positivism case studies. In B. Glassner & J. D. Moreno (Eds.), *Qualitative-quantitative distinctions in the social sciences* (pp. 57-77). Netherlands: Kluwer.

Singer, M. (1992). The application of theory in medical anthropology: An introduction. *Medical Anthropology, 14*(1), 1-8.

Spradley, J. P. (1979). *The ethnographic interview.* New York: Holt, Rinehart & Winston.

Strauss, A. L. (1987). *Qualitative analysis for social scientists.* Cambridge, UK: Cambridge University Press

Tripp-Reimer, T., & Cohen, M. Z. (1991). Funding strategies for qualitative research. In J. M. Morse (Ed.), *Qualitative nursing research: A contemporary dialogue* (pp. 243-256). Newbury Park, CA: Sage.

van Manen, M. (1990). *Researching the lived experience.* London, Ontario: Althouse.

Werner, O., & Schoepfle, G. M. (1987). *Systematic fieldwork* (Vol. 2). Newbury Park, CA: Sage.

Dialogue

The Democracy of Interpretation

DREHER But if I come up with a conclusion—"There's no effect from prenatal exposure to crack"—someone can always do more research and possibly say, "There is, in fact, an effect from prenatal exposure." In other words, my findings are open to refutation. But if you take a Freudian theory, for example, and the psychiatrist says, "How do you feel about your father?" And the patient says, "I hate my father!" The psychiatrist writes, "Unrepressed hatred of father." Or the patient could say, "I love my father!" And the psychiatrist could write, "Repressed hatred of father." Two opposite events are interpreted to mean the same thing. That's not science.

Now, I'm not saying that nonscientific knowledge hasn't made an extraordinary contribution. Religious knowledge, Freudian theory, probably some of the greatest grand theorists that we know are not open to refutationn. But I think that's OK. They make a contribution to knowledge building. But it's just not science.

SANDELOWSKI Well, if we use that definition, we have to look at all qualitative research as interpretive, and then we have to say it's not scientific.

DREHER I use science in a fairly precise way. To be called scientific, the results have to be open to refutation—the results have to be refutable. If you do have this democracy of interpretation, if any interpretation is a correct interpretation, it's not open to refutation.

It reminds me of an example. I was riding the bus one day in Jamaica, and the driver stopped to show us where the market truck had plunged about 200 feet down a bank the night before. The four men who were in the truck walked away from the accident. Everyone said, "Oh, God is good! God is good!" So I asked, "Well, what if the men had been killed. Would God be bad?" And they said, "No, God would still be good. It's God's way." Well, if you use the same interpretation to explain opposite phenomena, it can't be a scientific explanation. It's a religious explanation.

MAY Actually, we might be stuck on this problem of refutability. Theory is not refutable. Theory exists. It may be bad. It may be limited. I generate theory. The theory exists. The theory itself cannot be refuted. It can be tested in its pieces and parts. But there is no complete test for The Theory.

MORSE So it has to be revised—

MAY Right! So the failure to support the hypotheses revises the theory. So maybe that's where we are stuck when we are talking about refutability.

DREHER Yes—and the specific aim of writing a proposal is, as far as I'm concerned, absolute clarity. The clearer you are about exactly what you are doing, holding no misconceptions that you actually are getting inside people's heads; that you are dealing with reports and accounting for, somewhere in the methodology, for what the reporting itself does to what's being reported.

4

The Proof Is in the Pottery:
Toward a Poetic for Qualitative Inquiry

MARGARETE SANDELOWSKI

How I got into this whole area of reading other than science or health literature is, first of all, because my background is American studies—it combines history and literature. And the one thing that always impressed me about the scholarship in that field was not only that it is what we would call rigorous and beautifully done, so far as marshaling your evidence and your argument, but also that the writings are just beautiful pieces of literature, and that was always a goal for me. I wanted to write like that. The other thing is, in my work with infertile couples, I got into this narrative thing because one of the things I noticed was that it was very hard for me to do these conventional codes and categories. We followed these people over time, and even within the same interview, people seemed to contradict themselves or had different versions of the same event. I talked with an anthropologist, and she got me onto explanatory models, and through that I went into looking at literature on narrative. By looking at that, it became very hard for me to see science and art as very different anymore, and I started to think: How would we be advantaged by looking at the continuities between things that we have been taught or that we tend to see as very different? And it is not to deny that there are differences. So I said, "Let's look at this a different way. Instead of doing an either/or approach, let's see where the continuities are," and from that came this chapter. In this chapter I was trying to convey the continuity idea; also that being artful was not a flaw or a fault. There is this underlying thing, that if you are doing artful work, it is somehow not being faithful to your data. So I was trying to change people's thinking that art and science are not necessarily two clearly distinct things.

The pot carries its maker's thoughts, feelings, and spirit. To overlook this fact is to miss a crucial truth, whether in clay, story, or science. (Krieger, 1991, p. 89)

Those of us actively engaged in human studies research, especially in that domain of inquiry called qualitative research, live in what anthropologist Clifford Geertz (1988, p. 11) referred to as a "nervous present": one characterized by "profound epistemological skepticism" (Dillard, 1982, p. 132), much "methodological soul-searching," and a certain "moral hypochondria" (Geertz, 1988, p. 137). Over the last two decades, our faith in the claims of science to truth and objectivity has been shaken further by the (re)discovery of the subjective nature and storied quality of science: that "science was no longer privileged or pure" (Myerhoff & Ruby, 1982, p. 7). We are like the scientist who operates like a tightrope walker—not looking at our feet to avoid acknowledging that we are operating in midair (Dillard, 1982, p. 55). Or we are like Humpty-Dumpty, unable to recapture the "seamless innocence" we once had about the scientific enterprise or, perhaps, like the centipede who became paralyzed after being asked to consider the difficulty in moving all of its legs (Myerhoff & Ruby, 1982, p. 2).

As increasingly self-conscious and newly reflexive inquirers coming to terms with the subjectivities of science and the ineluctable role of the inquirer in the creation of knowledge, we strive for both a cool (but not cold) detachment from and warm (but not too hot) engagement with the subjects/co-researchers/informants/respondents/participants in our studies. We live the "oxymoron (of) participant observer" (Van Maanen, 1990, p. 3); we both assert and deny our own signature and voice—our "authorial presence"—in the findings of our studies. We claim to be both "there"—inextricably part of what we observe—and "here"—appropriately removed from it (Geertz, 1988).

Like the ethnographers Geertz described, we are confronted with the problem of making science out of biography, theory out of lives. Indeed many of us who do qualitative research undoubtedly experience (but, perhaps, have yet to name) the acute unease of trying accurately to render—in the service of theory-based practice—and passionately to evoke—in the service of empathic understanding and literary communication—elements of the lives we observe.

I believe that one critical factor at the heart of this new "methodological caution" (Dillard, 1982, pp. 12-13) and "authorial uneasiness" (Geertz, 1988, p. 14) is the location of the varieties of projects that have come to be known as qualitative research on the fault line presumed to exist between art and science. Art is presumed to begin where science stops (Brown, 1977), and scientific and artistic approaches to qualitative research are believed to differ essentially in their aims, sources of data, forms of representation, degree of license permitted the artist/scientist, and criteria for appraisal (Eisner, 1981).

Yet when we look at art and science with a view toward discerning similarity, as opposed to difference, the differences appear less as differences than as variations on common themes. Indeed, as sociologist Robert Nisbet (1976) remarked, the impulse to conceive of art and science as diametrically opposed human projects is very recent; until the 19th century, there was little consciousness in Western thought of art and science as separate domains. The creative imagination and operations of Michelangelo were presumed to be similar to those of Kepler. Moreover, as sociologist Richard Brown (1977) argued, there are many advantages to assuming an "aesthetical view" of human studies knowledge for resolving contemporary and often tedious methodological debates: for adopting a framework within which the "pioneering" artist and scientist are both recognized as involved in "making paradigms through which experience becomes intelligible" (p. 2). For these social scientists, art and science have an "essential affinity" (Brown, 1977, p. 2) or "kinship" (Nisbet, 1976, p. 9) that may be more valuable to emphasize than the techniques and modes of demonstration that separate them.

The value of this emphasis on the kinship between art and science in understanding and doing qualitative research is the subject of this chapter. What we have not fully come to terms with in our efforts to develop science for practice is that what we strive for is not "scientism," or a science devoid of its art, but rather a science with the "spirit of discovery and creation" left in (Nisbet, 1976, p. 4). By neither denying nor minimizing the kinship between art and science, qualitative researchers have available to them the distinctive opportunity and even obligation to show the way toward a poetic for inquiry: toward a science that both acknowledges and celebrates its art.

Science and Story, Theory and Theater

We may find evidence of the rediscovered unity between art and science in descriptions of science in terms of concepts drawn from the arts, especially literature. A variety of social scientists have described the narrativity and rhetoric of scientific description and explanation: drawing parallels between science and story and theory and theater, and exposing the imagery, metaphor, synecdoche, narrative stance, portraiture, and landscape in scientific activity (Hunter, 1990; Richardson, 1990a; Sandelowski, 1991). For example, science and art are united in discussions of dramaturgical approaches to the study of human phenomena (Cochran, 1986; Cochran & Claspell, 1987) and in the dramaturgical analysis of social life (Hare & Blumberg, 1988). Social critic Susan Sontag (1989, p. 5) found the "trappings of metaphor" in scientific representations of tuberculosis, cancer, and AIDS. Sociologist Joseph Gusfield (1976) discovered the "comedy and pathos" in research on drinking and driving and analyzed the dramatic elements of the conventional research report. Sociologist Susan Krieger (1991) described social science as an "interpretive activity" whereby scientists "make up stories to fit the world" (p. 16).

Feminist scholars have been particularly effective in describing the "narrative structures" of scientific descriptions of human reproduction that reprise masculinist social assumptions about gender relationships (Beldecos et al., 1988; Tuana, 1988). In the area of reproductive biology, scientists have "constructed a romance" between egg and sperm (Martin, 1991, p. 485), and "sperm tales" emerge as "variants of heroic quest myths" (Beldecos et al., 1988, pp. 63-64). In the "breathless prose" (Martin, 1991, p. 486) of scientific "fairy tales," female reproductive processes are "cast" (p. 488) to gendered type.

Finally, sociologist Robert Nisbet (1976) evoked the unity between art and science by describing the changing "styles" in both art and science. Just as medieval art can be distinguished from Renaissance art, so can styles and fashions characterizing 19th-century science be distinguished from those of modern science. When Marx and Weber described the socioeconomic and political conditions of their times and the prototypical worker and bureaucrat, they created "landscapes" and "portraits" as compelling and evocative as any novelist or painter. Indeed, according to Nisbet, artists often deal with larger social issues that are only later taken up by scientists. Moreover, as he further noted, nothing resembling what we know as the "scientific method" led to the grand sociological theories that remain so influential today. Nisbet also observed that the word *theory* comes from the same Greek root as the word *theater.* As he concluded: "A tragedy or comedy is, after all, no less an inquiry into reality, no less a distillation of perceptions and experiences, than a hypothesis or theory that undertakes to account for the variable incidence of murder or marriage" (p. 12).

Kinship

In all of these efforts and in the many others like it in contemporary social science literature, we find it hard to deny the unity between "realms of meaning" (Phenix, 1964) that we have become accustomed to viewing as worlds apart. The kinship of art and science can be affirmed in their mutual beginnings in the creative act. Indeed what we typically have called discovery is creation. Joseph Chilton Pearce (1971) observed:

> To be given ears to hear and eyes to see is to have one's concepts changed in favor of the discipline. A question determines and brings about its answer just as the desired end shapes the nature of the kind of question asked. This is the way by which science synthetically creates that which it then "discovers" out there in nature. (p. 7)

Jerome Bruner (1979) argued that new facts are rarely discovered in the sense of being "encountered in an uncharted sea of ignorance," or, if they seem to be encountered this way, it is almost always because of some "hypothesis about where to navigate" (p. 82). As he observed:

> Discovery . . . favors the well-prepared mind. . . . The history of science is studded with examples of men "finding out" something and not knowing it. . . . Discovery . . . is in its essence a matter of rearranging or transforming evidence in such a way that one is enabled to go beyond the evidence so reassembled to new insights. . . . It is often not even dependent on new information. (p. 82)

Similarly philosopher Nelson Goodman (1978) noted that "worlds are as much made as found . . . knowing, as much remaking as reporting" (p. 22). Importantly, as he further argued: "Perceiving motion . . . often consists in producing it. Discovering laws involves drafting them. Recognizing patterns is very much a matter of inventing and imposing them. Comprehension and creation go on together" (p. 22).

Art and science are also akin to each other in their search for truth, in that they both represent reality, and in the presence of aesthetic criteria governing both domains. There still exists the misconception that only science is concerned with truth, reality, events "out there," objectivity, explanation, and proof, whereas art is concerned only with beauty, symbols, feelings "in here," subjectivity, interpretation, and insight (Brown, 1977, p. 26). Embedded in these dichotomies are the presumptions that there are rules for doing science but not for doing art, and that facts, truth, and reality can be strictly distinguished from fancy, fiction, and the imaginary.

Like all such statements of either/or, these notions efface certain continuities and persistent paradoxes. For example, Goodman (1978) argued for the truth of an apparent paradox: the "fabrication of fact." He observed that although there are circumstances in which it is important to distinguish falsehood and fiction from truth and fact, we cannot do it "on the ground that fiction is fabricated and fact found" (p. 91). Facts are by themselves "things made" (Brown, 1977, p. 35). Moreover, given the made-up quality of all human attempts to know, the lines drawn between art and science do not "coincide with the line between subjective and objective" (p. 140). Margenau (1973) described the scientist's arrangement of selected facts in fanciful hypotheses and theories: facts "opaque" until "made significant by theoretical meanings" (p. 167). Bruner (1979) described the neutrino as a "fruitful fiction" (p. 62). If both fact and fiction are instances of fabrication, and if fabrication is "an ordering or rearrangement of selected materials from the actual world" (Dillard, 1982, p. 148), the novel can be seen as less different from (although certainly not the same as) a scientific theory. Indeed it becomes possible to argue that "after all, science is in one (rather attenuated) sense 'mere' art" (Dillard, 1982, p. 61).

Both scientist and artist are concerned with illuminating reality, exploring the unknown, and "creating and peopling worlds" (Krieger, 1979, p. 175). Interestingly, artistic truths are often more true to life than scientific ones, providing us with visions of human nature more resonant with our own experiences than any psychological, sociological, or other conventionally scientific rendering of it. How many times have we encountered a line in a poem or short story or novel or narrative account in a qualitative research report that we know captures the essence of a person or incident more faithfully than the volumes of frankly scientific description we have also read that may provide a sense of understanding, but no personal recognition? Furthermore, as biologist and feminist critic Ruth Hubbard reminded us (1982), science often "renders suspect" (p. 19) the very truths, or sense experiences, that contradict its definitions of reality. As she observed: "If we want to be respectable inhabitants of the Euclidian world, every time we see railroad tracks meet in the distance we must 'explain' how what we are seeing is consistent with the accepted definition of reality" (p. 19).

What differentiates the arts from the sciences is not the search for truth per se, but rather the kinds of truths that are sought. Science typically is concerned with propositional truths, or truths about something. Art is concerned with universal truths, with being true to: even with being more true to life than life itself (Hospers, 1946). Whereas the scientist and the historian must be faithful to and may take few liberties with the known facts and chronological sequence of events in a situation, the artist strives to be true to something beyond the bare realm of facts. The artist often searches for the universal in the one, striving to eliminate the trivial, transient, and other particular elements that impede the comprehension of some essential feature of human nature (Hospers, 1946). The greatest fictional characters, from Shakespeare's Hamlet to Ibsen's Nora, are those who, though not existing in real life, still reveal recurring or dominant human tendencies: the secrets of the human heart that we have shared and with which we can readily identify. Like a scientifically drawn typology (Schneider & Conrad, 1981) of people who also do not really exist, such characterizations apply to no one, but to many persons. Even wildly fanciful departures from camera truth in paintings (consider Picasso's or Dali's work) may, in part, be in the service of fidelity to the subject matter (Hospers, 1946).

Moreover, what distinguishes art from science is not the presence of literary and rhetorical (persuasive) devices in the one and their absence in the other. Indeed "rhetoric historically precedes and categorically incorporates science" (Hunter, 1990, p. 4); and the novel and research report are both modes of representing reality, not of presenting reality itself (Krieger, 1983). Scientists no less than artists attempt to persuade their audiences of the value/validity of their findings by employing speaking and writing strategies to stake their claims. Indeed the popular view of science as objective and truthful rests on the success of this "claims-making activity" (Aronson, 1984, p. 1) and traditional "linguistic practices" (Mishler, 1990, p. 420). The conventional research report is no less a "highly stylized art form" (Krieger, 1991, p. 117) than the novel or poem. Such strategies as the use of the passive voice and the third person, strict separation of method from findings and findings from interpretation, strict accounting of steps followed for data collection and analysis, and recurring appeals to significance and validity are intended to persuade the readers that what they are reading is science and not art, that the findings reported are objective and uncontaminated by the heart and mind of the researcher.

Yet despite scientific claims to the contrary, in neither science nor art can the self be denied or is language a neutral medium for communication. Rather, as Dillard (1982) reminded us, language "is itself like a work of art" (p. 70), selecting, abstracting, exaggerating, ordering, and, ultimately, missing its mark. In neither science nor art does language "signify things as they are" (p. 70), but rather as they are perceived as being by the observer. In addition, ethnography and history and science are what ethnographers, historians, and scientists speak and write; findings become findings when they are disseminated as findings.

Moreover, what distinguishes art from science is not the absence of evaluative criteria in one domain and the presence of them in the other domain, but rather the nature of the criteria. Traditional practices and aesthetic rules govern the process, content, and form involved in both artistic and scientific production. We also can verify artistic truths, not empirically, but rather against our own experiences, feelings, and observations of human conduct, against the "shock of recognition" (Bruner, 1979, p. 72) that a work engenders in us.

In both art and science, we make aesthetic choices, selecting frames of reference and modes of representation for reasons beyond their scientific or artistic merits. If we are honest, we must admit that our choice of a scientific theory is not necessarily (or even often) made because it is the best fit for the data, but rather for its aesthetic appeal to some part of us, for the "fondness" and "comfort" it evokes in us, and for the feeling that we can do something with it that fits us (Krieger, 1991, p. 22).

Accordingly science cannot claim such things as truth, rigor, or explanation solely for itself; and art cannot claim such things as beauty, imagination, and poetic license solely for itself. Whether we are motivated by impulses to make our work more scientific or artistic, we still make it up. As Nisbet (1976) concluded, both scientist and artist often strive to leave the "ordinary world of perception and . . . common sense," longing to escape the everyday in order to seek an "intensity of understanding" (p. 12). Both a theory and a novel are "escapes," not from reality or truth, but from the "conventionalities and literalnesses" of everyday life. Bruner (1979) observed that the creative poet, mathematician, and scientist "disengage from that which exists conventionally" to engage in what "they construct to replace it" (p. 24).

At the Crossroads

In *Composing a Life,* a book traversing anthropology and autobiography, Mary Catherine Bateson (1989) observed: "The most creative thinking occurs at the meeting places of disciplines. At the center of any tradition, it is easy to become blind to alternatives. At the edges, where lines are blurred, it is easier to imagine that the world might be different. Vision sometimes arises from confusion" (p. 73). Qualitative research is located at the meeting place between art and science, concerned with finding truths about and committed to representations that are true to its subject matter. Precisely because qualitative work is located at this crossroads, those of us engaged in it have choices to make. We may "refuse" (Krieger, 1983, p. 176) the art in qualitative work, or we may celebrate it, acknowledging and working with the ambiguities it creates.

Refusing the Art

We refuse the art by furthering efforts to scientize qualitative research only to make it more credible to those in the center of scientific tradition: to make it recognizable to them as science. I am reminded here of Henry Higgins's lament concerning why a woman could not be more like a man. Making over qualitative research solely for this purpose serves to reinforce the cultural legitimacy that things called science are granted and that things called not-science are not.

We may refuse the art by maintaining a methodological emphasis on, or by fetishizing, rules that give priority to redundant and generic expositions of technique over the production of works that incorporate singular imagination, analytic power, and elegance. I am reminded here of the difference between the technician and the artist: between the figure skater who gets a perfect score in the compulsories but gives a mediocre performance in the freestyle, and the skater who fails to perform the perfect figure eight but who excites in the freestyle. Although rules are certainly important for the novice entering a new terrain, rules also valorize conformity and trivialize art. "Intellectual craftsmanship" (Mills, 1959, p. 195) involves moving beyond, but not necessarily against, the rules learned as a novice. As sociologist C. Wright Mills (1959) maintained, we can only be trained in what is already known. Although training is necessary to understand the logic of various modes of inquiry (Morgan, 1983) and what rules may not be bent or broken, it also may "incapacitate" (Mills, 1959, p. 212) us in the creative enterprise. The refusal of the art in our research projects is evident in the dogged persistence in equating imagination and creativity with methodological anarchy. Philosopher Alice Koller (1981) observed:

I begin to see that the whole idea of a method for discovering things is *ex post facto* . . . Like Leonardo's "method" for teaching his pupils how to sketch the faces they saw on the street. He categorized all foreheads, all eyebrows, all shapes of eyes, every conceivable aspect of the human face, then numbered them, and gave the list to his pupils. Instead of sketching faces when he saw them on the street, the pupil took a description of the face in terms of items on the list: Eyebrow 22, Nose 64. The pupil was supposed to sketch the face later from the list of aspects checked off. And Leonardo was perplexed when his pupils couldn't make their sketches resemble the faces they had seen, because his sketches looked like the faces he saw and he had given his pupils his foolproof method. But it wasn't a method at all. He had no method; he just knew how to draw. (pp. 88-89)

We refuse the art in our science when we forget that rules of method serve us, but only to a certain point, after which they may enslave us.

Celebrating the Art

We celebrate the art when we strive for the wisdom and confidence that will permit us to cast off methodolatries: to "bridge the chasm that lies between the safe inadequacy of what (we have) been taught and the fulfillment that (we) uncertainly sense will exist on the other side." The only way is to "make a leap" to the other side; we can then "throw down a footbridge, (our) method," for others to follow and move beyond (Koller, 1981, p. 94). As a fictional detective also concluded, "Every good investigator in the world, criminal or scholarly, has to take a sudden leap—that is, if he or she is good at what they do" (Cross, 1990, p. 193). Without that leap, we remain mere "fact grubber(s)" (p. 193) and rule followers.

Celebrating the art permits us to turn to nonscientific sources of knowledge (literature, art, and literary and artistic criticism) as data themselves and to use theory imaginatively (including theories of fiction, dance, and music) to frame and enhance analysis. Celebrating the art permits us to experiment with forms of representing findings that best reprise the experiences we wish to convey.

Qualitative researchers give in and give themselves up to the "temptations" (Krieger, 1983, p. 176) of art. They may do this by showing the way to a "poetic" for inquiry: reaffirming the art in research design, and making a knowledge system that is "phenomenologically true to" the people and events observed, "hermeneutically self-conscious" of the methods and interests of its creators, and with the scope and explanatory power to guide practice (Brown, 1977, pp. 1-2).

The Burdens of Authorship

Qualitative researchers can move toward this poetic by celebrating and working with the subjectivities of inquiry and by confronting the burdens of authorship, including the recognition that (a) the presentation of findings is inseparable from our interpretation of data, (b) rules for "writing up" (Wolcott, 1990) research affect what we can write about, and (c) how we present our findings always involves aesthetic and sometimes even moral choices (Richardson, 1990b). As writers of lives, we choose whether we will tell "realist tales" in the traditional mode of science, or "confessional" or "impressionist tales" in the mode of autobiography, poetry, or painting (Van Maanen, 1988). We choose whether to emphasize such features as character, dialogue, scene, event, or action. Consider May's (1980) rendering of fathering types (a grounded theory project), Koenig's (1988) description of scene and action in the routinization of a technological innovation (an ethnography), Bergum's (1989) evocation of the inner lives of women becoming mothers (a phenomenology), or Paget's (1982) account of a physician's account of a medical error (a narrative analysis).

When we consider who the authority is in our research projects—the ones studied or the ones who will author the research report—we choose whether to privilege our own or their voices and points of view. When we consider the audience for our work, we choose whether to emphasize methodological rigor or "aesthetic resonance" (Richardson, 1990a, p. 117). We choose whether to emphasize "factual accuracy, theoretical sweep, imaginative grasp, or moral depth" (Geertz, 1988, p. 133). When we present something that we have observed as a strategy or as a typology, as an antecedent, condition, or outcome, we are choosing to represent it in a certain way; we are not simply reporting an external reality. Whatever claims we may wish to make to being scientists, we are ineluctably also storytellers and writers disseminating our fictions.

The Burdens of Readership

Qualitative researchers also celebrate the art by clarifying the burdens of scholarly (as opposed to lay) readership. Indeed these readers also have obligations to prepare themselves to evaluate and appreciate what they are reading: to recognize the varieties of ways phenomenology or grounded theory or ethnography or narrative analysis can be interpreted and executed but still remain what their authors claim them to be, to grasp what authors are attempting, and, if the readers are also reviewers, to assist them in their efforts. Readers have an obligation not to dismiss work simply because it does not conform to ruled expectations and to understand that a work that is imaginative can also be true. Most importantly, the reader has an obligation to know what the burden of the author of a qualitative work is vis-à-vis the reader and other kinds of researchers. For example, in most kinds of qualitative work, it is the burden of the reader, not of the writer, to decide whether elements of the work are generalizable or transferrable to other people and circumstances. However, it is the burden of the writer to provide readers with enough information to make this determination, should they wish to do so.

License

Celebrating the art in qualitative research is not an imprimatur for anarchy or for ignorance. Qualitative researchers are not free to make wild forays into fancy; they make, but cannot fake. Nor are they free to be ignorant of the logic and aesthetic of the varieties of research strategies encompassed by the label *qualitative research.*

Celebrating the art in qualitative research does not give anyone the license to fail to know about or to fail to acknowledge the work of other people in one's own and other disciplines in presenting one's work, or to fail to compare one's findings (including theoretical formulations) with relevant ones presented by other researchers, no matter their research orientation. Qualitative research is not a license to reinvent the wheel in the service of some misguided notion of bracketing one's assumptions or maintaining a pristine and pure atheoretical state. Such putative innocence of other people's work only makes the researcher guilty of breaking the cardinal rules of scholarship: Know thy field and give credit where credit is due.

Moreover, qualitative research does not permit anyone the license to claim, for example, that he or she reached "informational redundancy" or "saturation" of a theoretical category after talking with or observing a few people of vastly different social circumstances only one time. Such a claim reveals a clear and unsupportable violation of rule—a dangerous lack of understanding of the meaning of key concepts in certain kinds of qualitative work.

In addition, celebrating the art in qualitative work means preventing the displacement of analysis by clichéd renderings of method or by dictionary-like lists of categories (albeit, with definitions and an illustrative quote or two). Because of the very limited space provided for research reports in many research journals, explications of method should be as brief and to the point as possible and should never take over the report. Category lists are essential components toward some end—for example, instrument development, or the production of a phenomenology or an ethnography or theory—but they are not ends in themselves. If they were, then researchers could submit for publication their computer sheets with the unworked, or uninterpreted, results of the statistical tests they have run.

Moreover, notwithstanding the limitations of language to express meaning, artful qualitative work does not give anyone the license to make up word collages (consisting of unintelligible rows of words connected by hyphens) when perfectly good words already exist to convey an idea with both accuracy and elegance. The quintessential qualitative piece (I do not include the valuable kind of work done in the service of constructing items for an instrument in this category) is both representative and evocative; it tells an interesting and true story, it provides a sense of understanding and sometimes even personal recognition, and it conveys some movement and tension—something going on, something struggled against. A connection is made between the categories invented. Often a controlling metaphor or image ties observations together. There is a reason for the words chosen.

Significantly, qualitative research was never intended to be a mode of inquiry chosen by default, as a haven for those unable or unwilling to do other kinds of inquiry or to do the rigorous and considerable work involved in producing any masterful product. Wolcott observed (1990), "Qualitative approaches beckon because they appear easy or natural"; they seem to promise that one can become an "instant researcher" (p. 11). Moreover, although qualitative research mandates a kind of conceptual and verbal playfulness that we often associate with literature, it does not confer a license to do anything that one pleases in its name. Like any other serious project, a qualitative piece indeed may be judged as good or bad in terms of certain canons of inquiry and aesthetics in the same way that a novel, drama, or conventional scientific product may be judged. Our dilemma, then, is to educate ourselves—as doers, critics, and consumers of research— to recognize the difference.

Coda and Confession

I have always been more drawn to research papers that look more like finely crafted "romances" than "lab reports" (Geertz, 1988, p. 8). Undoubtedly that preference comes from obtaining a doctorate in a humanities field (American studies) that emphasizes history and literature and whose classic works have such titles as *Machine in the Garden* (Marx, 1964) and *Virgin Land* (Smith, 1950). I learned that scholarship can be both rigorous and imaginative, true and beautifully rendered. Consequently I am drawn to a research report that reads like a novel: one that tells a good story that is coherent, consistent, and believable but that is also aesthetically and intellectually satisfying. I have always felt some discomfort with efforts to make qualitative inquiry look and sound more scientific, as if being artistic was a serious flaw in the search for a truthful foundation for practice.

In my own work with infertile couples, I have tried to represent their stories in more creative ways. For example, in a paper about adoption waiting (Sandelowski, Harris, & Holditch-Davis,

1991), I sought to create a literary tableau of waiting, to reprise in substance and form the romance and tension of this experience as I interpreted it from couples' stories. I drew from conceptualizations of time in sociology and fiction to frame both the interpretation and presentation of the information they provided. A strict scientific description would have been less true to the emotional content of their experiences and to my response to their stories. Admitting the kinship between art and science is not a failing, but rather a directive to develop the kinds of imaginative and critical skills we associate with artists.

I have only lately realized that I never aspired to be a scientist, but rather a certain kind of writer. When you talk with me about my research, do not ask me what I found; I found nothing. Ask me what I invented, what I made up from and out of my data. But know that in asking you to ask me this, I am not confessing to telling any lies about the people or events in my studies/stories. I have told the truth. The proof for you is in the things I have made—how they look to your mind's eye, whether they satisfy your sense of style and craftsmanship, whether you believe them, and whether they appeal to your heart.

References

Aronson, N. (1984). Science as a claims-making activity. In J. W. Schneider & J. I. Kitsuse (Eds.), *Studies in the sociology of social problems* (pp. 1-30). Norwood, NJ: Ablex.

Bateson, M. C. (1989). *Composing a life.* New York: Plume.

Beldecos, A., Bailey, S., Gilbert, S., Hicks, K., Kenschatt, L., Niemczyk, N., Rosenberg, R., Schaertel, S., & Wedel, A. (1988). The importance of feminist critique for contemporary cell biology. *Hypatia, 3,* 61-75.

Bergum, V. (1989). *Woman to mother: A transformation.* Westport, CT: Bergin & Garvey.

Brown, R. H. (1977). *A poetic for sociology: Toward a logic of discovery for the human sciences.* Cambridge, UK: Cambridge University Press.

Bruner, J. S. (1979). *On knowing: Essays for the left hand* (expanded ed.). Cambridge, MA: Belknap.

Cochran, L. (1986). *Portrait and story: Dramaturgical approaches to the study of persons.* New York: Greenwood.

Cochran, L., & Claspell, E. (1987). *The meaning of grief: A dramaturgical approach to understanding emotion.* New York: Greenwood.

Cross, A. (1990). *A trap for fools.* New York: Ballantine.

Dillard, A. (1982). *Living by fiction.* New York: Harper & Row.

Eisner, E. W. (1981). On the differences between scientific and artistic approaches to qualitative research. *Educational Researcher, 10,* 5-9.

Geertz, C. (1988). *Works and lives: The anthropologist as author.* Stanford, CA: Stanford University Press.

Goodman, N. (1978). *Ways of worldmaking.* Sussex, UK: Harvester.

Gusfield, J. (1976). The literary rhetoric of science: Comedy and pathos in drinking driver research. *American Sociological Review, 41,* 16-34.

Hare, A. P., & Blumberg, H. H. (1988). *Dramaturgical analysis of social interaction.* New York: Praeger.

Hospers, J. (1946). *Meaning and truth in the arts.* Chapel Hill: University of North Carolina Press.

Hubbard, R. (1982). Have only men evolved? In R. Hubbard, M. S. Henifin, & B. Fried (Eds.), *Biological woman: The convenient myth* (pp. 17-45). Cambridge, MA: Schenkman.

Hunter, A. (Ed.). (1990). *The rhetoric of social research: Understood and believed.* New Brunswick, NJ: Rutgers University Press.

Koenig, B. A. (1988). The technological imperative in medical practice: The social creation of a "routine" treatment. In M. Lock & D. Gordon (Eds.), *Biomedicine examined* (pp. 465-496). Dordrecht, The Netherlands: Kluwer.

Koller, A. (1981). *An unknown woman: A journey to self-discovery.* New York: Bantam.

Krieger, S. (1979). Research and the construction of a text. *Studies in Symbolic Interaction, 2,* 167-187.

Krieger, S. (1983). Fiction and social science. In S. Krieger, *The mirror dance: Identity in a women's community* (pp. 173-199). Philadelphia: Temple University Press.

Krieger, S. (1991). *Social science and the self: Personal essays on an art form.* New Brunswick, NJ: Rutgers University Press.

Margenau, H. (1973). The method of science and the meaning of reality. *Main Currents in Modern Thought, 29,* 163-171.

Martin, E. (1991). The egg and the sperm: How science has constructed a romance based on stereotypical male-female roles. *Signs: Journal of Women in Culture and Society, 16,* 485-501.

Marx, L. (1964). *The machine in the garden: Technology and the pastoral ideal in America.* New York: Oxford University Press.

May, K. A. (1980). A typology of detachment/involvement styles adopted during pregnancy by first-time expectant fathers. *Western Journal of Nursing Research, 2,* 443-453.

Mills, C. W. (1959). *The sociological imagination.* London: Oxford University Press.

Mishler, E. G. (1990). Validation in inquiry-guided research: The role of exemplars in narrative studies. *Harvard Educational Review, 60,* 415-442.

Morgan, G. (Ed.). (1983). *Beyond method: Strategies for social research.* Beverly Hills, CA: Sage.

Myerhoff, B., & Ruby, J. (1982). Introduction. In J. Ruby (Ed.), *A crack in the mirror: Reflexive perspectives in anthropology* (pp. 1-35). Philadelphia: University of Pennsylvania Press.

Nisbet, R. (1976). *Sociology as an art form.* New York: Oxford University Press.

Paget, M. A. (1982). Your son is cured now: You may take him home. *Culture, Medicine, and Psychiatry, 6,* 237-259.

Pearce, J. C. (1971). *The crack in the cosmic egg: Challenging constructs of mind and reality.* New York: Pocket Books.

Phenix, P. H. (1964). *Realms of meaning.* New York: McGraw-Hill.

Richardson, L. (1990a). Narrative and sociology. *Journal of Contemporary Ethnography, 19,* 116-135.

Richardson, L. (1990b). *Writing strategies: Reaching diverse audiences.* Newbury Park, CA: Sage.

Sandelowski, M. (1991). Telling stories: Narrative approaches in qualitative research. *Image: Journal of Nursing Scholarship, 23,* 161-166.

Sandelowski, M., Harris, B. G., & Holditch-Davis, D. (1991). "The clock is ticking, the calendar pages turning, and we are still waiting": Infertile couples' encounter with time in the adoption waiting period. *Qualitative Sociology, 14,* 147-173.

Schneider, J. W., & Conrad, P. (1981). Medical and sociological typologies: The case of epilepsy. *Social Science and Medicine, 15A,* 211-219.

Smith, H. N. (1950). *Virgin land: The West as myth and symbol.* Cambridge, MA: Harvard University Press.

Sontag, S. (1989). *Illness as metaphor and AIDS and its metaphors.* New York: Anchor.

Tuana, N. (1988). The weaker seed: The sexist bias of reproductive theory. *Hypatia, 3,* 35-59.

Van Maanen, J. (1988). *Tales of the field: On writing ethnography.* Chicago: University of Chicago Press.

Van Maanen, J. (1990). Great moments in ethnography: An editor's introduction. *Journal of Contemporary Ethnography, 19,* 3-7.

Wolcott, H. F. (1990). *Writing up qualitative research.* Newbury Park, CA: Sage.

Dialogue

On Qualitatively Derived Intervention

MAY Given that the gold standard in health science is the randomized clinical trial, how do we argue when the provisional knowledge base is still theory, it is still putative, tentative? How do we explain the move quickly to intervention, the move quickly to as yet not verified scientific reasoning? Quantitative researchers actually have the same problem. I say, "You have 300 citations showing that bed rest doesn't work." The flip side is, they are going to do bed rest until they get something better. You have the same problem. You are never going to get the gold standard. You are never going to get scientific proof of efficacy. Yet you know in your gut that this works!

SWANSON We had a range of people in our program—people in their leather and 16 earrings, and a physician, and so on—and the feedback that we got from the leaders was the same old stuff! "Only one partner; PRACTICE SAFER SEX; settle down—same old stuff that you get in the doctor's office. I THOUGHT THIS WOULD BE SOMETHING DIFFERENT! I thought there was some hope here! We're not going to buy this!" As caregivers, we need to hear that. We need to start opening up and facing it. Preaching from a pulpit is not working! It's not working. We need to hear their voices.

CAREY At least they are telling you. There was someone in New York who thought her program wasn't working. At the beginning 60% were using condoms, but after 3 months it was down to 20%. Right? WRONG! At the beginning they didn't trust her, and now they are telling her the truth.

MAY But how do we do this? Do you keep the quantitative end completely blind to the qualitative end and then say, "Guess what, you're right! You're right!" Or do you take a deep breath and say, "Our measures are cock-eyed, we cannot trust the outcomes, but we know in our gut what we saw when we looked in his eyes." It may be that what we have to do is exactly what you've done—to say, "Guess what, normal science ain't doing it." So we do midcourse corrections, and we are doing it on purpose. And we hope that our theory building was good enough to help us from hurting people with this intervention. And it may be that this is the best we can do. But I warn you that I have gotten railroaded on this very same issue—[they say] "How dare you introduce a new protocol" (which is how physicians see it)—"How dare you take the risk, when what you have is tentative, putative, theory unverified," and I say, "Do you hear what you are saying? You guys are basing bed rest [to prevent premature labor] on dog studies, and you are accusing me of moving too quickly!" Or we are going to let the qualitative insight drive clinical protocols. That's going to be a biggie!

5

Inside the Black Box:
Theoretical and Methodological Issues
in Conducting Evaluation Research
Using a Qualitative Approach

JANICE M. SWANSON
LINDA CHAPMAN

I got into qualitative evaluation when I was doing a post-doc with Anselm Strauss, and Anselm says that there is this black box, and what we are doing throughout La-La land in health care is measuring people when they go into an intervention and when they come out, and we know we can describe the next person coming through the door in the clinic. We know what we want, but we don't know what happens to them as they are going through the intervention. So I put a qualitative evaluation—process evaluation—in my last grant. There are many examples in the literature, and most of them are what Fine and Kidder call a Small "q," which is adding a few questions in that were to enlighten people about the hypotheses. But the Big "Q" is coming up within a theoretical piece that is really going to enhance our knowledge, our evaluations. I found very few Big Q studies. And then I found that almost no one embedded a Big Q component within a quasi-experimental study. (That was encouraging?!!—and now I know why!). So in this chapter I have addressed about half of the 50 or so issues associated with process evaluation.

AUTHORS' NOTE: This research was funded by the National Center for Nursing Research, R01NR01637, National Institutes of Health. An earlier version of this chapter was presented at the 120th Annual Meeting of the American Public Health Association, Washington DC, November 9, 1992. The authors wish to thank Virginia Yee, Supervising Public Health Nurse, and staff, Health Center Number 5, City and County of San Francisco, for assistance with this project.

The effects of social interventions are seldom fully known. In the health field, and in nursing in particular, we spend more time doing than knowing. The purpose of evaluation research is to increase our knowledge of our interventions. Evaluation research may be carried out by using quantitative methods, qualitative methods, and a combination of quantitative and qualitative methods (Guba & Lincoln, 1989; Patton, 1986, 1987).

Evaluation research seeks to understand the mechanisms that underlie successful interventions. Quantitative approaches traditionally have been used to seek to demonstrate the effects or outcomes of an intervention. In this mode, evaluation of an intervention has involved measuring participants before they entered a "black box" and then measuring them again as they emerged from the black box (Broadhead, 1980; Chen, 1990; Chen & Rossi, 1983). What actually occurs during the intervention may largely remain a black box, as it is generally unknown to the evaluation researcher. Although the field of evaluation research has been dominated in the past by the use of quantitative methods, the qualitative paradigm is respected by large segments of the evaluation community and is being increasingly adopted (Guba & Lincoln, 1989). Two major problems have plagued the black box approach as a singular approach to evaluation: (a) the atheoretical nature of the majority of the work in this field and (b) results showing little or no effect from an intervention.

Chen (1990) pointed out that the field of evaluation research, though multidisciplinary, has been largely atheoretical. Lipsey, Crosse, Dunkle, Pollard, and Stobart (1985) reviewed a sample of 175 evaluation studies and found that most studies, even though they represented a variety of journals, academic affiliations, and program areas, lacked evidence of use of prior theory. The result, what Chen and Rossi (1983) referred to as a "cookbook" approach to evaluation, is a simple input/output, or black box, evaluation. Such an approach may assess whether a program works but offers no insight into the transformation processes between the inputs and outputs of a program. Kidder and Fine (1987) discussed the differences between qualitative work in evaluation as of two types: the Big Q and the Small q. The Big Q is hypothesis-generating inductive fieldwork. The hypotheses and sets of questions change as the work progresses. The Big Q results in such work as an ethnography or a grounded theory and contributes to theory development. The Small q involves the insertion of open-ended questions into a survey or experiment. The questions are asked of everyone, usually in the same order, and serve to enrich the responses to questions asked to test hypotheses stated at the outset of the study. The major distinction, according to Kidder and Fine (1987), is that studies using the Small q are "looking for answers," whereas studies using the Big Q are "looking for questions" (p. 60). The predominant use of the Small q in the field of evaluation research has been a hindrance to the development of theory through the use of qualitative methods. As stated by Judd (1987), "Theoretical knowledge about social behavior and the social factors that are responsible for those behaviors" is needed (p. 26). The lack of theory "greatly diminishes the explanatory power of evaluation" (Mullen & Iverson, 1986, p. 158).

Another problem that has plagued evaluation research is its tendency to show that many programs have had little or no effect. In most fields, competent evaluators have been frustrated over the "lack of results" of their program evaluations (Weiss, 1972, 1987). Cronbach, in 1975, called for archives of descriptive information to be filed to combat the costly waste of data in the face of "nonsignificant" effects:

> We cannot afford to pour costly data down the drain whenever effects present in a sample "fail to reach significance." . . . Let the author file descriptive information, at least in an archive, instead of reporting only those selected differences and correlations that are nominally "greater than chance." Descriptions encourage us to think constructively about results from quasi-replications, whereas the dichotomy significant/nonsignificant implies only a hopeless inconsistency. . . . There are more things in heaven and earth than are dreamt of in our hypotheses, and our observations should be open to them. (p. 156)

The practice of evaluation is changing (Guba & Lincoln, 1989). An alternative methodological paradigm, or naturalistic inquiry, has evolved from work in qualitative methodology, primarily from anthropology, phenomenology, symbolic interactionism, and ethnomethodology (Patton, 1986). Guba and Lincoln (1989) described four generations of evaluation as they have evolved historically: (a) Measurement was the focus of first-generation evaluation following World War I, and the role of the evaluator was to administer, score, and interpret tests; (b) description was the focus of second-generation evaluation at mid-century, and the role of the evaluator was to describe an individual, group, or program in light of objectives stated in behavioral terms; (c) judgment was the focus of third-generation evaluation in the 1960s, and the role of the evaluator was to judge merit and worth on the basis of standards and models; and (d) responsiveness is the focus of fourth-generation evaluation, in which the role of the evaluator is to seek out the claims, concerns, and issues of the stakeholders (persons who have something "at stake" in the outcome) and, through consensus, negotiate needed improvements and change. The prediction of variables and the preselection of methods and instruments are not possible in fourth-generation evaluation because of the variation in the issues, claims, and concerns put forth by the stakeholders. What is required is observation and interaction by the evaluator. The evaluator uses multiple methods of data collection, including participant observation, interviewing, and review of documents. Sampling may include both theoretical (Glaser & Strauss, 1967) and purposive (Patton, 1980). Interpretive analysis is concurrent with data collection, and the final product is the process, generated collaboratively with the stakeholders.

As reflected above, it is difficult to monitor ongoing process by using quantitative methods. As stated by Guba (1987):

> There are very few quantitative indices that can assess ongoing process; indeed, it was the utter inability of physicists to deal with process within the atom that gave rise to the black box model of research: alter inputs and assess resulting outputs to infer process that cannot be observed directly. (p. 28)

Observation of process in the human sciences is possible, and qualitative research methods can be used to describe these processes (Guba, 1987). Qualitative methods are used to interpret the meanings of both participants and nonparticipants, those who designed the intervention and those who carried it out, and the multiple realities of each in a given situation (Mullen & Iverson, 1986). These meanings are learned, or "socially constructed"

(Berger & Luckmann, 1967). Evaluation research using qualitative methods has process as a goal and seeks to understand what has happened inside the black box, or how and why the effect has occurred, so that interventions might be modified. Explanation is the goal of this method (Judd, 1987).

The concept of the use of multiple methods, common in the social sciences, is also common in evaluation research (Judd, 1987). Those who support comprehensive evaluation recommend the integration of multiple approaches through the use of both quantitative and qualitative methods (Mullen & Iverson, 1986). Judd (1987) stated that some (e.g., Cronbach et al., 1980) "have argued that the most important function of evaluation research is to modify treatments so that they achieve their desired goals more efficiently and effectively. If this is a primary evaluation goal, then process evaluations are a necessary addition to outcome evaluations" (p. 24). As stated by Reichardt and Cook (1979), evaluation, to be comprehensive, must be "process as well as outcome oriented, exploratory as well as confirmatory" (p. 18). Although the combination of the two methods in a single research endeavor is highly recommended and holds great promise, in reality it is rarely undertaken (Judd, 1987).

The purpose of this chapter is threefold: (a) to demonstrate the effectiveness of fourth-generation evaluation, (b) to compare quantitative to qualitative approaches to evaluation, and (c) to present theoretical and methodological issues encountered in conducting evaluation research using a qualitative approach—specifically, grounded theory (Chenitz & Swanson, 1986; Glaser & Strauss, 1967). Because the process evaluation using grounded theory was embedded within an outcome evaluation using a quasi-experimental design, we also describe one attempt to integrate quantitative and qualitative approaches in evaluation research. Many issues in conducting a qualitative evaluation and in combining both quantitative and qualitative methods in evaluation have been explored by experts in the field (Chen, 1990; Fetterman, 1984; Goetz & LeCompte, 1984; Guba & Lincoln, 1989; Patton, 1987, 1990). The following issues are addressed and illustrated from an ongoing study combining both quantitative and qualitative approaches to evaluation: theoretical issues, and methodological issues related to design, goals, and analysis.

Background

Qualitative approaches to evaluation research are gaining attention in the fields of social science (Livingood, Woodhouse, & Natale, 1991; Woodhouse & Livingood, 1991), including nursing (Burnside, 1990; Frenn, Borgeson, Lee, & Simandl, 1989; Wilson, 1982). Although qualitative evaluation research has been promoted by social scientists for some time (Broadhead, 1980; Fetterman, 1984; Patton, 1987, 1990), its promotion in nursing has been recent and minimal (Murdaugh, 1989; Sarnecky, 1990a, 1990b; Swenson, 1991).

In an early study, Wilson (1982) followed Mosher and Menn's (1978) outcome evaluation of an alternative treatment center for schizophrenics with a process evaluation of that center. The process evaluation generated a substantive theory called "infracontrol," which explained how persons with the diagnosis of schizophrenia and their related problems of social control were managed within a nontraditional community environment. In a later study, Frenn et al. (1989) described the concept of *repatterning,* a process of lifestyle change in clients who participated in a cardiac rehabilitation program. The study had no quantitative evaluation component. In a doctoral dissertation, Burnside (1990) compared the efficacy of a reminiscence group, a "Dear Abby" treatment control group, and a no-treatment control group on fatigue, affect, and life satisfaction among women over 65 years of age who were living independently. The quantitative evaluation yielded no statistically significant differences among the groups. A qualitative evaluation of the eight groups was carried out by using semantic analysis and grounded theory. Findings that contribute to the building of theory include a description of categories that identified major themes within the group sessions, the most important meanings of the reminiscence group experience to the participants, and the effect of the reminiscence group experience. These studies used grounded theory in the generation of categories or process in the outcome evaluation. No study describing an intervention imbedded within an experimental or quasi-experimental study was found in the nursing literature.

One area in particular that may benefit by knowledge of process—what occurs inside the black box—and outcomes is that of health education aimed at the promotion of sexual health in the era of the acquired immunodeficiency syndrome (AIDS) epidemic. Although some programs have been successful in changing people's sexual behavior, they have been limited largely to studies of white, middle-class gay men in Western cultures since the advent of the AIDS epidemic (Becker & Joseph, 1988; Joseph et al., 1987; Valdiserri et al., 1987; Valdiserri et al., 1989). The use of qualitative approaches in studies of high-risk sexual behavior has been both advocated (Aral et al., 1991; Herdt & Boxer, 1991) and demonstrated (Dorfman, Derish, & Cohen, 1992; Siegel & Krauss, 1991; Wermuth, Ham, & Robbins, 1992).

The Research Study

Genital herpes, the largest source of genital ulcerative disease in the Western world (Schmid, 1990), may place persons at high risk of human immunodeficiency virus (HIV) infection (see Corey, 1990, for a review). The purpose of the study was to describe the process and test the outcomes of nurse-led psychoeducational group interventions to lower sexual health risks (knowledge, attitudes, and behavior) and to improve psychosocial adaptation (depression, mood states, self-concept, self-concealment, self-disclosure, self-efficacy, and responses to genital herpes) in young adults with the chronic disease genital herpes (Swanson, 1992). Findings from an earlier descriptive study of the adaptation of young adults to living with genital herpes in which 70 young adults were interviewed and given questionnaires measuring psychosocial adaptation provided the basis for the quasi-experimental study (Swanson & Chenitz, 1993; Swanson, Remy, Chenitz, Chastain, & Trocki, in press). In the intervention study, 252 young adults with genital herpes were inducted into the study, filled out questionnaires, and were given pamphlets on genital herpes, AIDS, and safer sex for ethical reasons and to control for information received from the media and health care providers. They were assigned to either an experimental group that participated in three 90-minute nurse-led psychoeducational group sessions or a control group. All participants were followed up for repeat data collection at 3 and 6 months. Forty participants (two groups of participants in the experimental and control conditions) in the larger project agreed also to participate in a qualitative evaluation. Those in the experimental group agreed to videotaping of their group sessions (one person refused to participate because the sessions were to be videotaped). Following the data collection sessions, all 39 were interviewed by using open-ended interviews, and their interviews were tape-recorded. Data also included feedback sessions with the nurse group facilitators and the review of related documents and consumer materials.

Issues in Conducting a Qualitative Evaluation: Theoretical Issues

Initially the theories on which our study was based were those of young adult development and the task of achieving intimacy (Erikson, 1963) and of symbolic interactionism, which holds that the development of self is an interpretive process and occurs through discourse with one's social world (Blumer, 1969). Our dual purpose—to describe the process and to test the outcomes of psychoeducational interventions—led us to a quasi-experimental design to test the outcomes of the interventions and to an interactionist approach (Blumer, 1969; Broadhead, 1980) to describe the process. The interactionist approach would overcome the limitations of the black box design by offering "a methodology designed to explicate the internal processes and problems, events, meanings, and situations that make up the interaction between a program and its clients" (Broadhead, 1980, p. 35). Although our planned use of grounded theory potentially would contribute a needed substantive theory—the Big Q—to the field of evaluation research and give us information on how and why the outcome occurred, we were faced with the dilemma that a set of theoretical assumptions very different from those integral to an experimental approach was needed for the interactionist approach.

Examining Underlying Assumptions. The very assumptions of a positivist paradigm for social research may be found to be at variance with the assumptions about the nature of human interaction discovered in the pursuit of process. As stated by Mullen and Iverson (1986), evaluation researchers using quantitative methods may "apply theory inadequately and set objectives that reflect only a part of the actual effects that could have been predicted" (p. 155). Exploration, at least, will cause the researcher to question these underlying assumptions, as in the following example.

Most participants in the study came to the group intervention stating a desire to learn how to manage living with genital herpes for many reasons. A primary reason was fear of rejection by a partner, which would lead to increased stigma and isolation. Participants informed us they thought they could learn how to control their recurring outbreaks, how to protect their partner(s) by disclosing they had herpes, and how to negotiate the practice of safer sex. The goals of these participants were congruent with our theoretical base. Learning to manage would include a timely disclosure and conjoint practice of safer sex that would decrease sexual risk taking and increase psychosocial adaptation. Interaction with partner(s) and acceptance by partner(s) would increase their chances for achievement of intimacy.

This assumption of the major goals and theoretical base of our intervention would have gone unchallenged had we not had the qualitative evaluation component in our study. For example, we found that not all participants thought the above position reflected their views. Some participants stated they felt differently. Other ideologies were held that rivaled Erikson's (1963) postulate of the achievement of intimacy as a developmental task of the young adult. For example, persons in the sex industry were interested in managing their disease to prevent transmission to clientele. Angry feminists were interested in exercising their sexual freedom with many partners "as men have done for centuries" and denied that they sought an intimate relationship with a partner. These realities have led us to reexamine the assumptions of our study and the theory that underlies our intervention. Our dilemma is captured by Buchanan (1992) in a paper on the uneasy alliance of combining quantitative and qualitative methods of research:

> Positivists want to test hypotheses that will enable them to predict and control human behavior; the goals of a positivist social science are achieved through experiments. . . . The ends of an interpretive social science are achieved in the process itself of engaging people in dialogue. . . . The value of an interpretive social science derives from

its ability to aid people in improving their own skills of autonomy and participation in community life. (pp. 130-131)

Multiple Realities. The differences between quantitative and qualitative research methods are philosophical and a matter of no little debate (Chen, 1990; Guba & Lincoln, 1989; Mullen & Iverson, 1986). As stated by Mullen and Iverson (1986), "Quantitative methods have developed largely to confirm or verify theory, whereas qualitative methods have been developed to discover theory" (p. 150). The discovery of theory involves exploring the multiple realities of the actors in a changing social scene by engaging them in dialogue and being open to their interpretations of the world. Again the process of conducting the process evaluation superimposed on an outcome evaluation opened our eyes to the multiple realities that would tell us why our intervention had the effect it did and how it might be improved.

In the quasi experiment, precise, well-defined goals (specific aims or one reality) were set at the onset; a highly select sample had to be chosen and participants randomized into experimental and control groups, an intervention with a set curriculum had to be carried out, participants had to attend two out of three of the intervention sessions, and instruments of exact measures had to be selected and administered by a research assistant within a narrow window of time. In the interactionist approach, multiple realities in the form of multiple goals, problems, meanings, and situations became evident from the onset. For example, the group facilitators' goals were to cover the "facts" in the curriculum, whereas the goals of the participants were to exchange stories of their and others' experiences, to discuss their feelings, and to share strategies for living with herpes. An "unstudied curriculum" that we had not designed at times evolved. Through the use of the Big Q, we sought the multiple realities of people's lives, and we found them. For example, strategies were shared that reflected the realities of the lives of the participants; they included how to lie to a partner without having to disclose an outbreak of herpes in order to coerce a partner to practice safer sex: "Even if you're on the pill, you know, I might lie . . . even though I take the birth control pill and stuff, I might say, 'I don't have any,' you know, and suggest that we use a condom and spermicide." Again Buchanan (1992) captured our dilemma:

Positivist research is instrumental. It does not concern itself with questions about the goals or ends of human life, but only with the means to achieve goals set outside the research process. Ends and means are seen to be separate. The process of determining that drug use should be eliminated [or safer sex adopted] is unrelated to the process of determining how to do it. Research focuses on discovering the most effective or efficient means to an established end. Questions about whether or not the target population shares that goal are not part of the research process. (p. 131)

Another example involves the researchers' and group facilitators' noticing of subtle variations in the intervention as it inevitably evolved. The group facilitators reported to us that they became more experienced and hence more relaxed with each group they led. Of course, the group members changed in each series of group sessions they led, and sites varied between two locations. Because our primary training was in qualitative research methods using grounded theory, we were neither surprised nor alarmed at the multiple goals, the subtle variations in the delivery of the intervention, the multiple outcomes, and multiple consequences observed for the actors involved. When wearing our "quantitative hats," however, it was somewhat alarming to be a witness to such variation, when our reading and interpretation of clinical field trials had led us to believe that the goals and intervention remained constant throughout a study. We now read the flawless reports of major clinical trials with more interest and ask many more questions. Questions we ask ourselves include, Would we have known about the multiple realities—that is, the goals and evolution of our intervention—had we not entered the participants' world through qualitative study? Did we, in some way, cause this phenomenon? Or is this merely the hidden multiple reality behind every clinical trial that fails to carry out a qualitative analysis of the intervention? This hidden reality can be described only by qualitative data. As stated by Mullen and Iverson (1986):

Programs tend to drift away from their protocols. The program personnel, anxious to achieve success, may make midcourse corrections based on early perceptions of how well they are doing. A harried clinical staff for whom the program represents extra work may slacken their effort. You need qualitative data to detect these changes. (p. 156)

Kidder and Fine (1987), in a chapter on combining quantitative and qualitative methods, concluded:

> The more divergent the methods are, the greater the likelihood that the traits or concepts under study will also diverge. Field work and other Qualitative methods that permit the researcher to generate and revise hypotheses en route also permit the concepts or traits to evolve as the research progresses. . . . Field work and other methods with the Q writ large . . . increase the chance of obtaining multiple rather than identical stories. (pp. 72-73)

As the research using qualitative methods progresses, the evolution of the concepts, the multiple stories, and the divergent traits present the following dilemma to the investigators: the need to grapple with the underlying theoretical assumptions set at the onset of the study versus the generation of theory from the shared meanings and interpretations that come about through interaction.

Methodological Issues: Design

Driving the Study. Weiss (1987) stated that a "qualitative evaluation would proceed from the participants' view of the world, rather than from the bureaucratic perspective" (p. 43). In contrast to Weiss' statement, we found, in embedding a qualitative evaluation within a quasi-experimental study, that the research design, rather than the participants, drove the study. The design of the outcome evaluation virtually drove the study. The study, a randomized clinical trial, used a pretest, posttest repeated measures design, in which was embedded a qualitative evaluation of the intervention, generating a process using grounded theory. Judd (1987) recommended that process evaluations be "developed routinely in planning outcome evaluations" (p. 39) but noted that "process evaluation is rarely incorporated into outcome evaluation studies" (p. 37). Judd gave two primary reasons for this neglect. The first reason concerns the funding agency that defines the primary role of the researcher as "one of justifying a social intervention by demonstrating its utility" (Judd, 1987, p. 38). The second reason concerns the methodological demands of incorporating a process analysis into an outcome evaluation.

Funding. In the current fiscal crisis, nearly all funding agencies are making cutbacks in monies allocated to research. Our experience of cutbacks included an initial cut of 6 months of funding that had been allocated largely to the analysis of the qualitative data. Due to the nature of our design, in which we were locked into recruiting a sufficient number of participants to meet the needs for demonstrating a desired effect size and allow for attrition, an all-or-nothing approach had to be taken for the outcome evaluation. To preserve the integrity of the outcome evaluation, later annual cutbacks in funding preyed on the resources needed for the ongoing analysis of the process evaluation, which we felt was viewed as secondary to our outcome evaluation by the funders. Methodological demands of embedding a process evaluation into an outcome evaluation also occurred.

Study Eligibilities. Methodological dilemmas arose at the onset of the study in terms of eligibilities for participation in the study. The methodological requirements for sampling included screening of potential participants based on strict criteria for participation. Broadhead (1980) pointed out that "in resolving the methodological requirements of randomization, goal operationalization, and pre- and post-testing, the application of an experimental design in evaluating a given program results in fundamental transformations of the program itself" (p. 24). Conflict-laden problems, according to Broadhead, include "the withholding of services from otherwise eligible clients" (p. 24). The study was limited in meeting the needs of the quantitative evaluation; that is, it may have recruited persons with genital herpes not representative of persons with the disease in the community, a not uncommon problem in a quasi-experimental study. It was limited also in meeting the needs of the qualitative evaluation; that is, it recruited persons with genital herpes who did not represent a complete range and variation of persons with the disease in the community.

Although the criteria for eligibility for participation in the study were given in the proposal for the study, the meaning of the consequences of the eligibility criteria became evident to the investigators only as recruitment of participants progressed and feedback from the intake sheets and recruiter revealed the nature of the self-selected sample. For example, responses to the newspaper advertisements included calls from persons in their 60s and 70s who gave impassioned or, at times, angry pleas to be allowed into the study because they, too, were in and out of relationships and had problems disclosing to a partner and living with the disease. We were, in fact, accused of ageism. This limitation, although necessary to the experimental design, had repercussions in the analysis phase of the qualitative data as it limited theoretical sampling, an integral component of grounded theory. With a total of 39 participants in the qualitative phase of the study, we had sufficient data to show range and variation and could find the necessary cases for dimensionalizing categories. We were unable to go beyond the confines of the criteria for participation in the study for persons, for example, who had not consulted a health professional about their disease or who were under 18 or over 35 years of age.

Randomization. The requirement of the design for randomization presented us with a dilemma that we failed to anticipate. Fetterman (1982) described an ethical dilemma related to an insensitive design in a national evaluation study. The study evaluated workforce programs that would aid in knowledge development in the employment and training of high school dropouts and potential dropouts from disadvantaged backgrounds (largely low-income minority teenagers). The incident occurred when a young woman, during a transcontinental call, was moved to tears after receiving a letter assigning her to the control group, thus denying her treatment in the program, which she perceived as a chance, perhaps her only chance, to function within the system. Similar concerns were expressed during interviews with rejected students and parents at each site. Likewise, what we were not prepared for were the accounts of the informants in the control group of the meaning of being a member of the control group. Poring over the transcripts and recalling the interviews we had conducted individually with control group members revealed the anguish and, at times, anger they felt when not assigned to the experimental group sessions. The reality of the informants' lives as members of the control group at the 3-month and 6-month interviews caused much reflection and introspection. For example, a male informant at the 3-month interview responded to the interviewer's question, "Why did you join the research project, and what did you hope to get from being in it?"

> Well, initially I was hoping that I would, you know, learn some more about herpes and you know, maybe understand it better. And that's happening a little bit. . . . I was kind of interested in if I would have gotten in one of those group sessions, because you know, I've never actually been to a group session about herpes, and you know, there's only one person that I know right now who has herpes and I'm afraid to tell her that I have herpes cause I don't want her to feel like she gave it to me. . . . It would be good to talk to her about her experience with herpes and how she deals with it . . . but I can't, like, I can't like find a comfortable way to ask her about that.

In conducting the interviews and/or reading the transcripts, we came to know the informants in the control group as persons, not merely as identification numbers. It would have been easier to deal with the fact that they were in the control group if they were just numbers. It was harder to deal with the fact that our study design prevented them from receiving information about genital herpes, carrying out exercises on how to disclose to a partner, and discussing safer sex and how to bring this topic up with a partner. We wrote into our design that we would offer the psychoeducational groups to the control group members *if our findings made a statistically significant difference in the experimental group.* Although our preliminary findings suggest the group intervention made a difference in outcomes, we are left with two dilemmas: The first is trying to reach a highly mobile young adult population of control group members, more than 2½ years following the time when the first participants were inducted into the study. The second dilemma is that we ask ourselves why the decision to offer the group intervention to the control group should rest on the findings of the outcome evaluation and not on the findings of the process evaluation. In future studies the intervention could be offered to the control groups as soon as data collection is completed, independent of qualitative or quantitative results.

Goals

Midstream Changes. According to Buchanan (1992), process evaluation has a different set of goals for social research than does outcome evaluation. Our project started with very specific goals stated as specific aims, hypotheses, and research questions in our proposal. Goal operationalization clearly was presented in the proposal, too, in the form of definitions of terms, operationalization of terms, and instruments carefully chosen or developed to meet the needs of the study. As the study progressed, however, it became evident, in the course of analysis of the qualitative data, that we could not measure what was becoming evident as important at this later point in the study. Midstream changes to correct program deficiencies were needed but were not possible. For example, the participants in the psychoeducational groups stated a specific desire for more than three group sessions, as they believed they were just beginning to "open up" when the groups ended (one group session continues to meet). Another example is that feedback from the 18-year-old participants who were in the same group as those "much older," the 35-year-olds, was difficult to untenable. Only then did it dawn on us that 35 was nearly twice the age of 18 and that a generational difference would be of concern to some.

Uncharted Territory. We also realized there were limitations to our goals for the study. Our dilemma was that the goals, processes, problems, and consequences related to the intervention—what we were analyzing by using qualitative methods—were vastly complex and, it appeared to us, somewhat new material. We suddenly found ourselves asking, Was it foolhardy for us to have predicted outcomes for the quasi-experimental phase of the study when we were, in effect, exploring uncharted territory? Furthermore, we were asking nurses—public health, school-based clinic, and college health, and all carrying a caseload of patients with STDs—to conduct an intervention to bring about change in people's lives that the nurses were not overly experienced with and for which there is yet no science to guide their practice. For example, during the training session of the group facilitators, the nurses were asked to report on a homework project assigned to them to carry out the previous week. They were instructed to purchase condoms and to be prepared to present their experience and their feelings related to the experience at the training session. As they shared their experiences, it became evident that the majority of the nurses had not purchased condoms; their accounts were both comical and revealing. One nurse asked her teenage son to buy the condoms for her; another admitted she had "filched" them from work. Still another picked them off a stand at the drugstore and took them to the clerk, only to observe several other customers already in line. Embarrassed, she returned to the back of the store, placed the condoms in the bottom of a basket, and proceeded to pile many other items, which she confessed she did not need, on top of the condoms to make them invisible, and returned to the check-out stand and paid for her purchases, the condoms included. Yet the nurse group facilitators continued with the training and proceeded to lead the psychoeducational groups and taught safer sex as they were doing so in their professional practice. Our experience raised many questions: Do we continue as we have in the past? Is the level of sexual comfort of the nurse-facilitator important to leading the psychoeducational groups? Do we give the nurses more experience (increase our training)? Or do we wait for the science to catch up with our work? In future studies, would early qualitative work better serve to direct our quasi-experimental work?

Analysis

Investigator-Led Objectivity. Issues arose related to analysis. For example, there was no question that a qualitative analysis team whose members had studied grounded theory under mentorship of one of its founders, Anselm Strauss, would generate a grounded theory from the study that explained the process(es) experienced by the participants in the psychoeducational groups. In the original proposal, an outside consultant (an expert in grounded theory) was to have led the qualitative analysis team. Due to unforeseen circumstances, this person was not available to direct the analysis, and the reconfigured team included members who also were directing and managing the quantitative evaluation. The dilemmas revolved around the following issues:

Could the project personnel who designed the study, wrote the curriculum, trained the group facilitators, and were involved in the quantitative evaluation also carry out the qualitative evaluation? Could they be objective enough to carry out the qualitative evaluation? As the literature described both quantitative and qualitative phases of evaluation by the same research team (Burnside, 1990; Dorfman et al., 1992), we decided to proceed with the evaluations. We decided that although the qualitative team was aware of the preliminary findings based on aggregate data, until the grounded theory was completed, the qualitative evaluators would not examine any individual responses to questionnaire items so as to prevent bias. The next phase of the evaluation, however, will compare quantitative and qualitative responses in order to gain insight into contradictory findings.

Focus/Scope. The next questions faced by the qualitative evaluation team in the process of generating a grounded theory included the following: Was the unit of analysis the group or the individual? Would we account for interaction and change only within the group sessions, or would we include a description of or a theory of the experience of the controls? Would the grounded theory account for change in the young adults in both experimental and control groups over the 6-month period? Another question faced was, Would we "evaluate" (judge) the group sessions and how they were conducted? Would we "evaluate" the group facilitators? After reviewing the literature and our theoretical base, symbolic interactionism, the team decided that the context of the groups, such as the social structural features (e.g., where, when, and how the groups were conducted) and the interaction of the individual members and the entire group with the group facilitator, were all crucial to the qualitative analysis. Also the process by which the persons in the control groups changed and short-term (3-month) and long-term (6-month) consequences for persons in both the experimental and control groups were also important to the qualitative evaluation.

Mechanics. The mechanics of the analysis also posed dilemmas. For example, we originally had planned to select randomly the two sets of experimental and control participants for the qualitative evaluation. However, due to the constraints of the

sites chosen (only one had videotaping capacity) and the necessity of spacing the two groups to increase the time or allow
enough time for the analysis of the qualitative data, we were
unable to do so. The resulting dilemma was that even with the
planned spacing of the qualitative data collection phases of the
study (8 months apart), we still did not allow sufficient time to
analyze fully the data from the first round of data collection
before the second round took place; in effect, we were flooded
with data. Although a power analysis yielded the appropriate
size of the quantitative sample and allowed for a reasonable
percentage of the sample to drop out of the study, the qualitative
sample of 39 informants, though reasonable for a grounded
theory study, was complicated by the time series design; the
total of three interviews to be conducted with these informants
over the 6-month period (plus attrition) resulted in 115 interviews by Week 26, an inordinately large number of interviews
for a grounded theory study. Although this dilemma was handled
by treating the three interviews of each informant over the 6
months as a case study, it did not cut down on the total numbers
of pages of transcription that needed to be reviewed, coded, and
categorized.

Range and Variation. Broadhead (1980) pointed out that an
interactionist approach focuses on the dynamics of an intervention and is "designed to seek out and take variation and diversity
into account" (p. 34). Our discovery of range and variation
served to inform us of how much more complex the process we
were attempting to study was than we had ever imagined, and
pointed out to us the need for even more in-depth study than we
had realized we needed. An example relates to the serendipitous
finding of reports of substance use by the participants in our
study. We discovered quite unexpectedly, in the content of the
interviews in the first phase of the study, that substance use was
high in these young adults. Because substance use is a risk factor
or marker for risky behavior and has been associated with risky
sexual behavior and the acquisition of STDs, including HIV
seropositivity (Swanson et al., in press), we had developed a
scale of substance use and had included it in this second phase
of the study. We also had included a brief section in the psychoeducational group curriculum on drug awareness and educa-

tion and distributed a referral sheet with local agencies offering related services. We did not know how the connection between alcohol, drugs, and sex would be taken by the majority of the young adults: How sensitive would they be to this issue? Would they be offended? Or would they think it "on target" and find it helpful? Although we knew that our sample was probably at high risk due to substance use, feedback on the perceived appropriateness of this addition to the intervention from the young adults could be gained only from them. Despite being cautioned by a consultant who had worked with persons with genital herpes not to address the issue of substance use as it was too sensitive an issue for persons who were already feeling "one down" due to a diagnosis of the disease, we thought the accounts of substance use and its association with risky sexual behavior by informants in the first phase of the study and by the links suggested in the literature warranted the addition of this topic in the risk assessment questionnaires and in the intervention. Information regarding the appropriateness of this addition, the attitudes of the informants toward the topic, and insight into how substances were used and for what purpose could be gained only through the qualitative evaluation. The following excerpt from one of the psychoeducational group sessions illustrates how the qualitative evaluation informed us of the response to the addition and also contributed insight as to the context of drug use, conditions for its use, and strategies of drug use in relation to the disease.

My whole sexual history has been totally mixed with drugs and alcohol and I've been really thinking about this lately because of the first questionnaire that I filled out and I started thinking about the connection between . . . I've also gotten pregnant a lot of times and stuff like that and there's a really obvious, profound connection between my being high and not protecting myself, period . . . I smoke marijuana regularly. I drink beer with my friends . . . and I think it took those substances for me to be able to let go and have sex. . . .

I'd have this whole thing set up where I'm going to use this condom . . . Well, you know, after six beers, I didn't care. And so, it's a big deal and it's a big connection.

Just from my own experience, I never really got into any kind of trouble, so to say, with drugs and sex, cause I learned a long time ago that under the influence of drugs I just can't get active sexually . . . I've had to lay off everything just because . . . I went on a binge last year and it just really brought my immune system down and I was breaking out all the time. I had to quit smoking. My asthma came back . . . and I had to quit everything pretty much, you know, so I wouldn't be so unhealthy and breaking out, wheezing and coughing. The only thing I haven't given up is alcohol. I have to admit that's probably increased . . . The way I feel is, man you know, I got struck down with this damned thing at a young age. I need something . . . just one escape, now and then . . . a little bit of a release now and then.

I've used MDMA [ecstacy] for two days straight as soon as I have an outbreak or symptoms . . . But, I mean, it's due to stress, but if I don't have any stress, I don't have any problems . . . I, like when I contracted it, you know, and I was having my outbreaks, I drank a lot and I did a lot of drugs and that was probably part of it. But now, once I got rid of a lot of stress, I don't . . . I manage it a lot easier. I mean, MDMA is a drug and it helps me get rid of the stress.

Somebody mentioned alcohol. I mean, I drink a lot of alcohol, I'll admit it. I don't think I have a drinking problem but I drink a lot and party a lot. But, is that a direct effect of bringing out the herpes again? Cause if it is, I'm going to stop.

The resulting dilemma faced by the team, once informed of the even greater use of alcohol and illicit drugs among our participants than we had found in the previous phase of the study was, How adequate was our intervention? Should we have devoted more time to processing this topic? Too little is known about how substances are used as a strategy for living with genital herpes to even ask the correct questions in a later survey. Our range and variation around the category "use of illicit drugs" demands further exploration via in-depth, open-ended interviews.

The Nature of Change. Broadhead (1980) stated that although an experimental approach to evaluation "may be capable of measuring change, it does not inform the researcher of the basic social processes integral to a program under evaluation; nor does it reveal 'why' or 'how' the independent variable results in the changes observed" (p. 35). Weiss (1987) stated that, from a qualitative evaluation, one learns not only what processes are related to changes in the group under study but also what factors prevent people from implementing what they learned. A case study drawn from the data will serve to illustrate factors that "prevented" one respondent from implementing what she learned. It reflects a process that this respondent, as all, experienced in implementing what she learned from the group intervention.

Shirley, a 19-year-old student, reported in her baseline interview that she was not in a relationship when she contracted herpes from a "friend of a friend" who was in town from a nearby state, visiting for the weekend. Her interview 3 months later revealed that, during the interim 3 months, she had managed to establish a relationship of 2 months' duration with a partner, a major step for her. What prevented her from implementing what she had learned in the psychoeducational group—to make a timely disclosure of her diagnosis to a partner—was a process that took time. We had identified that a process accounted for the gap between her goal—to tell a partner of her disease—and the realities of her life. Although she was deemed successful by the quantitative measure in terms of disclosing to a partner at 3 months following her baseline interview and experiencing the intervention, she was unsuccessful at 3 months in terms of sustaining the relationship. Although she successfully had told her partner she had herpes, he was furious that she had waited 2 months to inform him and had placed him, unknowingly, at risk for herpes during that time. His fury culminated in his immediate termination of the relationship.

> He was extremely upset with me because I had waited to tell him. And that was basically the end of it . . . even though I knew he would be really angry and I knew that he probably wouldn't want to be involved with me anymore, I figured I had to like say it to someone the first time and get that over with and I'm glad that I told him. I mean, I regret not telling him from the beginning, but I'm glad I didn't wait any longer . . . I mean, he was really upset . . . I'm glad though, because it just made me realize that I can't make that mistake again . . . [I must] discuss it with every potential sex partner.

She, was, in effect, "successful" at disclosing but was "unsuccessful" in terms of timing and the maintenance of the relationship. She nevertheless stated that, as a result of the experience, "I almost feel like more confident about it, not as scared or ashamed as I had been."

Although the quasi-experimental design virtually drove the study methodologically, the process evaluation nevertheless illuminated the questions of how and why the group psychoeducational interventions resulted in the observed changes. Without the process evaluation, the black box would have remained opaque, at best. Our dilemma is, in the next phase of our study, how do we "measure" a complex process, or do we "measure" it?

Conclusions and Recommendations

Although the study team faced dilemmas repeatedly in the attempt to embed a qualitative evaluation within a quasi-experimental study, the team members believe that they have overcome the limitations of a black box design and that they have gained insight into the "internal processes and problems, events, meanings, and situations that make up the interaction between a program and its clients" (Broadhead, 1980, p. 35).

Success has been reported with the use of qualitative evaluation during the past 30 years (see Weiss, 1987, for a review) in many fields, including education, psychology, sociology, anthropology, health planning, and human organization. Mental health professionals are using both quantitative and qualitative approaches in the evaluation of federally funded AIDS prevention programs with intravenous drug users and their partners in cities throughout the United States (Schensul & Weeks, 1991).

Nursing, it seems, is less likely to report activity involving qualitative evaluation. Yet, as pointed out by Swenson (1991), fourth-generation evaluation may be "more consistent with a nursing paradigm than with a traditional, scientific, medical paradigm" (p. 79). It may be also that nursing, as a young science, has had a propensity to lean heavily on quantitative methods. It may be also that nursing does not yet have a cadre of investigators with the background and expertise to carry out qualitative investigations, although interest in qualitative methods is growing. Even more so, nursing may lack investigators who have expertise in both quantitative and qualitative methods and who then could apply them to evaluation research. Training is needed in both paradigms to do combination projects. Researchers should be encouraged to do postdoctoral fellowships in the paradigm opposite from their doctoral preparation. The development of teamwork also is needed, with members of the team having expertise in both paradigms. Faculty teams that can serve as role models are needed as well.

The existing cadre of nurse anthropologists, phenomenologists, medical sociologists, grounded theorists, and other qualitative researchers is needed for theory-generated process evaluation. Needed is theory-generated process evaluation that calls for the Big Q, which is looking for questions, rather than the Small q, which is looking for answers.

Qualitative research usually is relegated to "an epistemologically subordinate role" (Buchanan, 1992, p. 118). There is a need to deal with the cultural gap between the adherents of qualitative research and those of quantitative research (Steckler, McLeroy, Goodman, Bird, & McCormick, 1992). Kidder and Fine (1987) pointed out that questions about whether quantitative and qualitative methods are compatible and/or are complementary and can withstand methodological scrutiny must be viewed as questions about two distinct cultures. Whereas one culture is accused of "navel gazing," the other is accused of "number crunching" (Kidder & Fine, 1987, p. 57). Although Kidder and Fine (1987) shared with others, such as Cronbach et al. (1980), Goetz and LeCompte (1984), and Reichardt and Cook (1979), the belief that synthesis between the two cultures will allay the distrust one has for the other, they "want to preserve the significant differences between the two cultures. Instead of homogenizing research methods and cultures, we would like to see researchers become bicultural. Rather than 'closing down the conversation' about quantitative-qualitative differences, we want to sustain it" (pp. 57-58).

For nursing to move ahead and to generate theory that will enhance the "explanatory power of evaluation" (Mullen & Iverson, 1986), nursing needs to become "bicultural," and it needs sufficient funding to support process evaluation and literature that addresses methodology related to process evaluation and the combination of outcome and process evaluation. Books on analysis of various methods (quantitative and qualitative) and books and articles on the pros and cons of combination studies exist, but there is a dearth of books on the methodology of combining methods.

Nursing, unlike medicine, is faced with developing a body of literature that is heavily devoted to addressing human behavior and behavioral change. The demands on nurses in the current AIDS epidemic illustrate this point. For example, nurses are charged with preventing the spread of the AIDS epidemic through teaching safer sex practices, which for many persons means behavioral change. Yet little literature supports behavioral change as an outcome of interventions with heterosexual persons, persons of color, and persons of low socioeconomic status. Negative results from quantitative evaluations of such programs are almost expected. Qualitative evaluation of such programs could provide the insight needed into the substance of these programs, the "how" and the "why" behind the evaluation of a program as a "success" or a "failure." As evidenced in the study dilemmas posed here, behavior change is a process that cannot be captured in a true/false or Likert scale response to an item or even to a bank of items on a questionnaire. Truth as contained in shared meanings and interpretations is needed. Qualitative evaluation holds great promise for the science, for the profession, and for the health of the populations we serve.

References

Aral, S. O., Wasserheit, J. N., Green, S. B., Judson, F. N., Sparling, P. F., & NIAID Study Group on Integrated Behavioral Research for Prevention and Control of Sexually Transmitted Diseases. (1991). Part III: Issues in evaluating behavioral interventions. In J. N. Wasserheit, S. O. Aral, & K. K. Holmes (Eds.), *Research issues in human behavior and sexually transmitted diseases in the AIDS era* (pp. 367-371). Washington, DC: American Society for Microbiology.

Becker, M. H., & Joseph, J. G. (1988). AIDS and behavioral change to reduce risk: A review. *American Journal of Public Health, 78,* 394-410.

Berger, P. L., & Luckmann, T. (1967). *The social construction of reality.* Garden City, NY: Doubleday.

Blumer, H. (1969). *Symbolic interactionism.* Englewood Cliffs, NJ: Prentice Hall.

Broadhead, R. S. (1980). Qualitative analysis in evaluation research: Problems and promises of an interactionist approach. *Symbolic Interaction, 3,* 23-40.

Buchanan, D. R. (1992). An uneasy alliance: Combining qualitative and quantitative research methods. *Health Education Quarterly, 19,* 117-135.

Burnside, I. M. (1990). *The effect of reminiscence groups on fatigue, affect, and life satisfaction in older women* (Doctoral dissertation, University of Texas at Austin). (University Microfilms No. 9031528)

Chen, H. T. (1990). *Theory-driven evaluations.* Newbury Park, CA: Sage.

Chen, H. T., & Rossi, P. H. (1983). Evaluating with sense: The theory-driven approach. *Evaluation Review, 7,* 283-302.

Chenitz, W. C., & Swanson, J. M. (1986). *From practice to grounded theory: Qualitative research in nursing.* Menlo Park, CA: Addison-Wesley.

Corey, L. (1990). Genital herpes. In K. K. Holmes, P. Mardh, P. F. Sparling, P. J. Wiesner, W. Cates, S. M. Lemon, & W. E. Stamm (Eds.), *Sexually transmitted diseases* (pp. 391-413). New York: McGraw-Hill.

Cronbach, L. J. (1975). Beyond the two disciplines of scientific psychology. *American Psychologist, 30,* 116-127.

Cronbach, L. J., Ambron, S. R., Dornbusch, S. M., Hess, R. D., Hornik, R. C., Phillips, D. C., Walker, D. F., & Weiner, S. S. (1980). *Toward reform of program evaluation: Aims, methods, and institutional arrangements.* San Francisco: Jossey-Bass.

Dorfman, L. E., Derish, P. A., & Cohen, J. B. (1992). Hey girlfriend: An evaluation of AIDS prevention among women in the sex industry. *Health Education Quarterly, 19,* 25-40.

Erikson, E. (1963). *Childhood and society.* New York: Norton.

Fetterman, D. M. (1982). Ibsen's baths: Reactivity and insensitivity (A misapplication of the treatment-control group design in a national evaluation). *Educational Evaluation and Policy Analysis, 4,* 261-279.

Fetterman, D. M. (1984). *Ethnography in educational evaluation.* Beverly Hills, CA: Sage.

Frenn, M. D., Borgeson, D. S., Lee, H. A., & Simandl, G. (1989). Life-style changes in a cardiac rehabilitation program: The client perspective. *Journal of Cardiovascular Nursing, 3,* 43-55.

Glaser, B. G., & Strauss, A. L. (1967). *The discovery of grounded theory.* Hawthorne, NY: Aldine.

Goetz, J. P., & LeCompte, M. D. (1984). *Ethnography and qualitative design in educational research.* New York: Academic Press.

Guba, E. (1987). Naturalistic evaluation. In D. S. Cordray, H. L. Bloom, & R. H. Light (Eds.), *Evaluation practice in review* (New directions for program evaluation, No. 34, pp. 23-43). San Francisco: Jossey-Bass.

Guba, E. G., & Lincoln, Y. S. (1989). *Fourth generation evaluation.* Newbury Park, CA: Sage.

Herdt, G., & Boxer, A. M. (1991). Ethnographic issues in the study of AIDS. *Journal of Sex Research, 28,* 171-187.

Joseph, J. G., Montgomery, S. B., Emmons, C., Kessler, R. C., Ostrow, D. G., Wortman, C. B., O'Brien, K., Eller, M., & Eshleman, S. (1987). Magnitude and determinants of behavioral risk reduction: Longitudinal analysis of a cohort at risk for AIDS. *Psychology and Health, 1,* 73-96.

Judd, C. M. (1987). Combining process and outcome evaluation. In M. M. Mark & R. L. Shotland (Eds.), *Multiple methods in program evaluation* (pp. 23-41). San Francisco: Jossey-Bass.

Kidder, L. H., & Fine, M. (1987). Qualitative and quantitative methods: When stories converge. In M. M. Mark & R. L. Shotland (Eds.), *Multiple methods in program evaluation* (pp. 57-75). San Francisco: Jossey-Bass.

Lipsey, M. W., Crosse, S., Dunkle, J., Pollard, J., & Stobart, G. (1985). Evaluation: The state of the art and the sorry state of the science. In D. S. Cordray (Ed.), *Utilizing prior research in evaluation planning* (pp. 7-28). San Francisco: Jossey-Bass.

Livingood, W. C., Woodhouse, L. D., & Natale, J. (1991). The ALERT partnership evaluation: Enhancing health program evaluation with qualitative techniques. *Family and Community Health, 14,* 28-35.

Mosher, L. R., & Menn, A. (1978). Community residential treatment for schizophrenia: Two-year follow-up. *Hospital and Community Psychiatry, 29,* 715-723.

Mullen, P. D., & Iverson, D. C. (1986). Qualitative methods. In L. W. Green & F. M. Lewis (Eds.), *Measurement and evaluation in health education and health promotion* (pp. 149-170). Palo Alto, CA: Mayfield.

Murdaugh, C. L. (1989). Nursing research. *Journal of Cardiovascular Nursing, 3,* 56-58.

Patton, M. Q. (1980). *Qualitative evaluation methods.* Beverly Hills, CA: Sage.

Patton, M. Q. (1986). *Utilization-focused evaluation.* Beverly Hills, CA: Sage.

Patton, M. Q. (1987). *How to use qualitative methods in evaluation.* Newbury Park, CA: Sage.

Patton, M. Q. (1990). *Qualitative evaluation and research methods.* Newbury Park, CA: Sage.

Reichardt, C. S., & Cook, T. S. (1979). Beyond qualitative versus quantitative methods. In T. Cook & C. S. Reichardt (Eds.), *Qualitative and quantitative methods* (pp. 7-32). Newbury Park, CA: Sage.

Sarnecky, M. T. (1990a). Program evaluation part 1: Four generations of theory. *Nurse Educator, 15,* 25-28.

Sarnecky, M. T. (1990b). Program evaluation part 2: A responsive model proposal. *Nurse Educator, 15,* 7-10.

Schensul, J. J., & Weeks, M. (1991). Ethnographic evaluation of AIDS-prevention programs. In National Institute on Drug Abuse (Ed.), *Community-based AIDS prevention: Studies of intravenous drug users and their sexual partners* (pp. 110-120). Rockville, MD: NOVA Research.

Schmid, G. (1990). Approach to the patient with genital ulcer disease. *Medical Clinics of North America, 74,* 1559-1572.

Siegel, K., & Krauss, B. J. (1991). Living with HIV infection: Adaptive tasks of seropositive gay men. *Journal of Health and Social Behavior, 32,* 17-32.

Steckler, A., McLeroy, K. R., Goodman, R. M., Bird, S. T., & McCormick, L. (1992). Toward integrating qualitative and quantitative methods: An introduction. *Health Education Quarterly, 19,* 1-8.

Swanson, J. M. (1986). The formal qualitative interview for grounded theory. In W. C. Chenitz & J. M. Swanson (Eds.), *From practice to grounded theory: Qualitative research in nursing* (pp. 66-78). Menlo Park, CA: Addison-Wesley.

Swanson, J. M. (1992). Genital herpes and prevention of human immunodeficiency virus (HIV) infection: The report of a study in progress. *Journal of the Association of Nurses in AIDS Care, 3,* 4-10.

Swanson, J. M., & Chenitz, W. C. (1993). Regaining a valued self: The process of adaptation to living with genital herpes. *Qualitative Health Research, 3,* 270-297.

Swanson, J. M., Remy, L., Chenitz, C., Chastain, R., & Trocki, K. (in press). Illicit drug use in young adults with genital herpes. *Public Health Nursing*.

Swenson, M. M. (1991). Using fourth-generation evaluation in nursing. *Evaluation and the Health Professions, 14,* 79-87.

Valdiserri, R. O., Lyter, D. W., Kingsley, L. A., Leviton, L. C., Schofield, J. W., Huggins, J., Ho, M., & Rinaldo, C. R. (1987). The effect of group education on improving attitudes about AIDS risk reduction. *New York State Journal of Medicine, 87,* 272-278.

Valdiserri, R. O., Lyter, D. W., Leviton, L. C., Callahan, C. M., Kingsley, L. A., & Rinaldo, C. R. (1989). AIDS prevention in homosexual and bisexual men: Results of a randomized trial evaluating two risk reduction interventions. *AIDS, 3,* 21-26.

Weiss, C. H. (1972). *Evaluating action programs*. Boston: Allyn & Bacon.

Weiss, C. H. (1987). Evaluating social programs: What have we learned? *Society, 25,* 40-45.

Wermuth, L., Ham, J., & Robbins, R. L. (1992). Women don't wear condoms: AIDS risk among sexual partners of IV drug users. In J. Huber & B. E. Schneider (Eds.), *The social context of AIDS* (pp. 72-94). Newbury Park, CA: Sage.

Wilson, H. S. (1982). *Deinstitutionalized residential care for the mentally disordered*. New York: Grune & Stratton.

Woodhouse, L. D., & Livingood, W. C. (1991). Exploring the versatility of qualitative design for evaluating community substance abuse prevention projects. *Qualitative Health Research, 1,* 434-445.

Dialogue

Basic Versus Applied Ethnography

LEININGER As we continue to move to develop and use nursing theories, we also need to develop our own methodologies. This is an important trend in nursing. I think that as we move forward to establish research-based nursing knowledge, nurses will develop new research methods that will fit the theory being systematically examined or tested. Ethnonursing is the first example of nursing research method developed to fit the theory of culture care phenomena. Nursing can establish its contributions to research methods and encourage future nurses to pursue similar goals for generating substantive discipline knowledge.

MUECKE To me the issue really is that we are sitting on the horns of a dilemma. We have got the weight of history, so to speak, on our shoulders and on our heads saying, "It's your standard," and yet, we are out there practicing and trying to inform nursing practice through this work—

STERN You're right! You're right—and those "old guys on the hill" criticize you for not doing classical work, right? And you know that you've got something that's more important, more relevant!

LEININGER I think it would be interesting, Marjorie, to trace this trend historically of how nurse-anthropologists have changed research methods in anthropology over time to nursing research uses. Nurse-anthropologists have focused on studying health and care phenomena. Non-nurse anthropologists were slower in this area and pursued their academic cross-cultural interests. While nurses are teasing out health and care phenomena, some are not always making their methods and strategies fully known to nurse researchers. Some nurses are saying they are following ethnographic methods but have not discussed how they have altered the method to study nursing phenomena. How nurses conceptualize cultural care and health phenomena with qualitative approaches and strategies often is limitedly known in the literature. Such methodological changes from anthropology to nursing methods, I find, are fascinating to discover. They occur for a number of good reasons and over time. Such historical changes are of great interest to scholars of nursing.

6

Evaluation Criteria and Critique of Qualitative Research Studies

MADELEINE LEININGER

One thing that is becoming clearer in research assessments is the confusion between critique and evaluation. In looking at this problem, I find that many assessments are reviews, more than the use of critiques and evaluations. *Critiques* reflect the use of critics who assess a piece of work without external criteria. In contrast, a research *evaluation* requires the use of external explicit criteria. One of the problems we should address is, Why is it so difficult for qualitative researchers not to use qualitative criteria? I have always believed in and worked toward the goal to have evaluation criteria fit the paradigm. In my 30-some years conducting qualitative research, I hold we must develop and use criteria that fit the qualitative paradigm, rather than use quantitative criteria for qualitative studies. It is awkward and inappropriate to re-language quantitative terms or to relabel them as validity or reliability and use them for quantitative evaluations. Unfortunately students are taught to use quantitative criteria for qualitative studies, and this instruction seriously confounds and confuses the purposes of qualitative criteria. It therefore is time for nurses to assert their autonomy and to use qualitative criteria to evaluate qualitative paradigm studies. Without this position, we will continue to have noncredible, inaccurate, and questionable findings for qualitative studies. It is time to change practices!

The purpose of this chapter is to discuss critical issues and principles related to the use of evaluation criteria and critiques of qualitative paradigmatic research in order to advance and establish credible research outcomes. It is my contention that far more understanding and commitment must be given to the use of specific qualitative research criteria in order to establish substantive research outcomes.

It is imperative to use qualitative evaluation criteria to assess qualitative methods within the qualitative paradigm (Leininger, 1990, 1991b, 1992; Lincoln & Guba, 1985; Reason & Rowan, 1981). For example, qualitative researchers should not rely on the use of quantitative criteria such as validity and reliability to explain or justify their findings. Such dependence reflects a lack of knowledge of the different purposes, goals, and philosophical assumptions of the two paradigms. Because the paradigms are so radically different, a misuse of criteria of each paradigm poses critical problems and greatly curtails the development of credible and valid outcomes.

Few authors explicitly identified and discussed the uses and importance of qualitative criteria to evaluate their qualitative research studies. Rather, conditions for use of evaluating qualitative studies and the characteristics of what constituted "good" qualitative research were presented. Some authors, such as Morse (1991), identified important questions and areas one might use to assess a qualitative study, such as the significance of the research, the methods used, and ethical standards of qualitative research. However, no specific evaluation criterion was identified, discussed, and used. In some articles the term *criterion* was used, but often improperly. For example, in Cobb and Hagemaster's (1987) article "Ten Criteria for Evaluating Qualitative Research Proposals," the authors actually were addressing process, conditions, and concerns they labeled "evaluative categories." These categories, however, were not evaluative criteria. These authors really were addressing conditions and processes related to the use of broad categories for writing a proposal or to assess a proposal. They spoke about expertise of the researcher, problem and research questions, purpose, literature review, data collection, sample of data analysis, and so forth. Although research conditions and processes are important to consider for a qualitative study, they do not meet the definition or expectations of an evaluation criterion to assess a qualitative study.

In further review of the literature, qualitative nurse researchers, such as Aamodt (1983), identified and discussed domains of study. Aamodt discussed the domains of discovery, assumptions, and context as contributions to nursing and as criteria. During the past few decades, qualitative researchers have posed questions about appraising qualitative studies, such as, Was trust established with the informants? Who were the informants and how many? and Did the researcher review the literature before beginning the study? These questions are like stepping stones to conduct a sound qualitative study. They also can be viewed as preconditions to guide the researcher in developing a study, but they are not specific criteria to evaluate a completed work.

LeCompte and Goetz (1982) linguistically reworded reliability and validity criteria to evaluate qualitative research studies. Such practices violate the philosophy, purpose, and intent of the qualitative paradigm, which is to discover in-depth meanings, understandings, and quality attributes of phenomena studied, rather than to obtain quantitative measurable outcomes. Of more concern, in several qualitative books (e.g., Werner & Schoepfle, 1987) no specific criteria are identified or discussed. Thus a major dimension to evaluate qualitative studies has been the *absence of specific criteria to determine a standard or a rule on which to make accurate assessments about qualitative research.* Accordingly the credibility of qualitative research findings becomes obscure or unsubstantiated.

The greatest concern today is that many qualitative researchers are using quantitative criteria to interpret, explain, and support their research findings without realizing the questionable practice or the inappropriateness of such efforts. Using quantitative criteria to evaluate qualitative studies is clearly inconsistent with the philosophy, purposes, and goals of each paradigm and reduces the credibility of the findings. *Qualitative research criteria must be used to fit with the philosophical assumptions, purposes, and goals of the qualitative paradigm.* Using quantitative criteria such as validity and reliability that have been developed within the logical positivism ideology and using the scientific method to measure and make generalizations about quantitative findings are inappropriate means to substantiate qualitative findings. Such terms as *criterion, critique, evaluation,* and *reviews* will help us understand further these paradigmatic issues.

Definition of Terms and Their Uses

In the *American Heritage Dictionary* (1991, p. 341), *criterion* refers to "a standard rule or test on which a judgment or decision may be based." Stated in a research context, a *criterion* refers to "an external standard with preselected rules or norms by which one evaluates a piece of work, project, or research study." To assess a research study, it is important to differentiate the concepts of *evaluation* and *critique,* as these terms are confused with *criterion. Evaluation* refers to "a systematic process by which one deliberately assesses a piece of work using preformulated external standards or criteria with the goal of judging whether a piece of work adequately meets specified criteria or expectations" (*American Heritage Dictionary,* 1991, p. 469). In contrast, the term *critique* refers to a scholarly judgment of another's work by a recognized critic or scholar of stature regarding the general quality of written or nonwritten work according to the critic's areas of expertise, intellectual astuteness, and philosophical commitments (Leininger, 1968). Critics are well recognized in a particular field or subject domain. They usually have had extensive experiences to judge a particular work being appraised. A *review* is a descriptive summary or narrative account of some piece of work without a critique or systematic evaluation (Leininger, 1968). Most frequently, nursing research studies tend to be reviewed, rather than receive a critique.

Evaluation criteria are essential to assess qualitative studies; the researcher must realize that this necessity requires establishing preselected criteria by experts' decisions, consensus, or agreed-on terms. The goal is to use the evaluation criteria to determine whether a study or work meets specified standards and expectations.

Currently still too few researchers are using specific evaluation criteria to assess qualitative studies. Without the use of

evaluation criteria, the credibility of qualitative s
uncertain and indefensible. Qualitative researche
What specific evaluation criteria should be used t
tative research in order to substantiate the finding   ... can I
determine whether my findings are supported or not supported
with the criteria being used? How might my work be contrasted
with similar research studies using the same qualitative criteria?
These questions and others help the researcher realize the importance of using evaluation criteria to document and assess
qualitative paradigm findings. For without the use of explicit
evaluation criteria for qualitative studies, the findings can be
subject to doubt, questioning, and nonconfirmable findings.

Status and Principles Related
to Qualitative Studies in Nursing

Today it is encouraging that many nurse researchers are discovering new ways of knowing nursing phenomena (Duffy,
1986). Many are moving away from dependence on logical positivism and the quantitative paradigm. This movement has occurred because quantitative research often led to limited benefits
to discover, explain, and interpret the central and dominant domains of nursing phenomena especially related to human care,
health, and well-being. As early as 1960, I conducted ethnographic
research and helped open the door to transcultural care research
in nursing. Teasing out vague, subjective, and intersubjective
aspects of human care through language expressions, worldview,
ethnohistories, and social structure factors has led to many new
concepts, interpretive insights, knowledge domains, and specific findings to provide culturally congruent care (Leininger,
1970, 1991a). It took persistence and continuous focus on using
qualitative research methods to generate a new generation of
nurses who were different from the quantitative methodologists.
Moreover, the development and use of ethnonursing permitted
nurses to establish methods appropriate to nursing research and
theory (Leininger, 1990, 1991b).

Through the years it has been interesting to hear graduate
nursing students and faculty identify why quantitative research
methods were not too helpful in discovering difficult and covert

nursing phenomena. Some of their frequent comments were as follows: Quantitative paradigm studies "reduced or eliminated discovering what real humanistic nursing is about"; "It made me feel detached from knowing nursing and care phenomena"; "It overemphasized and misled my investigations because I had to use large random samples, many measurement scales, and statistical analysis"; "I kept testing and measuring nursing phenomena that were impossible to measure"; "I kept avoiding what I knew was potentially relevant to nursing as human care and well-being"; "I had to write my research findings using scientific jargon that omitted what clients and families actually said or told me"; "The preselected variables tested were not what was of interest or most important to me or in nursing"; and "I never felt I was studying and reporting the true meanings and understandings of the people regarding human caring and health in different environments in which nurses work with people." Nurses realized how important qualitative studies were to advance nursing knowledge and to study phenomena of interest to nurses and nursing. With the advent of qualitative studies, a wealth of new and valuable insights has been generated, and more nurses are committed to knowing and understanding the use of qualitative research methods. The need remains, however, for nurses to value and use specific qualitative evaluation criteria within the tenets of the qualitative paradigm to advance and perfect their research endeavors.

It also has been encouraging to know that the status of qualitative studies has increased largely due to publication outlets that are now reporting qualitative research findings, such as *Qualitative Health Research* and *Journal of Transcultural Nursing*. With such journals, faculty, students, and clinicians are able to share their qualitative research findings and to receive recognition. This is a major achievement, for prior to the 1980s, most "pure" of any qualitative studies in nursing were considered to be nonscientific and unacceptable in most publications in nursing research journals unless they were laced with statistical or quantitative measures. It has been most encouraging to see traditional quantitative nursing journals gradually accepting some qualitative articles. As true scholars of nursing, these researchers should not relinquish what they believe is important to advance new areas in nursing. At the same time, these researchers must recognize the many thorny academic, methodological, and unresolved issues related to getting qualitative methods accepted.

Guiding Principles

Many of the issues in nursing and other disciplines are the misuse of the philosophical assumptions, purposes, and goals of the quantitative and qualitative paradigms. Currently one often finds two major principles violated by researchers due to ignorance or denial of the paradigm's philosophical premises and purposes. The first principle to uphold is that *quantitative and qualitative paradigms have different philosophic premises, purposes, and epistemic roots that must be understood, respected, and maintained for credible and sound research outcomes.* Both qualitative and quantitative paradigms have entirely different philosophic assumptions and purposes that lead to different goals, different uses of research methods, and the need for different criteria to fit with each paradigm (Leininger, 1985, 1990, 1991b; Lincoln & Guba, 1985). A full awareness of this first principle makes it imperative that critiques and evaluations be consistent with the philosophic tenets of each paradigm and that the methods used are derived from or congruent with the paradigm purposes. Although this principle has been discussed and substantiated in the literature by several qualitative experts (cited above), the principle remains vaguely understood, valued, and upheld by qualitative researchers as they select methods and ways to evaluate their work.

The second important principle to uphold is that *one cannot mix research methods across qualitative and quantitative paradigms, but one can mix methods within each paradigm* (Leininger, 1990, 1991b). Mixing methods, goals, and purposes across the paradigms violates the intent and philosophic purposes for each paradigm. Some researchers mix qualitative and quantitative research methods with triangulation, or what I call "multiangulation," by using many methods, different scales or instruments, and often different statistical formulas. The idea that "more is better" and "blend the methods" tends to prevail without full awareness of the purposes and potential outcomes of each paradigm its methods and uses. Such practices violate the integrity, purposes, and epistemic roots of each paradigm and lead to a misuse of methods. This misuse can only lead to inaccurate, questionable, and meaningless research findings. With such practices, the philosophic tenets, axioms, and purposes of the two paradigms become eroded, and the work becomes noncredible. The researchers can, however, mix qualitative research methods within a particular paradigm, as this would be consistent with the philosophic tenets and purposes of each paradigm. For example, with the qualitative paradigm, the researcher could mix ethnonursing with life histories and audiovisual methods to study a domain of inquiry, as these methods are congruent with the qualitative paradigm. But to mix ethnography with an experimental or quasi-experimental quantitative method would be inconsistent with the purposes and assumptions of the paradigms.

I find that, in nursing, there is a desire to mix methods across paradigms "to be open" and to show that one must try to use many methods and prove their effectiveness regardless of their purposes. Often no explicit reasons are given for the use of several methods, nor is a full explanation given for how each method was used. Such practices patently violate the purposes of the paradigms. I find that the two paradigms, if used as philosophically based, tend to complement each other and lead to new and different knowledge. We need to encourage nurse researchers to discover the complementary reality of the paradigms and to not keep mixing methods across the two paradigms. The misconception of "using all methods available" or that "diversity will reveal the truths" is a myth and often leads to questionable and unsubstantiated findings. Often the mixing of methods across paradigms occurs because nursing faculty who teach research methods have never had a substantive or advanced qualitative research course. Instead these faculty teach what they think will be best to "integrate both methods" without full awareness of the philosophical bases for each paradigm. Some nursing faculty have said blatantly that they used qualitative findings to support vague quantitative findings or findings that are meaningless or insignificant statistically. Such practices are of deep concern and reflect the critical need to educate faculty and researchers about the differences between the two paradigms and their proper uses.

Some researchers, however, contend that "mixing and matching" of the two paradigms and their respective methods is a controversial issue and see no reason to resolve the matter. Some researchers are continuing to combine qualitative and quantitative research paradigms, such as noted in the work of LeCompte and Goetz (1982), Goodwin and Goodwin (1984), and De Groot (1988). In studying these authors' work and viewpoints, it is clear that they do not seem to understand the philosophic bases of each paradigm. De Groot (1988), a doctoral nursing student, provided a creative approach to problem solving by using both paradigms side by side. However, the conceptualization model and philosophic reasons were questionable and violate the premises and purposes of each paradigm. The "mix and match syndrome" will continue to be an issue until qualitative nurse researchers learn through advanced seminars and experts in qualitative research the philosophic roots and purposes of each paradigm.

As more nurse researchers study the benefits of "pure" qualitative research studies without feeling compelled to add quantitative methods or measurement outcomes, these researchers will see the tremendous power and strengths of qualitative research and will become confident in their work. Most assuredly, qualitative studies that are not tainted or confounded with quantitative statistical methods are much needed to obtain in-depth insights about the "truths" and meanings of many unknowns in nursing. Granted, some "numbers" can be and are used in qualitative studies for directional orientation, but statistical formulas and statistical treatments generally obscure and reduce obtaining meaningful qualitative findings. Nurses should be aware that such uses of statistical formulas not only obscure the purposes and goals of qualitative studies but also limit arrival at full understandings, meanings, expressions, interpretations, and explanations of qualitative phenomena (Guba, 1990; Leininger, 1985, 1991a, 1991b; Lincoln & Guba, 1985). Discrete measurable outcomes and generalizations are not the goal of the qualitative paradigm.

Qualitative Criteria:
Definitions and Purposes

During the past three decades, I have identified and defined six central and important criteria to evaluate qualitative paradigm studies. These criteria have been used by a number of nursing and anthropology students for several years. In developing and studying the criteria, it was important to consider that they could be applicable to all research methods used within the qualitative paradigm. It was my belief that the qualitative paradigm should have evaluation criteria that flowed from its philosophy and purposes. They should be useful for qualitative research methods within the paradigm. The six criteria can be used with all qualitative research methods to research findings. For example, qualitative research methods, such as phenomenology, life history, ethnography, grounded theory, ethnonursing, ethnoscience, metaphoric inquiry, and ethnohistory, would use the six criteria if one fully understands the scope and nature of each criterion. It is true that linguistic terms or phrases for each qualitative method may vary, but the criteria can be used with all qualitative methods. For example, in ethnography and ethnonursing methods, one often refers to "thick" or "in-depth" data. In grounded theory, the term may be "dense" data, which has a similar meaning to thick data. "Saturation" is another term used in phenomenological studies, but it is also used or referred to as "redundancy," or as "an exhausted area" with other methods such as life histories, ethnography, critical theory, and ethnoscience methods. Hence the terms or emphases on each criterion may vary, but similarities in meanings or interpretations make the criteria relevant to all methods within the qualitative family paradigm. Commonalities among the qualitative methods lead to commonalities in the use of the criteria.

With the use of the six criteria, there may be more qualitative data to give evidence to a specific criterion than with a different criterion, but still the six criteria have meaning and are appropriate for all qualitative methods. Having the six criteria used with all qualitative research studies increases the credibility, accuracy, and common family relationships within the qualitative paradigm. Specific qualitative criteria are long overdue to increase the scholarly bases and understandings generated from qualitative studies. Without some common criteria to evaluate qualitative methods, only highly idiosyncratic or particularistic and vague research outcomes can be found in qualitative-related studies. The basic assumption is that some common evaluative criteria needed to be used consistently and explicitly with all qualitative paradigmatic studies and that these six criteria have congruence and are appropriate within the philosophy of the qualitative paradigm.

The criteria stated below are recommended as qualitative criteria to be used in supporting and substantiating qualitative studies. The six major evaluation criteria and definitions developed over time are as follows (Leininger, 1987, 1990, 1991b):

1. *Credibility* refers to the "truth," value, or "believability" of the findings that have been established by the researcher through prolonged observations, engagements, or participation with informants or the situation in which cumulative knowing is the "believable" or lived-through experiences of those studied. Credibility refers to the truth as known, experienced, or deeply felt by the people being studied (emic or local) and interpreted from the findings with co-participant evidence as the "real world," or the truth in reality (this includes subjective, intersubjective, and objective realities). Etic (or outsiders' views) are studied in relation to emic perspectives.

2. *Confirmability* refers to the repeated direct participatory and documented evidence observed or obtained from primary informant sources. Confirmability means obtaining direct and often repeated affirmations of what the researcher has heard, seen, or experienced with respect to the phenomena under study. Confirmability includes getting evidence from informants about findings by the researcher or interpretations. Restating ideas or instances to those who have shared their ideas are ways to confirm ideas throughout the study. "Audit trails" (Lincoln & Guba, 1985) or "periodic confirmed informant checks" and "feedback sessions" (Leininger, 1990) directly from the people are important means to establish confirmability of the data. How researchers confirm what they have seen, heard, or experienced may vary with cultures, situations, contexts, and with material and nonmaterial sources. Pictures, actual and repeated instances, voice inflections, and nonverbal communication are some indicators of confirmability.

3. *Meaning-in-context* refers to data that have become understandable within holistic contexts or with special referent meanings to the informants or people studied in different or similar environmental contexts. Situations, instances, life events, or lived-through experiences with particular meanings that are known to the people in their environment are important indicators. This criterion focuses on the contextualization of ideas and experiences within a total situation, context, or environment. The significance of interpretations and understandings of actions, symbols, events, communication, and other human activities as they take on meanings to informants within their lived context or the totality of their lived experiences support the criterion.

4. *Recurrent patterning* refers to repeated instances, sequence of events, experiences, or lifeways that tend to be patterned and recur over time in designated ways and in different or similar contexts. Repeated experiences, expressions, events, or activities that reflect identifiable patterns of sequenced behavior or expressions or actions over time are used to substantiate this criterion. Numbers or percentages of occurrences also can substantiate this criterion.

5. *Saturation* refers to the full "taking in of occurrences" or the full immersion into phenomena in order to know it as fully, comprehensively, and thoroughly as possible. Saturation means that the researcher has done an exhaustive exploration of whatever phenomenon is being studied. It may refer to getting dense or thick (in depth and breadth) data to know fully whatever has been observed, presented, or discovered. The researcher finds no further explanation, interpretation, or description of the phenomenon under study by the informants. In fact, there tends to be a redundancy in which the researcher gets the same (or similar) information on repeated inquiries. Informants often state: "There is no more to tell you, as I have said all I know or what is known about this topic." Hence redundancies and duplication of similar ideas, meanings, experiences, and descriptions occur from informants so that no more information is forthcoming.

6. *Transferability* refers to whether particular findings from a qualitative study can be transferred to another similar context or situation and still preserve the particularized meanings, interpretations, and inferences from the completed study. Because the goal of qualitative research is not to produce generalizations,

but rather in-depth understandings and knowledge of particular phenomena, the transferability criterion focuses on general similarities of findings under similar environmental conditions, contexts, or circumstances. Similarities to another similar situation can contribute to extending knowledge uses. It is the researcher's responsibility to establish whether this criterion can be met in a similar context while preserving the original particular findings from a study.

Each of the above criteria is congruent with the philosophic purposes and goals of qualitative studies. It is extremely important for the researcher to understand each criterion before initiating a qualitative research study, because the criteria then can be used with documentation throughout the study, rather than at the end of an investigation. The only research method that was declared qualitative but that developed by using both qualitative and quantitative perspectives was grounded theory. This creation appears related to Glaser and Strauss' (1967) intellectual orientations and discipline preparation, as one is a mathematician and the other a social scientist.

Some Illustrative Uses of the Six Criteria

In using the six criteria, there is some variability of evidence for each qualitative criterion in relation to the particular research method being used. In addition, the knowledge and skills of the researcher vary with the use of the criteria. As the researcher uses the criteria with different methods, it is important to reflect on each criterion with the findings and to document the particular criterion with the data. For example, with phenomenology and its branch of hermeneutics, the criteria of saturation, meanings-in-context, and credibility will be used heavily, and the criteria of confirmability and recurrent patterning may be used less. In most qualitative research methods, all criteria generally are used. The domain of inquiry, length of time studying the phenomena, and the skill of the researcher will lead to some differences in the extent of using each criterion. Several qualitative studies using all of the criteria can be found in Bohay (1991), Cameron (1990), Finn (1993), Leininger (1991a), Luna (1989), Rosenbaum (1991), Stasiak (1991), and Wenger (1988).

It requires a conscientious and deliberate effort to use the six criteria as one begins the analysis of data from the beginning of the study until the end. Although the six criteria can be used with all qualitative methods, some criteria are used more fully than others. Much depends on the skills of the researcher to document the use of the criteria with the emerging findings.

When using the above qualitative research criteria, the researcher can document ways to check and recheck each criterion with the informants or the situation. As with all qualitative studies, the researcher usually returns to informants throughout the data collection period to confirm the findings and to recheck particular findings. I have found that most informants like to participate in the rechecks, as it reaffirms their active participation and their desire to make the findings meaningful, accurate, and credible. Most informants are quite capable of correcting errors in interpretation of facts and of giving further examples to make their ideas clear to the researcher. The researcher's etic (or outsider's) views may be different, but they also may be shared with informants and reported in special ways in the final analysis. Accordingly the report should be written with the criteria so that it can be understood by the users (the general public and researcher's worlds). Hence the report may be written for different audiences and purposes. Nonetheless the research report still must give evidence of reflecting the findings and meeting the qualitative research criteria.

Although all six criteria are defined and discussed above, a few examples of specific criteria such as credibility, confirmability, and meaning-in-context will be highlighted to understand more fully their uses. The criterion of *credibility* as truth, or what is believable and known to the informants and that becomes discovered and known to the researcher, is one of the most important criteria to understand and use in a qualitative study. For this criterion and others, the researcher keeps in mind that *the informants are the primary gatekeepers* and *the researcher is the secondary gatekeeper* for information and to substantiate findings. These primary gatekeepers know their worlds, which may be quite different from the researcher's world. The researcher has the task to grasp the informants' world in its fullest known, credible, or believable ways to them, which is often a difficult challenge for the researcher. Grasping what is "true," "known," or the "truth" to informants in their lived environmental context or history requires active listening, reflection, and empathetic understanding. There may be a strong tendency for credibility to be that of the researcher or to have the truth fit the researcher's interests, theoretical orientation, interest, and experiences. The goal is to enter the informants' world, which takes time, patience, reflection, and audit trails to check and recheck what is truth or believable to informants. This process requires moving from emic to etic data and from my "stranger to trusting friend" model with the informants to establish fully what is credible or believable to the people (Leininger, 1985). Establishing a trusting relationship is an important precondition to qualitative study, but not as a criterion. This point differs from that of Lincoln and Guba (1985), who use "trustability" as a criterion.

Time is not always the key ingredient in establishing any of the criteria. Much depends on the preparation and skill of the researcher, who has had good mentorship with an experienced qualitative methodologist, or one who knows and has used the method several times. The researcher mentor is invaluable for developing and perfecting the skills of the researcher and for arriving at credible interpretations. With such a skilled qualitative mentor and prepared researcher, one usually can be guided to move in and be with informants for shorter spans of time and get accurate and credible data.

The researcher must remain cognizant of emic (local) perspectives and how such data may contrast with etic (external) perspectives, which are often researcher views. These concepts are extremely helpful in establishing the criteria of credibility, meaning-in-context, and saturation. The researcher's skills in checking and rechecking emic and etic data differences and similarities with their own language and with that of the informants is critical for getting credible data. These findings usually contribute to confirmable, recurrent patterning and meaning-in-context. The researcher's skill "in getting to the emic truths" requires some cultural knowledge and sensitivity, respect for the informants, skills in interviewing and observing, and ethical considerations. It also requires that the researcher (a) let the informants interpret what is credible to them and (b) not impose his or her interpretations onto the statements. For example, in

an ethnographic and ethnonursing study of urban Italian families, I found that the truth or credibility about the "evil eye" was
the harm "caused" by etic, or non-Italian neighbors who recently
moved into the traditional Italian community. The evil eye was
not an illness of envy of the child, but rather a social threat to
adults. This finding was established and made credible and
confirmed by several emic (local) and etic narratives from informants and by direct observations within the families and with
the newcomers in the community. Meaning-in-context became
clearly evident with the evil eye as the informants gave full,
detailed, and many narrative stories about living situations in a
multicultural community. Credibility, confirmability, and meaning-
in-context were established with the evil eye that was different
from the textbook accounts of the Italians and of other cultures.

In our changing world, with many proclaimers and authorities
about what is truth, one realizes that absolute truth or credibility
may be very difficult to establish with informants and contexts.
Nonetheless the researcher seeks to discover and know the
truths as known to those being studied. The search for truths
through the qualitative research paradigm includes subjective,
objective, and transcendental ideas. Accordingly qualitative researchers have come to realize that credibility, or the truth, may
not always be "out there" but may be in the beliefs and values of
the people that may require skills to explicate and understand.
This perspective is helpful in teasing out this knowledge bearing
on what people believe in or value. A perspective is the integrated and comprehensive way people look out on life and the
world about them, including common beliefs, values, and lived
experiences. In Bateson's work (found in Brockman, 1977), the
following statements have had meaning in relation to the concept of *perspective* and to support criteria related to credibility
and confirmability:

> The word "objective" becomes, of course, quite quietly obsolete, and
> at the same time the word "subjective," which normally confines
> "you" within your skin, disappears as well. It is, I think, the debunking
> of the objective that is the important change. The world is no longer
> "out there" in quite the same way that it used to seem to be. . . .
>
> I have to use the information that which I see, the images or that
> which I feel as pain, the prick of a pin, or the ache of a tired

muscle—for these too are images created in their respective modes—that all this is neither objective truth nor is it hallucination. There is a combining or marriage between an objectivity that is passive to the outside world and a creative subjectivity, neither pure solipsism not its opposite.

Consider for a moment the phrase, the opposite of solipsism. In solipsism, you are ultimately isolated and alone, isolated by the premise "I make it all up." But at the other extreme, the opposite of solipsism, you would cease to exist, becoming nothing but a metaphoric feather blown by the winds of external "reality." . . . Somewhere between these two is a region where you are partly blown by the winds of reality and partly an artist creating a composite out of inner and outer events. (p. 245)

The above ideas are philosophically helpful to reflect on when difficult aspects of what constitutes holistic credibility and understandings are of interest. Schwartz and Ogilvy (1980) contended that researchers need to move away from notions of splitting objectivity and subjectivity and to use the notion of perspective. This integrated and holistic perspective concept is especially important because our Western tendency is to dichotomize our world into subjects and objects. To get to holistic credible meanings and understandings in contexts, we need to remain conscious of such efforts.

Another major area that needs to be examined is a comparison of the advantages and disadvantages of mini, small-scale qualitative studies with maxi, large-scale studies using the six criteria with documented outcomes. Mini ethnonursing studies are valuable for clinical studies and are generating nursing knowledge. In many instances they are replacing major ethnographic studies in clinical settings. The large-scale maxi ethnonursing studies are valuable but usually require the skills of doctorally prepared researchers because they tap broad knowledge areas about worldview, social structure factors, historical, and environmental influencers related to nursing and health care dimensions. For example, the domain of protective care for Mexican-Americans with action uses has been well identified and confirmed with a mini ethnonursing study. In contrast, the study of protective care and the epistemics and ontology of care embedded in the social structure, in the worldview, and in environmental protective caring modes requires considerable skill to explicate and analyze complex data sets. Documenting the findings with saturation, credibility, and meaning-in-context takes skill and analytic synthesis strategies for maxi ethnonursing studies. Hence different purposes, goals, and results can be found with the use of mini or maxi ethnonursing studies.

One would be remiss not to identify this unresolved issue: The road to research funding still remains paved figuratively with quantitative cement. This institutional ethos of using logical positivism continues to be a major hurdle for obtaining grants for "pure" qualitative studies without imposing validity and reliability criteria. We also need expert peer reviewers prepared in qualitative studies who are not prepared to relinquish their philosophic tenets of the qualitative paradigm. Using quantitative evaluative criteria for qualitative criteria refutes the very purposes, the epistemic integrity, and the ontological attributes of qualitative paradigmatic research.

In looking to the future, I would predict that the next generation of qualitative researchers will have passed the current transitional stage of accommodating two paradigms in a research study, as their knowledge base will be stronger for understanding the differences between the two paradigms. By then, qualitative researchers will have learned to use explicit qualitative criteria. We will see many more nurses and other researchers conducting qualitative studies, as they are so natural to humanistic lifeways. Researchers will have the confidence to use specific evaluation criteria to fit the qualitative paradigm, and they will be comfortable with and want expert critiques of their work. These trends will greatly increase our understanding of people, cultures, human expressions, and life conditions. If the integrity of each paradigm is maintained, I further predict that one will see how the two paradigms complement each other and provide major differences in research findings, which will, in turn, enrich the discipline's knowledge and practice goals. We still need brave, bold, and knowledgeable qualitative researchers and mentors ready to face these new areas to support and make highly visible qualitative research methods and the use of qualitative criteria for full knowledge discoveries. The future looks promising.

In this chapter I discussed the importance of preserving and maintaining the purposes, goals, and philosophic assumptions of the qualitative research paradigm and of using qualitative research methods and criteria appropriate to the paradigm. I defined the terms *evaluation criteria, critique,* and *review* with different purposes and characteristics. The serious problem of mixing paradigms and research methods was discussed with deep concern that it violates the purposes, goals, and integrity of each paradigm. In addition, this problem continues to perpetuate ambiguities and outcomes of research from each paradigm. The use of triangulation or multiangulation paradigm methods confounds the intent of each paradigm and lessens the credibility and meaningful interpretation of findings. Six specific qualitative criteria were defined, and some illustrations were given to clarify the use of the criteria within the qualitative paradigm. The use of quantitative criteria such as validity and reliability remains inappropriate for qualitative studies. I hope that in the next century many of the issues presented here will be resolved to advance knowledge for many disciplines and their efforts to grasp a full understanding of their central discipline interests and of the wider world of human beings and cultural lifeways.

References

Aamodt, A. (1983). Problems in doing nursing research: Developing criteria for evaluating qualitative research. *Western Journal of Nursing Research, 5*(4), 399.

American Heritage Dictionary. (1991). Boston: Houghton-Mifflin.

Bohay, I. (1991). Culture care meanings and experiences of pregnancy and childbirth of Ukrainians. In M. Leininger (Ed.), *Culture care diversity and universality: A theory of nursing* (pp. 203-230). New York: National League for Nursing Press.

Brockman, J. (1977). *About Bateson.* New York: E. P. Dutton.

Cameron, C. (1990). *An ethnonursing study of health status of elderly Anglo-Canadian wives providing extended caregiving to their disabled husbands.* Unpublished doctoral dissertation, Wayne State University, Detroit.

Cobb, A. K., & Hagemaster, J. N. (1987). Ten criteria for evaluating qualitative research proposals. *Journal of Nursing Education, 26*(4), 138-143.

De Groot, H. A. (1988). Scientific inquiry in nursing: A model for a new age. *Advances in Nursing Science, 10*(3), 1-21.

Duffy, M. E. (1986). Qualitative research: An approach whose time has come. *Nursing and Health Care, 7*(5), 237-239.

Finn, J. (1993). *Professional nursing and generic care of childbirthing women conceptualized within Leininger's cultural care theory and using Colaizzi's phenomenological method.* Unpublished doctoral dissertation, Wayne State University, Detroit.

Glaser, B., & Strauss, A. (1967). The discovery of substantive theory: A basic strategy underlying qualitative research. *American Behavioral Scientist, 8*(6), 5-12.

Goodwin, L., & Goodwin, W. (1984). Qualitative vs. quantitative research or qualitative and quantitative research. *Nursing Research, 33*(6), 379.

Guba, E. (1990). *The paradigm dialogue.* Newbury Park, CA: Sage.

LeCompte, M., & Goetz, J. (1982). Problems of reliability and validity in ethnographic research. *Review of Educational Research, 52*(1), 31-60.

Leininger, M. (1968). The research critique: Nature, function, and art. *Nursing Research, 13*(5), 444-449.

Leininger, M. (1970). *Nursing and anthropology: Two worlds to blend.* New York: John Wiley.

Leininger, M. (1985). Nature, rationale, and importance of qualitative research methods in nursing. In M. Leininger (Ed.), *Qualitative research methods in nursing* (pp. 1-26). New York: Grune & Stratton.

Leininger, M. (1987). Importance and uses of ethnomethods: Ethnography and ethnonursing research. In M. Calhoun (Ed.), *Recent advances in nursing/research methodology* (Vol. 1, pp. 12-35).

Leininger, M. (1990). Ethnomethods: The philosophic and epistemic bases to explicate transcultural nursing knowledge. *Journal of Transcultural Nursing, 1*(2), 40-51.

Leininger, M. (1991a). Culture care of the Gaadusup Akuna of the Eastern Highland of New Guinea. In M. Leininger (Ed.), *Culture care diversity and universality: A theory of nursing* (pp. 231-280). New York: National League for Nursing Press.

Leininger, M. (1991b). Ethnonursing: A research method with enablers to study the theory of culture care. In M. Leininger (Ed.), *Culture care diversity and universality: A theory of nursing* (pp. 112-116). New York: National League for Nursing Press.

Leininger, M. (1992). Current issues, problems, and trends to advance qualitative paradigmatic research methods for the future. *Qualitative Health Research, 2*(4), 392-415.

Lincoln, Y., & Guba, E. (1985). *Naturalistic inquiry.* Beverly Hills, CA: Sage.

Luna, L. (1989). *Care and cultural context of Lebanese Muslims in an urban U.S. community: An ethnographic and ethnonursing study conceptualized within Leininger's theory.* Detroit, MI: Wayne State University.

Morse, J. (1991). Editorial: Evaluating qualitative research. *Qualitative Health Research, 1*(3), 283-286.

Reason, P., & Rowan, J. (1981). *Human inquiry: A source book of new paradigm research.* New York: John Wiley.

Rosenbaum, J. (1991). Culture care theory and Greek Canadian widows. In M. Leininger (Ed.), *Culture care diversity and universality: A theory of nursing* (pp. 305-340). New York: National League for Nursing Press.

Schwartz, P., & Ogilvy, J. (1980). *The emergent paradigm: Changing patterns of thought and belief* (Analytical Report No. 7, Values and Lifestyles Program). Menlo Park, CA: SRI International.

Stasiak, D. (1991). Culture care theory with Mexican-Americans in an urban context. In M. Leininger (Ed.), *Culture care diversity and universality: A theory of nursing* (pp. 179-202). New York: National League for Nursing Press.

Wenger, A. F. (1988). *The phenomena of care of the Old-Order Amish: A high context culture.* Unpublished doctoral dissertation, Wayne State University, Detroit.

Werner, O., & Schoepfle, G. M. (1987). *Systematic fieldwork: Foundations of ethnography and interviewing* (Vol. 1). Newbury Park, CA: Sage.

Dialogue

Good Phenomenology Is . . .

HUTCHINSON When you are teaching students, you have to think about what is "good." Some studies take you on a journey, whereas others provide only limited definitions, almost like a tautology. When we are teaching students, we need models.

SANDELOWSKI When you evaluate a phenomenology as "good," you are clearly giving a message that you do like this and you don't like that. It seems that there is a "beauty" criterion that is more important here than some other kind of qualitative product. And it has to ring true—some kind of fidelity criteria.

MORSE Some have their students write seven drafts, or whatever. How do you know when to say, "Stop!"?

RAY Well, I have a student right now who is probably on the final draft. It is beautiful. It is artistic. It is knowledge generating. The person has a powerful background in philosophy and knows what it is—has worked at it—knows the dilemmas associated with the various approaches to the methods in terms of the combination of phenomenology and hermeneutics. There's theory generation—which is controversial. And figuring out what does that mean in the context of being human—you know, how does this particular mode of understanding relate to the human condition in general. There's art in it. It's complex.

BOYLE That's a helpful list!

7

The Richness of Phenomenology: Philosophic, Theoretic, and Methodologic Concerns

MARILYN A. RAY

The richness, really, is how well somebody else can use it. Does this make sense to somebody else? Does this have any relevance or validity in the context of my practice? Or maybe I learned more about the philosophy of something. So every individual who approaches phenomenological writing may, in fact, get something different from it. Phenomenological writing could be descriptive in the Husserlian sense, or interpretive (hermeneutical). As text, however, it is open to multiple interpretations. It might not be the same for each one of us, just as when each one of us is reading these chapters, because we will each come to these with our own interpretive lens.

In phenomenology, excellence rests on a dialogue of key philosophic approaches to phenomenology, creativity, and reflective insights of phenomenologists. What is distinctive about the phenomenologic tradition is discussed in this chapter by examining phenomenologic inquiry beginning with Husserlian and Heideggerian thought. Within the transcendental (descriptive) and hermeneutic (interpretive) traditions, the consequences of both descriptive and interpretive approaches to phenomenology are clarified. Common philosophic, theoretic, and methodologic concerns are noted, and the credibility or truth value of phenomenologic research is discussed.

Phenomenology and *hermeneutics* are becoming familiar terms in nursing inquiry. As qualitative research has gained in popularity in recent years, a wide range of perspectives has been presented and has been adopted wholly or adapted in part from the ideas of major philosophers or human scientists.

What is phenomenology? In many respects this question is as old as the question, What is philosophy? and is centered in the ontologic question, What is being? Phenomenology also relates to the epistemologic question, How do we know? The method and mode of analysis (reflection) are similar to those of philosophy (Stapleton, 1983). Thus phenomenology is, first and foremost, a philosophy or a variety of distinctive, yet related, philosophies. But it also is concerned with approach and method. Husserl (1970), the father of phenomenology, considered phenomenology to be all three—a philosophy, an approach, and a method. By examining ideas within the phenomenologic and hermeneutic traditions and hermeneutic-phenomenology, we can see the different foci of phenomenology. The Husserlian tradition or eidetic phenomenology is epistemologic and emphasizes a return to reflective intuition to describe and clarify experience as it is lived and constituted in consciousness (awareness) (Husserl, 1970). The hermeneutic-phenomenologic tradition or interpretative approach is ontologic, a way of being in the social-historical world where the fundamental dimension of all human consciousness is historical and sociocultural and is expressed through language (text). Hermeneutic-phenomenology is central to Gadamerian, Heideggerian, and Ricoeurian philosophies (Gadamer, 1990; Heidegger, 1962; Ricoeur, 1981).

The Phenomenologic Tradition

Phenomenology derives from the Greek word *phenomenon,* which means "to show itself," to put into light or manifest something that can become visible in itself (Heidegger, 1962, p. 57). "Phenomenology attempts to disclose the essential meaning of human endeavors" (Bishop & Scudder, 1991, p. 5). In conformity with the philosopher Husserl's attitude, phenomenology relates to the question, How do we know? It is epistemologic inquiry into and commitment to describing and clarifying the essential structure of the lived world of conscious experience (the experiential content of "originary" experience) by reflexively meditating on the origins of experience. Thus the essence of a thing as it "is meant," or what makes something what it is without preconceptions or prejudices (historical traditions) (Husserl, 1970), is revealed.

Husserl's aim was the avoidance of all conceptually bound and theoretically constructed beginnings. He posited a philosophical, descriptive approach of a return to capturing the essence of consciousness in itself (Stapleton, 1983). What is important about Husserl's phenomenology is the claim that consciousness is a realm of absolute being where the starting point for philosophical reflection in the most immediate way is not theory or history, but "a description of the presence of man in the world, and the presence of the world for man" (Stapleton, 1983, p. 9). The entire spiritual force of Husserl's phenomenology is conferring meaning by the knowing ego (or self) reflecting on itself, by bracketing or holding in abeyance one's preconceptions about the world and seeking to attain the genuine and true form of the things themselves (Hammond, Howarth, & Keat, 1991). In this sense phenomenologic language is descriptive, and its purpose is to make the originary experience evident through reflection to clear intuition. Direct apperception, or clear intuition, is the means to the constitution of phenomena "as meant," or "seeing" its meaning in consciousness (Stapleton, 1983).

Husserl was interested in the ideal of philosophy as a rigorous science and claimed that by using the method of epoche or bracketing (holding in abeyance) one's presuppositions or theories and by deep reflection, one could seek the roots or beginnings of knowledge in the subjective processes, "in the things themselves." According to Husserl, these processes lay deep within the consciousness of the knowing subject to whom these phenomena appeared (Husserl, 1970, 1973; Kohak, 1978; Spiegelberg, 1982). He called this philosophic activity "transcendental subjectivity" (Spiegelberg, 1982, p. 77), whereby *transcendental* can be understood as conferring meaning by the knowing ego, or self, reflecting on itself. The transcendental subjective process is achieved by seeking to attain the genuine and true form of the things themselves. The realm of the transcendental being, thus, is that of pure ego and what it knows. It is called transcendental because of its presuppositionless relationship to the world (bracketing or suspending one's presuppositions about the world) so as to come to know what makes a thing what it is, thus providing the basis for the world's existential status (Hammond et al., 1991).

The key positions in Husserlian transcendental phenomenology and his phenomenologic beginning are the orientation toward being *of* the world, and the concept of *certitude* or nonrelativistic evidence. Thus, by employing a presuppositionlessness approach (bracketing in consciousness our knowledge of the world), we allow ourselves to found with certainty our judgments about the reality of our experience without a relationship to historical traditions or theories of the world. Furthermore it allows us to found an appreciation for those judgments through reflective intuitive *givenness* (which is the meaning of the thought from within) (Hammond et al., 1991; Stapleton, 1983). From Husserl's point of view, all crucial distinctions within our experience should be made within the transcendental or presuppositionless ego that allows for the provision of certitude or for obtaining a secure foundation for describing experience and gaining knowledge of the world as it is (Hammond et al., 1991).

Hermeneutic-Phenomenology

Phenomenology was reinterpreted radically as hermeneutical or interpretive by Heidegger, a student and critic of Husserl. Hermeneutical or interpretive phenomenology does not seek evidence first "as it is in itself" as foundational, but instead discloses the *horizon* by uncovering the presuppositions. This disclosure makes prior understanding of Being (presence or something that is) possible and, hence, the questioning of the meaning of Being *in* the world. Phenomenology as interpretive in the Heideggerian sense is the preontological understanding of Being (What is it that supplies the possibility for the question of the meaning of Being?) (Stapleton, 1983 p. 121).

The central distinction between the Husserlian and Heideggerian approaches is that Heidegger articulates the position that presuppositions are not to be eliminated or suspended, but are what constitute the possibility of intelligibility or meaning. Therefore, Being, as such, already is present *in* the world (Being of the questioner, which he refers to as the *Dasein*). The *Dasein* (the possibilities of Being in the world or being-there) guides the question that is made explicit and is interpreted as a possibility to be realized (Stapleton, 1983). Heidegger, thus, moved away from the Husserlian transcendental (presuppositionless) idea of finitude to an *ontological* idea of finitude that is made possible by the prior understanding of "Being *in* the world" (*Dasein*), rather than *of* the world.

Being in the world is disclosed as *care* (Sorge)—that which makes possible in temporality, earnest questioning. A person who needs to question or to philosophize is finite seeing. In other words, interpretation is grounded existentially in understanding and is itself one of the possibilities of Being itself (Heidegger, 1962). Despite differences in how they stressed the importance of their foundations, what both Husserl and Heidegger continued to ask, as did the ancient philosophers, was, What is Being? (Stapleton, 1983, p. 126).

Gadamer (1990) further drew on the ideas of Heidegger and articulated a hermeneutic in both the context of temporality and the historicity of human existence. In this sense, hermeneutics illuminates the modes of being in the world where the realm of understandability in which persons interact is interpreted through their use of language. Understanding is the fundamental way people exist in the world (Gadamer, 1990). By recognizing the role of historical influences or horizons of meaning of past traditions, human experience is understood in a new way. In other words, by recognizing the universality of language use (text) as the carrier of everything (cultural-historical influences) that people incorporate in the process of understanding, then understanding originates in the linguistic experience of the world (Gadamer, 1990).

Ricoeur (1981) offered the broadest definitions of phenomenology and hermeneutics. His conception supported the Husserlian, Heideggerian, and Gadamerian views by stating: "Phenomenology remains the unsurpassable presupposition of hermeneutics. On the other hand, phenomenology cannot constitute itself without a hermeneutical presupposition" (Ricoeur, 1981, p. 101). He showed that the belongingness to the world is the interpretive experience itself and that all understanding is mediated by interpretation (Ricoeur, 1981). Ricoeur's theory of interpretation deepened our understanding of the relationship between the ontology of human reality (being in the world) and the epistemology of what is to be known (being of the world) and secures the link between understanding meaning and self-understanding.

Hermeneutic-phenomenology, in particular the philosophy of Ricoeur, awakens our sensitivity to ourselves in the world—as participants in an active communicative ontology (Reeder, 1988). It provides the richness to understand the human condition in the changing yet continuous social-historical reality in which we find ourselves. Additionally philosophers such as Merleau-Ponty, Habermas, and others in North America have contributed to the advancement of contemporary phenomenology and hermeneutics.

A leading human scientist, van Manen (1990), introduced and explicated a hermeneutic-phenomenologic approach grounded in German and Dutch philosophic traditions. Van Manen advanced the notion that human science research could not be separated from the textual practice of writing. The practical nature of pedagogy and semiotics (the signification of language and text orientation) are employed in such a way that they engage the researcher in pedagogic reflection (on how one lives with children as parents, teachers, or educators). Van Manen's research method, however, is influential in all of the human sciences because it clearly articulates the interrelationship of phenomenology, hermeneutics and semiotics, and a research process of textual reflection that contributes to understanding practical action.

Common Philosophic, Theoretic, and Methodologic Problems in Phenomenologic-Hermeneutics

Because phenomenology attempts to disclose the essential meaning of human experience, the philosophy and approach are well suited to nursing inquiry (Bishop & Scudder, 1991). Although the philosophic foundations are complex, knowledge of these major philosophic traditions facilitates clarification and understanding of philosophic, theoretic, and methodologic concerns in nursing human science research. In terms of the following presentation, phenomenology may be discussed separately or in conjunction with hermeneutics.

Philosophic Concerns

A serious concern in phenomenologic inquiry in the nursing literature relates to the lack of philosophical understanding of phenomenology on the part of many researchers. Phenomenology often is misused or is used to refer to the qualitative paradigm (e.g., Lincoln 1992; Lincoln & Guba, 1985). Although this misuse may be true, in part, because phenomenology does disclose the meaning of human experience and qualitative research addresses both human experience and meaning, not all qualitative research or approaches are phenomenological. In determining excellent phenomenology, the researcher needs to communicate some knowledge of the phenomenological traditions as advanced by the key philosophers or other scholars who have interrelated key phenomenologic ideas. To attempt a phenomenologic study without having knowledge of its philosophic foundations and, especially, the practice of the analytic process of reflection would invalidate or severely impede a study's credibility.

Theoretic Concerns

In phenomenology, theoretic concerns arise within three spheres: (a) whether or not there is or should be theory at all, (b) theory emerging from the reflective analysis of data (narrative text), and (c) theory that guides the research process. In general the role of theory in phenomenology is controversial. Because phenomenology arises from the reflective analysis of the meaning of the lived world of experience, it is temporal in the Husserlian sense and is both temporal and historical (interpreted as a process of theorizing) in the Heideggerian and Gadamerian senses. Some phenomenologists, such as van Manen (1990), believe that although interpretive theorizing is acceptable, theory, as such, is antithetical to phenomenology. Others, such as myself, believe that theory, rather than being the conceptual sum of its parts, reveals a process of possibilities that, when captured as insight and represented as a narrative or model, belongs to the inner structure of meaning and under-standing (Gadamer, 1990; Ray, 1990, 1991).

A theoretical position from reflective insight communicates a relationship between the human experience represented in the text as themes, metathemes or metaphor, and compassion and self-understanding with the whole of the human condition. In this sense a theory captured from human experience is not isolated to the number of participants in a study or from human knowledge or emotion arising at the point in time of the research study. Rather it demonstrates a powerful representation or unity of meaning of belongingness and interconnectedness to the whole of the human condition both historically and universally, as Gadamer claims.

A unity of meaning generated through reflective insight is similar to holographic theory (Briggs & Peat, 1984), where in each part (the explicate order) the whole can be seen and discovered and is, therefore, a part of and can be expressed as a whole (the implicate order). Reflective insight theory becomes important in an epistemologic sense because its aim is not only to express the meaning of a particular life-world experience but also to enhance, develop, and advance the discipline under study as a human science by capturing the meaning of the human experience as a universal. This position of the universality of the subjectivity of human experience is not subjectivity toward an object, but rather subjectivity toward the history of its influence (Gadamer, 1990; Outhwaite, 1985; Thompson, 1981). This the-oretic position helps alleviate the problems raised about subjec-tivity and objectivity, about the idea that the subjective (e.g., a phenomenologic study of a few individuals at a point in time) is individualistic and idiosyncratic, and that the objective (a logical positivist position) is disciplined, methodical, and generalizable.

The universality of subjectivity brings into light the idea that every language-use (expression) represents something common to many in a culture or to the human condition of many cultures and is, thus, part of the objective mind. Everyone who acts, acts in a common sphere and is connected by something people have in common. Because we are human beings, it is possible to understand what it is like to be another human being; all human beings are rooted in the social world that makes possible the understanding a human being would have of another's personal or social reality.

Universality in understanding is not only a perspective of a human science but also the fundamental way human beings exist in the world (Outhwaite, 1985). The two central positions in hermeneutics advanced by Gadamer (1990)—(a) prejudgment (one's preconceptions or prejudices or horizon of meaning that is part of our linguistic experience and that make understanding possible) and (b) universality (the persons who express themselves and the persons who understand are connected by a common human consciousness, which makes understanding possible) are, thus, significant in understanding how hermeneutic-phenomenologic theory can be advanced.

In turning to theory that guides phenomenological research, the work of nursing scholars such as Parse (1981, 1987, 1992) and Watson (1985) has been the most popular. Parse's (1992) *theory of becoming* relates to the existential or processual nature of the interrelationship among human beings, living, and health; Watson's (1985) *theory of caring* relates to norms, ideals, and a metaphysics of transpersonal caring interaction. Both scholars use their own phenomenological methods adapted, in part, from traditional philosophic foundations of phenomenology or adaptations from phenomenological psychology. The methodologic processes of Parse and Watson, though not articulated by them, can be illuminated by a discussion of Gadamer's hermeneutic circle (Outhwaite, 1985). This process involves historicity (theoretical preconceptions or prejudgments) as part of the researcher's experience. This historicity contributes to making possible an understanding of a new horizon of meaning. The new data of experience articulated in a research study using Parse's or Watson's theories, for example, become a part of hermeneutic reflection and, thus, are part of the hermeneutic circle. Hermeneutic reflection consists of the dialectic of interpreting the meaning of the research data (text) as a dynamic movement toward further understanding. It is a dialogic-dialectic interpretive encounter with the research data (text) by reflecting on the parts (themes) and moving to the meaning of the whole in relation to the respective theory. Meaning, rather than being captured as it is in itself as in Husserlian phenomenology, or

interpreted as being read into the text as in traditional hermeneutics, should be read *out of* the text where the text itself is a
part of historical influences or past traditions (theory that guides
the study). Within this historicity or, in other words, within historical interpretative reflection, is a fusion of horizons (mediation)
in the methodological approach that makes possible the further
understanding and enhancement of a particular theory.

In excellent phenomenology, a knowledge of what theory
means and why or how is used methodologically is
critical. Again knowledge of the key philosophies of both phenomenology and hermeneutics, as well as the theory under
study, provides the clue to the approach and to what informs the
approach and the researcher.

Methodologic Concerns

Methodologies advanced in phenomenology differ in a variety
of ways. The approach, study participants, research question,
data generation, and reflective analysis and theory development
all contribute to problems in evaluating whether phenomenology can be considered as excellent. The qualitative researcher
embarking on the use of phenomenology as a method today
rarely encounters a discussion of phenomenology as we have
seen it, without dealing with the complexity of the topic or the
apparent possibilities of contradiction in the philosophic approaches, especially now that hermeneutics also has become an
important resource for nursing inquiry. What becomes clear as
one reads journal articles or chapters on the subject, or research
studies on whether a study can be judged as excellent or has
credibility is the issue of approach.

Giorgi (1970) stated that "by approach is meant the fundamental viewpoint toward man and the world that the scientist brings,
or adopts, with respect to his work as a scientist, whether this
viewpoint is made explicit or remains implicit" (p. 126). Although as Giorgi (1970) explained, the task of making explicit
all of the characteristics of the researcher's approach is impossible, it is useful to make explicit whatever one can. Each
researcher has a particular attitude or orientation to methodology from philosophical knowledge or lack of it that is carried
into the work and that implies a certain way the study will be

accomplished. Thus the issue of approach affects the research process and the results and, ultimately, its classification as excellent or not. Once the philosophic approach has been established, other aspects of the research, such as the participants, the research question, the data generation, the reflective analysis, and the theory development, may be problematic.

In excellent phenomenology, the nature of study participants should be explicated. They may be the researcher, a singular person, a group of people (usually a small number of 8 to 12) who are involved in a similar experience, or even material objects such as a work of art or photographs or a videotape recording. Again the phenomenologic or hermeneutic approach to understanding is important. Is the study descriptive (Husserl, 1970), interpretive (Gadamer, 1990; Heidegger 1962), or both (Bishop & Scudder, 1991; Ray, 1991; Ricoeur, 1981; van Manen, 1990)? What is to be captured is the meaning of experience, and, as previously discussed, there are different ways to understand and capture the meaning of experience.

Because of phenomenology's temporal nature and its idea of consciousness as intentional (Husserl, 1970), the self is the recognized bearer of responsibility of experience firsthand (Reeder, 1989). This idea holds true for both the researcher and the study participants. Experience of things or phenomena include sense perception (seeing, hearing, touching, tasting, and smelling) and other phenomena, such as believing, remembering, anticipating, judging, intuiting, feeling, caring, loving, imagining, and willing. An act of consciousness includes these multiple modes of awareness (Reeder, 1989). In other words, the internal time, the moment of the unitary present (the "now") in a conscious act—the just-past and the about-to-be, what Husserl called, respectively, retentions (rememberings) and protentions (anticipations)—are an intrinsic part of the temporal ordering of conscious processes (Kohak, 1978). What is important here is intentional consciousness. The objects of conscious experience are always integral; consciousness is always of something, always related to consciousness of things of the world. This integral evidence of the multiple modes of awareness, for example, can be expressed by study participants in terms of colors as imagined, energy as felt, symbols as remembered, and health as desired (Reeder, 1984, 1989) and illuminates the relationship between the knower and the known as one (Reeder, 1984). The integral evidence that is distinguished from purely objective evidence espoused in positivism, thus, incorporates a reflexive element—the "recognition of the role of the active mind in coming to know the world" (Reeder, 1989, p. 179)—humankind's self-reflection (Husserl, 1970). In this sense, the experience expressed by study participants, whether past, present, or anticipated, is the nature of the data, and those data are captured and transcribed as text. All interview data transcribed as text are subject to the particular philosophic approach that the researcher started with—descriptive, interpretive, or both—and will determine the nature and method of analysis. Issues related to eidetic phenomenology or descriptive phenomenology and the concept of the *bracketed interview process* are explained later.

If a researcher is interested in a transformative experience, such as pregnancy or illness, the participants' lived world of experience through understanding the temporal process of consciousness could be captured either at significant times of the transformative process or after the transformation through the recall experience of the study participants themselves. This choice can be decided mutually by the researcher and participants. These phases could be viewed as "portraits" or "snapshots" of experience. Benner (1984) called particular phases "exemplars" or "paradigm cases." Methodologic language is not universal; it varies with different researchers and often creates problems for reviewers or readers of scholarly journals, especially those who generally do not review or publish phenomenologic studies. Methodologic language should be consistent throughout the report.

Although cultural experiences may benefit from ethnographic inquiry, phenomenology may be used for a large cultural study. The notion of intentional consciousness as the vessel of history and culture and the "holder" of conscious experience in cultural knowledge, thus, can be captured both descriptively and hermeneutically.

Research or interview questions in phenomenology center around meaning (What is the meaning of an experience?) and analogy (What is it like to experience?). Children generally respond to the questions of analogy, while adults can express meaning. In an eidetic or descriptive phenomenologic study, during the interview process and descriptive phase of analysis to intuit the meaning of experience of the study participants, researchers would hold in abeyance their past experience or knowledge and future anticipations of a phenomenon to allow data (the things themselves) to show themselves "as meant." Thus, even though consciousness of something is the essence of an intentional consciousness, how a researcher understands and uses bracketing is critical to the efficacy of eidetic phenomenology.

In a bracketed or presuppositionless interview, research questions are not predetermined, but rather flow within a clue-and-cue-taking process (Ray, 1990, 1991) after the initial meaning or analogy question is asked. The phenomena of experience are probed with the participant until "the thing itself" is illuminated and described. If, however, the research approach is considered to be hermeneutical, questioning can include conceptual, theoretical, or historical traditions as part of the questioning process. Research questioning during the interview process again must be framed by an understanding of the approach selected. The art of questioning is the art of thinking (Gadamer, 1990).

Data analysis is a reflective process and involves a sensitive attunement to opening up to the meaning of experience both as discourse and as text. Presuppositionless description of meaning via intuitive, reflective insight is the mode of reflective analysis in Husserlian descriptive phenomenology. In contrast, the disclosure of meaning through the hermeneutic-phenomenologic process is a combination of description, thematic interpreting, and metaphoric insight as the product "given" to the researcher by the text (van Manen, 1990).

Ricoeur (1981) communicated most extensively about discourse, ordinary language, and written texts in phenomenology. He attempted to reconcile the presuppositionless and interpretive phenomenologic gulf of Husserlian and Heideggerian methodology. As an example, the semantics of discourse and the concept of the *text* provided Ricoeur with the foundation for the development of his theory of interpretation (Thompson, 1981). Ricoeur employed the processes of the constructive reflective dialectic of distanciation, a presuppositionless description (opening up of the text of experience to "see" the experience as it is in itself), and engagement (interpretation of the experience) that is rooted in the properties of the text. By the process of sense (what the text says in itself) and reference (what the text is about), the understanding or conscious horizon of the researcher would be expanded to appropriate meaning. Ricoeur (1981) included that the use of metaphor transformed the referential dimension to redescribe reality in the text.

Ricoeur's theory, thus, articulated how understanding of the whole of the phenomenon of textual discourse could be actualized (Reeder, 1988; Ricoeur, 1981; Thompson, 1981). The dialectic of interpretation of the text allows for several possible interpretations and, finally, culminates in an act of understanding. This understanding is actualized in the recognition of ourselves-in-the-world through our linguistic nature as human beings (Reeder, 1988). This belongingness or the engagement of ourselves as interpreters in a social-historical world is what makes appropriation of meaning or self-understanding possible. An actuality, thus, is expansion of the conscious horizons of meaning of the researcher or persons reading the textual account (Reeder, 1988; Ricoeur, 1981; Thompson, 1981).

Themes, metathemes, or metaphor and interpretive theory from textual discourse illuminate the meaning of an experience as it is lived; "no conceptual formulation or single statement can possibly capture the full mystery of this experience" (van Manen, 1990, p. 92). The process of interpretation points only to an aspect of the phenomenon (van Manen, 1990). The important thing in phenomenologic reflection is commitment and authenticity. Bergum's (1989) and Olson's (1993) works show clearly how researchers "see" and live their data—where research and writing, where the description and gathering of kinds of understanding are given authentic form and a sign of presence that discloses the depth of meaning (van Manen, 1990).

Credibility of Phenomenologic Research

Credibility and affirmation of phenomenologic research can be understood best by Heidegger's (1972) concept of truth as unconcealment and Ricoeur's idea that truth of the text may be regarded as the world it unfolds (Thompson, 1981). A phenomenologic researcher can recognize that his or her description or interpretation is correct because the reflective process awakens an inner moral impulse (Bollnow, 1974).

Phenomenologic meaning is revealed by the examination of two processes of integral evidence—evidence of a person who is engaged in firsthand experience in the world, and experience that is deeply reflected on or brought into awareness by the experiencing person (Reeder, 1989). "When something is evident, it is 'certain'; and it 'excludes doubt' in the sense that in experiencing something as certain one does not at the same time experience it as doubtful" (Hammond et al., 1991, p. 21). "Truth is, in the broadest sense, the deeply painful event wherein the veils that conceal are torn away and a man sees reality as it is" (Bollnow, 1974, pp. 10-11). Ricoeur emphasized that truth was inseparable from being. His theory of interpretation, thus, led from a descriptive phenomenology of explanation of the text (distanciation) to a concrete ontology of self-understanding by demonstrating that interpretation of the text makes possible the actualized meaning of the text (Reeder, 1988; Spiegelberg, 1982; Thompson, 1981).

In essence, Heidegger's idea of unconcealment and Ricoeur's idea of the world unfolded in the appropriation of meaning in interpretation deepen our understanding of the relationship between the ontology of human reality (being in the world) and epistemology (what is to be known). Unconcealment and appropriation of meaning of text secure the link between understanding meaning and self-understanding, which not only occurs within the researcher but also is a point of reconciliation between interviewees and readers of the research. Credibility, thus, is a validating circle of inquiry, what Buytendijk (a European phenomenologist) refers to as the "phenomenological nod"—where the description and interpretation of experience are something we can nod to and recognize as experiences that we had or could have had (van Manen, 1990, p. 27). Hermeneutic-phenomenology, thus, awakens our sensitivity to ourselves in the world—as participants in an active communicative ontology (Reeder, 1988).

Summary

The discussion of key philosophers in phenomenology and hermeneutics shows us that the task of the transcendental and interpretive analytic is to make explicit our being *of* and *in* the world, respectively. I attempted to show the relationship between "going to the thing itself"—the phenomenon—and the moral nature of the reflective process that allows for the revelation of truth through a deeper penetration into a horizon that makes meaning possible. The richness of phenomenology is found in communicating about this "thing in itself." Its excellence is in scrupulous philosophical scholarship and, in essence, reveals an aesthetic—a beautiful object—where the phenomenon and the reflection are united in an illuminating way" (Halliburton, 1981).

References

Benner, P. (1984). *From novice to expert.* Menlo Park, CA: Addison-Wesley.

Bergum, V. (1989). *Woman to mother: A transformation.* Granby, MA: Bergin & Garvey.

Bishop, A., & Scudder, J. (1991). *Nursing: The practice of caring.* New York: National League for Nursing Press.

Bollnow, O. (1974). The objectivity of the humanities and the essence of truth. *Philosophy Today, 18*(1), 3-18.

Briggs, J., & Peat, F. (1984). *Looking glass universe: The emerging science of wholeness.* New York: Simon & Schuster.

Gadamer, H-G. (1990). *Truth and method* (J. Weinsheimer & D. Marshall, Trans.) (2nd rev. ed.). New York: Crossroad.

Giorgi, A. (1970). *Psychology as a human science.* New York: Harper & Row.

Halliburton, D. (1981). *Poetic thinking.* Chicago: University of Chicago Press.

Hammond, M., Howarth, J., & Keat, R. (1991). *Understanding phenomenology.* Oxford, UK: Basil Blackwell.

Heidegger, M. (1962). *Being and time* (J. MacQuarrie & E. Robinson, Trans.). New York: Harper & Row.

Heidegger, M. (1972). *On time and being* (J. Stambaugh, Trans.). New York: Harper & Row.

Husserl, E. (1970). *The crisis of European sciences and transcendental phenomenology* (D. Carr, Trans.). Evanston, IL: Northwestern University Press.

Husserl, E. (1973). *Experience and judgment* (L. Landgrebe, Rev. & Ed.; J. Churchill & K. Ameriks, Trans.). Evanston, IL: Northwestern University Press.

Kohak, E. (1978). *Idea and experience: Edmund Husserl's project of phenomenology in ideas* (Vol. 1). Chicago: University of Chicago Press.

Lincoln, Y. (1992). Sympathetic connections between qualitative methods and health research. *Qualitative Health Research, 2*(4), 375-391.

Lincoln, Y., & Guba, E. (1985). *Naturalistic inquiry.* Beverly Hills, CA: Sage.

Olson, C. (1993). *The life of illness: One woman's journey.* Albany: State University of New York Press.

Outhwaite, W. (1985). Hans Georg Gadamer. In Q. Skinner (Ed.), *The return of grand theory in the human sciences* (pp. 21-39). New York: Cambridge University Press.

Parse, R. (1981). *Man-living-health: A theory of nursing.* New York: John Wiley.

Parse, R. (1987). *Nursing science: Major paradigms, theories, and critiques.* Philadelphia: W. B. Saunders.

Parse, R. (1992). Human becoming: Parse's theory of nursing. *Nursing Science Quarterly, 5*(1), 35-42.

Ray, M. (1990). Phenomenological method for nursing research. In N. Chaska (Ed.), *The nursing profession: Turning points* (pp. 173-179). St. Louis: C. V. Mosby.

Ray, M. (1991). Caring inquiry: The esthetic process in the way of compassion. In D. Gaut & M. Leininger (Eds.), *Caring: The compassionate healer* (pp. 181-189). New York: National League for Nursing Press.

Reeder, F. (1984). Philosophical issues in the Rogerian science of unitary human beings. *Advances in Nursing Science, 8*(1), 14-23.

Reeder, F. (1988). Hermeneutics. In B. Sarter (Ed.), *Paths to knowledge: Innovative research methods for nursing* (pp. 193-238). New York: National League for Nursing Press.

Reeder, F. (1989). *Conceptual foundations of science and key phenomenological concepts. Nursing theory, research, and practice* (Summer research conference monograph). Detroit: Wayne State University, College of Nursing.

Ricoeur, P. (1981). *Hermeneutics and the human sciences* (J. Thompson, Ed. & Trans.). New York: Cambridge University Press.

Spiegelberg, H. (1982). *The phenomenologic movement: A historical introduction.* The Hague: Martinus Nijhoff.

Stapleton, T. (1983). *Husserl and Heidegger: The question of the phenomenological beginning.* Albany: State University of New York Press.

Thompson, J. (1981). *Critical hermeneutics: A study in the thought of Paul Ricoeur and Jurgen Habermas.* New York: Cambridge University Press.

van Manen, M. (1990). *Researching lived experience.* Albany: State University of New York Press.

Watson, J. (1985). *Nursing: Human science and human care.* Norwalk, CT: Appleton-Century-Crofts.

Dialogue

Clarifying Phenomenological Methods

HUTCHINSON One risk is that students take Benner and then take their qualitative data and fit it into Benner's categories. So it's a kind of matching scenario. That's what comes through these dissertations—"Oh, I have just discovered expert practice in psychiatric nursing," or whatever, and then it becomes deductive.

BOTTORFF I think there are two issues here: On one hand you have Sally's concern about people fitting their data with the theoretical framework, "discovering" something; and on the other hand you have theorists saying that the methods that you can use to explore this are phenomenology, so it is confusing to people to know when it is OK to use phenomenology under the umbrella of these theoretical frameworks and when it's not.

RAY Well, the way that I have used a particular theory in phenomenological research, such as Parse, is related to the idea of the use of presuppositions or prejudgment—or what Gadamer calls prejudice or horizon of meaning. The theory is used positively, as part of the data of conscious experience. That makes interpretation and understanding possible in the first place. This notion is hermeneutical or hermeneutic-phenomenology, and not purely descriptive phenomenology, which rules out presuppositions because of the commitment to bracketing or holding in abeyance presuppositions (in this case a theory). Thus the use of theory in a phenomenological study needs to be used in conjunction with the hermeneutical perspective, rather than stating that it is just phenomenological. It's a thorny issue. So at the time when we are trying to simplify our understanding of this type of very difficult information (philosophy), at the same time it becomes more complex.

BOYLE For those of us who want answers, is what you are saying, there aren't any? [laughter]

KNAFL But this is something doctoral students need to know—this is tough stuff, very abstract, and very conceptual.

RAY For an eidetic (descriptive) phenomenological study, you don't bracket your awareness, you bracket your presuppositions. You bracket some kind of theorizing about a phenomenon, and then you bring it back after you move it into a hermeneutic. But if you solely use hermeneutics, you can interpret out of the nature of any theory because it's considered a prejudgment that makes interpretation possible.

8

Schools of Phenomenology: Implications for Research

MARLENE ZICHI COHEN
ANNA OMERY

As you know, phenomenologists are not noted for their clear language, and one of the issues we struggled with was how to make phenomenological philosophy more accessible. The other issue was the comprehensiveness. When we started writing this chapter, we wrote about the three phases of phenomenological philosophy and all of the philosophers in these phases; we quickly realized that we would have a three-volume set. So we decided to focus on Heidegger and Husserl, in part, because the research that is reported by using phenomenological methods most often refers to those philosophers.

Phenomenological research is increasingly appreciated in social science research. Along with the increased use of this method has come discussion about appropriate criteria for evaluating phenomenological research. Better understanding of the philosophical basis of phenomenology may enable better evaluation of the quality of phenomenological research. The purpose of this chapter is to show the effect of phenomenological philosophy on research in the social sciences. This we accomplish by briefly reviewing the philosophy of Husserl and Heidegger, the two key influences in phenomenological research. A review of phenomenological methodologies and how they are reported in social science research follows.

Spiegelberg (1982) used the term *movement* in his history of phenomenological philosophy to show it is a philosophy that has changed considerably over time, both across different philosophers and within each philosopher. Indeed Spiegelberg hoped his book would rectify the idea that a solid body of teaching or a unified philosophy is subscribed to by all phenomenologists. However, common features are found among the varieties of individual philosophers. Husserl and Heidegger are the focus of this chapter because their work has had the most influence on phenomenological research.

The Phenomenology of Edmund Husserl: Eidetic Phenomenology

Phenomenology in our sense is the science of "origins," of the "mothers" of all cognition: and it is the maternal-ground of all philosophical method": to this ground and to the work in it, everything leads back. (Husserl, 1971/1980, p. 69)

Husserl is the founder and central figure of the phenomenological movement. Phenomenology includes more than Husserl's philosophy, and his philosophy changed considerably across time. Spiegelberg (1982) traced this development in detail; Cohen (1987) traced this history more briefly.

Four constants through Husserl's philosophy have been described (Spiegelberg, 1982). The first was the *ideal of rigorous science.* Husserl had a sense of mission that did not waver. He hoped that philosophy, after its reorganization, would be able to help even objective scientists clarify and critique their unclarified fundamental concepts and assumptions. This philosophy would restore contact with the deeper concerns of people and science.

The second constant in Husserl's work was his *philosophic radicalism.* The starting point for Husserl was his idea that human experience contains a meaningful structure. Philosophy is made of ontology and epistemology. *Ontology* is concerned with the nature and relations of being, whereas *epistemology* is the study or theory of the nature and grounds of knowledge, especially with reference to its limits and validity. Husserl's epistemology involved the study of essential, or a priori, structures of possible beings. His eidetic, or descriptive, phenomenology sought universal essences, their structure and relations, based on the eidetic reduction. The phenomenology of essences seeks to secure absolute insights into the what, or essence, of whatever is given intuitively in experience. The task is to elucidate the general essence of the phenomena being investigated to yield a concrete descriptive analysis. The study of the general essence of consciousness and of its various structures presupposes the conception of general essences.

Husserl's work was redirected toward phenomenology after his son died in World War I. He believed that science needed a philosophy that would restore its contact with deeper human concerns. His philosophical radicalism means going to the "roots," or "beginnings," of all knowledge—to its ultimate foundations. He sought a philosophy without presuppositions.

The third constant for Husserl was the *ethos of radical autonomy.* He believed that people were responsible for themselves and for their culture.

The final constant in Husserl's philosophy was the *respect for wonders,* and he said, "The wonder of all wonders is the pure ego and pure subjectivity" (1913/1952, p. 75). The central focus was the being that is aware of its own being and of other beings.

Phenomenological intuiting, or *anschauung,* is a meaningful aspect of Husserl's philosophy. *Anschauung* ("looking at") is the ultimate test of all knowledge. It can involve imagination, memory, or real cases. It is close to the idea of logical insight based on careful consideration of representative examples.

Husserl used the Greek term *epoche* for the phenomenological reduction. The Greek term was used by the ancient Sceptics for suspension of beliefs. The phenomenological reduction is a new method of suspension of belief. It serves the purpose of obtaining unadulterated phenomena that are attainable in the "naive," or "natural," attitude, the everyday, unreflected attitude of naive belief (Husserl, 1960). This reduction prepares us for critical examination of what, undoubtedly, is given before our interpreting beliefs enter in. With the reduction, we are led back to the origins of phenomena; these origins are lost in the haste of our everyday thought.

Reduction involves two stages (Spiegelberg, 1982). The first stage, *eidetic reduction,* is reduction from particular facts to general essences. Although Husserl did not give detailed instructions on how to accomplish this reduction, it has been interpreted to mean dropping references to the individual and particular. The second stage, the transcendental or *phenomenological reduction proper,* frees phenomena from all transphenomenal elements. This stage allows phenomena to come directly into view, rather than to be viewed (and distorted) through our preconceptions because we temporarily suspend the natural standpoint (or natural attitude). Husserl used the mathematic metaphor of bracketing for this suspension of belief.

Life-world (Lebenswelt), the world of lived experience, is an important concept that was found posthumously in Husserl's unpublished work (Spiegelberg, 1982). This world of everyday experience is not immediately accessible in the "natural attitude." We take for granted so much of what is commonplace that we often fail to notice it. To really see what surrounds us requires phenomenological study. This task is central to the phenomenological tradition.

The intentionality of consciousness (awareness) is another key aspect of Husserl's phenomenology. *Intentional* means directedness toward an object. Because consciousness is in the world and is always intentional (is always "consciousness of" something), the study of experience reveals consciousness.

Husserl's phenomenology studies experience to reveal consciousness. With the use of phenomenological reduction, we can uncover and describe the fundamental structures of our lifeworld. Husserl claimed that a true science follows the nature of what has to be investigated, not its methodological preconceptions (Bolton, 1987). Bolton argued that phenomenology allows investigators to understand and express the necessary relationship between data of empirical investigation and the concepts used to organize and direct these data. Although the method of eidetic variation and phenomenological analysis practiced by Barritt, Beekman, Bleeker, and Mulderij (1983, 1984), Giorgi (1985), van Manen (1984), and others has been shown to be useful, Bolton argued that failure to understand how concepts and methods of data gathering and inspection relate might yield phenomenological positivism.

The Phenomenology of Martin Heidegger: Ontological Phenomenology

Men alone of all existing things . . . experience the wonder of all wonders: that there is being (*das Seiendes ist*). (Heidegger, 1951, p. 42)

It will do Heidegger an injustice if this chapter (section) nowhere sounds extremely strange. (Llewelyn, 1985, p. 3)

Introduction

As with Husserl, Heidegger sought, through phenomenology, to redefine and center the mission of philosophy. Heidegger moved away from Husserl's thoughts, however, because he saw the primary focus of philosophy as ontological, while Husserl's focus was epistemological. (*Metaphysics* is a philosophy made up of ontology and epistemology. *Ontology* is concerned with the nature and relations of being. *Epistemology* is concerned with the nature and grounds of knowledge.) Bringing together thoughts from the phenomenological, ontological, and hermeneutical (interpretive), Heidegger defined *philosophy* as the universal phenomenological ontology based on the hermeneutic of human being (Spiegelberg, 1982). This ontological phenomenology reveals that truth is to be found in the world interpreted hermeneutically (Langan, 1970). The primary phenomenon that phenomenology uncovers is the meaning of Being (*Sein*), which has become victim of the usual forgetfulness of the ontological difference between Being (*Sein,* or presence) and being (*Dasein,* or "being there").

Distinguishing Being from being has been done most clearly by those interpreting Heidegger's work. According to these interpretations, *Sein,* or Being, is presence in the world, as opposed to being, or "being there" (*Dasein*), which signifies people (beings) who comprehend this presence. Being, a phenomenon itself, is the presence in the world through which truth is self-determined. It is the ground of all beings. People and Being are interdependent; all persons (beings) need Being, and Being needs beings (persons). They subsist together. The unique distinction of persons is that they stand as beings not only in the midst of Being but also as beings exposed to nonbeing—that is, death.

One unique feature of Heidegger's philosophy is that he saw the task of phenomenology as destruction. This destruction means looking past the normal, everyday meanings of life to see the larger meaning in Being. This destruction liberates us from unconscious servitude to our metaphysical past (Spiegelberg, 1982). This destruction loosens and removes the hardened tradition of our everyday being in order to detect the truth of our Being.

Phenomenology, for Heidegger, meant primarily a notion of method, a mode of approaching the objects of philosophical research, rather than a specific, unique philosophical method (Heidegger, 1927/1962). This "method" does not identify the qualitative content of the particular objects of philosophical research, but the mode of approaching them. It is a methodological approach making us see what is otherwise concealed, of taking the hidden out of its hiding, and of detecting it as "unhidden"—that is, as truth (Spiegelberg, 1982).

Husserl's Contributions to Heidegger

Martin Heidegger already was struggling with the basic themes of his work—Being/being, time, and history—when he sought out Edmund Husserl. Grappling with this ontological problem, Heidegger realized that phenomenological method could provide the basis for his study of our everyday being in the world. For Heidegger the central idea of Husserl's phenomenology was expressed in the watchword *Zu den Sachen* (to the things themselves) (Llewelyn, 1985; Spiegelberg, 1982). This central idea provided at least a partial solution to the ontological problem with which Heidegger struggled.

From the very start, however, Heidegger claimed the freedom to develop his own version of the phenomenological approach (Spiegelberg, 1982). Heidegger voiced criticisms of the way Husserl had constituted phenomenology, especially by emphasizing description, rather than understanding (*verstehen*), as its basis. He disassociated himself from the eidetic and the transcendental approaches.

For Heidegger, eidetic phenomenology was, at best, useless, and at worst, spurious. He was convinced that philosophers could not make a fresh start until they identified and neutralized the metaphysical preconceptions that distorted the very formulations of their philosophical problems—in fact, even the descriptions of their phenomena. For Heidegger, phenomenology should not garner new information or provide knowledge hitherto simply nonexistent; it is intended to appropriate and interpret a meaning already implicit in the lived experience as its truth (Burch, 1989).

Husserl's interest was primarily in the epistemological question, What do we know as persons? Heidegger's interest was in the ontological question, What is Being, and what are the foundations for philosophizing and phenomenologizing in the midst of it? Heidegger shifted the foundation of phenomenology from the eidetic, or essential, to Being (Burch, 1989; Kvale, 1984; Spiegelberg, 1982). Heidegger (1951) wrote, "Man alone of all existing things . . . experiences the wonder of all wonders: that there are things-in-being" (p. 42). In contrast, as noted earlier, Husserl (1913/1952) wrote, "The wonder of all wonders is the pure ego and pure subjectivity" (p.75). Heidegger's wonder was objective Being; Husserl's wonder was subjective consciousness.

Heidegger's Ontological Phenomenology

In actuality, it is not Being (*Sein*) itself that Heidegger claimed to be searching, but the meaning (*Sinn*) of Being (Spiegelberg, 1982). This search for meaning is both unique and fundamental to the human because humans are privileged entities who are concerned about being and thus have a certain understanding of the meaning of Being, however defective, from the very start. Humans are fundamentally "ontological." *Being and Time* (1927/ 1962), Heidegger's seminal work, is, then, an examination of the meaning of Being by way of an analysis of the being of the human animal.

Being/Being. For Heidegger, *Being* referred to the presencing, or self-manifesting, of entities. Collective beings, or humanity, is *Dasein,* the temporal-historical world in which entities can manifest themselves, or "be." Neither being nor *Dasein* can be understood as the particular entities in or of themselves; rather they are the conditions necessary for the specific entities to appear (Zimmerman, 1989). *Dasein* stands outside itself, ahead of itself, toward beings of a different kind from itself, and with beings of its own kind. The phenomenological analytic is done to elucidate the particular manner of being within *Dasein.* An everyday world of *Dasein* that is different from our own can be understood only by imagining variations on the general formal structure that individuals discover in their own *Dasein* (Llewelyn, 1985). The results of this analysis of *Dasein* is not being as an object over subjectivity (as in traditional science); rather this analysis illuminates the being in which we already are standing; that is, the being that is disclosed is not merely the being of an object, but our own being—that is, what it means to *be,* or Being (Palmer, 1969).

In constituting itself, Being constitutes a truth not yet realized within the lived experience. Phenomenology necessarily affirms the existential structure (lived experience) where truth is first accessible and against which truth must be tested (Bolton, 1987). And yet, in constituting itself, it must determine a truth already immanent in the intelligibility of lived experience and thus in some sense an integral part of our everyday understanding.

Like the forest that cannot be seen for looking at the trees, Being is obscured by being in the everyday world. For Heidegger, we live in, and in fact are nothing but, a clearing (*Lichtung*) in the midst of Being, implying that around this clearing, Being remains a dark jungle. Heidegger made a special point of emphasizing that Being, particularly in the case of human being, is fundamentally particularized (Spiegelberg, 1982). Western philosophy and civilization have become more and more diverted from a contemplation of Being to a study and, finally, the technical use and subjugation of beings.

Modern science, along with the totalitarian state, was interpreted as the necessary consequence of modern technology and its subjugation. Science became a degeneration of "thinking" because it does not really think at all. Metaphysics, science, and technology increasingly took the place of what properly should be called ontology, or the study of Being. The result is that the human being usually lives in complete oblivion of the question of Being (Spiegelberg, 1982).

Time. Being was essentially temporal for Heidegger. Yet time is nothing apart from Being. The idea of timelessness, and especially of an eternal Being, was for Heidegger meaningless. *Time* was introduced as "the possible horizon for an understanding of Being" (Spiegelberg, 1982, p. 351). Time is the frame of reference and, as a result, the key to understanding (Spiegelberg, 1982). The passage of temporality and time makes up the sense of human being. At best one might understand it as the setting, or matrix, of our being. As human beings we are ahead of ourselves toward the possibilities of future existence, are immersed in the facticity of our past, and "fall for" the escapes of our present.

Existence, Mood, and Being Toward Death. Heidegger's concepts of *human being* and *temporality* are linked closely with his concept of *existence.* In the strict sense, however, existence, or the possibility of being or not being oneself, is only one of several basic features of human being. As Heidegger saw it, existence is a nontheoretical affair that can be handled only by actual existing. The essence of human being lies in its existence—that is, in its possibilities to choose different ways of being. Human being is always oriented toward future possibilities of its own.

The historicity of human beings' existence consists primarily of individuals' fates based in their own determination within an inherited, yet chosen, frame of possibilities. The center of gravity of historicity lies in the future, for human beings are oriented toward the future and, ultimately, toward their only authentic possibility—death. There is both impotence and freedom in such an existence.

Heidegger used the term *angst* for humanity's awareness of its mortality, its ontological nothingness. In *Being and Time,* Heidegger (1927/1962) spoke of the necessity for courageous, resolute being-toward-death as a necessary condition for human *Dasein* to become authentic. Authenticity is how life/existence is constituted in response to angst; it is manifested in the uncertain struggle that constitutes the day-to-day existence of being.

Anxiety is described now as the condition that is behind our everyday escape from angst into small talk, curiosity, and ambiguity. It is interpreted as a pulling away from the nothing. The unique distinction of humans that Heidegger identified was that they are beings who stand in the midst of Being and also find themselves exposed to the possibility of nonbeing and, in this sense, can transcend the mere fact of their being.

It is the function of phenomenology to understand anxiety as the fundamental mood of the human situation and to bring out this structure. Anxiety always is concerned about the existential possibilities of the human being caught by its facticity and trying to escape into everyday existence. It shows human beings diverted by the world of their present, yet tied to their past, while still primarily reaching out into the future, into which they find themselves "thrown." This "thrown-ness" is not a mere brute fact of human birth. It represents an intimate part of our way of being, even though it usually is pushed into the background.

Truth, for Heidegger, was primarily no longer a property of propositions but of Being itself. In fact, truth is a process by which Being opens up to the human being in the face of nothingness. Being and truth are so intimately related as to be a single, basic theme (Spiegelberg, 1982).

If Being is basic fundamental structure (the truth of human being), then consciousness and knowledge are only modifications of this underlying fundamental relationship between Being and being. As a result, thinking loses its character as an independent, spontaneous activity and, instead, consists as an acceptance and listening to the voice of Being.

For Heidegger, no method could enforce the revelation of the truth. At best, method can only prepare the way of truth in the thinker. Nowhere is this statement truer than in the case of scientific method, for science does not discover original truth but merely develops what already is known. Additionally it is not given to our thinking to force our way into Being, but it is Being that reveals itself by its own initiative, its speaking to us (*Zuspruch*). We can do nothing but either resist or accept it in "mellow tranquillity" (*Gelassenheit der Milde*) (Spiegelberg, 1982, p. 374).

Heideggerian Hermeneutics

For Heidegger, *hermeneutics* was simply the interpretive method that leads the investigating glance back from naively conceived beings to Being itself. It is the method by which being is transcended toward Being.

Heidegger believed that Being has a tendency to fall (or possibly to be pushed by human beings in their angst) into oblivion. As a result, human beings have an inherent tendency toward *Verfallen*. The world of *Verfallen* may be understood as a kind of decay of existence, of infatuation with everyday detail, and of denial of the nothingness. Yet it is a characteristic of hermeneutics that it has to take its starting point in this everyday mode of human being. It is in and from the everyday experience that the sense of Being is recovered and made apparent (Langan, 1970).

The concern of Heidegger's hermeneutic is to uncover the hidden phenomena and, particularly, their meanings. As with eidetic phenomenology, hermeneutics presupposes that what is to be interpreted has meaning. Yet the aim of hermeneutic phenomenology is different and more ambitious then eidetic phenomenology. Hermeneutic's goal is discovery of meaning that is not immediately manifest to our intuiting, analyzing, and describing. Interpreters have to go beyond what is given directly. Yet, in attempting this, they have to use the ordinary, everyday given as a clue for meanings that are not given, at least not explicitly.

Thus every interpretation of ordinary items in daily life is related to a frame or relevance that embraces it, implies a preview looking toward anticipated meanings, and requires conceptual patterns for it. Precisely what is discovered in the phenomenology of everydayness is that there are neither any essences of things nor any pure meaning-giving ego distinct from the existential structures. Because the totality has no essence, no determinate "what it is" that could fix a horizon within which it is ultimately to be understood, hermeneutic interpretations always must be based on (be within the horizon of) such understanding as we already have; that is, they initially must be based in our pre-phenomenological everyday understanding (Dreyfus & Haugeland, 1979).

For Heidegger, then, hermeneutics was the interpretive method by which one goes beyond mere description of what is manifest and tries to uncover hidden meanings by anticipatory devices. Even more important than the technique, however, is the fact that this is the method by which beings are rescued from *Verfallen* and being is transcended toward Being.

Heideggerian Phenomenology
as a Research Method

As a philosopher, Heidegger saw hermeneutics as a philosophical method, not a scientific one. Early, while Heidegger was still in contact with Husserl, indications were that he strove toward "scientific" thinking. But after World War II, Heidegger abandoned all pretense of being "scientific" (Spiegelberg, 1982; Zimmerman, 1989).

Indeed Heidegger rebelled against method. An indication of the nonmethodical character of Heidegger's new "thought" in the 1950s and 1960s is his repudiation of the term *research.* To him, research was the mark of modern science, which he saw as excessively preoccupied with itself and its method. The researcher is actually a technician in the service of the conquest of the world by humans, the subjects. Reflection, which Heidegger contrasted to this research as the proper task of philosophy, apparently cannot be described in terms of a clear and teachable method (Spiegelberg, 1982).

It fell to others to define what the hermeneutic was to become as a research method. It would be interesting if we could speak with Heidegger about his views of the current extensions of his ideas in the social sciences.

Phenomenological Research Methodology:
Eidetic (Descriptive) and Hermeneutic (Interpretive)

Eidetic, or descriptive, phenomenology and hermeneutic, or interpretive, phenomenology are distinctive schools of thought. The methodologies that are founded in these schools are as distinctive. The uniqueness between the eidetic and phenomenological methodologies lies not in the specific techniques applied but in the goals and tasks of the affiliated research methods.

Eidetic phenomenology as a research method rests on the thesis that there are essential structures to any human experience. These structures are what constitute any experience. Each unique experience is made up of distinctive structures that pattern the specific experience uniquely. When these structures are apprehended in consciousness, they take on a meaning that is the meaning (or truth) of that experience for the participants.

The goal of eidetic phenomenology, then, is description of the meaning of an experience from the perspective of those who have had that experience—that is, to describe the meaning of an experience from the worldview of those who have had that experience and as a result now have a meaning attached to it. Researchers bracket their presuppositions, reflect on the experiences that were described, and intuit or describe the essential structures of the experiences under study.

This eidetic description is not, however, just an individual, subjective perspective of the experience or opinion of a meaning. It is a description of a meaning that is eidetic, that is fundamental and essential to the experience no matter which specific individual has that experience. This eidetic constitution or description of the meaning of the experience can be achieved only through reduction. *Reduction* is the process of putting aside the natural world (one could even say the world of interpretation) in order to see the phenomenon as it is in its essence. Reduction is the process of looking at the experience naively, without the preconditions, the prejudices, and the biases that one usually brings to any description. A variety of techniques have been developed to achieve reduction in phenomenological research. The most common of these techniques is to identify and articulate assumptions prior to data collection and analysis.

Hermeneutics as a research method rests on the ontological thesis that lived experience is itself essentially an interpretive process. The phenomenological task is one of explicit ontological self-interpretation (Burch, 1989). Hermeneutics as research methodology is a way of systematically dealing with interpretations (Bolton, 1987). Understanding and possibilities are the outcome of interpretations; these are linked to cultural norms.

For those who practice hermeneutics, constitutive analysis is not just watching the phenomena form themselves in consciousness, but rather is a figure-structure action of interpretation (Spiegelberg, 1982). It is a more spontaneous act of perception by which sense is brought from the historical horizons to crystallize in a gestalt-forming of the thing (*das Ding,* in Heideggerian terms), whose meaning can be fully interpreted only through its history (Langan, 1970).

The concept or subject under investigation possesses its meaning because of the context we supply for it. The conceptual meaning is placed within the context of a relatedness to things in the world, which precedes and always transcends that meaning. The notion of "being-in-the-world" is inescapable if any justice is to be done to the way concepts are formed (Bolton, 1987).

Method, where it exists, is focused on the unequivocal and systematic in the interpretations of meaning. The interpretation is understood to occur in context. Both the everyday experience of the subject and the researcher are participants in this context.

What is missing from current descriptions of hermeneutic research methods, however, is a sense of Being. The goal is to understand the *Verfallen* world of being, rather than to understand Being. Current hermeneutic investigators, in their shift toward the epistemological questions or science, have shifted away from Heidegger's ontological phenomenology. They have abandoned the philosophical quest for the meaning of Being, with hermeneutics constituting the method by which that quest is to be actualized. For the research method that is hermeneutics, Being is now assumed. The systematic interpretative methodology that is hermeneutic research has priority over the quest for Being, if indeed the quest still even exists.

Schools of Phenomenology:
Research Applications

Phenomenological philosophy has been applied in a variety of ways to guide research. Various schools have developed with differences in approaches. Three of these traditions have been used extensively in social science research. The goal of these phenomenological studies is to obtain fundamental knowledge of phenomena: the eidetic structure (when guided by Husserl or the Duquesne school), or interpretation of phenomena to bring out hidden meanings (when guided by Heidegger or Heideggerian hermeneutics), or some combination of these goals (when guided by the Dutch school).

Approaches developed by researchers from the Duquesne school, including Giorgi, Colaizzi, Fischer, and van Kaam, often are referred to by social science researchers. This label of the "Duquesne school" is used loosely because not all who originally worked at Duquesne University remain in Pittsburgh. Adrian van Kaam founded the doctoral program of the Psychology Department at Duquesne University in 1962. He and others in the department based their work on existential-phenomenological psychology (Giorgi, Fischer, & Von Eckartsberg, 1971).

The Dutch phenomenology of the "Utrecht school," the phenomenology of such scholars as Langeveld, Buitedijk, and Linschoten, also has been translated and applied to social science research. Barritt et al. (1983, 1984) and van Manen (1990) wrote particularly clear and helpful texts describing Dutch phenomenology and its use in research. Their work also has been referred to by social science researchers.

One difference between the Dutch phenomenology and the Duquesne tradition is that the Duquesne researchers focus on eidetic description, whereas the Dutch approaches combine features of descriptive and interpretive phenomenology. However, individual researchers and schools of researchers have applied the philosophy and have used variations in methods and forms of reporting so that there is more variety in the use of these methods than this description might imply.

A third tradition has been called "Heideggerian hermeneutics." Diekelmann, Allen, and Tanner (1989) described a seven-stage process of analysis. This interpretive approach is based on Heideggerian phenomenology (Heidegger, 1962). The intent of this tradition is to reveal frequently taken for granted shared practices and common meanings.

Reports of Research

A review of selected recent research reports from 13 journals revealed interesting trends in discussion of the phenomenological methods used. Very few discussed methods in relation to phenomenological philosophers. Giorgi (1989), Sass (1990), and Tien (1992) are exceptions; they refer us to either Husserl or Heidegger.

Researchers most often cited secondary sources to reference their methods. These sources included the approaches described above as the Duquesne school, Dutch phenomenology, and Heideggerian hermeneutics. Examples of researchers who referred to the Duquesne school include Ablamowicz (1992); Angus, Osborne, and Koziey (1991); Beck (1991, 1992); Becker (1987); Bowman (1991); Brice (1991); Columbus and Rice (1991); Denne and Thompson (1991); Forrest (1989); Guglietti-Kelly and Westcott (1990); Ling (1987); Rose (1990); and Sandelowski and Pollock (1986). Examples of researchers who referred to the Dutch school (including Barritt et al. and van Manen) are Cohen and Sarter (1992), Forrest (1989), Rose (1990), and Whetstone and Reid (1991). Forrest (1989) and Rose (1990) referred to both the Duquesne school (Colaizzi) and the Dutch school (van Manen). Heideggerian hermeneutics has been used by Benner (1984); Benner, Tanner, and Chesla (1992); Benner and Wrubel (1989); Diekelmann (1989, 1990, 1991, 1992); and Kondora (1993).

A number of reports lacked a discussion of the method or lacked references to support the method that was described in general terms. For example, articles in the journal *Phenomenology + Pedagogy* do not include detailed discussions of methods, yet it is a well-respected journal in phenomenology. Examples of reports that either had no description of method or a very brief description are Carrere (1989); Cohen, Craft, and Titler (1988); Connolly (1987); Davidson (1992); Johnson (1988); Marr (1991); Osborne (1989); Ots (1990); Radley (1991); Smith (1987); and Smith (1989).

Some researchers described the methods by using language from other methods, most often grounded theory (e.g., Bennett, 1990; Drew, 1986; Moch, 1990; Mulcahey, 1992). More troubling were those that described methods inconsistent with phenomenology. For example, Breault and Polifroni (1992) used cognitive dissonance as their theoretical framework, and Whetstone and Reid (1991) used Orem as their theoretical framework. It is appropriate to use theories as part of phenomenological research to show how the research might enhance the theories or as part of the interpretation. However, guiding a phenomenological study with a theoretical framework is not consistent with this approach, which values going to the "things" or phenomena themselves, as opposed to going to concepts, theories, or other derivatives from immediate experience.

The space constraints of writing for journal publication are troubling for phenomenologists. It is impossible to discuss completely both the method used and the results in a way that allows the reader access to the data that are needed for a rich phenomenological report. Perhaps for this reason some journals, such as *Phenomenology + Pedagogy,* have an editorial policy that eliminates discussion of methods or publish manuscripts that include only a very brief discussion of methods.

The language of phenomenologists has never been described as clear. This complexity may account for researchers using the language of other traditions when describing techniques that are common to many approaches. Space constraints and the feeling that reviewers need precise descriptions of methods may lead researchers to describe methods by using set steps. However, this tactic could lead to the "phenomenological positivism" that Bolton warned against, in which researchers fail to understand how concepts and methods of data gathering and inspections relate. Researchers who use techniques by rote, without understanding their base, will be unlikely to advance our science.

The inconsistent combinations of theoretical frameworks with phenomenological approaches may reflect a lack of understanding of phenomenology. Reading the entire report often reveals that the researcher has not adhered to the method. The realities of a practice discipline may require that research methods (specific techniques or steps) be altered to fit clinically important questions. Concerns about method ought to be less important than concerns about methodology (theoretical understanding and articulation of method) when practice realities serve as an additional guide. However, practice concerns cannot substitute for an appreciation for the underlying philosophy. Spiegelberg introduced the idea of "cooperative research" in a series of workshops from 1965 to 1971 (Churchill, 1990). He advocated that phenomenologists work together to eliminate the limitations of private investigations. The dialogal approach used in Seattle is one model for this cooperation (Halling & Leifer, 1991). Our work indeed will be advanced by fostering cooperation, entering each others' perspectives, and pointing out aspects that have been overlooked.

References

Ablamowicz, H. (1992). Shame as an interpersonal dimension of communication among doctoral students: An empirical phenomenological study. *Journal of Phenomenological Psychology, 23*(1), 30-49.

Angus, N. M., Osborne, J. W., & Koziey, P. W. (1991). Window to the soul: A phenomenological investigation of mutual gaze. *Journal of Phenomenological Psychology, 22*(2), 142-162.

Barritt, L., Beekman, A. J., Bleeker, H., & Mulderij, K. (1983). *A handbook for phenomenological research in education.* Ann Arbor: University of Michigan, School of Education.

Barritt, L., Beekman, T., Bleeker, H., & Mulderij, K. (1984). Analyzing phenomenological descriptions. *Phenomenology + Pedagogy, 2*(1), 1-17.

Beck, C. T. (1991). Undergraduate nursing students' lived experience of health: A phenomenological study. *Journal of Nursing Education, 30*(8), 371-374.

Beck, C. T. (1992). The lived experience of postpartum depression: A phenomenological study. *Nursing Research, 41*(3), 166-170.

Becker, C. S. (1987). Friendship between women: A phenomenological study of best friends. *Journal of Phenomenological Psychology, 18,* 59-72.

Benner, P. (1984). *From novice to expert: Excellence and power in clinical nursing practice.* Menlo Park, CA: Addison-Wesley.

Benner, P., Tanner, C., & Chesla, C. (1992). From beginner to expert: Gaining a differentiated clinical world in critical care nursing. *Advances in Nursing Science, 14*(3), 13-28.

Benner, P., & Wrubel, J. (1989). *The primacy of caring: Stress and coping in health and illness.* Menlo Park, CA: Addison-Wesley.

Bennett, M. J. (1990). Stigmatization: Experiences of persons with acquired immune deficiency syndrome. *Issues in Mental Health Nursing, 11,* 141-145.

Bolton, N. (1987). Beyond method: Phenomenology as an approach to consciousness. *Journal of Phenomenological Psychology, 18,* 49-58.

Bowman, J. M. (1991). The meaning of chronic low back pain. *AAOHN Journal, 39*(8), 381-384.

Breault, A. J., & Polifroni, E. C. (1992). Caring for people with AIDS: Nurses' attitudes and feelings. *Journal of Advanced Nursing, 17,* 21-27.

Brice, C. W. (1991). What forever means: An empirical existential-phenomenological investigation of maternal mourning. *Journal of Phenomenological Psychology, 22*(1), 16-38.

Burch, R. (1989). On phenomenology and its practices. *Phenomenology + Pedagogy, 7,* 187-217.

Carrere, R. A. (1989). Psychology of tragedy: A phenomenological analysis. *Journal of Phenomenological Psychology, 20*(1), 105-129.

Churchill, S. (1990). Considerations for teaching a phenomenological approach to psychological research. *Journal of Phenomenological Psychology, 21*(1), 46-67.

Cohen, M. Z. (1987). A historical overview of the phenomenological movement. *Image: Journal of Nursing Scholarship, 19*(1), 31-34.

Cohen, M. Z., Craft, M. J., & Titler, M. (1988). Families in critical care settings: Where fear leads to silence. *Phenomenology + Pedagogy, 6*(3), 147-157.

Cohen, M. Z., & Sarter, B. (1992). Love and work: Oncology nurses' view of the meaning of their work. *Oncology Nursing Forum, 19*(10), 1481-1486.

Columbus, P. J., & Rice, D. L. (1991). Psychological research on the martial arts: An addendum to Fuller's review. *British Journal of Medical Psychology, 64*, 127-135.

Connolly, M. (1987). The experience of living with an absent child. *Phenomenology + Pedagogy, 5*(2), 157-172.

Davidson, L. (1992). Developing an empirical-phenomenological approach to schizophrenia research. *Journal of Phenomenological Psychology, 23*(1), 3-15.

Denne, J. M., & Thompson, N. L. (1991). The experience of transition to meaning and purpose in life. *Journal of Phenomenology Psychology, 22*(2), 109-133.

Diekelmann, N. (1989). The nursing curriculum: Lived experiences of students. In *Curriculum revolution: Reconceptualizing nursing education* (NLN #15-2280). New York: National League for Nursing Press.

Diekelmann, N. (1990). Nursing education: Caring, dialogue, and practice. *Journal of Nursing Education, 29*, 300-305.

Diekelmann, N. (1991). The emancipatory power of the narrative. In *Curriculum revolution: Community building and activism* (NLN #15-2398). New York: National League for Nursing Press.

Diekelmann, N. (1992). Learning-as-testing: A Heideggerian hermeneutical analysis of the lived experiences of students and teachers in nursing. *Advances in Nursing Science, 14*(3), 72-83.

Diekelmann, N., Allen, D., & Tanner, C. (1989). *The NLN criteria for appraisal of baccalaureate programs: A critical hermeneutic analysis.* New York: National League for Nursing Press.

Drew, N. (1986). Exclusion and confirmation: A phenomenology of patients' experiences with caregivers. *Image: Journal of Nursing Scholarship, 18*(2), 39-43.

Dreyfus, H., & Haugeland, J. (1979). Husserl and Heidegger: Philosophy's last stand. In M. Murray (Ed.), *Heidegger and modern philosophy* (pp. 222-238). New Haven, CT: Yale University Press.

Forrest, D. (1989). The experience of caring. *Journal of Advanced Nursing, 14*, 815-823.

Giorgi, A. (1985). Sketch of a psychological phenomenological method. In A. Giorgi (Ed.), *Phenomenological and psychological research* (pp. 8-22). Pittsburgh, PA: Duquesne University Press.

Giorgi, A. (1989). An example of harmony between descriptive reports and behavior. *Journal of Phenomenological Psychology, 20*(1), 60-88.

Giorgi, A., Fischer, W., & Von Eckartsberg, R. (Eds.). (1971). *Duquesne studies in phenomenological psychology* (Vol. 1). Pittsburgh, PA: Duquesne University Press.

Guglietti-Kelly, I., & Westcott, M. R. (1990). She's just shy: A phenomenological study of shyness. *Journal of Phenomenological Psychology, 21*(2), 150-164.

Halling, S., & Leifer, M. (1991). The theory and practice of dialogal research. *Journal of Phenomenological Psychology, 22*(1), 1-15.

Heidegger, M. (1951). *Was ist Metaphysik?* (6th ed.). Chicago: Henry Regnery.

Heidegger, M. (1962). *Being and time* (J. Macquarrie & E. Robinson, Trans.). New York: Harper & Row. (Original work published in 1927)

Husserl, E. (1952). *Ideas pertaining to a pure phenomenology and a phenomenological philosophy. First book: General introduction to a pure phenomenology* (F. Kersten, Trans.). Boston: Martinus Nijhoff. (Original work published in 1913)

Husserl, E. (1960). *Cartesian meditations* (D. Cairns, Trans.). The Hague: Martinus Nijhoff.

Husserl, E. (1980). *Ideas pertaining to a pure phenomenology and a phenomenological philosophy. Third book.* (F. Kersten, Trans.). Boston: Martinus Nijhoff. (Original work published in 1971)

Johnson, E. (1988). A phenomenological investigation of fear of the dark. *Journal of Phenomenological Psychology, 19,* 179-194.

Kondora, L. (1993). A Heideggerian hermeneutical analysis of survivors of incest. *Image: Journal of Nursing Scholarship, 25*(1), 11-16.

Kvale, S. (1984). The qualitative research interview: A phenomenological and hermeneutical mode of understanding. *Journal of Phenomenological Psychology, 14*(2), 171-198.

Langan, T. (1970). The future of phenomenology. In F. J. Smith (Ed.), *Phenomenology in perspective* (pp. 1-15). The Hague: Martinus Nijhoff.

Ling, J. (1987). Persuasion-in-teaching. *Journal of Phenomenological Psychology, 18,* 73-89.

Llewelyn, J. (1985). *Beyond metaphysics? The hermeneutic circle in contemporary continental philosophy.* Atlantic Highlands, NJ: Humanities Press.

Marr, J. (1991). The experience of living with Parkinson's disease. *American Association of Neuroscience Nurses, 23*(5), 325-329.

Moch, S. D. (1990). Health within the experience of breast cancer. *Journal of Advanced Nursing, 15,* 1426-1435.

Mulcahey, M. J. (1992). Returning to school after a spinal cord injury: Perspectives from four adolescents. *American Journal of Occupational Therapy, 46*(4), 305-312.

Osborne, J. W. (1989). A phenomenological investigation of the musical representation of extra-musical ideas. *Journal of Phenomenological Psychology, 20*(2), 151-175.

Ots, T. (1990). The angry liver, the anxious heart, and the melancholy spleen. *Culture, Medicine and Psychiatry, 14,* 21-58.

Palmer, R. E. (1969). *Hermeneutics.* Chicago: Northwestern University Press.

Radley, A. (1991). Solving a problem together: A study of thinking in small groups. *Journal of Phenomenological Psychology, 22*(1), 39-59.

Rose, J. F. (1990). Psychologic health of women: A phenomenologic study of women's inner strength. *Advanced Nursing Science, 12*(2), 56-70.

Sandelowski, M., & Pollock, C. (1986). Women's experiences of infertility. *Image: Journal of Nursing Scholarship, 18*(4), 140-144.

Sass, L. A. (1990). The truth-taking-stare: A Heideggerian interpretation of a schizophrenic world. *Journal of Phenomenological Psychology*, *21*(2), 121-149.

Smith, C. (1987). Letting go. *Phenomenology + Pedagogy*, *5*(2), 135-146.

Smith, S. J. (1989). Operating on a child's heart: A pedagogical view of hospitalization. *Phenomenology + Pedagogy*, *7*, 145-162.

Spiegelberg, H. (1982). *The phenomenological movement* (3rd ed.). The Hague: Martinus Nijhoff.

Tien, S. S. (1992). Psychogenesis: A theory of perinatal experience. *Journal of Phenomenological Psychology*, *23*(1), 16-29.

van Manen, M. (1984). Practicing phenomenological writing. *Phenomenology + Pedagogy*, *2*, 36-69.

van Manen, M. (1990). *Researching lived experience*. London, Ontario: Althouse.

Whetstone, W. R., & Reid, J. C. (1991). Health promotion of older adults: Perceived barriers. *Journal of Advanced Nursing*, *16*, 1343-1349.

Zimmerman, M. (1989). The thorn in Heidegger's side: The question of national socialism. *Philosophical Forum*, *20*(4), 325-365.

Dialogue

On Emic and Etic

SANDELOWSKI It is a mistake to say you are doing ethnography and just do interviews. I think the idea is that it's a series of strategies, that whatever gets you the information, such as census reports, or asking the postmistress, or what have you. But if anything, it must include participant observation in some way.

DREHER I also think the emic/etic trap is a real bear, because it's so often misused. While it is true that the emic perspective is the insider's perspective, and it is simple to say that the etic perspective is the outsider's perspective—it's actually the difference between what people say and what people do. And then it becomes very important that both are captured in an ethnography. Women tell me, for example, that their ideal family size is two children—I believe them, and I think they believe it, too. But then, the etic reality is that they have six. Well, then it becomes very interesting from the ethnographer's perspective—it's not just that I observed they have six—*they had six!*

BOYLE And that's what makes it so interesting.

DREHER But I review a lot of proposals and what they often say is that emic is good and etic is bad. The etic piece is this horrible empirical observer who is coming in and doesn't know anything until he gets inside the emic head. And that's not the case at all!

9

Styles of Ethnography

JOYCEEN S. BOYLE

Are styles the same as types? As characteristics? I just munched
them altogether and plowed ahead. I think we would agree that
any good ethnography is always holistic; it is always contextual;
it is always reflexive. It always deals in some way with the
emic-etic question. But then there are all these other ways that
you could classify it too. And those are just some of the things I
tried to do.

In this chapter the origins, purposes, and similarities and differences in the types and methods of ethnography are discussed.
First, the major characteristics of ethnography are explored, as
an emphasis on particular features sets the stage for both the
kind and quality of ethnography produced. Next, a classification
of the different types of ethnographies is proposed, followed by
a discussion of the methods used to collect and analyze data in
ethnographic studies. This discussion highlights the epistemological differences within ethnographic research. Although this
chapter is not about methods per se, the epistemological foundations of a study should exert a powerful and continuous
influence on the purpose of the study, the methods of data
collection, and the procedures for data analysis.

Origins of Ethnography

Hughes (1992) observed that the term *ethnography* has dif-
fused widely to other contexts of inquiry from its original

intellectual source. Historically ethnography evolved in cultural anthropology, with a typical focus on small-scale societies. Two classic ethnographies produced in the early days of anthropology (and now reprinted) are Bronislaw Malinowski's *Argonauts of the Western Pacific* (1961) and Franz Boas's *The Kwakiutl Ethnography* (1966). However, as Werner and Schoepfle (1987a) observed, when the number of anthropologists increased and the number of tribal peoples diminished, ethnographers found other social units appropriate for description. Now ethnography's theoretical and methodologic contributions are applied in diverse naturalistic settings by ethnographers from numerous disciplines, including nursing and other health professions.

As nursing moved into academic settings in the 1960s, a number of nurses in the Nurse Scientist Program obtained their doctoral preparation in anthropology and encouraged the use of ethnography in nursing. Madeleine Leininger and Pamela Brink are two individuals who come to mind who consistently have urged the use of qualitative methods in nursing, particularly the use of ethnographic methods. Leininger (1970) urged the blending of nursing and anthropology using a research method that she termed "ethnonursing" (Leininger, 1985). Other nurse-anthropologists, such as Aamodt, Glittenberg, Kay, Kavanagh, Lipson, Morse, Muecke, and Tripp-Reimer, have used ethnography or ethnographic methods to explore issues or problems of interest to nursing. Some, such as Morse (who is trained in both nursing and anthropology), Roberson, and myself, are prepared in nursing and have used ethnography or ethnographic methods to examine phenomena within the nursing paradigms. Nursing ethnographies usually have focused on health beliefs and practices and how these are related to other social factors.

However it is conducted or by whom, an ethnography is always informed by a concept of *culture*. Ethnography is based on the assumption that culture is learned and shared among members of a group and, as such, can be described and understood (Morse, 1992). Culture, of course, has multiple definitions, and the ethnographer's theoretical orientation influences how she or he makes inferences from what people say and do. The concept of *culture* enables the ethnographer to go beyond what people say and do to understand that shared system of meanings we call culture.

What Is Ethnography?

Werner and Schoepfle (1987a, 1987b) began their two-volume discussion of ethnography by stating, "An ethnography is what ethnographers do" (p. 42). They explained that ethnography is any full or partial description of a group—*ethno* ("folk") and *graphy* ("description"), a "description of the folk," if you will. The usual images associated with ethnography bring to mind a book or monograph about "primitive," or at least an exotic, people. Thus ethnography is not only a research technique but the term also is used to describe the product of an investigation.

Hughes (1992) stated that, in its original usage, the term *ethnography* was applied to a localized group of people who shared many similar social and cultural characteristics. Usually members of this group had a strong sense of solidarity with each other, based on common factors of language, residence, social relationships, and religious and political beliefs and practices. This usage still seems to be more or less in style at the present time. An ethnography focuses on a group of people who have something in common, although in current ethnographies the commonalities may differ from traditional ones; participants in an ethnography may share a work site, a lifestyle, a nursing home, or a management philosophy.

Agar (1980) was more specific in his definition of ethnography; like Hughes (1992), Agar noted that ethnography is both a process and a product. He said that, as a product, an ethnography is usually a book. The focus of the book is on a particular social group, and the discussion is fairly broad. Agar (1980) explained, "There will be a dash of history, something about the various environments—physical, biological and social—and some detail on the things the group does and the beliefs they hold" (p. 1). Agar observed that, as a process, ethnography is how an ethnographer attempts to learn about or understand some human group, and the name for "doing ethnography" is *fieldwork*.

Distinguishing Characteristics of Ethnography

The question, What is ethnography? often arises and frequently produces confusion. Many of us would like to assume that some prototype exists, but the lack of consensus indicates there are many variations of ethnography. Most textbooks on fieldwork suggest ethnography contains aspects of both art and science. Agar (1980) said it very emphatically: "Without science, we lose our credibility. Without humanity, we lose our ability to understand others" (p. 13). Nevertheless all ethnographies have certain hallmark characteristics. Not everyone will agree that the characteristics I list are exclusive, but I think that most ethnographers will agree with most of them, although any one ethnographer may emphasize one over the others. The characteristics often are overlapping and interrelated. I separate them into somewhat artificial distinctions for some clarity. The characteristics of ethnography that I discuss are (a) the holistic and contextual nature of ethnography, (b) the reflexive character of ethnography, (c) the use of emic and etic data, and (d) the end product that we call ethnography.

Holistic and Contextual

An ethnography is holistic, and contextualizing the data involves placing observations and interview data into a larger perspective. A central tenet of ethnography is that people's behavior can be understood only in context; that is, in the process of analysis and abstraction, the ethnographer cannot separate elements of human behavior from their relevant contexts of meaning and purpose. Indeed it is this context that provides for the understanding of human behavior. Hammersley and Atkinson (1983) observed that the context includes far more than the physical environment, as "any account of human behavior requires that we understand the social meanings that inform it" (p. 9). To do that, the ethnographer needs to do more than just describe behavior; she or he must understand *why* the behavior takes place and *under what circumstances.*

Fieldwork is the hallmark of ethnographic research—working with people for long periods of time in their natural setting. Participant observation characterizes most ethnographic research and is critical to effective fieldwork. *Participant observation* combines participation in the lives of the people under study with maintaining some professional distance that allows for adequate observation and recording of data. Ideally participation observation is immersion in the culture or way of life of a group; often the ethnographer lives and works in the community for a long period of time—6 months to several years. Agar (1980) suggested that, in ethnographic research, there is always an emphasis on direct personal involvement with the people in the study. Long-term residence helps the ethnographer learn the basic beliefs, fears, hopes, and expectations of the people under study and provides an opportunity to observe people as they go about the tasks of daily living. In some applied settings, participation observation is often noncontinuous and consists of short periods of intensive observation spread out over a long period of time. Participant observation sets the stage for other techniques, such as interviews, life histories, and other data collection procedures. However it is done, if it is done well, participant observation provides the baseline of meaning and the contextual data for the ethnography.

Ethnography, then, is *labor intensive*. It is not simply a series of interviews that are analyzed qualitatively; ethnography always involves prolonged, direct contact with group members. Learning something about a social group implies an apprenticeship role. By its very nature, an apprentice's role cannot be done for you. As Agar (1980) pointed out, it is difficult to allow another screen between yourself and the person from whom you are supposedly learning. A good ethnography attempts to describe as much as possible about a cultural or social group. The description might include the group's history, religion, politics, economy, environment, and how the group relates to the social units under study. This holistic orientation demands a great deal of time in the field, gathering the kinds of data that create a picture of the whole. Hughes (1992) stated that, in ethnography, "the goal of the inquiry is a *rounded,* not *segmented* understanding. It is comprehensive in intent" (p. 443). A primary purpose of this holistic approach is to make explicit the interrelationships among the various systems and subsystems in the group under study, generally through an emphasis on the contextualization of data.

Most ethnographies are sprinkled liberally with direct quotations from informants that summarize or illustrate a point the ethnographer is trying to make. Indeed "letting informants speak for themselves" is an important part of writing up the ethnography.

Bernard (1988) jokingly observed that using selected anecdotes and comments from informants helps the reader understand quickly what it took the ethnographer months or years to figure out. Using direct quotes to illustrate the study's findings looks easy, but it actually can be very complicated. Atkinson (1992b) suggested that the ethnographer should edit the narrative into a coherent text so that it is fluent, coherent, and readable. He described this process as "textual conversion." In my experience, novice ethnographers tend to become very close to their data, and they want their readers to read all of it. I have read drafts of papers that contain extensive quotations intended to reproduce the original interview data or the field notes; unfortunately they offer little in the way of analysis. The trick is to develop your analysis first, tell your reader what it is, and then illustrate it with selected quotes from your informants.

Contrary to a belief commonly held among health professionals, an ethnography may include quantitative data and analyses, although such an ethnography is not common in health literature. Bernard's *Research Methods in Cultural Anthropology* (1988) contains chapters on quantitative data analysis, including multivariate analysis. One characteristic of an ethnographic method is, typically, numerous sources of data. When only different qualitative data sources are used, I am comfortable labeling this process "triangulation," although sometimes in health-related literature that term refers to a mix of qualitative and quantitative methods. Ethnographers make copious field notes about what they observe, conduct different kinds of interviews that yield different types of data, consult documents, collect life histories, and use questionnaires, projective techniques, and a variety of other measures that do not require participant observation. Like any good researcher, a good ethnographer will use appropriate methods to analyze the variables under study. Thus findings from an ethnography may or may not follow a strictly qualitative format.

At the present time, many ethnographers use qualitative computer software programs to assist in data management. Tesch (1990, 1991) provided an overview of the various software programs that can be used in the management of qualitative data. The data analysis that the ethnographer employs may vary according to the type of ethnography she or he is conducting, or, at the very least, it may vary according to the kind of data collection procedures she or he uses. Exactly how the ethnographer sorts and sifts the data, searches for types, classifies, sequences, and processes the data to come up with patterns of the whole again depends somewhat on the type and focus of the ethnography and the skills and preferences of the ethnographer. The aim of this process is to assemble or reconstruct the data in a constructive and comprehensible fashion, putting it together into meaningful patterns, categories, and relationships. However it is done, if it is done well, an ethnography presents a holistic conception of a social group within its relevant contexts of meaning and purpose.

Reflexivity

Ethnography has a *reflexive* character, which implies that the researcher is a part of the world that she or he studies and is affected by it. In explaining this reflexivity, Hammersley and Atkinson (1983) observed that the distinction between science and common sense, between the activities of the researcher and those of the researched, lies at the heart of both positivism and naturalism. They suggested that both (extreme) positions "assume that it is possible, in principle at least, to isolate a body of data uncontaminated by the researcher, either by turning him or her into an automaton or by making him or her a neutral vessel of cultural experience" (p. 14). Good ethnography is somewhere between these two extremes. The ethnographer does not take data at face value, but instead considers it as a field of inferences in which hypothetical patterns can be identified and their validity tested.

Ethnography as a process always consists partly of participant observation and partly of conversation or interview (Werner & Schoepfle, 1987a). It is the mix of the two, or rather the interface between the two, that leads to the reflexivity described by Hammersley and Atkinson (1983). Werner and Schoepfle (1987a) explained it this way:

> As ethnographers, we try to do more than just describe the cultural knowledge of the native. We try to understand and, if possible, explain. We need to be able to explain how the natives could possibly

view the world as they do. The paradox of this situation is that all description, understanding, and explanation of the natives' cultural knowledge is based fundamentally on two disparate, incompletely transmittable, presumptive systems of knowledge—the knowledge of the native and the knowledge of the ethnographer. (p. 60)

They observed that "this combination of insider/outsider provides deeper insights than are possible by the native alone or an ethnographer alone. The two views, side by side, produce a 'third dimension' that rounds out the ethnographic picture" (p. 63). Thus good ethnography produces theory from the reflexive nature of the ethnographic experience. A good ethnography is always more than just a description—it is a theoretical explanation. The level and power of the theory vary according to the scope and focus of the ethnography.

Emics and Etics

Emics and *etics* are common terms in ethnography, and they are related directly to the previous discussion of reflexivity. The *emic perspective*—the insider's view, or the informant's perspective of reality—is at the heart of ethnographic research. Obviously the insider's view of what is happening and why is instrumental in understanding and accurately describing situations and behaviors. The *etic perspective* is the outsider's framework, the researcher's abstractions, or the scientific explanation of reality. One important purpose of etic, sociocultural research is to develop standardized instruments to measure sociocultural variables (Davis, 1992). It is also important to note, however, that the etic perspective—the outsider's view—is what ethnographers see or observe as they go about their fieldwork. Although emic perspectives may not always conform to an "etic" viewpoint, both views are important in helping the ethnographer understand why members of that particular group do what they do, and both are necessary if the ethnographer is to understand and accurately describe situations and behaviors. Both views help the ethnographer develop conceptual or theoretical interpretations.

In the past, anthropologists used the term *natives* to refer to the people they studied, and they wrote about the "native's" or the "emic" point of view. More recently, as the focus of ethnographies has broadened to include other kinds of social groups, the term *informant* has been used to describe members of a sample, although that term also has some rather negative connotations. Morse (1991b) argued for the use of the term *participant* in qualitative studies conducted by social scientists, because *participant* reflects the nature of the discourse and relationship between the researcher and the individuals who participate in the kinds and types of studies that are being conducted in many qualitative studies. The "participant's view" is the emic view.

A discussion of emic and etic perspectives requires some explanation of the diverse trends and theories in anthropology. Although this explanation simplifies the situation greatly, some anthropologists who are interested primarily in the emic viewpoint use cognitive/ethnoscience methods to collect and analyze data and give primacy to interview data. These studies usually result in taxonomies, componential or domain analyses, or cultural themes (Spradley, 1979). Agar (1980, 1986), Spradley (1979), and Werner and Schoepfle (1987a, 1987b) gave good, in-depth descriptions of ethnoscience. Other anthropologists placed their data into an etic or scientific framework. Generally speaking, this second group of anthropologists tends to emphasize data from observations and informal interviews and espouses the etic or scientific views of reality. Harris (1968, 1979), a leading proponent of an etic view known as "cultural materialism," has written extensively on the emic-etic dichotomy and the differences in their epistemological stances. Most ethnographers use both perspectives, collecting data from the emic perspective of their informants and then trying to make sense of it—in terms of both the informants' perspectives and their own etic or scientific analysis. I will return to the discussion of emics and etics later in this chapter when I discuss the analysis of ethnographic data. To understand how ethnographic data are analyzed, it is necessary to be clear about the epistemology of the study—that is, whether the final analysis represents the emic or the etic point of view.

The Product of Ethnography

Lastly, but of concern to health professionals who conduct ethnographies, is, What is the end product? Is it an ethnography?

Morse (1991a) raised a series of questions about qualitative research, including ethnography. Is ethnography simply a method
that includes techniques for data collection and analysis? Is
ethnography just a method that anyone can learn to use well? Or
must ethnography be used within the context of anthropology's
theoretical assumptions and perspectives? Is it possible to produce an ethnography that does not offer a cultural explanation?
Do health researchers need some kind of formal training in
anthropology to appropriately apply cultural theory?

Spradley (1979), whose *The Ethnographic Interview* is used
frequently by health researchers, stated:

> The essential core of ethnography is this concern with the meaning
> of actions and events to the people we seek to understand . . . people
> make constant use of these complex meaning systems to organize their
> behavior, to understand themselves and others, and to make sense out
> of the world in which they live. These systems of meaning constitute
> their culture; *ethnography always implies a theory of culture* [italics
> added]. (p. 5)

To continue with this discussion, perhaps, I would need to
write a book on anthropology. I do not intend to do that, nor do
I want to find myself derailed into an explanation of the nature
of knowledge in nursing or the other health sciences. There does
seem to be general agreement that nursing and health problems
and situations for which health professionals use qualitative
methods differ from the situations and contexts of interest to
most anthropologists. Some of these differences and concerns
were addressed rather provocatively in Thorne's (1991) discussion
of methodological orthodoxy in qualitative nursing research.

My best answer to some of the earlier questions posed by
Morse is that some cultural concepts and theories commonly
used in anthropology enrich both the data collection and the
analysis of ethnographic studies of nursing and health phenomena. At the same time, health ethnographers bring their own
scientific traditions, training, and socialization to an ethnographic undertaking. Like all research methods, the more the
ethnographer knows about how to do an ethnography, the better
the study. There are different kinds of ethnography, if you will,
and some of these kinds of ethnography produce knowledge that

can be used by nurses and other health professionals in their practice settings. Some ethnographies are "more ethnographic" than others (see Wolcott, 1990). Some are more useful to health professionals than others. For example, I believe that Golander's (1992) ethnography of elderly residents in a nursing home has immediate application to nursing practice because this study helps us understand how residents think and feel and why they behave as they do. Nurses then can respond more appropriately. Some ethnographies are more theoretical and abstract in terms of the cultural theories they produce. Some tell us why nations go to war or why cultures evolve and change, and other ethnographies, such as Germain's (1979) ethnography of a cancer unit, tell us about a place where nurses work and interact with patients. The value of ethnography or even ethnographic methods in nursing or other health professions lies in the pragmatic outcomes for both theory and practice.

Classification or "Types" of Ethnographies

As "doing ethnography" evolved from the early focus on small tribal societies to today's studies, the methods, techniques, focus, and theories of ethnographic research have changed. Numerous factors have influenced these changes. Certainly the expansion of knowledge in the social sciences, linguistics, computer sciences, and statistics have been influencing factors. In addition, national and international trends in politics, economics, education, and other areas have shaped the types and foci of ethnographies.

Probably the most important factor that influences the type of ethnography that is conducted is the social unit the ethnographer chooses to study. Because numerous disciplines employ ethnography or ethnographic methods, obviously the social units under study can vary considerably (see Hughes, 1992). In addition, the skills and training of the ethnographer influence the kind of ethnography she or he produces. For example, an ethnographer whose epistemological stance is that a culture should be studied through language will emphasize the emic view and will use analytic techniques derived from ethnoscience. This kind of ethnography will result in taxonomies, componential domains, and other forms of semantic analyses.

Even within anthropology are numerous possibilities for classifying ethnographies, and there does not seem to be any kind of general agreement. For example, building on Haekel's (1970) earlier classification system, Werner and Schoepfle (1987a) suggested two "taxonomies" of ethnographies. Taxonomy I consists primarily of processual ethnographies that describe social processes—either functionally and synchronically, or diachronically. Taxonomy II classifies ethnographies along binary features such as rural/urban, single theme/multiple theme, and so on (see Figure 9.1). For the purposes of this chapter, I selected some categories from Werner and Schoepfle's (1987a) Taxonomy I in an attempt to describe common types of ethnographies, as well as those that I believe are most useful to health professionals. All of the types of ethnographies I describe are *processual* and can be divided into four distinct subtypes: *holistic, particularistic, cross-sectional,* and *ethnohistorical* ethnographies. The result may be somewhat overlapping; in the attempt to categorize, one always risks blurring some crucial distinctions. Even Werner and Schoepfle (1987a) admitted to some "crosscutting" of classificatory systems.

Processual Ethnographies

Processual ethnographies are those ethnographies that describe some aspects of the social processes. Social processes can be described functionally and synchronically—for example, explaining how parts of a culture or social system are interrelated within a limited period of time and ignoring the historical antecedents. Or social processes can be explained diachronically, as is the case with ethnohistory. An *ethnohistorical account* describes current events or social processes as the result of historical events.

The defining features of processual ethnographies were discussed earlier in this chapter. They are holistic, contextual, and reflexive in nature. They usually include both emic and etic data, and the focus is on a group of people who share similar social and cultural characteristics.

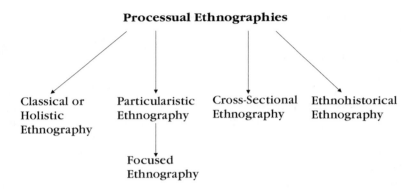

Figure 9.1. Processual Ethographies
SOURCE: Werner & Schoepfle (1987a). Reprinted with permission.

Holistic or Classical Ethnography

The holistic approach is considered by anthropologists world-wide to be the hallmark of classical ethnography. Some authors, such as Haekel (1970), have argued that the holistic approach, by its very nature, must focus on *entire* social groups and that the written product or outcome is *always* a book or a mono-graph. The goal of holistic ethnographies is the description of an entire cultural system. The ethnographer looks beyond the mere parts of a culture to how those parts work together, both statically as patterns, and dynamically as interactive processes. Again the traditional classics in anthropology come to mind: Boas's (1966) ethnography of the Kwakiutl and Malinowski's (1961) study of the Trobriand Islanders. Many of the early anthropologists followed their lead, and their ethnographical works would fall into this category. If health or healing were mentioned, they usually were subsumed in descriptions of the supernatural, magic, sorcery, or religious ceremonies.

Particularistic Ethnography

Instead of applying ethnographic methods to the study of an entire culture, Werner and Schoepfle (1987a) suggested that the current trend in anthropology is to *apply the ethnographic, holistic approach to any social unit or isolatable human group.* Professional articles or monographs, rather than a book, may very well be the result. As examples of particularistic ethnography, Werner and Schoepfle (1987a) cited Wolcott's (1973) use of ethnography in a school setting, Caudill's (1958) ethnography of a psychiatric hospital, and Germain's (1979) ethnography of a cancer unit. The ethnography of small groups (fewer than 15 members) has been called "microethnography" (Werner & Schoepfle 1987a).

McFeat (1974) described "small group cultures" and suggested that the ideal size may be about five members. An example from sociology of an ethnographic focus on a small group is White's (1943) *Street Corner Society.* Particularistic ethnographies may deal only with small groups and/or parts of a culture, but even this narrower focus is described *holistically* or in a *rounded* manner (Hughes, 1992)—that is, within the contextual setting.

Leininger (1985) used the terms *mini ethnography* to describe a narrow area of inquiry and *maxi ethnography* to describe a more general, classical study. Morse (1991a) suggested that *focused ethnography* be used to describe the topic-oriented, small-group ethnographies found in the nursing literature. Thus, as Morse observed, the unit of ethnography in nursing can be a hospital unit (Germain, 1979) or a support group of patients (Lipson, 1980, 1982) or, more recently, a nursing home (Golander, 1992). These *particularistic* ethnographies focused on a social unit or processes within a small group and generally identified and helped us understand the cultural rules, norms, and values and how they are related to health and illness behavior. Such ethnographies have generated descriptive theories about phenomena of interest and concern to health professionals. The scope of most nursing and health ethnographies is such that they can be presented in an article-length format. Two nursing enthnographies have been published in book form: Germain's *The Cancer Unit* (1979) and Street's *Inside Nursing* (1992).

Thorne (1991) suggested that nurse ethnographers rarely conduct whole ethnographies. If she means *holistic* ethnographies, she might be right, although I would suggest that a few nurse ethnographers' dusty dissertations on university shelves represent holistic ethnographies. However, Thorne made a valid point when she observed that most nurse ethnographers draw on ethnographies from other anthropological research to contextualize their discrete findings within the larger picture. She stated, "In this way, details of specialized inquiries into such questions as health behaviors or healing rituals can be interpreted in the context of linguistic patterns, kinship rules or seasonal nutritional variations understood from the composite picture of the cultural whole" (p. 182).

Cross-Sectional Ethnography

Although cross-sectional ethnographies appear to be holistic, the focus is actually quite different. In describing this classification, Werner and Schoepfle (1987a) suggested that the best-known example of a cross-sectional ethnography is Spradley's (1970) *You Owe Yourself a Drunk*. Spradley selected tramps for his unit of study because they possess an integrated culture with a well-developed terminology. Werner and Schoepfle (1987a) noted, "Spradley did not study *a group of interacting tramps*. He studied a cross-section of all tramps" (p. 49). Another example of a cross-sectional ethnography identified by Werner and Schoepfle is Goffman's (1961) sociological study of asylums—a cross-sectional study of institutions. Werner and Schoepfle predicted that, with the trend toward applied anthropology and the use of ethnography in other disciplines, cross-sectional designs of increasing sophistication undoubtedly will become more common.

Ethnohistorical Ethnography

Ethnographies usually are written in a fictionally ethnographic present, with the present tense of verbs used throughout the ethnography—the ethnographic present. This usage makes the ethnography appear as if all of the described events had taken place at the same time. According to Werner and Schoepfle (1987a), many ethnographies follow this format of a synchronic description of a culture, while others follow a more ethnohistorical form. An ethnohistorical ethnography describes the cultural reality of the present as the historical result of events in the past. A most unusual and creative approach in the use of the ethnohistorical approach to examine nursing phenomena is

Villarruel and Ortiz de Montellano's (1992) article "Culture and Pain: A Mesoamerican Perspective." They explored beliefs related to the experience of pain within ancient Mesoamerica by examining primary and secondary sources concerned with Aztec and Mayan civilizations. They stated, "This method combines the use of diachronic, or historic, sources or strategies with synchronic, or theoretical, abstractions derived from existing data in an effort to provide a more complete understanding of a cultural or social phenomenon" (p. 24). Their study provides a historical understanding of Mexican-American meanings, expressions, and care associated with pain.

Other Classifications

Werner and Schoepfle (1987a) suggested that ethnographies can be classified by other distinguishing characteristics (see Table 9.1). For example, binary features—a given feature and its opposite—can be used. Thus there are holistic/particularistic ethnographies, urban/rural ethnographies, single theme/multiple theme ethnographies, and so on. Or ethnographies can be classified by spatial or geographical dimensions. There are ethnographies of fire stations, school rooms, and nursing units, and ethnographies of villages, cities, or even nations. Ethnographies can be classified by language (native/translated) or by theory (explicit/implicit or strong/weak) or in numerous other ways. There are even photographic and film ethnographies. Classifications are arbitrary, at best.

Ethnographic Analyses

Ethnographic analysis—in fact, all scientific analysis—is the search for patterns in data and for ideas that help explain the existence of those patterns. Bernard (1988) observed:

> The word "analysis" has two meanings. On the one hand, it means making complicated things understandable by reducing them to their component parts. This is *descriptive analysis.* On the other hand, it means making complicated things understandable by showing how their component parts fit together according to some rules. This is *theory.* (p. 317)

TABLE 9.1   Some Binary Features for Classifying Ethnographies

Binary Ethnographies	
Holistic	Particularistic
Urban	Rural
Multiple theme	Single theme
Native language	World language
Multi level	Single level
Native organization	Ethnographer organization
Full description	Sketch
Analytic	Synthetic

SOURCE: Data from Werner, O., & Schoepfle, G. M. (1987a). *Systematic Fieldwork: Ethnographic Analysis and Data Management* (Vol. 1) (pp. 51-55). Newbury Park, CA: Sage. Copyright 1987 by Sage Publications, Inc. Reprinted with permission.

Exactly how the patterns are identified and the explanation of how the component parts fit together varies in ethnographic research.

Werner and Schoepfle (1987a) emphasized the distinction between the epistemology of observation and interview in ethnographies. This epistemology is related directly to the earlier discussion of emic and etic viewpoints. Remember that emic views are insiders' accounts usually obtained from direct interviews with informants. Etic accounts are the outsider's or ethnographer's theoretical views, and the emphasis in data collection and analysis is placed on observational data and scientific viewpoints. At the one extreme position, the cultural materialists claim that theory and observation are primary and interviews secondary—if interviews are considered at all. At the other extreme position is the cognitive/ethnoscience view that culture can be studied best through language, and thus the emphasis is on interviews. The emic, or insider's view, is that human beings have an understanding of their own actions, values, and feelings and that is the overriding prerequisite for understanding what they do. A strict emic view is that cultural knowledge is accessible only through language. To emphasize this latter point, Werner and Schoepfle (1987a), proponents of the ethnoscience, or emic, epistemology, even stressed the methodological importance of viewing interviews as "ethnographic data" and observations as "predata" and treating each form of data in a different manner.

As I have mentioned previously, somewhere between the two extremes are most ethnographers who have a preference for one over the other. This epistemological preference influences both the data collection and the analysis in ethnography. In any ethnography, the researcher must be clear about her or his own epistemological preference, and that preference should be equally clear to the readers or audience. It is also important that the ethnographer be clear about the emic and etic sources of data and how they are presented. An excellent contrast of the use of both emic and etic options in the same ethnography is Davis's (1992) "The Meaning of Menopause in a Newfoundland Fishing Village."

In an attempt to describe how epistemology influences data collection and analysis, I divided the discussion of ethnographic analyses into three general headings: ethnoscience, content analysis, and the more orthodox approach, which I labeled "text" or "descriptive" analysis. Not all ethnographies have such clear boundaries. It is possible to combine different types of ethnographic analyses as long as the ethnographer is clear about what she or he is doing and makes it equally clear to the reader.

Ethnoscience

Ethnoscience, or cognitive, ethnographies emphasize the emic view and give primacy to interview data. Ethnoscience was developed in the 1950s and was based on techniques used in linguistics. Early proponents (Goodenough, 1956; Pike, 1954; Sturtevant, 1964) suggested that ethnoscience would achieve the preciseness and scientific credibility that had been associated with linguistics. Ethnoscience ethnographies result in taxonomies or in decision models, causal chains, and other more complex semantic systems, such as componential analysis or domain analysis. There are several excellent and detailed texts, such as Werner and Schoepfle's *Systematic Fieldwork: Foundations of Ethnography and Interviewing* (1987a) and *Systematic Fieldwork: Ethnographic Analysis and Data Management* (1987b). Agar (1980, 1986) and Spradley (1979) also can be consulted by readers interested in more details. In this chapter, I rely on Bernard's (1988) text because, in my opinion, its section on ethnoscience is presented in a clear and understandable manner.

Taxonomies. Folk taxonomies and folk definitions or native classifications are basic to cognitive ethnoscience. In particular, taxonomies are one of the most commonly used techniques in an ethnoscience analysis. Bernard (1988) described a native taxonomy as

> a description of how people divide up domains of culture, and how the pieces of a domain are connected. By "domain" I mean simply a list of words in a language that somehow belong together.
>
> Some domains are very large and inclusive, others are small and narrow; some lists are known to all speakers of a language, while others represent highly specialized knowledge. (pp. 336-337)

We use folk taxonomies all the time to order our experiences and to guide our behavior. When we walk into a supermarket and look for the dairy section, it is because we know that is where to find the yogurt we want to purchase. Folk taxonomies are constructed with a *frame elicitation* technique. Once the ethnographer has identified a domain of interest, the next step is to construct a list of terms that signify parts of the domain. This enumeration is done by using the frame "What kinds of _____ are there?" (Bernard, 1988, p. 338). The blanks can be filled with kinds of cars, fruits, illnesses, classes, or whatever it is that the ethnographer wants to understand. Folk taxonomies are constructed from information provided by a number of informants and to obtain some idea of the range of variation and areas of consistency about how people think about this particular domain. A common way to display taxonomies is with a branching tree diagram.

Bernard (1988) warned that generating a taxonomy can be a very complex process. Interinformant variation is common, as different informants may use different words to refer to the same category of things. Category labels may not be simple lexical terms; instead they may be complex phases. In addition, there may be categories for which informants have no label at all. There may be overlap and indeterminacy in categories, as a word or a phrase can be placed in two or more categories. One way to deal with the complexity of taxonomies is a technique known as componential analysis.

Componential Analysis. Componential analysis is a formal qualitative technique for studying meaning that is based on linguistics (Bernard, 1988). There are two objectives. The first is to specify the conditions under which a native speaker of a language will call something (e.g., a fruit, a car, a person) by a particular term. The second objective is to understand the cognitive process by which native speakers decide which of several possible terms they should apply to a particular thing. This technique helps the investigator understand the meanings that people attach to terms in their languages. Componential analysis can be used to determine meaning in taxonomies by enabling the ethnographer to predict what classification label will be assigned to some object.

Componential analysis can be used for other ethnoscience approaches. For example, *taxonomic analysis* lets us predict which class of things some new thing will be assigned to; *decision analysis* allows us to predict which of several behavioral options people will take under specific circumstances. Aamodt (1991) described how linguistic expressions can be used within ethnoscience or semantic ethnography (the term she prefers) to generate knowledge that is useful in nursing.

One of the best-known descriptions of componential analysis is Spradley's (1979) *The Ethnographic Interview.* Spradley, coming from the epistemological stance of ethnoscience, placed interview data first in data analysis. In fact, if you read carefully Spradley's description of his method, no participation observation seems to be involved. Spradley (1979) was very specific about his description of "ethnographic analysis." It includes (a) making a domain analysis, (b) asking structural questions, (c) making a taxonomic analysis, (d) asking contrast questions, (e) making a componential analysis, and (f) discovering cultural themes.

Spradley (1979) defined *cultural theme* as "any cognitive principle, tacit or explicit, recurrent in a number of domains and serving as a relationship among subsystems of cultural meaning" (p. 186). According to Spradley, cultural themes are elements in the cognitive maps that make up a culture. They are larger units of thought that consist of a number of symbols linked into meaningful relationships. They usually are stated as assertions and are common assumptions that people believe and accept as true and valid, and they have a high degree of generality and apply to numerous situations. On the one hand, Spradley suggested that any particular cultural scene will have both minor and major themes. On the other hand, Benedict, in *Patterns of Culture* (1934), attempted to explain entire cultures on the basis of a single, all-encompassing theme.

Content Analysis

Content analysis is a catch-all term covering a variety of techniques for making inferences from text data (Bernard, 1988). Like other kinds of qualitative analysis, a formal content analysis is labor intensive. Content analysis can be used with interview data or to analyze other kinds of "text" data, such as newspaper editorials, songs, advertisements, and so on. Most often, it involves categorizing each word or phrase in a text with labels that reflect such concepts as *aggression, denial, caring,* and so on. Once this is done, a computer program can run through the data and count things or determine the likelihood of one concept, such as *caring,* appearing in the same paragraph as another, such as *nurse.* This process also can be done laboriously by hand. The word counts for concepts can be compared to determine differences in the frequency of the concepts. Usually the assumption is that when the researcher conducts a content analysis, some counting is done, although that is not always the case because not all researchers agree that "counting" strengthens the analysis.

Different forms of content analysis have been described by Wilson (1989), who provided a detailed account of how to conduct a content analysis. Wilson divided content analysis into two types: (a) semantic content analysis (manifest) and (b) feeling tone, or inferred content analysis (latent). In a latent content analysis, the researcher goes beyond what was said or written and infers meaning of something. Some studies may involve both manifest and latent analyses.

Wilson (1989) identified three basic elements in any kind of content analysis: (a) deciding what the unit of analysis will be, (b) borrowing or developing the set of categories, and (c) developing the rationale and illustrations to guide the coding of data into categories. Like Bernard (1988), Wilson also suggested that cross-tabulations can be correlated with frequencies of responses in each category.

According to Downe-Wamboldt (1992), content analysis has external validity as a goal. Because validity has to do with what is being measured and how well it is measured, Downe-Wamboldt described how to strengthen content validity in content analysis. Her suggestions and examples ranged from relying on a panel of experts to the use of statistical procedures such as factor analysis to identify clusters of related variables in text data. Most researchers who use content analysis believe that counting cases or occurrences of a topic is a way of improving both the precision and the completeness of the research. However, approaches such as Downe-Wamboldt's run the risk of substituting numbers for rich description and contextualization, thus defeating the purpose of ethnography. The emphasis in ethnography should be on holistic description and interpretation, not on measurement. Counting can be used in qualitative research (Stern, 1991), but the investigator must be clear about the purpose of the study and the appropriate ways to enhance reliability and validity (Morse, 1991a).

Ethnographic Text or Descriptive Analysis

In an ethnography that uses a traditional approach to data analysis, the analysis process starts very early in the data collection and continues throughout the project. As the ethnographer develops ideas, she or he tests them against observations; the ideas are modified and then are tested again. Tesch (1991) stated, "The main purpose of this type of analysis is to achieve deeper insight, to search for commonalties across the study participants or sites, to explore uniqueness, and to interpret the meaning of the discovered patterns" (p. 319).

The analysis process in a traditional approach to ethnography uses data from both participation observation and informal or more structured interviewing. Hughes (1992) observed that the interplay of questions and participation observation—a "back and forth" process of data collection and analysis—is a generic feature of traditional ethnographic methods. In describing this process, he said:

The interview is used, of course, but in a style that differs from that usually found in other behavioral sciences. The interview is free flowing, "open-ended," responsive to the information and cues provided by the "subject" or "informant." The researcher does not simply ask questions; questions are asked *when they are appropriate and when there is something to ask about.* Typically no preset and tightly structured questionnaire "schedule" is employed (at least not initially). A survey instrument developed prior to the fieldwork implies that the researcher already knows what the most salient relevant and possibly fruitful questions are *that would serve as points of entry into understanding a theretofore unmapped situation.* (p. 444)

At the same time, the researcher does hold preexisting theoretical interests, and these interests guide the questions and observations. Answers to the questions and observational data are used to develop more inquiries and hunches. Bernard (1988) described this process of data collection and analysis as "a constant validity check" (p. 320). He explained that it involves switching back and forth between the etic perspective (your assumptions, your ideas, your questions, and your explanations) and the emic viewpoint (your observations, informants' reports, and interviews) and testing the first against the second. As a result, the data consist of interview data, both formal and informal, and field notes from participant observation. It may include other sources, such as diaries or other documents.

Typically the ethnographer reads the preliminary data and identifies patterns, trying to understand how the data relate to what she or he expected and to identify any inconsistencies or contradictions between accounts provided by informants. Exactly how this is done and what the end product looks like vary according to the skills, background, theoretical orientation, and training of the ethnographer. According to Hammersley and Atkinson (1983), after the beginning analytic categories are developed, the next task is to develop them into a theoretical scheme by finding links between the concepts and adding new ones. This is the strategy they refer to as the "constant comparative method," a term usually associated with grounded theory. They stated:

Each segment of data is taken in turn, and, its relevance to one or more categories having been noted, it is compared with other segments of data similarly categorized. In this way, the range and variation of any given category can be mapped in the data, and such patterns plotted in relation to other categories. As this process of systematic sifting and comparison develops, so the emerging model will be clarified. (p. 180)

Tesch (1990) described this sorting and sifting process as *decontextualizing and recontextualizing* text data. She explained that the ethnographer identifies categories and instances within the data. This approach disaggregates the text (notes or transcripts) into a series of fragments, which then are regrouped under a series of thematic headings. In a practical sense, it is often a matter of physical fragmentation or cut-and-paste. Atkinson (1992a) observed, "The actual technology employed may vary; from computer storage and retrieval, to punch cards and knitting needles, to file cards, to cardboard shoe boxes, to manila folders" (p. 455). From this beginning activity, the analytic categories can be defined by the ethnographer, or concepts can be adapted or borrowed from existing theories.

Conclusion

The style and method of ethnography are a function of the ethnographer, who brings her or his own scientific traditions, training, and socialization to the research project. An ethnography is also a function of the group with which the ethnographer is working (Agar, 1986). Like other scientists, ethnographers write for specific audiences, and this focus influences what the final product looks like. Whether they use ethnoscience or more traditional methods of analysis, books, professional and lay journal articles, essays, methodological papers, and even films or photographs are all possible products of ethnography.

Most ethnographies are written in a narrative format and are broad, holistic, and naturalistic in intent. An ethnography can be presented as a natural history or a chronology, a format that allows the ethnographer to use the passage of time for a linear arrangement of the final text. The presentation may include different levels of generality or inclusiveness, from the general to the particular or vice versa. Some ethnographers separate the ethnography (the data and cultural description) from the analysis. Other ethnographers follow a thematic approach and describe a limited number of major components or social institutions.

However it is presented, an ethnography provides insights about a group of people and offers us an opportunity to see and understand their world. The results may be "thick description," interpretive ethnography, or theories or models that help us explain and understand human behavior.

References

Aamodt, A. M. (1991). Ethnography and epistemology. In J. M. Morse (Ed.), *Qualitative nursing research: A contemporary dialogue* (rev. ed., pp. 40-53). Newbury Park, CA: Sage.

Agar, M. H. (1980). *The professional stranger: An informal introduction to ethnography*. New York: Academic Press.

Agar, M. H. (1986). *Speaking of ethnography* (Sage University Paper Series on Qualitative Research Methods, Vol. 2). Beverly Hills, CA: Sage.

Atkinson, P. (1992a). The ethnography of a medical setting: Reading, writing, and rhetoric. *Qualitative Health Research, 2,*(4), 451-474.

Atkinson, P. (1992b). *Understanding ethnographic texts* (Sage University Paper Series on Qualitative Research Methods. Vol. 25). Newbury Park, CA: Sage.

Benedict, R. (1934). *Patterns of culture*. Boston: Houghton-Mifflin.

Bernard, H. R. (1988). *Research methods in cultural anthropology*. Newbury Park, CA: Sage.

Boas, F. (1966). *The Kwakiutl ethnography* (H. Codere, Ed.). Chicago: University of Chicago Press.

Caudill, W. (1958). *The psychiatric hospital as a small society*. Cambridge, MA: Harvard University Press.

Davis, D. L. (1992). The meaning of menopause in a Newfoundland fishing village. In J. M. Morse (Ed.), *Qualitative health research* (pp. 145-169). Newbury Park, CA: Sage.

Downe-Wamboldt, B. (1992). Content analysis: Method, applications, and issues. *Health Care for Women International, 13,* 313-321.

Germain, C. (1979). *The cancer unit: An ethnography*. Wakefield, MA: Nursing Resources.

Goffman, E. (1961). *Asylums: Essays on the social situation of mental patients and other inmates*. New York: Anchor.

Golander, H. (1992). Under the guise of passivity: We can communicate warmth, caring, and respect. In J. M. Morse (Ed.), *Qualitative health research* (pp. 192-201). Newbury Park, CA: Sage.

Goodenough, W. (1956). Componential analysis and the study of meaning. *Language, 32,* 195-216.

Haekel, J. (1970). Source criticism in anthropology. (T. A. Tatje & E. M. Schepers, Trans.). In R. Naroll & R. Cohen (Eds.), *A handbook of method in cultural anthropology* (pp. 147-164). New York: Columbia.

Hammersley, M., & Atkinson, P. (1983). *Ethnography: Principles in practice.* New York: Tavistock.

Harris, M. (1968). *The rise of anthropological theory.* New York: Thomas C Crowell.

Harris. M. (1979). *Cultural materialism: The struggle for a science of culture.* New York: Random House.

Hughes, C. C. (1992). "Ethnography": What's in a word—Process? Product? Promise? *Qualitative Health Research, 4,* 439-450.

Leininger, M. M. (1970). *Nursing and anthropology: Two worlds to blend.* New York: John Wiley.

Leininger, M. M. (1985). Ethnography and ethnonursing: Models and modes of qualitative data analysis. In M. Leininger (Ed.), *Qualitative methods in nursing* (pp. 33-71). New York: Grune & Stratton.

Lipson, J. G. (1980). Consumer activism in two women's self-help groups. *Western Journal of Nursing Research, 2*(1), 393-405.

Lipson, J. G. (1982). Effects of a support group on the emotional impact of cesarean childbirth. *Prevention in Human Services, 1*(3), 17-29.

Malinowski, B. (1961). *Argonauts of the Western Pacific.* New York: E. P. Dutton.

McFeat, T. (1974). *Small-group cultures.* New York: Pergamon.

Morse, J. M. (1991a). Qualitative nursing research: A free for all? In J. M. Morse (Ed.), *Qualitative nursing research: A contemporary dialogue* (rev. ed., pp. 14-22). Newbury Park, CA: Sage.

Morse, J. M. (1991b). Subjects, respondents, informants, and participants? (Editorial). *Qualitative Health Research, 1*(4), 403-406.

Morse, J. M. (1992). Ethnography. In J. M. Morse (Ed.), *Qualitative health research* (pp. 141-144). Newbury Park, CA: Sage.

Pike, K. (1954). *Language in relation to a unified theory of the structure of human behavior* (Vol. 1). Glendale, CA: Summer Institute of Linguistics.

Smith, A. F. (1992). *Inside nursing: A critical ethnography of clinical nursing practice.* Albany: State University of New York Press.

Spradley, J. P. (1970). *You owe yourself a drunk: An ethnography of urban nomads.* Boston: Little, Brown.

Spradley, J. P. (1979). *The ethnographic interview.* New York: Holt, Rinehart & Winston.

Stern, P. N. (1991). Are counting and coding *a cappella* appropriate in qualitative research? In J. M. Morse (Ed.), *Qualitative nursing research: A contemporary dialogue* (rev. ed., pp. 147-162). Newbury Park, CA: Sage.

Sturtevant, W. (1964). Studies in ethnoscience. *American Anthropologist, 66,* 99-131.

Tesch, R. (1990). *Qualitative research: Analysis types and software tools.* New York: Falmer.

Tesch, R. (1991). Computer programs that assist in the analysis of qualitative data: An overview. *Qualitative Health Research, 1*(3), 309-325.

Thorne, S. E. (1991). Methodological orthodoxy in qualitative nursing research: Analysis of the issues. *Qualitative Health Research, 1*(2), 178-199.

Villarruel, A. M., & Ortiz de Montellano, B. (1992). Culture and pain: A Mesoamerican perspective. *Advances in Nursing Science, 15*(1), 21-32.

Werner, O., & Schoepfle, G. M. (1987a). *Systematic fieldwork: Foundations of ethnography and interviewing* (Vol. 1). Newbury Park, CA: Sage.

Werner, O., & Schoepfle, G. M. (1987b). *Systematic fieldwork: Ethnographic analysis and data management* (Vol. 2). Newbury Park, CA: Sage.

White, B. F. (1943). *Street corner society.* Chicago: University of Chicago Press.

Wilson, H. S. (1989). The craft of qualitative analysis. In H. S. Wilson (Ed.), *Research in nursing* (2nd ed., pp. 394-428). Menlo Park, CA: Addison-Wesley.

Wolcott, H. F. (1973). *Man in the principal's office: An ethnography.* New York: Holt, Rinehart & Winston.

Wolcott, H. F. (1990). Making a study "more ethnographic." *Journal of Contemporary Ethnography, 19*(1), 44-72.

Dialogue

Sorting Out the Styles . . .

LIPSON How come there are so many papers in ethnography on needing to classify? It just occurred to me that because it's so varied, we are all trying to grapple with what's common and what's different. And why are there all these fights about grounded theory, for example? Is that because there are Glaser, Strauss, and that whole school, and people who are elaborating on it, stretching it, as opposed to ethnography, that has official different types?

STERN It's [grounded theory] newer. It's fairly recent.

MAY And grounded theory doesn't have the whole disciplinary weight behind it. Anthropology is ethnography, at least from the naive perspective. That is what I think of when I think of anthropology. You could take a whole course on sociology without tripping over grounded theory. And I think that's the difference.

BOYLE Why are ethnographies that are done by nurses different? Are they different? Some of them are, some of them are not. If we are to ask for some blind reviews, some you could recognize, and others none of us could. Now some would say—and I don't disagree—that ethnography *always* implies a theory of culture, but I would like to think that I do something differently because I'm not contributing to theories of culture; I'm contributing to my own discipline of nursing.

LIPSON But it seems that there are a lot of ethnographic methods that are used by nurses that don't always look at something cultural, but are practically always informed by something cultural. It's an underlying non-said thing.

BOYLE Oh, I agree.

MAY That's interesting. When you said I think nurses produce a different kind of ethnography, I immediately thought of grounded theory where there is a *fine*-ness in the observations—it's not necessarily in the findings, not necessarily in description or the theory building, but there is a fine-grained quality about the grounded theory nurses do, as opposed to those that are done by others. And I concluded that it comes from use of self and being smart about people.

186

10

On the Evaluation of Ethnographies

MARJORIE A. MUECKE

With this chapter I want to say that it is time to acknowledge that we are dealing with two different types of ethnography, not just short and long, mini and maxi, versions of the same thing. On the one hand, we have academic anthropology. It has a variety of schools of thought about what ethnography is, but they all say that doing ethnography takes a long time and emerges from the local context. And then on the other hand, we have these other ethnographies, the ones done with a specific question in mind, the ones with a clear purpose, the ones that are applied in intent. They are programmatic and pragmatic. When you are a health professional doing or reading an ethnography, you ask, So what? So what does it tell me about xyz? You look to these mini, focused, particularistic descriptive studies in a moral way; you want them to show the humanity in whoever is being described. And you want them to answer some question. So in this chapter the challenge for me is coming up with evaluation criteria for this second type of ethnography, this spin-off from academic anthropology's ethnography that has been adapted by health professionals, particularly by nurses, to health care needs. What criteria will show the richness, the value, the strengths of these ethnographies? How are we to assess them for the best they have to offer?

AUTHOR'S NOTE: I especially appreciate the constructive suggestions on earlier drafts of this chapter from two nurse-anthropologist colleagues whose work I esteem, Dr. Joyceen Boyle and Dr. Juliene Lipson.

The 1980s witnessed a renaissance of ethnography, taking this emblem of sociocultural anthropology into the realms of other social sciences, nursing and related health sciences, literature, agricultural development, and even policy making.[1] In the process, ethnography has been transformed by anthropologists and nonanthropologists, has been applied to novel situations, and has reached new audiences. At the same time, qualitative studies have become a legitimate and desired research approach in nursing education and research literature (Burns, 1989; Morse, 1987). With this rising prevalence of ethnography, journal editors, grant reviewers, students, dissertation committees, and program planners are asking, *What makes an ethnography good?*

Although evaluation criteria have been codified for one type of ethnography (Werner & Schoepfle, 1987a), there is no single standard form of ethnography. Criteria for evaluating ethnographies have not kept pace with the proliferation of ethnographic forms. Within anthropology, for example, I detect at least four major schools of thought about ethnography. First is the original structural-functionalist form, now referred to as *classical ethnography,* or the holistic description of a foreign,[2] relatively bounded (socially, geographically, and/or linguistically) group of people that is achieved through the researcher's long-term participant observation in the group. Next, the "new ethnography," or *systematic ethnography,* was developed in the 1960s by ethnosemanticists (also known as cognitive anthropologists). Then *hermeneutic ethnography* was elaborated by Weberians such as Clifford Geertz, who defined the concept *thick description,* which has become a standard for good (or better) ethnographies. Most recently, *critical ethnography* has emerged, representing the influences of postmodernist and feminist thinking. Outside academic anthropology, another, quicker version has emerged in community-oriented health sciences such as nursing, public health, and social work. These "rapid appraisals" or *focused ethnographies* may be conducted for purposes other than academic, particularly for program development in health services.

Even prior to this renaissance, differentiating better from poorer ethnographies was no easy task. Evaluation of ethnographies has been problematic, in part, because the standards for scientific studies were applied to but did not fit them.

Although anthropologists recognized that ethnography was unsuited to the evaluation methods and criteria of the physical sciences (Agar, 1980, 1986), others, particularly grant reviewers and funders, tended to resort to those criteria for lack of better direction. In vain they sought a priori hypotheses and methods to test predictability; in vain they expected to see in ethnography the linear logic of proceeding from hypotheses to data collection and then to data analysis and statement of findings. The recent proliferation of types of ethnography raises questions about what ethnography is (Clifford & Marcus, 1986). Anthropologists have come to acknowledge that ethnographies may vary by the background (e.g., theoretical, cultural, educational) of the ethnographer, by the group reported on, and by the audience targeted (e.g., other scholars, policy makers, funders, governments); but the variation tends to confuse the nonanthropologist. The ability to differentiate a good from a less good or poor ethnography may be more problematic for those outside than inside academic anthropology for several reasons. These include the different purposes of ethnographies in other fields and the different methodological premises in the tradition of the field that adopts ethnography as a form of knowing. Perhaps what is a good ethnography for academic anthropologists is not the best ethnography for health scientists. This is the central question of this chapter.

A description of anthropologic ethnography in its major variations and a proposal of criteria for its evaluation are given in the first section of this chapter. Then a similar process is undertaken with the focused ethnography of nursing and related health sciences. I conclude the chapter with an acknowledgment of differences in ethnographies but also of similarities that distinguish all ethnographies from other inductive epistemologies, particularly from the closely related approach of grounded theory.

Anthropologic Ethnographies

An *ethnography* is a written description of a people that focuses on selected aspects of how they lead their routine, remarkable, and ritual lives with each other in their environment, and of the beliefs and customs that comprise their common sense about their world. Ethnographic description reveals the depth and intricacy of a human society in its local environment.

For anthropologists, ethnography is not a method; it is a product. There is no essential ethnographic protocol of discrete steps to follow, no necessity for an orderly transformation of information into ethnography (although, as is discussed, there are ways to make information gathering and processing systematic). In fact, some of the best ethnographies were written with minimal note taking. Edmund Leach's classic 1954 study *The Political Systems of Highland Burma* even was written without field notes because of their accidental loss in the field.

The ethnographer starts with "what's there" in its empirical reality and, then, through long-term participant observation learns and analyzes its local meanings (Spindler, 1970; Spradley, 1980). "What's there" can be any of a wide variety of types of information, including written texts (e.g., poetry, media, verbal transcriptions); maps, film, drawings, or other visual representations; oral recitations; and music. The ethnographer gathers a variety of data types that go beyond the visible facts and that identify the experiential connections that link those facts in people's lives (Bruyn, 1966, pp. 174-197). For most anthropologists, "ethnography is a lifelong endeavor" (Aamodt, 1991, p. 41). The form of knowing it depicts is an exquisitely attuned pattern recognition acquired through comprehensive long-term study. This in-depth experience enables the ethnographer to identify, probe, and then understand ambiguities in meanings observed, to arrive at a gestalt that portrays the cultural "stuff" of the people.

Instead of a set of indispensable data analysis procedures, the ethnographer (and there is characteristically a single researcher or a single married pair) lives a process of analyzing data while collecting them, engaging in an iterative process of gathering and verifying information. Aamodt (1983, p. 394) pointed out that this exploratory iterative process is the reason why, in research proposals to do ethnographic study, "the questions may be unclear, the objectives ambiguous, and the final outcome uncertain." While gathering data in the field, the ethnographer is the equivalent of a multivariate analyst, sorting and exploring on the basis of implications of comparative and contrastive information. Knack and insight are the ethnographer's basic tools in the collection and analysis of the data. In ethnographic work, "much evidence for comprehension is accumulated in unscheduled, informal ways" (Agar, 1986, p. 56) and arrived at intuitively. The ethnography culminates in a translation of "what's there" into a summary interpretive document of the "grammar" that implicitly guides the people's ways of living with each other and continuing their society.

An ethnographic account may take a variety of forms: a write-up as a book, report, or article; an oral narrative as in a lecture; or a visual display such as in a museum, a film, or a video. Its ultimate purpose is to make the social action of a society or of a subunit of society comprehensible to an audience of another society or to the rest of the same society. The purpose of an ethnography is introductory and instructive. It also conveys at least two moral messages: (a) Despite our differences, we are all human; and (b) the range of human capacity is broad, and human social diversity may be essential for sustained life on this planet. This moral dimension suggests one criterion for recognizing a good ethnography: *It should be a tool for enabling us to take a more understanding account of whomever we perceive as "The Other," or "Not Me."*

Anthropologists have spun variations around this core understanding of ethnography. A summary of four major schools of anthropologic thought follows to answer, subsequently, the question, *What standards for evaluating ethnographies would prevail despite major differences in theoretical conceptualization of ethnography?*

Classical Ethnography

Classical ethnographers aim for comprehensive descriptions of people's material constructions and perspectives. The people studied are assumed to share a common culture. The descriptions reformulate the raw "facts" into simpler and more universal terms and categories, such as kinship, trade systems, and rituals. A classical ethnography is a product of a prolonged sojourn during which the researcher resides with the community being studied and observes and documents while directly participating in selected activities. The classical ethnographer typically selects one or a few persons from the group for more intensive and focused interviewing over time. These *key informants* are highly influential over the ethnographer and the resulting content of the ethnography; the voices of other informants tend to be subsumed under the authoritativeness of the key informants.

Crucial to a classical ethnography is the credibility of the ethnographer. Although, in an effort to attain objectivity, the researcher's subjectivity is withheld intentionally from the text, the extent of her or his association with the people studied is an important informal index of her or his trustworthiness as an ethnographer. Facility in the language(s) of the informants is basic to the ethnographer's credibility, although when this fluency is not feasible, use of local interpreters is acceptable.

Examples of this type of ethnography are Margaret Clark's (1959) *Health in the Mexican-American Culture: A Community Study;* Carol Germain's (1979) *The Cancer Unit: An Ethnography;* Colin Turnbull's (1961) *The Forest People: A Study of the Pygmies of the Congo;* and George and Louise Spindler's series of case studies in anthropology published by Holt, Rinehart and Winston in the 1960s and early 1970s.

Systematic Ethnography

Systematic ethnographers aim to define the structure of culture, rather than to describe a people and their social interaction, emotions, and materials. This school criticizes classical ethnographies for being too global and unsystematic. Proponents believe that a good systematic ethnography provides a truthful schema of the characteristic ways that the people studied organize their knowledge. Fidelity to the informants' knowledge is the paramount criterion for evaluation. The image of local knowledge portrayed should be so clear that it produces "a photograph rather than an impressionistic painting" (Werner & Schoepfle, 1987a, p. 23). The aim of systematic ethnography is to discover "the native point of view," to learn the "cognitive maps" that shape the people's behavior as members of a particular group, to develop "an ethnographic algorithm which, if followed, would make it possible . . . to pass (physical appearance aside) for a native" (Geertz, 1973b, p. 11). This aim is thought to be achievable through rigorous semantic analysis, where the primary data are folk taxonomies of words and naming units and contrast sets of terms. Formalized data collection techniques and database management are required skills, and demonstration of competence in applying them is essential.

Examples of good systematic ethnography include several classics: Charles Frake's (1961) "The Diagnosis of Disease Among the Subanun of Mindanao," Horacio Fabrega and Daniel Silver's (1973) *Illness and Shamanistic Curing in Zinacantan: An Ethnomedical Analysis,* and James Spradley's (1970) *You Owe Yourself a Drunk: An Ethnography of Urban Nomads.* Works on methodology and methods have been published more recently: James Spradley's (1979) *The Ethnographic Interview;* Oswald Werner and Mark Schoepfle's (1987b) *Systematic Fieldwork: Foundations of Ethnography and Interviewing* and its sequel of the same year, *Systematic Fieldwork: Ethnographic Analysis and Data Management* (1987a); and David Fetterman's (1989) *Ethnography: Step by Step.*

Interpretive Ethnography

Interpretive ethnographers believe that ethnographic analysis should discover the meanings of observed social interaction. They are intellectual descendants of Max Weber. For them, ethnography is quintessentially analytic and interpretive, rather than methodological (Wolcott, 1980). This school criticizes ethnoscientists for locating culture in people's minds, for reducing it to private psychology, and for not being able to determine whether their descriptions are really what people think or merely an observer's approximations.

For this school, good ethnography provides "thick description"[3] of human behavior and leads the reader through analyses of the myriad inferences and implications of the embeddedness of behavior in its cultural context. Ethnography as cultural analysis is "guessing at meanings, assessing the guesses, and drawing explanatory conclusions from the better guesses, not discovering the Continent of Meaning and mapping out its bodiless landscape" (Geertz, 1973b, p. 20). It takes ethnography to higher levels of analytic power, with the best thick description being analytically elegant: "It is not necessary to know everything in order to understand something" (Geertz, 1973b, p. 20). The ethnographer's inference from and insight into implicit "webs of significance"

(Geertz, 1973b) make an otherwise dizzying compendium of detail coherent to the reader. The outcome is an ethnographic description that renders the people "accessible: setting them in the frame of their own banalities, it dissolves their opacity" (Geertz, 1973b, p. 14). What distinguishes better ethnographies from poorer ones can be assessed by "the power of the scientific imagination to bring us into touch with the lives of strangers" (Geertz, 1973b, p. 16).

Prototypic examples of interpretive ethnography come from the late 1960s and 1970s: Mary Douglas's (1966) *Purity and Danger: An Analysis of the Concepts of Pollution and Taboo* and her (1970) *Natural Symbols: Explorations in Cosmology;* Clifford Geertz's (1973) *The Interpretation of Cultures;* and Victor Turner's (1975) *Revelation and Divination in Ndembu Ritual.*

Critical Ethnography

Critical ethnographers see ethnography as a fiction, an invention created by the interactions of the ethnographer and the informants, who are considered to be co-authors and creatures of their own times and cultures. This stance disagrees with the assumptions of classical ethnographers and ethnoscientists that culture is "out there" to be discovered. Critical ethnographers reason that because ethnography is wholly interpretive, different ethnographers would create different accounts and, therefore, that any interpretation is only one possible reading of the culture studied (Noblit & Hare, 1988, p. 14). This school criticizes its predecessor—interpretive ethnography—for essentializing, for "rounding off" observations to an integrated core, and thereby for excluding contrary voices that keep culture alive and ever-changing.

Critical ethnographers hold that the ethnographer is inevitably participant throughout the text and its construction. They believe that ethnography is subjective, reflecting the stance, values, and awareness of its scribe. The dynamic and mutual influence of ethnographer and research field on each other is referred to by the term *reflexivity.* Good ethnographies are explicit about the nature of the reflexivity that shaped them (Lamb & Huttlinger, 1989). Critical ethnography is thought to present an impressionistic collage, an image that represents only a particular moment and context, not the holistic culture of interpretive ethnographers.

Two schools have emerged within the scope of critical ethnography: postmodernist and feminist. At the risk of simplistic contrast, postmodernist ethnographers are concerned fundamentally with rhetoric, with the form of the description; they view both the writing and reading of ethnography as creative processes. Marjorie Shostak's (1981) pathbreaking *Nisa: The Life and Words of a !Kung Woman* exemplifies their stand (Clifford & Marcus, 1986); another "new ethnography" is Lorna Rhodes's (1991) *Emptying Beds: The Work of an Emergency Psychiatric Unit.* Feminist ethnographers, in contrast, are oriented primarily toward minimizing their own exploitation of their informants and of exposing the forces of oppression against the less privileged groups of society. Two excellent examples of feminist ethnography are Wolf's (1992) *A Thrice-Told Tale: Feminism, Postmodernism and Ethnographic Responsibility* and Street's (1992) *Inside Nursing: A Critical Ethnography of Clinical Nursing Practice.*

Evaluating Anthropologic Ethnographies

What has emerged from these shifts in thinking about ethnography is a recognition that ethnographies are neither wholly inductive nor wholly objective. Ethnographies are shaped by the historical circumstance, by the subjectivity and conceptual stance of the ethnographer, as well as by the particular people with whom the ethnographer works. Many anthropologists now consider the belief that ethnography is an accurate, objective portrayal of a unified society an obsolete simplification: " 'Cultures' do not hold still for their portraits. Attempts to make them do so always involve simplification and exclusion, selection of a temporal focus, the construction of a particular self-other relationship, and the imposition or negotiation of a power relationship" (Clifford & Marcus, 1986, p. 10). However, there are still better and poorer ethnographies: "There is no question that field work is highly personal and each cultural immersion unique. But the product of ethnographic work is a public ethnography. The public deserves to know how we compile an ethnography and what standards we use to measure its minimum adequacy" (Werner & Schoepfle, 1987b, p. 310). Encouraged by the latter sentiment, I proceed to suggest criteria that are applicable to all four types of anthropologic ethnography discussed above.

Proposed Criteria for Evaluating Anthropologic Ethnography

1. The ethnography demystifies the people studied to the point of rendering their behavior coherent to the reader. An ethnography:
    a. demystifies and explains, not merely describes;
    b. interprets one social group to its larger society or to another society;
    c. increases understanding of the common humanity of all people.
2. The people described would, in general, find it an honest and caring depiction of them in their situation (Sanjek, 1990, p. 18; Werner & Schoepfle, 1987a, p. 310).
3. The conceptual orientation of the ethnographer in constructing the ethnography is acknowledged and coherently linked to the study and its field material.
4. The relationship of the ethnographer to the people in the field is explicitly assessed for its influence on the information reported.
    a. The anonymity and integrity of informants is protected throughout the ethnography unless specific informants requested or consented to be identifiable in the ethnography, as may particularly be the case with famous or public figures.
    b. The sources of the ethnographer's information are sufficiently clear for the reader to assess the adequacy, appropriateness, and breadth of coverage of the data.
    c. The data were collected and recorded in the primary language or dialect of the informant and were translated with utmost care to preserve the meaning believed to have been intended.
5. Ethnographic depth is achieved through thick description. *Thick description* analytically explores, compares, and contrasts diverse perspectives and sources of information in the corpus of field data. It tests links and adjusts inferences to form a coherent interpretation that engenders understanding of differences.
    a. The information was acquired through the ethnographer's continuous participant observation in the field or situation studied.

    b. The information was obtained from a variety of sources. The personal sources ranged from the most informal and casual to that of trusted collaborator. The material sources ranged from the informal mundane artifact or note to the formal text. The rationale is that "a blend of formal, informal, and casual interviews . . . guarantees a balance between accuracy and candor" (Werner & Schoepfle, 1987a, p. 331).

    c. The information was gathered accumulatively and cyclically, each gathering including comparative analysis with other information and leading to reformulations of questions.

6. The narrative is competent literature. This is a defining criterion for critical ethnography but holds for anthropologic ethnography in general because both understand that the style of writing itself embodies meanings that are implicit in the society of study. This criterion goes beyond the caveat of "descriptive vividness" in grounded theory that requires clarity, credibility, and depth of description (Burns, 1989; Glaser & Strauss, 1967). The criterion requires that the ethnographer demonstrate understanding of the constraints of her or his own and of the informants' rhetoric and conventional modes of expression on reports of fieldwork findings.

The 'literariness' of [ethnography] . . . appears as much more than a matter of good writing or distinctive style. Literary processes—metaphor, figuration, narrative—affect the ways cultural phenomena are registered, from the first jotted 'observations,' to the completed book, to the ways these configurations 'make sense' in determined acts of reading. (Clifford & Marcus, 1986, p. 4)

Ethnography in the Health Sciences

The emergence of the field of medical anthropology in the 1970s has brought a new purpose, focus, and approach to the canons of general anthropology, and to its defining product—ethnography. An ethnography conveys a coherent statement of a people's local knowledge. Local knowledge increasingly has been recognized as important for health care program development and as a guide to specific nursing interventions. However, the costs of research to attain local knowledge are high because of the lengthy (typically counted in years) fieldwork required. Prolonged fieldwork is incompatible with funding and service agencies' limited budgets and fixed time schedules. Planners' needs to fit their ideas to local contexts have given birth to a

pragmatic compromise called *rapid ethnographic appraisal.*
Nurses' needs to adapt their practice to clients' beliefs and
social context have resulted in the proliferation of *focused
ethnographies,* ethnographies that select a behavioral or belief
area for study of its meaning among a specific group of people.

Usually, *rapid ethnographic appraisals* are of communities,
involve multidisciplinary teams, and adopt techniques from other
fields in addition to anthropology. Rural development work, for
example, has integrated ethnographic methods and principles
with techniques from agriculture, forestry, geography, and journalism. Validity of findings is approached in several ways: (a) by
deriving information from a variety of perspectives and people,
(b) by supplementing open-ended interviews with direct observation, and (c) by applying an iterative process whereby acquired knowledge is subjected continually to testing and
reconfirmation with local people and their resources (Grandstaff,
Grandstaff, & Lovelace, 1987). Scrimshaw (Scrimshaw, Carballo,
Ramos, & Blair, 1991; Scrimshaw & Hurtado, 1988) developed a
highly structured field guide for rapid ethnographic appraisals
as the first step in developing community health programs; brief
but intensive prefieldwork training is required. The ethnographic
work is focused clearly on health-illness beliefs and practices, and
the local language is used in relation to them. The short time of
the study usually precludes developing relationships in the field
sufficiently to cultivate key informants (Bentley et al., 1988).

In nursing, *focused ethnographies* are becoming more common than anthropologic ethnographies because the research
motive is to develop nursing knowledge and practice. Like the
anthropologic model, focused ethnographies typically derive
from the fieldwork and conceptual orientation of a single researcher. Leininger (1985, pp. 34-36) termed small-scale, focused studies *mini ethnographies,* in distinction from the *maxi
ethnography* of anthropology. Germain (1986) distinguished
macroethnography, signifying broad, long-term studies of a
complex society, from *microethnography,* studies of "the sub-
units of single social institutions, of even a single family"(p.
147). Others prefer the term *focused ethnographies* because the
studies are problem focused and context specific (Magilvy,
McMahon, Bachman, Roark, & Evenson, 1987; Morse, 1987, pp.
17-18). To denote this as a genre of brief or partial ethnography,

I use the term *focused ethnography* in this chapter. Focused ethnographies are time-limited exploratory studies within a fairly discrete community or organization. They gather data primarily through selected episodes of participant observation, combined with unstructured and partially structured interviews. The number of key informants is limited; they are usually persons with a store of knowledge and experience relative to the problem or phenomenon of study, rather than persons with whom the ethnographer has developed a close, trusting relationship over time.

Whereas anthropologic ethnographies typically are published in book form, focused ethnographies are published in journals as articles. The number of journals accepting this type of research has burgeoned since the mid-1970s. Journals that specialize in publishing qualitative health research reports and the year of their founding are *Culture, Medicine & Psychiatry* (1977), *Medical Anthropology* (1977), *Medical Anthropology Newsletter* (1969, 1982), *Qualitative Sociology* (1978), *Medical Anthropology Quarterly* (1983), *Journal of Contemporary Ethnography* (1987), *International Journal of Qualitative Studies in Education* (1988), *Journal of Transcultural Nursing* (1990), and *Qualitative Health Research* (1991). Five other journals occasionally publish qualitative health research reports: *Image: Journal of Nursing Scholarship* (1968), *Advances in Nursing Science* (1978), *Western Journal of Nursing Research* (1979), *Health Care for Women International* (1979), and *Social Science & Medicine* (1979). In addition, master's degree theses contribute significantly to the store of focused ethnographies in nursing, although they have limited distribution (e.g., Anderson, 1986; Crassweller, 1986; Glidden, 1986). All of the articles published in the above journals are subject to peer review: hence the need for some consensus on what constitutes a good focused ethnography.

Even though, at the very least, 40 nurses (according to the *Council of Nursing and Anthropology Directory* for 1992) and unknown numbers of social workers and physicians have earned doctoral degrees in anthropology, much of whose ethnographic work fits the canons of anthropology, the ethnographies of the health sciences differ from anthropologic ethnography. Review of these differences, summarized in Table 10.1, suggests that different evaluation criteria may be appropriate for the two types of ethnography.

TABLE 10.1 Contrasts Between Anthropologic and Health Sciences Ethnographies

Contrast Topic	Health Sciences Ethnography	Anthropologic Ethnography
Purpose	Improve cultural appropriateness of professional practice	Deepen understanding of a people's social action
Definition of ethnography	As both methods for data collection and as product	As both a conceptual orientation and as product
Primacy of inductive methodology	Variable: Inductive methods may be used only after the topic of inquiry has been selected	Essential, the chief characteristic of anthropologic ethnography
Conduct of participant observation	At selected events/times only and for a limited period of time	Continuously, for a prolonged period, usually at least a year
Language of data collection	The researcher may not know the primary language of the informants; use of language interpreters is common	The researcher uses the primary language of the informants; use of interpreters is rare but acceptable in certain situations
Access of informants to the ethnographer	Informants usually live and work separately from the residence and worksite of the ethnographer	Informants have regular immediate access to the ethnographer's life space
The nature of knowing	Contrast and comparison, identification of pattern in narratives	Inference, insight, intuition developed as a function of being engaged with the context and text

Evaluating Health Science Ethnographies

If anthropologic ethnographies are used as the standard, assessment of focused ethnographies raises questions about epistemology in the health sciences. What can we really know through focused ethnographies? Because they are brief and limited in scope, can they yield knowledge that is as valid, coherent, and deep as anthropologic ethnographies? The following questions emerge:

1. Does the preselection of the problem or phenomenon of study compromise the inductive nature of the study too much? That is, can the problem be contextualized adequately within the confines of the scope of the briefer study?
2. Does the brevity of the ethnographer's contact with informants jeopardize the development of trust between ethnographer and informants?
3. How are the ethnographer's relationships to informants affected by working in a multidisciplinary team?
4. How is the ethnographer's competence in data analysis and interpretation affected by the short time allotted for fieldwork?
5. Does the ethnographer have sufficient personal involvement to experience the insight necessary for valid thick description?

Because focused ethnographies do not presuppose prolonged and comprehensive exposure to the society of study on its own turf, they are poorly matched with some of my proposed criteria for evaluating anthropologic ethnography, particularly those that concern use of language (4c), and thick description (5a, b, c). The criteria, the ethnography, or both need changing.

Anthropologic Criterion 4c: The data were collected and recorded in the primary language or dialect of the informant and were translated with utmost care to preserve the meaning believed to have been intended.

Given the variety of ethnic and linguistic groups with whom nurse and public health researchers come in contact, it is unreasonable to expect them to be competent in the language of all of the people they study. Nurse researchers studying groups in the United States have overcome their lack of facility in a language in a variety of ways. Kirkpatrick and Cobb (1990) and

Williams (1990), for example, relied on trained indigenous field assistants to gather field data and to assist in their analysis and interpretation. Capps (1991), Frye (1990), Lipson (1991), and Thompson (1991) worked effectively with intermittent use of bilingual interpreters. Other nurses, such as Brink (1982, 1989), DeSantis (1986), Dreher (1984, 1989), Kay (1977, 1979), and Muecke (1987) used their own bilingual skills to study groups with whom they share a language.

The language criterion for health science ethnographies need not be as rigid as for anthropologic ethnographies largely because health science researchers tend to conduct their studies in their home country, rather than abroad. When studying immigrant or refugee groups in the United States, it is likely that some of the people studied have some facility in the language of the researcher, and it is likely that many of the young people of the group are learning the researcher's language because it is the language of the public domain. The dual language competency of the people studied may give a researcher who speaks only the dominant language of larger society an entrée sufficient to pursue ethnographic investigation (e.g., Crassweller, 1986; Lipson, 1991; Luna, 1989; Rosenbaum, 1990). A compelling reason for not requiring expert bilingual competence is the alternative of not studying a people solely because of language differences, thereby relegating the group to continued isolation from and potential misunderstanding in health care. For health science ethnography, then, a criterion appropriate for language is: *In cross-language situations, measures taken to ensure common interpretation of meaning across languages are documented and limitations related to language are identified.*

Anthropologic Criterion 5: Ethnographic depth is achieved through thick description. Thick description analytically explores, compares, and contrasts diverse perspectives and sources of information in the corpus of field data. It tests links and adjusts inferences to form a coherent interpretation that engenders understanding of differences.

    a. *The information was acquired through the ethnographer's continuous participant observation in the field or situation studied.*
    b. *The information was obtained from a variety of sources.*
    c. *The information was gathered accumulatively and cyclically.*

Focused ethnographies that derive from prolonged periods of field research generally meet this criterion (Kay, 1982; Morse, 1989; Muecke, 1992a; Reeb, 1992; Rosenbaum, 1990).

The greatest risk of focused ethnographies is that the boundaries of their focus unknowingly exclude what is relevant. Ethnographies of all varieties should correct the problem common to deductive research of excluding the unrecognized but potentially powerful interpretation. With ethnographic research, the problem emerges when the initial scope of the study is too narrow. Anthropologic ethnographies must begin purposefully nondirected. This is a challenge for nurses because we have been socialized to think in terms of problem identification as a first step of inquiry and to practice. A student who wants to conduct a focused ethnography to find out why a particular ethnic group of women are not breast-feeding their infants, for example, should be counseled either to change the question (e.g., broaden it to how do infants get nourished in that group and why they get nourished that way) or to change the methodology to one more appropriate to the research question (e.g., a phenomenological study of the lived experience of breast-feeding).

Some health science ethnographies reach publication without meeting this criterion because they are unanalytic. What an ethnography teaches us emerges from the researcher's cumulative analysis of her or his data. Studies that report only what was explicit, that describe only things and behavior literally, are not ethnographic, but rather simply case descriptions (Muecke, 1992b). Similarly studies undertaken to examine specific behaviors or concepts, such as breast-feeding or isolation, lack the scope and opportunity of ethnographic work for realizing that another concept or issue altogether is more relevant for understanding the people studied. Studies that use ethnographic methods such as open-ended interviews or intermittent participant observation may or may not become good ethnographies, depending on the openness of the field-worker to contrary interpretations and on the analytic power of the write-up.

What is most important is that the people studied be contextualized comprehensively and accurately in their local symbolic, social, and physical environments. In general, the more complete the researcher's participation in the life-space of the people studied, the greater the value of the study because of the researcher's greater exposure to a variety of situations. Because the researcher is present when the unexpected happens, she or he can get caught in the same crises as the informants. Getting caught in an unexpected crisis with one's informants can be a powerful means of winning their confidence, as reported by Capps (1991) when her providing mouth-to-mouth resuscitation to a Hmong boy who subsequently survived his fall with no after-effects brought the leaders of the community to acknowledge her as a trustable, caring, and valuable outsider at the beginning of her fieldwork. Geertz (1973a) reported a similar episode when he and his wife fled from the police with the entire cockfight audience, thereby unwittingly gaining entrée to the Balinese village community they had gone to study. Such instances accelerate the ethnographer's incorporation into the group studied, achieving what villagers in India told Gerald Berreman when he went to study them: "You may be a foreigner and we only poor villagers, but when we get to know you we will judge you as a man among other men, not as a foreigner" (Adams & Preiss, 1960).

Conclusion

Although it is not a purpose of this chapter to compare ethnography with other forms of qualitative research, identifying some of the major contrasts can clarify the criteria for evaluating ethnographies by placing ethnography in the conceptual context of contemporary nurse researchers. For example, in contrast to the standards of grounded theory, neither rigor in documentation nor auditability of decision-making trails are required of an ethnography. In fact, identification of decision-making trails may be impossible because decisions may occur unintentionally and not be recorded or recallable (Wolf, 1992). The particular format of the rigor of documentation necessarily varies by ethnographer, but a canon of ethnographic fieldwork is the recording of field notes where raw observations and reflections on them are recorded (Sanjek 1990; Wolf 1992). A decision trail that would document all of the decisions involved in the transformation of raw data into the theoretical schema is not possible in ethnography because observations are analyzed continuously, as they are made, in the ethnographer's sleep, or mentally when pieced together at a subsequent "unrelated" event, and they are repeatedly rethought and reread in light of new observations. What is crucial for ethnography is that there be logical consistency in the development of the interpretation and that the logic be rooted in that of the people studied.

Making an ethnography also differs from producing a grounded theory or phenomenological study in the definition of data. Whereas the data to be analyzed for these other inductive approaches are necessarily in written form, this is not true for ethnography. My own study of child health in northern Thailand, for example, included children's drawings; psychological tests (Raven Colored Progressive Matrices, Draw-A-Person); medical laboratory tests (e.g., blood counts, fecal examinations); diet, family, and medical histories; performance in and attendance at school; serial anthropometric measurements; folklore; structured questionnaires; open-ended interviewing; and participant observation associated with long-term in-site residence (Muecke, 1976).

This chapter was not conceived as a primer in the evaluation of ethnography. It has identified the evaluation of the focused ethnography in nursing and related health sciences research as problematic. The work is not done. In the light of current trends, focused ethnography undoubtedly will increase in prevalence. We need to ensure that our understanding of what it is that makes ethnographies good grows apace with their numbers.

References

Aamodt, A. M. (1983). Problems in doing nursing research: Developing a criteria [sic] for evaluating qualitative research. *Western Journal of Nursing Research, 5*(4), 398-402.

Aamodt, A. M. (1991). Ethnography and epistemology: Generating nursing theory. In J. M. Morse (Ed.), *Qualitative nursing research: A contemporary dialogue* (pp. 40-53). Rockville, MD: Aspen.

Adams, R., & Preiss, J. J. (Eds.). (1960). *Human organization research.* Homewood, IL: Irwin.

Agar, M. (1980). *The professional stranger: An informal introduction to ethnography.* New York: Academic Press.

Agar, M. (1986). *Speaking of ethnography* (Qualitative Research Methods Series 2). Beverly Hills, CA: Sage.

Anderson, J. (1986). *Health-seeking behavior of Salvadoran refugees.* Unpublished master's thesis, University of Washington, Seattle.

Bentley, M., Pelto, G., Straus, W., Schumann, D., Adegbola, C., de la Pena, E., Oni, G., Grown, K., & Huffman, S. (1988). Rapid ethnographic assessment: Applications in a diarrhea management program. *Social Science and Medicine, 27*(1), 107-116.

Brink, P. (1982). Traditional birth attendants among the Annang of Nigeria: Traditional practices and proposed programs. *Social Science and Medicine, 16*(21), 183-192.

Brink, P. (1989). The fattening room among the Annang of Nigeria. *Medical Anthropology, 12,* 131-143.

Bruyn, S. (1966). *The human perspective in sociology: The methodology of participant observation.* Englewood Cliffs, NJ: Prentice Hall.

Burns, N. (1989). Standards for qualitative research. *Nursing Science Quarterly, 2*(1), 44-52.

Capps, L. L. (1991). *Concepts of health and illness of the Protestant Hmong.* Unpublished doctoral dissertation, University of Kansas, Department of Anthropology, Lawrence.

Clark, M. (1959). *Health in the Mexican-American culture: A community study.* Berkeley: University of California Press.

Clifford, J., & Marcus, G. E. (Eds.). (1986). *Writing culture: The poetics and politics of ethnography.* Berkeley: University of California Press.

Council of Nursing and Anthropology. (1992). *CONAA membership directory.* Baltimore: Author.

Crassweller, J. (1986). *The paradox of opium addiction among Southeast Asian refugees: Panacea or problem?* Unpublished master's thesis, University of Washington, School of Nursing, Seattle.

DeSantis, L. (1986). Infant feeding practices of Haitian mothers in south Florida: Cultural beliefs and acculturation. *Maternal-Child Nursing Journal, 15*(2), 77-89.

Douglas, M. (1966). *Purity and danger: An analysis of the concepts of pollution and taboo.* Boston: Ark.

Douglas, M. (1970). *Natural symbols: Explorations in cosmology.* New York: Penguin.

Dreher, M. (1984). School children and ganja. *Anthropology and Education Quarterly, 15*(1), 131-150.

Dreher, M. (1989). Poor and pregnant: Perinatal ganja use in rural Jamaica. *Advances in Alcohol and Substance Abuse, 8*(1), 45-54.

Fabrega, H., & Silver, D. (1973). *Illness and shamanistic curing in Zinacantan: An ethnomedical analysis.* Stanford, CA: Stanford University Press.

Fetterman, D. M. (1989). *Ethnography: Step by step.* Newbury Park, CA: Sage.

Frake, C. O. (1961). The diagnosis of disease among the Subanun of Mindanao. *American Anthropologist, 63,* 113-132.

Frye, B. (1990). The process of health care decision making among Cambodian immigrant women. *International Quarterly of Community Health Education, 10*(2), 113-124.

Geertz, C. (1973a). Deep play: Notes on the Balinese cockfight. In *The interpretation of cultures* (pp. 412-453). New York: Basic Books.

Geertz, C. (1973b). Thick description: Toward an interpretive theory of culture. In *The interpretation of cultures* (pp. 3-30). New York: Basic Books.

Germain, C. (1986). Ethnography: The method. In P. L. Marshall & C. J. Oiler (Eds.), *Nursing research: A qualitative perspective* (pp. 147-162). New York: Appleton-Century-Crofts.

Germain, C. P. H. (1979). *The cancer unit: An ethnography.* Wakefield, MA: Nursing Resources.

Glaser, B., & Strauss, A. L. (1967). *The discovery of grounded theory: Strategies for qualitative research.* Hawthorne, NY: Aldine.

Glidden, C. (1986). *Infant feeding practices among recently arriving Khmer mothers.* Unpublished master's thesis, University of Washington, Seattle.

Grandstaff, S., Grandstaff, T., & Lovelace, G. (1987). Summary report. *Proceedings of the 1985 International Conference on Rapid Rural Appraisal.* Khon Kaen, Thailand: Khon Kaen University, Rural Systems Research and Farming Systems Research Projects.

Hughes, C. C. (1992). "Ethnography": What's in a word—Process? Product? Promise? *Qualitative Health Research, 2*(4), 439-450.

Kay, M. (1977). Health and illness in a Mexican-American barrio. In E. Spicer (Ed.), *Ethnic medicine in the Southwest* (pp. 99-166). Tucson: University of Arizona Press.

Kay, M. (1979). Lexemic change and semantic shift in disease names. *Culture, Medicine and Psychiatry, 3,* 73-94.

Kay, M. (Ed.). (1982). *The anthropology of human birth.* Philadelphia: F. A. Davis.

Kirkpatrick, S., & Cobb, A. (1990). Health beliefs related to diarrhea in Haitian children: Building transcultural nursing knowledge. *Journal of Transcultural Nursing, 1*(2), 2-12.

Lamb, G. S., & Huttlinger, K. (1989). Reflexivity in nursing research. *Western Journal of Nursing Research, 11*(6), 765-772.

Leininger, M. (1985). Ethnography and ethnonursing: Models and modes of qualitative data analysis. In M. Leininger (Ed.), *Qualitative research methods in nursing* (pp. 33-71). New York: Grune & Stratton.

Lipson, J. (1991). Afghan refugee health: Some findings and suggestions. *Qualitative Health Research, 1*(3), 349-369.

Luna L. (1989). *Care and cultural context of Lebanese Muslims in an urban U.S. community.* Unpublished doctoral dissertation, Wayne State University, Detroit.

Magilvy, J., McMahon, M., Bachman, M., Roark, S., & Evenson, C. (1987). The health of teenagers: A focused ethnographic study. *Public Health Nursing, 4*(1), 35-42.

Morse, J. (1987). Qualitative nursing research: A free-for-all? In J. Morse (Ed.), *Qualitative nursing research: A contemporary dialogue* (pp. 14-22). Newbury Park, CA: Sage.

Morse, J. (1989). Cultural variation in behavioral response to parturition: Childbirth in Fiji. *Medical Anthropology, 12,* 35-54.

Muecke, M. A. (1976). *"Reproductive success" among the urban poor: A micro-level study of infant survival and child growth in northern Thailand.* Unpublished doctoral dissertation, University of Washington, Seattle.

Muecke, M. A. (1987). Resettled refugees' reconstruction of identity: Lao in Seattle. *Urban Anthropology, 16*(3-4), 273-289.

Muecke, M. A. (1992a). Mother sold food, daughter sells her body: Prostitution and cultural continuity. *Social Science and Medicine, 35*(7), 891-901.

Muecke, M. A. (1992b). Review of Wolf, ZR. *Western Journal of Nursing Research, 14*(4), 514-515.

Noblit, G. W., & Hare, R. D. (1988). *Meta-ethnography: Synthesizing qualitative studies* (Qualitative Research Methods Series 11). Newbury Park, CA: Sage.

Read, K. E. (1980). *Other voices: The style of a male homosexual tavern*. Novato, CA: Chandler & Sharp.

Reeb, R. (1992). Granny midwives in Mississippi: Career and birthing practices. *Journal of Transcultural Nursing, 4*(2), 18-27.

Rhodes, L. A. (1991). *Emptying beds: The work of an emergency psychiatric unit*. Berkeley: University of California Press.

Rosenbaum, J. (1990). Cultural care of older Greek Canadian widows within Leininger's theory of culture care. *Journal of Transcultural Nursing, 2*(1), 37-47.

Sanjek, R. (Ed.). (1990). *Fieldnotes: The makings of anthropology*. Ithaca, NY: Cornell University Press.

Scrimshaw, S., Carballo, M., Ramos, L., & Blair, B. (1991). The AIDS rapid anthropological assessment procedures: A tool for health education planning and evaluation. *Health Education Quarterly, 18*(1), 111-123.

Scrimshaw, S., & Hurtado, E. (1988). *Rapid assessment procedures for nutritional and primary health care: Anthropologic approaches to program improvement*. Los Angeles: UCLA Latin American Center and United Nations University.

Shostak, M. (1981). *Nisa: The life and works of a !Kung woman*. Cambridge, MA: Harvard University Press.

Spindler, G. (1970). *Being an anthropologist: Fieldwork in eleven countries*. New York: Holt, Rinehart & Winston.

Spradley, J. P. (1970). *You owe yourself a drunk: An ethnography of urban nomads*. Boston: Little, Brown.

Spradley, J. P. (1979). *The ethnographic interview*. New York: Holt, Rinehart & Winston.

Spradley, J. P. (1980). *Participant observation*. New York: Holt, Rinehart & Winston.

Street, A. F. (1992). *Inside nursing: A critical ethnography of clinical nursing practice*. Albany: State University of New York Press.

Thompson, J. (1991). Exploring gender and culture with Khmer refugee women: Reflections on participatory feminist research. *Advances in Nursing Science, 13*(3), 30-48.

Turnbull, C. (1961). *The forest people: A study of the Pygmies of the Congo*. New York: Simon & Schuster.

Turner, V. (1975). *Revelation and divination in Ndembu ritual*. Ithaca, NY: Cornell University Press.

Werner, O., & Schoepfle, M. (1987a). *Systematic fieldwork: Ethnographic analysis and data management* (Vol. 2). Newbury Park, CA: Sage.

Werner, O., & Schoepfle, M. (1987b). *Systematic fieldwork: Foundations of ethnography and interviewing* (Vol. 1). Newbury Park, CA: Sage.

Williams, H. (1990). Families in refugee camps. *Human Organization, 49*(2), 100-109.

Wolcott, H. (1980). How to look like an anthropologist without really being one. *Practicing Anthropology, 3*(2), 56-59.

Wolf, M. (1992). *A thrice-told tale: Feminism, postmodernism and ethnographic responsibility.* Stanford, CA: Stanford University Press.

Notes

1. Hughes (1992, p. 449) suggested that a main reason for the widespread use of the ethnographic method is its similarity to a case study approach to understanding human behavior: "A case study draws its power from the deep-seated human capacity—and *need*—to *anthropomorphize* perceived events in the human natural world—to empathize, not merely sympathize."

2. *Foreign* need not signify international borders. Much of the pluralist society of the United States may appear remote and exotic to "mainstream" society. Kenneth Read's urban ethnography of a gay bar, *Other Voices,* for example, exposed a lifestyle that, at the time of publication in 1980, was still largely hidden and secreted from social acknowledgment.

3. The construct equivalent to the ethnographer's "thick description" for grounded theorists is "density."

Dialogue

More on Muddling Methods

MAY There have been a lot of changes in grounded theory. It's as if when we get exited, stage left, dissertation in hand, the methods froze. And that's nonsense. But it looks like there is a lot of garbage out there, so I see your chapter, Phyllis, as drawing some lines in the sand about what innovation is theoretically sound, versus make-it-up-as-you-go-along. And make-it-up-as-you-go-along may be OK, but then you have to say, "I'm making-it-up-as-I-go-along, guys."

MORSE But it is very dangerous—

MAY Yes and no.

STERN But I say again that Glaser and Strauss made it up as they went along.

MORSE Yes, I know, but they were not students.

LEININGER Well, you grounded theorists—Do you think you are evolving something that is different from the original masters? And if so, what is it, and what are the issues?

STERN Well, Madeleine, what I think is that methods are personal. It's like a religion. Everybody believes their own. They may go to a certain church, but they go home and they pray their own way. You may not like it. Maybe my reputation will be smudged forever (because we do have it on tape), but people think differently, and they do have their own way of getting to some type of truth. And you have to do it your own way.

KNAFL This is so important, but it is something that we never talk about. The fit between the method and the person and the style and who you are and how you think and what your work style is.

SANDELOWSKI I think grounded theory always did have some range of variation and personal twist to it. However, just to put some brackets around it—not meaning "bracket" in the phenomenological sense—

WILSON The worst thing that is happening to me in my life is supervising doctoral students who are generating "The Nursing Process." They go out there, and they go through all the steps—one version or another of the procedures, and they "discover" assessing, intervening, and evaluating and call it a grounded theory. And I end up having to say, well you have several choices. Either you can rewrite your methodology chapter and say you are doing a content analysis, or you cannot graduate. Or you have to do your analysis over again. Or you can change your advisor.

STERN   Yes. Those are good choices!

MAY   Oh, the generational changes that we are going through! But I don't think the world knows about it. I would sit in seminar, and they would talk to me about the method, and I would have to go through a mental dictionary and say, "Wait a minute, what do you guys call that? We used to call it open coding. Do you still call that open coding?" So we now have come across the general forms of the process we have come to call grounded theory. And you have this form and you have that form, and they are different in some fairly interesting ways.

11

Eroding Grounded Theory

PHYLLIS NOERAGER STERN

There is a kind of glass called end-of-the-date glass, made by
taking all colors and throwing them in a pot and stirring it up. It
is quite a beautiful thing, but it is not any particular style or
pattern—it is just whatever you get. I get a lot of that as the
editor of a journal (*Health Care for Women International*) who
likes qualitative research. I see endless numbers of manuscripts
in which everything is all mixed up and they call it grounded
theory.

Pam Brink, speaking to a seminar group at Dalhousie University
(October 1989), claimed that I am the loosest grounded theorist
around. I have a hunch that, in my writings (Stern, 1980, 1984,
1991; Stern, Allen, & Moxley, 1982; Stern & Pyles, 1985), I am
just one of the most honest. Or it may be that Pam's reference
point is what I call the Straussian (after Anselm Strauss) school,
which differs in both process and product from the Glaserian
(after Barney Glaser) school I use. Glaser and Strauss developed
the method while both were at the School of Nursing of the
University of California, San Francisco, and wrote a book about
it—*The Discovery of Grounded Theory* (1967). Apparently they
thought they were using it the same way. Students of Glaser and
Strauss in the 1960s and 1970s knew the two had quite different
modus operandi, but Glaser only found out when Strauss and
Corbin's *Basics of Qualitative Research* came out in 1990,
whereupon Glaser wrote his second solo book on grounded
theory, *Basics of Grounded Theory Analysis* (1992). (The first,
Theoretical Sensitivity, was published in 1978.) Glaser clearly,

and rather dramatically, points out what the differences are and goes so far as to write that the Glaserian and Straussian methods should have different names: *grounded theory* for the Glaserian school, and *conceptual description* for the Straussian school. Students of Glaser or Strauss taught their own students according to the dictates of the mentor with whom they worked. This schism has lent its force to the erosion of grounded theory. A given conceptual framework developed by using the method of the Glaserian school may well be judged according to the Straussian model.

Another factor that contributes to the erosion of grounded theory stems from what I will call "minus mentoring"—mentoring that is either poor in quality or nonexistent. That is to say, the investigator learned it from a book or, more likely, a book chapter or, with no reference from which to work, decided to manipulate the data in any old way and name it grounded theory. Before we take this discussion further, it would be well to place grounded theory—whatever it is—within the milieu of the interpretive family of methods.

Interpretive Methods

Grounded theory is but one of the interpretive methods that share the common philosophy of phenomenology—that is, methods that are used to describe the world of the person or persons under study. The desired end product determines the method used. Ethnographers who accept a phenomenological perspective attempt to describe the culture of a given group as the individuals under study see it—an *emic* view. Sociologists hope to discover the major influences in the social world of a group of individuals, and those who name themselves phenomenologists attempt to describe the relationships between an individual's intrapsychic experience and the surrounding world at a given time. To find these various truths, investigators employ a multitude of ways-of-going, which they refer to as "methods." When existing methods fail, investigators tinker with their ways-of-going in pursuit of an explanation of a phenomenon that seems to them truthful, logical, and an addition to existing knowledge (Strauss & Corbin, in press).

Barney Glaser and Anselm Strauss were two such scholars. When they could not get at the true symbolic meaning of dying for individuals and their intimates, they started tinkering with existing sociological methods. They claim that awareness of their transgressions came over them only after the fact, at which point they wrote *The Discovery of Grounded Theory* (1967).

It may be that all seasoned researchers tinker with the method they use until it works for them. The point is that maybe it is not heresy; rather, it may be an effort to be true to the data and to develop an end product of quality and use. But then, isn't it okay to tell other researchers how one got to the end product? Perhaps one might have discovered a better way to address research problems from which other professionals could benefit.

Muddling Methods

Does this argument lend support to the minions of mediocrity who (a) write articles in which they claim to have developed a grounded theory but explain that their theoretical construct was arrived at using "ethnographic methods," as some authors do, or (b) tell us they used grounded theory techniques to gain the "lived experience" of the participants (Muret, 1990), or (c) report their data in percentages and never get beyond reporting semirelated categories? Not at all, because clearly these authors fail to understand the prescriptive of a single method and have simply "muddled methods" (Baker, Wuest, & Stern, 1992).

To explain, chances are good that when results are laid out in percentages, the investigator used content analysis methods to analyze qualitative data. As a rule of thumb, when researchers present their work as grounded theory and it is something else, the something else is usually content analysis, even when reported without percentages. It should be pointed out that as usually conducted today, content analysis falls out of the arena of interpretative research. I direct the interested reader to those authors who have dealt with the method extensively (Downe-Wambolt, 1992; Krippendorff, 1980; Stiles, 1978; Weber, 1985). For the sake of simplicity, I limit this discussion to the three most popular (as of this writing) and most often muddled methods in the social sciences—ethnography, phenomenology, and grounded theory. (There is that pseudomethod—grounded theory approach—which, rather than being a blending of methods, stands out as a slapdash procedure; that is, the investigator is too slovenly to learn the real thing. Put another way, close, but no cigar.)

Methodological Frameworks

Although there may be similarities in all interpretative methods, in that ethnographers, phenomenologists, and grounded theorists use observation and interview as a means for collecting data, the frameworks underlying the methods differ. *Ethnographers* approach the field armed with theory developed by generations of anthropologists and, therefore, turn their attention to the culture within the framework from a particular theoretical perspective. For example, they may be looking at the *structure* that creates order or to the *ritual* that is part of the identity of the culture and that, in effect, holds it in place; or they may be looking into the meaning certain *symbols* have for this group of people. The attention of the ethnographer then, is focused prior to entering the field.

Researchers who call themselves *phenomenologists* or hermeneutic phenomenologists seek guidance from existential philosophy of a particular school (e.g., Heidegger, 1975/1982; Merleau-Ponty, 1945/1962) in the interpretation of their data. Through careful study with an individual or individuals, they hope to discover the deeper meaning of "lived experience" for individuals in terms of their relationship with time, space, and personal history.

The framework for the *grounded theorist* is rooted in *symbolic interactionism* (Blumer, 1969; Mead, 1964/1934), wherein the investigator attempts to determine what symbolic meaning artifacts, clothing, gestures, and words have for groups of people as they interact with one another. From this viewpoint the investigator hopes to construct what the interactants see as their social reality. According to Fawcett (1991), grounded theorists also function within a framework in which the investigator assumes that individuals give them information they, the participants, consider accurate. The grounded theorist, though, enters the scene bereft of preformed theory; observation and questioning are guided by hypotheses generated in the field. Whereas the ethnographer may concentrate on ritual from beginning observations, the grounded theorist will only decide that ritual is primary to the social reality of a given population when individuals involved tell her or him that it is.

The Menace of Minus Mentoring

Why do researchers muddle these methods? Why do they take a perfectly good method like grounded theory and erode the earth from beneath it? What I think we have here is a generational erosion. In the 1960s and 1970s, students having read about grounded theory in a book or an article (Glaser, 1978; Glaser & Strauss, 1967; Wilson, 1977) found a professor, who again had only read an article or a book about it, willing to take them on. Those students have gone on to teach other students "grounded theory method," and their students' other students, and so on. The problem is that no matter how skilled the writer, interpretative methods have been described imperfectly. I suspect the reason is that grounded theory, being "half art and half science" (Leonard Schatzman, personal communication, 1980), or more art than science as Sandelowski (Chapter 4) argues, means that the description of how one does it (the method) has got to be elusive. The comparison can be made between interpretative research and any other art form (one can learn formulas for writing from a book, or techniques of perspective from a book), but unless one wishes to become the Grandma Moses of researchers (talented but primitive), one had best get oneself to a mentor who can be watched, can be watchful, can lead, can allow one to take the lead; in short, with whom one can engage in the love affair that is learning grounded theory.

Denying the value of artful interpretation of data has led to attacks on the foundations of the method by those whose view is obscured by their need for control over data. Data, in fact, will come willingly to artful explanation if one is dedicated to working *with* it rather than against it, or as Glaser (1992) puts it, if we let the theory emerge. Over the years researchers whose formative values stem from quantitative research have attempted to apply rules that impede, rather than advance, the gaining of new knowledge. A student auditor in one of my methods seminars once observed that "it seems like magic" when the theory starts coming. It seemed magical to her because she only observed, rather than getting her hands dirty with the data; the process of discovery remained a mystery. She could not see the interpretative steps involved in the process of analysis. It must be allowed, however, that it is the creativity in the act that brings the real truth of a social situation into being, and following grounded theory techniques is one way to approach this creative process. It is not the only way, but if one wishes to produce an end product that can be called a grounded theory, it may be the best way to go about it. The method is the ritual that ensures that the culture of the school will be preserved—in this case, the school of grounded theory.

Most importantly, the developed theory must be integrated: All of the parts need to fit together. The interpreter, the grounded theorist, would do all of this by using a process of *artful integrating*. The described theory would be as true to the social scene under study as the artful scientist could make it because it would have been derived from a problem identified by informants themselves, would relate ways in which informants solve the problem, and would have involved informants as participants in the study by processes of *checking back* and *revealing* the theory as it developed. Other qualities inherent in a well-drawn grounded theory are common to all interpretative methods: readability, personal voice, connectedness with the reader. Glaserian grounded theory alone would be expected to be immediately applicable to individuals and social groups who shared the problem under study, and would be expected to be testable. Strauss and Corbin (in press) downplay grounded theory's applicability.

Writing Up Grounded Theory

As written, grounded theory is laid out in recognizable ways. Because of the way the analysis is executed—the method—the author of the study report usually calls attention to the components of the theory—processes, categories, dimensions, and properties—by the use of italicized rubrics interspersed throughout the work. In addition, as part of a concluding section, the researcher may suggest that further study would allow for the discovery of other categories and dimensions, thus further defining the limits of the variables—for example, looking at another cultural group. The well-schooled grounded theorist never, ever makes excuses for the size of the sample or its characteristics. Were the numbers insufficient to saturate the categories for that particular aspect of the study, the researcher would have continued to collect data until satisfied she or he was hearing nothing new (for a recent example, see Hitchcock & Wilson, 1991).

Mentoring the Creative Act

But what about the creative act? Does creativity require a mentor? What the mentor does, I think, is create an atmosphere where the natural creativity we all possess can emerge. As Richards and Richards (1991) suggest: "The assumption is often made that themes are there waiting to be freed and that we will, of course, recognize an emerging theme as such when we see it happen. Neither assumption is justified by research experience" (p. 247).

Recognizing emerging themes is part of the "seems like magic" the student spoke of. I have insufficient words to describe the act of creation that is the magic. The sensation of insight seems relatively easy to put to paper. One usually reads that it includes a somatic response: It feels right or is like a thunderbolt. But the act of putting pieces together until suddenly the electricity arcs and the world is there to see and to take—how does one write that? (For further elaboration see Morse, Chap. 3.) Nevertheless, I do create. I get inspirational flashes, and sometimes I look good in front of my students. But how I do that, and if I ever will again, I do not know. Students often find it hard to believe, as they begin the research process, that they will develop a credible conceptual framework. And yet students manage to learn to perform the magic of creativity. The neophyte must watch the act and be able to relate it to her or his data. Having transcended the creative process, the neophyte becomes sufficiently proficient to conduct subsequent studies independently and to teach other neophytes: the see-one-do-one-teach-one of learning the tricks of any trade (Maxwell, 1979). Some noted scholar somewhere who has the time and inclination to read this may chortle, "I learned it all from a book, and I'm famous for my grounded theory studies." I would allow for only one. Two at the most. It may be possible to learn brain surgery from a book, but it is far from usual. And brain surgery is easier!

Book learners or those who have fallen victim to generational erosion tend to go part way with their analyses. Their reports suffer from incompleteness. Reviewers tend to find them thin; a typical comment is, "With such rich data, it's a pity the author has made such poor use of it." Usually book learners get no farther than categorizing the data. Or the central variable they claim explains the data just does not ring true. Students of grounded theory who have no mentor on campus would do well to contact a potential mentor by phone and/or to arrange a visit for consultation, thus beginning the love affair of learning. Printed words are but a poor replacement for the genuine article.

Modifying Methods

I have no problem with researchers tinkering with a given method or inventing a new one. What I cannot abide is the author who claims to have used grounded theory but whose end product is some kind of hybrid. Wilson and Hutchinson (1991) combined Heideggerian hermeneutics and grounded theory to great advantage. In this way they were able to get at both the social reality and the deeper, intrapsychic meaning in phenomena. But they took great pains to tell us just what they did. Beck (1992, 1993) used grounded theory and phenomenology on a single data set. Although one might argue that the data collection techniques should be different for each method of inquiry, at the very least, Beck let us in on what she had done. And that is the whole point, within the parameters of science: I really don't care what you do, just tell me about it. I might learn something.

Glaserian or Straussian Grounded Theory

When Barney Glaser gave up his chance for a tenure-track position at the University of California at San Francisco to make room for the addition of a professor of color to join the faculty, he went into business and became a successful corporation, thereby leaving Anselm Strauss to answer the multiple charges laid against grounded theory's seeming looseness, its lack of verification, and the tangled description of it in the *Discovery* book. The need to respond to critics, I think, led Strauss (1987) and Strauss and Corbin (1990) to modify their description of grounded theory from its original concept of emergence to a densely codified strictured operation.

My colleague Sharon Sims, who has used grounded theory in ways that portend applicability (Sims, Boland, & O'Neill, 1992), muses that Glaser and Strauss have both undergone a conversion experience—Glaser, whose background is in statistical analysis, insists on allowing the theory to emerge (a deceptively loose description of the process of discovery), while Strauss seems to have come all the way out of the Chicago school to a way of going that is tightly prescriptive (S. Sims, personal communication, April 2, 1993). Those close to the two researchers tell us that the differences in approach, though subject to evolution over the years, have been there from the beginning. Strauss "played theoretical games" as long as his current research partner, Juliet Corbin, can remember—some 14 or 15 years (J. Corbin, personal communication, April 13, 1993). These theoretical games are tangential to, but inspired by, the data. What allowed the careful description of the Straussian school was the writing style of Juliet Corbin. In *Basics of Qualitative Research* (Strauss & Corbin, 1990), Corbin gives us careful attention to detail, and, nurselike, she orders the description of Strauss' method in logical, easy-to-understand segments. Thus has another student paid homage to her mentor, much as Strauss did for Mead in 1964.

In Glaser and Strauss we have two brilliant men who both do important work. But they go about it in different ways. The crux of the dichotomy is, I think, that Strauss, as he examines the data, stops at each word to ask, "What if?" Glaser keeps his attention focused on the data and asks, "What do we have here?" Strauss brings to bear every possible contingency that *could* relate to the data, whether it appears in the data or not. Glaser focuses his attention *on* the data to allow the data to tell their own story. Strauss takes on a professorial tone as he suggests that although Glaser has been away from academia for 14 years, he has continued to do research and that it is only natural that he and the method would evolve (A. Strauss, personal communication, March 24, 1993). For his part, Glaser is adamant that Strauss' evolution is more correctly a departure from the original method, which makes no scholarly sense (B. Glaser, personal communication, February 12, 1993). In other words, to Glaser, the Straussian school represents an erosion of grounded theory.

Conclusion

In the end, whether grounded theory has evolved or eroded becomes a matter of ideology. Glaser sees in Strauss' work a fundamental change, while Strauss argues that a method that has become as popular as grounded theory is bound to change (Strauss & Corbin, in press). To me, a strict Glaserian (student paying homage to a mentor), Strauss and Glaser present fundamentally different methods. Strauss' students produce good and important work (Cohen, 1993), but it, too, is fundamentally different. The product seems bound to a single set of circumstances and fails to hint at that conceptual leap that, in time, becomes formal theory. Glaserian methodologists are getting a bit long in the tooth now, and our students are fewer. One hopes that readers of *Basics of Grounded Theory Analysis* (Glaser, 1992) can see beyond Glaser's tendency for tirade against what he considers to be the spiriting away and mangling of his method, to the clear exposition of the original grounded theory method of allowing theory to emerge.

As for the menace of minus mentoring, perhaps these few words of mine will help at least one pseudogrounded theorist kick the habit of antimethod methods. Get thee to a mentor.

References

Baker, C., Wuest, J., & Stern, P. N. (1992). Method slurring: The phenomenology/grounded theory example. *Journal of Advanced Nursing, 17,* 1355-1360.

Beck, C. T. (1992). The lived experience of postpartum depression: A phenomenological study. *Nursing Research, 41,* 166-170.

Beck, C. T. (1993). Teetering on the edge: A substantive theory of postpartum depression. *Nursing Research, 42,* 42-48.

Blumer, H. (1969). *Symbolic interactionism.* Englewood Cliffs, NJ: Prentice-Hall.

Cohen, M. H. (1993). The unknown and the unknowable: Managing sustained uncertainty. *Western Journal of Nursing Research, 15,* 77-96.

Downe-Wambolt, B. (1992). Content analysis: Method, applications, and issues. *Health Care for Women International, 13,* 313-322.

Fawcett, J. (1991). Approaches to knowledge development in nursing. *Canadian Journal of Nursing Research, 23,* 23-34.

Glaser, B. G. (1978). *Theoretical sensitivity.* Mill Valley, CA: Sociology Press.

Glaser, B. G. (1992). *Basics of grounded theory analysis.* Mill Valley, CA: Sociology Press.

Glaser, B. G., & Strauss, A. L. (1967). *The discovery of grounded theory.* Hawthorne, NY: Aldine.

Heidegger, M. (1982). *Basic problems of phenomenology* (A. Hofstadter, Trans.). Bloomington: Indiana University Press. (Original work published 1975)

Hitchcock, J. M., & Wilson, H. S. (1992). Personal risking: Lesbian self-disclosure of sexual orientation to professional health care providers. *Nursing Research, 41,* 178-183.

Krippendorff, K. (1980). *Content analysis: An introduction to its methodology* (4th ed.). Beverly Hills, CA: Sage.

Maxwell, E. K. (1979). Modeling life: The dynamic relationship between elder modelers and their protégés (Doctoral dissertation, University of California, San Francisco). *Dissertation Abstracts International, 39,* 7531A.

Mead, G. H. (1964). *George Herbert Mead on social psychology* (rev. ed.). Chicago: University of Chicago Press. (Original work published 1934)

Merleau-Ponty, M. (1962). *Phenomenology of perception* (C. Smith, Trans.). New York: Humanities Press. (Original work published 1945)

Muret, C. T. (1990). Transformation of provisional existence of unknown limit: A grounded theory. *Dissertations Abstracts International, 51,* 2820B. (University Microfilms No. DA9033)

Richards, L., & Richards, T. (1991). Computing qualitative analysis: A healthy development? *Qualitative Health Research, 1,* 234-262.

Sims, S. L., Boland, D. L., & O'Neill, C. A. (1992). Decision making in home health care. *Western Journal of Nursing Research, 14,* 186-197.

Stern, P. N. (1980). Grounded theory methodology: Its uses and processes. *Image: Journal of Nursing Scholarship, 12,* 20-23.

Stern, P. N. (1984). Using grounded theory method in nursing research. In M. Leininger (Ed.), *Qualitative research methods in nursing* (pp. 149-160). New York: Grune & Stratton.

Stern, P. N. (1991). Are counting and coding *a cappella* appropriate in qualitative research? *Qualitative nursing research: A contemporary dialogue* (pp. 135-148). Newbury Park, CA: Sage.

Stern, P. N., Allen, L. M., & Moxley, P. A. (1982). The nurse as grounded theorist: History process and uses. *Review Journal of Philosophy and Social Science, 7,* 200-215.

Stern, P. N., & Pyles, S. H. (1985). Using grounded theory methodology to study women's culturally based decisions about health. *Health Care for Women International, 6,* 1-24.

Stiles, W. B. (1978). *Manual for a taxonomy of verbal response modes.* Chapel Hill, NC: Institute for Research in Social Science.

Strauss, A. L. (1987). *Qualitative analysis for social scientists.* New York: Cambridge University Press.

Strauss, A. L., & Corbin, J. (1990). *Basics of qualitative research.* Newbury Park, CA: Sage.

Strauss, A. L., & Corbin, J. (in press). Grounded theory methodology: an overview. In Y. Lincoln & N. Denzin (Eds.), *Handbook of qualitative research.* Thousand Oaks, CA: Sage.

Weber, R. P. (1985). *Basic content analysis.* Beverly Hills, CA: Sage.

Wilson, H. S. (1977). Limiting intrusion: Social control of outsiders in a healing community. *Nursing Research, 26,* 103-110.

Wilson, H. S., & Hutchinson, S. A. (1991). Triangulation of qualitative methods: Heideggerian hermeneutics and grounded theory. *Qualitative Health Research, 1,* 263-276.

Dialogue

Questions About Focus Groups

KNAFL What are the advantages of a focus group compared with a one-to-one interview?

CAREY For a new topic, or if you are trying to take a topic to a new population, or if it's something where you want to get the thinking and the feeling and not just the behavior—such as, why don't people do breast self-examination—when it's not as likely to come out in a one-to-one interview, then the group dynamic will be a synergistic factor in bringing the information out. The negative aspect is how much are people going to hold back. It's a bit more of an art than a science, I think. When one person starts talking, then another realizes, "Oh, that happened to me!" so that the second person might report information that would not come up in an interview.

WILSON Is there a rule of thumb on numbers?

CAREY Well, if your group is articulate and will really speak up, you can have a big group. But if group members are 65 years old and their backs hurt, try three or four in a group because they won't have to share talk time as much. With the senior citizen group, we had four. With the HIV study, we had six or seven. And in another project on technology transfer, we had 15. In that study the group leader asked the first question and that's all—until she said it was time to stop. So it really depends on who the people are and what the topic is.

DREHER Do you think it would be leading the focus group to identify those who are reluctant to speak and to ask them their opinion about something, or should you let the group unfold naturally?

CAREY I think you have to guide it. In the presession milling about, pick out who is going to be dominant and who is not going to be dominant. Put the dominant person next to you so you can guide him or her a little. And put the shy ones across from you so you can encourage them nonverbally.

12

The Group Effect in Focus Groups: Planning, Implementing, and Interpreting Focus Group Research

MARTHA ANN CAREY

When I wrote this chapter, I started writing on the social-psychological aspects of focus groups, and I have not seen the social-psychological aspects published anywhere. I feel strongly that the fact of being in a group needs to be kept in mind when you are planning and running groups, and when analyzing the data. And if you do not, you are just missing a lot of impact on the data. And I also am amazed, from my own experience, how people will talk on tape about sensitive subjects. And I think sometimes a focus group is the best approach for a sensitive subject. It has advantages over the one-on-one interview in that you use the group interaction. In spite of the constraints, such as demand characteristics, this method is still very useful in health research.

Focus groups provide insight into beliefs and attitudes that underlie behavior. Data regarding perceptions and opinions are enriched through group interaction because individual participation can be enhanced in a group setting. In selected research settings, the data collected by using a focus group can be more informative than the data collected by other methods. The focus

AUTHOR'S NOTE: I would like to thank my colleagues Mickey W. Smith and Molly Engle for their insightful comments and the members of the focus groups for their participation in the research group technique is especially useful for studies of complex issues involving many levels of feelings and experience, such as studies of beliefs and attitudes of the causes of AIDS (Flaskerud & Calvillo, 1991; Irwin et al., 1991; Nyamathi & Shuler, 1990). Krueger (1988) described the focus group technique as collecting "richness of data at reasonable cost" (p. 177). The development of the focus group technique, first credited to the research program of Robert Merton and colleagues in the mid-1940s (Merton, Fiske, & Kendall, 1956), has been refined by market researchers into a powerful technique with commercial applications. Only recently have social science and health researchers begun applying this technique.

Underlying this technique is the rationale that, with proper guidance from the focus group leader, group members can describe the rich details of complex experiences and the reasoning behind their actions, beliefs, perceptions, and attitudes. The impact of the group setting can enhance the quality of the data elicited. Because the definition of a focus group is not precise, in this chapter I concentrate on concepts and issues including a brief review of the purpose and process of using focus groups, a description of psychosocial factors and the impact of these factors on planning and implementing focus groups, and on analyzing and interpreting the data.

Purpose and Process

In this section I briefly describe the purpose and process of using focus groups. For a more detailed description, a very readable and useful reference is Krueger (1988) (see also Kingry, Tiedje, & Freidman, 1990; Merton, Fiske, & Kendall, 1990; Morgan, 1988; Stewart & Shamdsani, 1990). In addition to the information drawn from the above sources, I add to this synopsis information from my experience using focus groups.

Although the term *focus group* has been used to include a range of techniques, the general field of social science research has come to broadly conceptualize this technique as follows: using a semistructured group session, moderated by a group leader, held in an informal setting, with the purpose of collecting information on a designated topic. Although a session may provide group members with information and a sense of social support, the sessions are not primarily intended to provide education or emotional support. The collection of personal experiences and beliefs related to the designated topic is the purpose of a focus group.

The focus group technique is especially well suited for problems in health research where complex clinical issues are often best explored through a qualitative approach. Focus groups as the sole source of data or in addition to other qualitative or quantitative methods should be considered for:

Needs assessment: especially to explore a new concern or for new population

Development or refinement of instruments: especially to identify domains, to obtain natural vocabulary for item generation for questionnaires, and to assess cultural appropriateness

Enrichment and exploration of the interpretation of research results: particularly if results appear contradictory

Focus groups can be described in terms of the number of members per session, the demographic characteristics of the members, the topic of interest, and the amount of structure imposed by the leader. The most important characteristic, however, is the nature of the group itself as expressed through the interaction of the members, the flow of the discussion, and the evolution of the experiences described.

The *leader* of a focus group session may be someone other than the researcher. An experienced researcher does not necessarily have the skills needed for leading a focus group (Greenbaum, 1991; Ringo, 1992). In marketing research, it often is recommended that the leader be an external person who is not known to the researcher. This distance can enhance the objectivity of the data collection.

The *session structure* comes from the guideline questions developed by the researcher and the leader's style of guiding sessions. The amount of structure and leader guidance varies with the preferences and professional experiences of the researcher and of the group leader. The leader monitors the group interaction and adapts plans accordingly. For example, a group that seems stuck on one aspect may be guided to the next guideline question, or a session that drifts off the target may be guided back. Further, the group leader may choose to follow the group's lead because important data often arise unexpectedly. Often a co-leader is used to assist with the logistics and to take notes on nonverbal behavior for use in data analysis. The leader takes only minimal notes for use during the session, such as points to come back to in a rapidly moving session.

Confidentiality is a special concern of focus group research because the nature of the group session may elicit information more personal than the members anticipated. The leader has the responsibility to monitor and intercede appropriately. In addition to the potential issues arising from collecting information on sensitive topics, focus group members may not readily understand the research process and the rationale for audiotaping or videotaping. Future use of the data and conditions of confidentiality should be described simply and carefully. For example, in a study of HIV patients (Carey & Smith, 1992), the leaders promised to erase the tapes within 24 hours. Written informed consent is generally not required because participation is voluntary and taking part in a session constitutes consent.

The use of focus groups involves the sequential phases of preparation, implementation, analysis, and interpretation. Errors in an early phase will affect later phases. For example, if member recruitment in the preparation phase is inappropriate, the members' participation in the session will not be optimal and, therefore, analysis and interpretation will be compromised.

Phase 1: Preparation

Preparation includes study of the research topic and the development of guideline questions; selection and recruitment of group members; logistic arrangements, including food, room, and tape-recording equipment; and leader preparation.

The researcher explores the research topic and formulates broad concepts to be explored. From these concepts three or four guideline questions are formulated that are used to guide the session. Each of these broad areas generally includes a few subquestions. These guideline questions often are used to guide the initial development of themes or categories in data analysis.

The amount of preparation time needed for the focus group leader and the researcher varies with the availability of information on both the research topic and the culture of the members. Familiarity and uniqueness of the members' culture and the research topic need to be considered when planning optimal preparation time. Some exploration of the research topic and the culture of the population is necessary to develop the guideline questions. This information is necessary for the leader to understand group members' contributions and to probe appropriately during the session. In some studies the process may begin with interviews and use this information to formulate guideline questions.

The next major step in the focus group process is the *selection and recruitment of group members*. Members are selected on the basis of their common experience related to the research topic—for example, parents of a child with a terminal illness. Usually the members are strangers who have no expectation of future interaction. Generally members are homogeneous in terms of prestige or status, such as occupation, social class, age, education, and family characteristics. This homogeneity is useful because people are more likely to share information with others who are seen as similar (Krueger, 1988). If the group is too heterogenous, the lower status members will defer to higher status members and not contribute fully. These psychosocial factors are discussed more fully in the next section.

Recommendations on optimal *group size* vary from 5 to 12 per session. Factors to consider include the sensitivity and complexity of the topic, and the abilities, expectations, and needs of the group members. A person is more likely to feel comfortable being part of a small group than a large group. Also, with a small group of 4 to 6, each member has a greater opportunity to talk. This opportunity to talk is important for elderly or ill individuals who may have some problems in contributing readily in a group setting. With a small group, the leader can more easily manage the group dynamics, process the information, and attend to each member. The disadvantage is that conducting additional smaller groups is more labor intensive because data can be collected from fewer people per session. However, collection of better quality data from fewer participants is a wise choice for virtually any study.

The *logistics* are very important to the successful use of focus groups. The arrangements and ambience should be chosen thoughtfully. The room should be comfortable and afford privacy so that few interruptions will occur. For some studies it may be helpful to hold the sessions off-site—that is, away from the physical setting associated with the research topic. This distance provides a psychological break and may encourage sharing of information.

Of surprising importance is the effect of *food,* regardless of how expensive or generous. In my experience, brownies were a hit with the military personnel, bagels and coffee were appreciated by elder citizens for a morning session in a senior center, and gourmet cookies went well with high school students. Food facilitates presession conversation and provides group members with something to do.

Presession chatting, often around the food table, helps break the ice, allowing the group leader to assess the members' characteristics in order to arrange optimal seating. *Seating* can affect the dynamics of the group. For example, a person who appears outspoken can be placed next to the leader so that the leader can better guide the level of participation of that member. A shy or very quiet person can be seated directly across from the leader so that the leader can provide encouragement by making eye contact and using other nonverbal behavior.

Recording equipment should be arranged as unobtrusively as possible. After an introduction outlining the purpose of the research, the leader asks permission to audiotape or videotape the session and explains the helpfulness of not having to take extensive notes and the desire to catch the important details of each person's contributions.

Mental preparation of the group leader greatly affects the smooth running of the session. The leader should know the introduction and the guideline questions so that he or she does not have to refer to notes. The leader's topic preparation should be adequate enough to permit him or her to understand and probe for important details and to perceive idiosyncratic meanings in members' contributions. However, if too well versed, the leader may find it difficult to be open to information from the members that is contrary to his or her current knowledge. Logistics should be organized in advance so that the leader is not distracted and can maintain as alert and calm a mental posture as possible. A calm mental state is an asset for the intense job of processing the group interactions during the session.

Phase 2: Implementation

The skill of the leader is crucial to implementation of the focus group and, therefore, to the usefulness of the research data. *Establishing trust* and an accepting atmosphere is imperative. The session introduction includes the purpose of the study, the nature of the organization conducting the study, how members were selected, and the planned use of the data. This presentation enhances trust and helps establish a congenial atmosphere for optimal sharing. The introduction also includes rules for the session: no derogatory statements about another member's contributions, and all experiences are valid and legitimate. The leader trains the group members for their role informally, as well as formally. Unspoken expectations for group behavior are conveyed by encouraging and limiting participation as appropriate. For example, a member who is long-winded is curbed gently, and attention is directed to a quieter member.

The leader encourages responses, does not endorse or agree with comments, and remains neutral to the content by monitoring his or her nonverbal, as well as verbal, behavior. It is important to be open to contributions that are contrary to previous comments. Because interaction among members leads to more synergistic exchanges than leader-member interaction, the leader encourages members to respond to each other. The leader may ask a question such as, "Have any of you had a similar experience?" The leader continually weighs the potential to be gained by following leads from the group and thereby deviating from the guideline questions.

Complexity of data requires attention from the leader as the session progresses. The leader attends to the nonverbal, as well as verbal, communication, especially by looking for nonconcurrence. Also monitored is the sequential context of participation at the group level by evaluating the relationship of each member's contribution to the total interaction and at the individual level by assessing the consistency of contributions for each member.

Knowing when and how to probe is the most important aspect of guiding the session. By probing, I mean seeking further information, more details based on personal experience. Lack of agreement between verbal and nonverbal communications, and inconsistent contributions can be the bases for probing. Personal and specific details improve the credibility and general quality of the data. The leader should consider the following questions in deciding when to probe: Is this a plausible story? Are the members' contributions logically consistent? Does the nonverbal communication match the verbal? When a member provides a general description, the leader follows up with a request for more details. "Think back" is a common device to put the members in the frame of mind to provide details.

The leader tries to be aware of his or her own relevant experiences, as well as the needs and expectations of the group members. The leader's past experiences affect his or her perceptions and, therefore, how the session is guided. *Being aware* is crucial to being as neutral as possible to the content. Members may become very uncomfortable with a part of a session, and the leader needs to intercede. In spite of a clear statement of purpose, members may expect the leader to rectify past injustices related to the research topic, and that expectation needs to be corrected. The leader can listen and commiserate but should not try to rectify problems except in extreme circumstances. Generally, after finishing the discussion of a guideline question and before going to the next question, the leader feeds back a summary of the discussion to the group to check out his or her perceptions. This is an opportunity for the members to clarify and correct the information. The leader, of course, uses common sense and tact in this process of feedback.

Phase 3: Analysis and Interpretation

As one approaches analysis and interpretation, it is useful to keep in mind that the purpose of using the focus group technique is to understand, from the perspective of the research participants, the meaning and nature of the research topic as fully as possible. Like other qualitative data, focus group data cannot appropriately be lifted out of context. For this type of data, the context includes the psychosocial setting, which is discussed in the next section.

The analysis and interpretation of focus group data can be very complex, and a thorough explication is beyond the scope of this chapter. Analysis is similar, in general, to other qualitative data analysis with the added dimension of the group context. (See Glaser and Strauss, 1967, for a basic reference on the grounded theory approach to qualitative data analysis.) By applying appropriate qualitative approaches for systematic and rigorous analysis and incorporating the relevant psychosocial concepts, the researcher can draw meaning from the data. In this section I discuss a few issues unique to analysis of focus group data.

The concern of *generalization* for focus group data analysis is similar to this concern in other qualitative data analysis. Krueger (1988) suggested that generalizations are likely to be appropriate for people in settings similar to the focus group members. It may be useful to the researcher to be able to make statements of a broad nature, such as most caregivers of Alzheimer patients find respite care necessary.

A group has a chemistry and a dynamic that are greater than the sum of the members. In a different mix of members, the data collected could, and likely would, be different. Specific data are not readily comparable across groups. Therefore, detailed comparison across sessions is not appropriate. It is more appropriate to examine broad themes across sessions. Such data are subject to psychosocial factors but are not invalid in the traditional meaning of construct validity (Messick, 1989). The data from a focus group session can be thought of as potentially incompletely collected. What is collected, though possibly subject to some constraints, represents the reality of the experiences of the group members.

The purpose of a study guides the researcher in selecting the methods of analysis and interpretation for this type of data. These methods range from a broad approach with the purpose of identification of general concepts to a very detailed analysis of transcripts. For example, in the development of a survey questionnaire, the identification of significant content domains and natural vocabulary would not require intense analysis. However, a very detailed analysis could be required when using focus group data as the sole source of data in a study of the health care experiences of Hispanic women who have limited English language skills. Further, much useful information can be obtained by researchers who do not have qualitative training, who do not do intensive analysis, and who are not doing research per se. For example, in marketing studies, new ideas for product development could be obtained with a very cursory examination of focus group data. Health researchers could use this technique in a similar manner.

The guideline questions can serve as the initial categories and can provide a common structure for analysis across sessions. As the researcher listens to the tape recording, watches the videotape, and/or reads the transcript, he or she looks for the direction and magnitude of these categories, as well as additional categories that emerge, themes that transcend the categories, and patterns of relationships between categories, themes, and individual characteristics. When using transcripts of a focus group session, the researcher needs to be mindful of the total group setting, the nonverbal data, and changes and discrepancies in a member's contributions. In a more intense analysis of transcripts of audiotapes or videotapes, the effect of being in a group can be overlooked unless special attention is paid to incorporating data from notes.

A group member's contribution often will elicit another member's contribution on the same topic, and this interaction is a major advantage of the focus group technique. Unless specifically asked or probed for, however, a potential contribution may actually not be provided. In analysis, a category or theme cannot be assumed to be absent merely because no relevant responses were mentioned in a session. Therefore, simple counts are not appropriate for this type of analysis due to the nature of data from a group setting.

Psychological Factors and Their Implications

Members in a group are interactive, dynamic suppliers of information. Participation is interactive in the sense that a member's contribution exists in a social context affected by previous statements and other factors, such as conformity and censoring, that are discussed later in this section. The dynamic group process is affected by personal needs, group chemistry, and the skills of the leader. The potential for collecting rich data by using a group format is supported by empirical evidence on task performance in a group setting versus an individual setting. In experimental problem-solving situations, new ideas emerged from group settings that were not evident in prior individual performance (Hill, 1982; Sussman et al., 1991).

The interactional nature of a group has positive and negative aspects. The major *positive aspect*—the opportunity to collect rich, experiential information by using group interactions—is the unique contribution of the focus group technique. The *negative aspects* arise from psychosocial factors that potentially limit the quality of the data. To draw valid meaning from focus group data, it is important to understand the impact of these factors on the data collected in a group setting, as contrasted with the data collected in other formats. In focus group research, the impact of psychosocial factors cannot be teased out of the data; rather, they are part of the contextual fabric that provides rich details, as well as presents challenges in analyses. In this section relevant psychosocial factors and their impact on the nature of the data are discussed.

First Impression

The format of most focus group studies consists of a single session of members who are initially unknown to each other and to the leader. An understanding of the developmental stages of a group over time is, therefore, not relevant. However, understanding the process of forming a first impression is very important in understanding the group data.

Initial judgments of group members are based on very little information. Because they occur at the beginning of a social interaction, members' first impressions of each other affect their contributions greatly and affect how members behave toward each other throughout the session. For example, if one member assesses another as dominant, he or she will tend to be more submissive, will contribute less, and will be less likely to describe an experience that is contrary to previous contributions in the session.

Status from characteristics outside the group session is brought to a session, is used in forming first impressions, has an impact on the group interactions, and consequently affects the data elicited. The professional positions of the group members affect the way the contributions are perceived and responded to by the other group members. Often group members with higher paying professional jobs use more "talk time"; that is, more time is used for their contributions than for those of other members.

Two factors involved in forming a first impression are (a) the state of the person judging and (b) perceptual bias. The first factor, the state of the person judging, has an impact when a person tends to project his or her own feelings and tends to be more sensitive to specific issues that relate to his or her own emotional state. If the person forming the impression is fearful about a specific topic, such as risk for cardiovascular disease, he or she will tend to judge the other members as more fearful about risk for cardiovascular disease than if he or she were not fearful.

The second factor, perceptual bias, occurs when one trait strongly colors the total judgment of a person so that another person is seen in a consistent way as all good or all bad. This factor is demonstrated in the classical experimental work "What Is Beautiful Is Good" (Dion, Berscheid, & Walster, 1972). This halo effect is seen when a person with a high status occupation is judged as more honest or more perceptive, for example, than if he or she were of lesser occupational status. The opposite effect occurs when a person of low socioeconomic status, for example a homeless person, is judged as less believable. These biases can serve to inhibit or promote a member's responses.

Censoring and Conformity

The *major pitfall* of the focus group technique is the potential impact of censoring and conforming. These processes occur when a person adjusts his or her own behavior in response to personal impressions of other group members and in relation to his or her own needs and history. In conforming, a person elects to tailor his or her contributions to be in line with perceptions of the group members and/or the leader. In censoring, a person withholds potential contributions, often due to a lack of trust of the leader, or the other members, or the future use of the data. Not only is it possible that members could conform or censor their input to be socially acceptable but also they may actually mentally reconstruct or "cognitively reframe" their experience on the basis of the ongoing dialogue. The classic conformity experiments demonstrated that having just one ally (someone who agrees with you) will often be adequate for a person to speak up about contrary information (Asch, 1951).

An example of censoring was evident in the contrast between focus groups my colleague and I conducted with HIV-positive military personnel (Carey & Smith, 1992). In the first setting the group members were not known to me, although my colleague knew many of them from his work on the hospital ward. I am certain a major factor in the rapport that was readily established was the fact that focus group members were aware that my colleague is HIV positive and medically retired from the military. This commonality and the fact that we both were known to the hospital personnel enabled us to collect information regarding drug use and sexual behavior. At each of the sessions, we obtained permission to tape-record and promised to erase the tapes within 24 hours. We had expected censoring, and although we are aware that some censoring could have occurred, we were surprised at the level of sensitive data we collected.

In contrast, when we went to an out-of-state hospital operated by a different branch of the military service, we had a different experience. Although we were introduced by my colleague's local counterpart who had arranged the session, we were not known to the other hospital staff or patients. At this session, we noted more reticence in contributing and less detail. Of particular interest was the nonverbal behavior that was characteristic of the outwardly cooperative and compliant group members—for example, arms folded across the chest, leaning back in the chair, less than usual eye contact, and few nods of agreement in response to others' contributions. As the session progressed, we noted a change in behavior toward more participation. We believe this change was probably due to increased trust in the leaders and in each other as the session progressed. In this focus group session, we were told of a recent internal security investigation that involved deception. The group members were, appropriately, very suspicious of any new endeavor such as this focus group.

Factors in Participation

Factors that affect conformity and censoring also affect other aspects of group participation. Being aware of the potential influence of these factors allows the researcher to better plan the sessions and interpret the data. These factors act at the levels of the individual and the group, and they interact across levels. Factors related primarily to the individual level include trust, deviancy, anonymity, commitment to own opinion expressed publicly, self-esteem, previous experience with groups, experience related to the topic, gender, affiliation need, concern for being evaluated, and need for social comparison (from Hastie, 1986). Group level factors are group size, group unanimity, history of agreement, and group cohesiveness.

Factors that have been demonstrated to influence group participation in studies of small group productivity are plausible influences in focus group sessions. These include incentives, threats, competition, task familiarization, coordination of members' input by the leader, and strategies for task solution (Hill, 1982; Laughlin, 1991). Also the age, ethnicity, and social class of the members and the leader are likely influences.

Ameliorations and Limitations

The focus group technique is not a consensus-building technique. However, some members may interpret their role in this way and may believe that each guideline question needs to be resolved by mutual agreement. A person uses the opinion of others in forming his or her own opinion (Krueger, 1988). The tendency toward consensus is particularly a problem when a member has not yet formed an opinion and his or her contributions are therefore likely to be affected by information in the group session. This "bandwagon" effect lessens the meaningfulness of the data.

Also of concern is exaggeration. In my experience and in my knowledge of others' work, exaggeration does not occur often and is fairly easy to recognize. An example was noted in a focus group session of senior citizens held at a residential center. These people did know each other and would have interaction in the future. The topic was health status after ambulatory surgery, and the purpose was to understand experiences in order to develop a questionnaire to be mailed to Medicare patients (Carey, 1990). One member described an experience that was inconsistent and implausible medically. The other members gently but firmly questioned him, and he revised his contribution. If the group members had not questioned the speaker, the leader could have done so. In choosing between the conflicting versions, I find the detailed, consistent version is the most creditable.

The social context of the focus group adds complexity to the qualitative data analysis. It is important to integrate session notes with the transcript in order to appreciate meaning that is not readily apparent in words. Affect, body language, and the sequential nature of the context generally are captured best in notes not in the transcript. Because group effects cannot be teased out of the data, they need attention in analysis. Group effects are explored best at the macro level, as contrasted with a micro level analysis of each contribution (or speech utterance) (Carey & Smith, in press). The more intensive analysis will tend to miss the focus on the group effects unless special efforts are made.

In evaluating the quality of the data, the researcher should consider the pattern within a member and within the group context. Being alert for possibility of conformity, the researcher should attend to the data early in the session and cautiously interpret changes after another member's related input. If censoring is thought to occur, such data may be interpreted as a lower bound of potential data.

The researcher can modify troublesome effects at least to some extent. A wealth of knowledge gained from experience and based on solid social psychology principles is found in a revised edition of the classic text by Merton, Fiske, and Kendall (1990). As suggested by these authors, the researcher can minimize the negative aspects and maximize the advantages by attending to the basic tenets: retrospection (think back to place the members in the context of the experience), range (breadth of experiences), specificity (detailed description), and personal context (individual meaning of actual experience).

The focus group technique is a useful research technique, and participants have reported that they find the sessions enjoyable, supportive, informative, and provide a sense of commonality of experience. The opportunity to have a voice in the topic of study makes participants feel important and empowered.

References

Asch, J. E. (1951). Effects of group pressure upon the modification and distortion of judgment. In H. Guetzkow (Ed.), *Groups, leadership, and men* (pp. 117-190). Pittsburgh: Carnegie Press.

Carey, M. A. (1990, August). *Cognitive aspects of questionnaire design: Surveying the elderly.* Paper presented at the American Psychological Association Conference, Boston, MA.

Carey, M. A., & Smith, M. W. (1992). Enhancement of validity through qualitative approaches: Incorporating the patient's perspective. *Evaluation and the Health Professions, 15*(4), 107-114.

Carey, M. A., & Smith, M. W. (in press). Keeping the group in focus in focus group research. *Qualitative Health Research.*

Dion, K., Berscheid, E., & Walster, E. (1972). What is beautiful is good. *Journal of Personality and Social Psychology, 24,* 285-290.

Flaskerud, J., & Calvillo, E. (1991). Beliefs about AIDS, health, and illness among low-income Latina women. *Research in Nursing and Health, 14*(6), 431-438.

Glaser, B., & Strauss, A. (1967). *The discovery of grounded theory.* Hawthorne, NY: Aldine.

Greenbaum, T. (1991). Outside moderators maximize focus group results. *Public Relations Journal, 47*(9), 31-32.

Hastie, R. (1986). Experimental evidence on group accuracy. In B. Grosman & G. Owen (Eds.), *Information pooling and group decision making* (pp. 129-264). Greenwich, CT: JAI.

Hill, G. (1982). Group versus individual performance: Are N + 1 heads better than one? *Psychological Bulletin, 91*(3), 517-539.

Irwin, K., Bertrand, J., Mibandumba, N., Mbuyl, K. et al. (1991). Knowledge, attitudes and beliefs about HIV infection and AIDS among healthy factory workers and their wives, Kinshasa, Zaire. *Social Science and Medicine, 32*(8), 917-930.

Kingry, R., Tiedje, L., & Freidman, L. (1990). Focus groups: A research technique for nursing. *Nursing Research, 39*(2), 124-125.

Krueger, R. (1988). *Focus groups: A practical guide for applied research.* Newbury Park, CA: Sage.

Laughlin, P. (1991). Collective versus individual induction: Recognition of truth, rejection of error, and collective information processing. *Journal of Personality and Social Psychology, 61*(1), 50-67.

Merton, R., Fiske, M., & Kendall, P. (1956). *The focused interview.* New York: Free Press.

Merton, R., Fiske, M., & Kendall, P. (1990). *The focused interview: A manual of problems and procedures* (2nd ed.). New York: Free Press.

Messick, S. (1989). Validity. In R. Linn (Ed.), *Educational measurement* (pp. 13-103). New York: Macmillan.

Morgan, D. (1988). *Focus groups as qualitative research.* Newbury Park, CA: Sage.

Nyamathi, A., & Shuler, P. (1990). Focus group interview: A research technique. *Journal of Advanced Nursing, 15,* 1281-1288.

Ringo, S. (1992). Only a real pro has skills to be a moderator. *Marketing News, 26*(1), FG1-FG2.

Stewart, D., & Shamdsani, P. (1990). *Focus group: Theory and practice.* Newbury Park, CA: Sage.

Sussman, S., Burton, D., Clyde, W., Stacy, A. et al. (1991). Use of focus groups in developing an adolescent tobacco use cessation program: Collective norm effects. *Journal of Applied Social Psychology, 21*(21), 1772-1782.

Dialogue

Using Videotaped Data

STERN It's interesting, but I think there is a caveat. There is always an editorial process that goes between the camera and the situation. I'm mindful of the riots at San Francisco State when I was a student there. When I walked out into the quad, I saw police on the roof with automatic guns pointed down at this crowd of students. When I saw it at home on the video screen, I saw a bunch of angry students and nothing of the context. So there's always a distortion.

BOTTORFF I feel that I got the best of both worlds, because I spent a lot of time on the unit before, during, and after the taping was going on. Although I wasn't formally doing participant observation, so to speak, I think informally I was. And this gave us a more complete perspective on patient behavior.

STERN So what you say is that you need a broader lens.

BOTTORFF I think that was helpful, but that is not to say that you could not use the video data alone and answer some very interesting questions.

LEININGER I think this is so important in nursing. When you think about such an opportunity we have in the observation area, really it's probably one of the most difficult skills we have [to acquire] even at the doctoral level—how do you do observations?—and now that there is technology to help do this, it is an excellent opportunity to explicate the method(s).

STERN But does that make it more real? If it's not real in the nontechnological experience of folks, is it truly how they think of their lives?

MORSE I don't see that slowing the tape down distorts it. I see a parallel between this and the transcription for the analysis of verbal data. That allows you to get at things that are probably implicitly recognized by the two people in the video that may not be recognized by a regular observer at normal speed.

STERN When I use the term *distort,* I don't necessarily mean it negatively. It's just not real life.

MORSE What it does is that it brings out these other layers.

MAY I felt as Phyllis did. When you described the interaction, they
could not remember it, but when they saw it, they remembered. I
think the same thing happens when you slow down a videotape;
of course, you will see things. The question is, at what level of
meaning is the seeing? Do we signify it? I'm not saying it's a bad
thing. I'm just saying that it changes what is available to the analyst.

MORSE I think the answer is, and there is a lot of evidence to show that
it is perceived and is a part of the interaction. Slowing it down and
looking at it in other ways makes it available to the analyst, just as
going through the transcript line by line and looking at the actual
meaning does. Just as if we wanted to recall what was said this
morning, we couldn't remember, but if we listened to the tape, we
would remember all the jokes.

STERN But w h a t   i f   w e   s p o k e   v e r y   s l o w l y . . .

13

Using Videotaped Recordings in Qualitative Research

JOAN L. BOTTORFF

Videotaping is an approach that is evolving, not only for health sciences, but for other disciplines as well. So I am not sure whether we have any definitive procedures or rules at this stage, but we are working on them. I started writing this chapter in the terms of some of the uses and advantages of using this approach, and then some of the "how to's" and things to be considered when using videotapes.

Qualitative researchers have made extensive use of direct observation to study behaviors and human experiences as they occur in the course of daily life in a variety of settings and contexts. In particular, the methodology of participant observation depends on direct observation as a basic strategy for data collection (Jorgensen, 1989). However, some circumstances call for observation beyond conventional strategies, such as when behaviors of interest are of very short duration, the distinctive character of events change moment by moment, or more detailed and precise descriptions of behaviors and/or processes than is possible with ordinary participant observation are required. Although photographs and film have been used in the past to enhance observations, advances in audiovisual technology have increased significantly the flexibility and ease with which behavior can be videotaped and analyzed, effectively opening new avenues for research. In particular, researchers conducting deductive quantitative studies of behavior have made extensive use of videotaped recordings (VTR). However, VTR can be a rich source of data for qualitative research as well if its use is accompanied by an awareness of its limitations, requirements, and assumptions. These considerations gradually are becoming more clearly defined as we attempt to use VTR to help us undertake more detailed observation and analysis of behaviors than has been possible by using more traditional observational methods. In this chapter I review the advantages and limitations of using VTR and provide some suggestions, based on my experience, on how VTR can be used in qualitative research.

The examples used are primarily from the nursing research literature, although VTR have been used to extend observational research in other disciplines. In particular, I draw on my own research experience in using VTR to study the ways nurses use touch to care for and comfort patients (Bottorff, 1992). This research was based on the assumption that, to increase understanding of touch as a dyadic interaction, detailed observations of a wide range of verbal and nonverbal behaviors (in addition to touch), including the timing and sequencing of behaviors as they occurred in unstaged daily nurse-patient interactions, were needed. Because the concept of *touch* is still poorly understood (Estabrooks, 1987; Estabrooks & Morse, 1992; Jones & Yarbrough, 1985; Weiss, 1979, 1986), an inductive qualitative approach was used to identify the significant behaviors that should be observed in touch episodes and to facilitate the development of rich descriptions that could serve as a conceptual basis for productive deductive research. To accurately record and examine the complexity of behaviors making up interactions that include touch events, film footage and sound track evidence of the interactions were needed for repeated viewing. VTR of nurse-patient interactions in a naturalistic setting were collected and analyzed to describe the patterns of touch in the context of interactions that are characteristic of nursing practice.

VTR: Advantages and Limitations

Grimshaw (1982) described the two principal advantages of using audiovisual recordings (such as VTR) as a research resource as being density and permanence. In comparison to the participant observer, who has access to all verbal and nonverbal behaviors that participants demonstrate but cannot simultaneously monitor all relevant cues or remember most when the moment has passed, VTR offer a unique advantage. In fact, the density of data collected with VTR is greater than with other kinds of recordings. It is important to recognize, however, that no record is ever complete, including VTR (Grimshaw, 1982). There are at least three reasons for this. First, any recording of behavior is incomplete because it is selective and because mechanical limitations are inherent in all recording devices and human observers. For example, microphones may not pick up all verbal behaviors, and individual cameras focused on facial expressions will not be able to record simultaneously gross body movements. When other cameras or equipment are added, a point is reached when the interaction becomes constrained (due to increased reactivity), again resulting in an incomplete record. Second, with VTR, as with human observers, it is not possible to discern the subjective content of the behavior being observed. Third, with recording devices and, to some extent, with participant observers, there is no sensitizing awareness of the historical context of the observed behaviors. Although some accommodation can be made for each of these deficiencies, it would nonetheless be erroneous to assume that VTR provide a complete record, despite the amount of potentially useful information that can be captured on VTR in comparison to other records. This limitation, however, may not be a major one because some information is carried through several channels of behavior (Grimshaw, 1982). More often than not, more information is captured on VTR than can be used and interpreted easily.

The second primary advantage of VTR is permanence, making it possible to review events as often as necessary in a variety of ways (e.g., real time, slow motion, frame by frame, forward, backward), each time directing attention to different features of what is occurring. In this way, no longer constrained by the sequential occurrence of events in real time, instances of similar recorded events at different points in time can be compared and contrasted easily. This capacity for a more thorough and complete analysis than is possible by using other means of observation is one of the major strengths of using VTR. In addition, the opportunity for deliberation prior to making interpretive judgments is enhanced, dependency on frequently occurring events as the best source of data is decreased, the analysis can be demonstrated to others, replications can be made, and alternative hypotheses can be evaluated (Erickson, 1992; Grimshaw, 1982). VTR also can be made available for secondary analysis to address entirely different questions, if this procedure has been negotiated beforehand with participants.

Two principal limitations are associated with the use of VTR: (a) the absence of contextual data beyond what is recorded and (b) the lack of opportunity to test emerging interpretive theories as an active participant in the scene (Erickson, 1992). These limitations may be overcome, to some extent, by collecting and analyzing demographic and historical data and by combining other data collection techniques (e.g., open-ended interviews, participant observation) with VTR. In my research on nurses' use of touch, the limitations of VTR were clearly apparent. Although the behaviors that comprise touching gestures could be observed directly, some dimensions of touch and touching are essentially private and, for the most part, unobservable. Inferences relating to emotional or affective states can be made with some degree of certainty from observational data, as has been done in studies of facial expressions (Ekman, 1992; Ekman & Friesen, 1975). The use of direct observation alone, however, was insufficient to understand all of the dimensions of touch. Consequently other data collection methods were used to provide supplementary data. In this study, tape-recorded, unstructured interviews with patients and selected nurses were conducted. Short videotaped segments were used in the interviews to elicit perceptions of the interaction, the meaning of touch, and subjective reactions to the experience. This technique was particularly useful because the videotaped segments were effective in helping participants remember the events and frequently stimulated valuable comments, thereby enriching and augmenting interview data. Others have used this approach and, as a result, were able to extend their analyses in interesting ways (McKay, Barrow, & Roberts, 1990; Pepler, 1984). The data from the interviews in my own study provided insight into the subjective experiences associated with touch, facilitated the interpretation of observed behavior patterns, and were used to validate analyses. Demographic and clinical data, along with field notes, were used to provide a solid contextual base for viewing and analyzing the interactions.

The collection and analysis of data by using VTR can be an expensive and time-consuming undertaking. Costs may be reduced by using equipment that is already in place, by renting equipment, and by using videotapes that are being collected for another purpose (e.g., for surveillance or quality assurance in hospital settings). In addition, the costs of data collection may be offset, to some extent, by the fact that the videotapes are likely to be a rich source of data for secondary analysis. Because most researchers using VTR focus on complex behavior patterns, however, the analysis remains labor intensive and, more frequently than not, is very time consuming. It is not unusual for 5 minutes of interaction to take 2 or 3 hours to analyze.

Optimal Data

Despite general agreement on the potential usefulness of VTR for research, there is less consensus on what constitutes maximally useful and valid data or how they should be collected. Although how and what is videotaped is tied inextricably to the questions asked and the behaviors of interest, several considerations are common to any study involving the use of VTR. Not unlike other data collection methods, researchers using VTR must strive to obtain as accurate a reproduction of events and behaviors as mechanically and humanly possible. This endeavor means minimizing distortions of observed behaviors and being vigilant for a wide range of threats to validity.

The key technical requirements of any VTR to be used for research purposes are a clear picture and clear sound. Making careful decisions regarding the type of equipment to be used and checking lighting conditions, microphone and camera placements, and sound and picture quality before regular recording begins is crucial. Continuing developments in audiovisual technology will have an impact on these decisions. Because it is essential that the time be recorded in hours, minutes, and seconds (or even smaller units of time in some instances) on VTR for the purpose of analysis, videocassette recorders with this function or time-date generators must be used. Also it is wise to use an additional videocassette recorder at the time of recording to provide backup VTR if researchers cannot afford the risk of losing data with a faulty videotape or machine.

The merits of filming with a fixed or moveable camera are still under debate and may depend on the focus and purpose of the study, the type of setting, and the characteristics of the participants. For example, in a study of Alzheimer patients in a nursing home, Lucero, Hutchinson, Leger-Krall, and Wilson (1993) used portable cameras to record the wandering behaviors of patients. In contrast, fixed cameras have been used successfully when the participants are likely to be more stationary (e.g., in studies of maternal-infant interaction or restrained nursing home patients). Alternatively, when participants move within a confined setting and the presence of an operator may influence behavior, fixed cameras equipped with remote control pan/tilt mechanisms may be the best alternative. Whichever method is used, keeping all of the bodies of the participants within the visual frame as much as possible makes for the most comprehensive research document (Erickson, 1992).

In my own study of nurse-patient interactions, the use of two video cameras proved to be effective and necessary. By using the remote control pan/tilt and a video switcher, it was possible to keep the nurse and patient in view, regardless of which side of the bed or where in the room the nurse was working, without drawing attention to the act of videotaping. Occasionally there was some delay in switching or moving cameras to obtain an adequate view and, therefore, some data were lost, especially if the nurse or patient was moving quickly (although this was not significant).

It is important to note that considerations regarding the type and placement of equipment always involves some trade-offs. For example, in my study the particular placement of cameras easily captured behaviors displayed by the patient. However, the nurse's face was not always clearly visible, especially when he or she focused directly on the patient with his or her back to the cameras. Repositioning cameras to capture these behaviors would have resulted in the loss of other data (e.g., the patient's face). Adding another camera was not considered to be a reasonable option because of cost and the fact that three or more cameras in one small private room would have been overwhelming for most participants. A partial solution when two cameras are used in similar situations may be the use of a "picture-in-picture" monitor or a split screen so that both images can be viewed simultaneously.

Because boundaries marking the "beginnings" and "endings" of events are often not clearly defined and require judgment calls by researchers, it is usually advisable to begin recording prior to the event of interest and to continue recording a few minutes after the event appears to have concluded. In some situations it simply may be more efficient to make a continuous VTR rather than attempt to record specific instances of behavior. This solution may be particularly relevant for qualitative researchers who may be unable to predict at this stage of their research when behaviors or events will occur or which behaviors will be of most interest. The additional cost involved in purchasing extra videotapes is often minimal and more than compensated for by a substantial reduction in the risk of missing important data. Nevertheless the time required for analysis can be significantly increased when this approach is used.

The representativeness of behaviors captured with VTR is influenced primarily by observer effects. Natural field observations with the naked eye or with a camera can have an intrusive effect on the persons who are observed and may change their behavior (Gross, 1991; Kendon, 1979; Lytton, 1971; Scaife, 1979; Scherer & Ekman, 1982), given that ethical constraints in most, if not all, situations do not permit covert VTR. Researchers must be aware of the factors that influence self-monitoring and determine the extent to which monitoring should be anticipated and allowed for in analyses.

In my study of nurse-patient interactions, VTR were collected in a clinical setting where research activity was an accepted and valued norm for both patients and staff. Nevertheless, because the use of VTR was an unusual practice in this clinical setting, we expected that people would be conscious about the way they looked and concerned about what they said or did while being videotaped. Because the success of the project depended on the voluntary cooperation of staff, patients, and visitors, it was extremely important to deal with these concerns. Several steps were taken to enhance acceptance of and reduce reactivity to the recording process. First, all participants were informed of the rationale for using VTR and how data collection would proceed so that they were prepared for the presence of the investigator and the recording equipment. Not surprisingly, the growing use of video cameras in homes, at sports events, and in business were important in facilitating the acceptance of explanations and justifications of the use of VTR in research. In addition, the video equipment was installed 1 month prior to the commencement of videotaping to help staff habituate to the presence of the cameras. Second, to protect participants from embarrassment or administrative repercussions, assurances were given that the VTR would remain confidential and that if photographs from the recordings were used in final reports, individual names would not be revealed. Third, the video cameras used for this research were placed on the wall in a patient room and were monitored from an adjacent area in an attempt to minimize the intrusiveness of the cameras, interference in patient care, and the influence of the presence of the investigator. Fourth, each patient was videotaped for a period of 72 hours, and nurses were videotaped for the duration of their shift, often over several days with either the same or different patients. It was unlikely, therefore, that participants would maintain atypical behaviors for the entire time they were being videotaped. Finally, the investigator was able to establish a relationship with participants that helped allay any anxiety or apprehension about being involved in this study. This last strategy was important and underlines the importance of following ethically responsible strategies to negotiate entry, not unlike those engaged in by skilled participant observers.

Throughout the data collection process, reactivity was monitored and the extent to which self-monitoring occurred was assessed in interviews with participants at the conclusion of the VTR. Comments to the investigator by a few staff members (e.g., "Are we likely to get an Academy Award?" "How am I doing?") reflected some of their sensitivity during data collection. However, all of the nurses who viewed a sample of their interactions with patients captured on videotape during follow-up interviews indicated that the selected episodes represented their usual way of doing things and that though they may have been self-conscious about the videotaping when they first entered the room, this quickly disappeared.

Similarly patients and their visitors were found to pay little attention to the fact that videotaping was in progress. Indications that participants simply "forgot about the cameras" because they were too busy or involved in their ongoing activities to worry about them are supported by others using similar videotaping methods in clinical settings (Morse & McHutchion, 1991) and other contexts (Grimshaw, 1982). It is also important to note that although some self-monitoring occurred, recorded behaviors were not recognized as atypical by participants or found to be unsuitable for analysis.

In summary, the problem of distortion of behaviors related to the use of VTR appeared to have been minimized in this study, with no elaborate technical efforts to reduce the visibility of recording. In settings where the use of video cameras are commonplace, reactivity will be less of a problem for researchers. For example, in many hospital emergency rooms, the activities of staff are videotaped on a daily basis for quality assurance programs.

Ethical Considerations

Proposals involving studies using VTR are scrutinized very closely by ethics review committees to ensure that the rights of participants are protected. In addition to the usual concerns surrounding informed consent, confidentiality is an important ethical issue. Strategies to maintain confidentiality (e.g., by protecting identities, restricting access to VTR) are critical to reducing the risk of harm related to embarrassment, and administrative or legal punishment to those studied (Erickson, 1992). In addition, procedures for informing participants about when videotaping is occurring must be delineated clearly, as well as how participants can stop the videotaping if they change their mind or wish some time out.

In videotaping nurse-patient interactions, the provision for time-out requests was important and usually involved intimate nursing care activities (such as bathing) or activities related to toileting. Because of the number of people who entered the patient's room during the usual course of the day, it was also necessary to make provision for accommodating those individuals who did not want to participate in the study with procedures for stopping the recording while they were in the room. Although the analysis of patterns of touching is limited by these missing data, it would not have been possible to do the study without this provision.

In some situations it may be necessary to use video editors to "erase" identifying features by distorting facial images to protect the identity of participants. Although important data may be lost with this process, researchers may be willing to make this compromise if the only remaining alternative is that the research cannot be conducted at all.

Data Analysis

As with other forms of qualitative research, some analytic work begins while the researcher is in the field. For example, analytic decisions underlie determining which events, persons, or behaviors are to be recorded or moving to greater visual or audio selectivity as data collection proceeds (Erickson, 1992). Most of the analytic work, however, takes places after the VTR are completed.

There are major differences in the theoretical positions and analytic strategies among researchers who work with VTR (e.g., see Birdwhistell, 1970; Duncan & Fiske, 1977; Scheflen, 1973), and some researchers argue that the analysis of VTR requires new theoretical assumptions, methodological procedures, and criteria for evaluation (Hood, McDermott, & Cole, 1980).

The approach to analysis described here is derived primarily from *ethology,* a disciplined observational method that facilitates the close study of behavior under natural conditions. This method, used in studying the behavior of insects, fish, birds, and other animals, has its origin in zoology and is demonstrated clearly in the classic studies by Lorenz, Tinbergen, and Pavlov (Eibl-Eibesfeldt, 1989). Recognizing that the ethologist's techniques of careful observation, including the "intent and candid gaze to which ethologists owe their success" (Medwar, 1976, p. 501), could be used to extend our understanding of human behavior, researchers have adapted ethological methods to the study of human behavior, as evidenced by their use in fields such as comparative psychology (especially in the study of child behavior), education, anthropology, psychiatry, and, more recently, nursing (Bateson & Hinde, 1976; Morse & Bottorff, 1990; Wolcott, 1992).

Ethological research includes both qualitative and quantitative approaches to the study of behavior (Slater, 1978). Characteristically ethological investigations begin with an inductive descriptive phase to identify and describe important segments and regularities in behavior. Much of the work of early ethologists reflected this inductive start, and their often lengthy but rich descriptions provided new insights into a variety of puzzling behavior patterns and their functional significance (Tinbergen, 1963). Many ethologists now have directed their attention to conducting more structured deductive and quantitative studies dealing with the causal explanation of observations. This trend, as well as the tendency for scientific journals to limit the amount of descriptive material reported, has decreased the amount of attention directed to the initial phase of ethology. Nevertheless its importance still is recognized as a foundation for quantifying behavior (Blurton Jones, 1972; Drummond, 1981; Eibl-Eibesfeldt, 1989; Hartmann & Wood, 1990; Tinbergen, 1963).

The methods of analysis discussed here take direction from the first inductive phase that characterizes ethology. Because the selection and description of relevant contours and boundaries in the naturally occurring flux of behavior are essentially an inductive process involving a sensitive and intuitive assessment and interpretation of behaviors using various levels of abstraction and integration (Drummond, 1981; Eibl-Eibesfeldt, 1989; Fourcher, 1979), this phase is referred to as *qualitative ethology*. To make these discoveries, ethologists approach behaviors as occurring in a particular context and think themselves into the minds of their subjects (a feat, some argue, that may involve a careful use of anthropomorphism in some studies of animals) to get a sense of what is "important" to the subject being observed (Bekoff & Jamieson, 1991; Fisher, 1991; Fourcher, 1979). This descriptive task involves more than compilation of an inventory of the objective manifestations of behavior (e.g., muscular movements). Observations also are used to draw conclusions about the organization of behavior. The ultimate aim of qualitative ethology is the development of an *ethogram,* a detailed textual description of the behavior patterns under study in natural settings (Eibl-Eibesfeldt, 1989; Martin & Bateson, 1986).

Although there is no consensus on what level behavioral analysis should begin, the starting point is the concrete event (Eibl-Eibesfeldt, 1989). Therefore VTR can be used to identify and characterize the most elemental behaviors, which, in turn, would be used to construct higher levels of behavior. Or as others may prefer, the VTR can be used to analyze behavior by moving downward through the behavioral organization, starting with the identification of complex goal-directed behavior and analyzing these to identify their component parts. It would appear, at this stage, that many qualitative researchers analyzing VTR choose the latter and, therefore, the guidelines suggested here for data analysis reflect this preference.

In qualitative ethology, the analysis of VTR begins not unlike other types of qualitative analysis, in an unstructured fashion to identify specific recurring behavioral patterns as units from the flow of behaviors observed (Lehner, 1979; Rosenblum, 1978). As VTR are reviewed, the researcher watches, listens, and asks questions about the recorded events to delineate distinct behavioral clusters or interactional segments. Such questions include, "What is going on here?" "How does this behavioral response or interaction differ from another?" "What are the characteristics of this type of response or interaction?" Writing the equivalent of field notes to describe observed activities, indicating verbal and nonverbal behaviors that may be of interest and the location of the event on the VTR for future reference, is helpful. To facilitate the search for events of interest, it is helpful to have a log of the major events that have been captured on videotapes, along with the time that each event was recorded, the counter number from the VCR, and any comments the researcher wishes to add.

Using this process to delineate behavioral clusters in my own study of nurse-patient interaction, I noted that interactions differed in nurse-patient proximity, the degree to which the nurse focused on the patient and/or caretaking tasks, and the ways patients participated in the interaction. Four recurring clusters of behaviors based on the apparent focus of the nurse in the interaction were identified (Bottorff & Morse, in press). Referred to as "types of attending," they were labeled *doing more, doing for, doing with,* and *doing tasks.* Segments of interactions that appeared to reflect the characteristics of each cluster were grouped. For ease of analysis, they could be dubbed onto a separate tape.

At the next stage, selected strips of the VTR in each grouping are studied intensely, with attention paid to subtle changes in behavior to identify boundaries in that segment's recorded behaviors and the important constituents of each behavior pattern. Verbatim transcripts of VTR also can be used to facilitate the analysis of the content and the expression of the vocalizations and linking these with nonverbal behaviors. Although transcriptions do not need to be sophisticated for some purposes, innovative computer-aided methods of transcribing videotaped speech and body motion are now available (e.g., Duncan & Sayre, 1991).

During this stage of analysis in my study of nurse-patient interactions, notations were made concerning who initiated the interaction, the condition of the patient, the use of eye contact, the proximity of the nurse and patient, the content of the conversation, the characteristics of the touch that was used, how and why the interaction ended, and all other relevant verbal and nonverbal behaviors. Interaction segments in each category then were compared and contrasted to determine consistencies and variations in this pattern of interaction as it was used with different patients, in different contexts, and by different nurses. For example, it was noted that the use of attending patterns did not depend entirely on the task being performed or the individual characteristics of the nurse.

The process of intensive and extensive observation is key to recognizing regularities of behavior (Kendon, 1979; Scaife, 1979) because confidence in identifying regularities increases if they are viewed repeatedly and in a variety of contexts. The use of

VTR definitely facilitates this process. However, the role of the researcher in recognizing and selecting regularities should not be underestimated. For example, perceptual biases, theoretical perspectives, or sampling techniques could lead to inadequate recognition and coverage of important regularities (Drummond, 1981; Eibl-Eibesfeldt, 1989). In addition, novel sampling techniques, such as using various playback speeds, could disclose new patterns not immediately apparent during normal observation or viewing (Eibl-Eibesfeldt, 1989; Scaife, 1979). Higher order regularities in behavior may be revealed by using the fast-motion procedure. Similarly, by viewing videotapes in slow motion or frame by frame, subtle changes in behavior may become apparent and, therefore, available for analysis. Although some may have reservations about the validity of behavior patterns recognized by using these techniques, the latter is not unlike the process of analyzing verbatim transcripts line by line in other types of qualitative research. Furthermore, Drummond (1981) argued that patterns or units of behavior identified at any speed are "natural" and valid if the study of them enhances our understanding of behavior.

From the preceding analysis, an ethogram or detailed description of the patterns of behavior observed is developed. In addition to the characteristics of behavior, these analytic descriptions include details or interpretations of the function, conditions, and consequences of each behavior and any variations noted. In some situations it may be possible to validate the analysis with participants or others who have similar experiences. Several examples of descriptions of behavior that have been developed by using qualitative ethology are available (Bottorff, in press; Bottorff & Morse, in press; Solberg & Morse, 1991).

The advantages of using a qualitative approach to analyze observational data in the form of VTR should now be more apparent. The use of qualitative methods ensures that the context in which particular behaviors or interactions occur is preserved and, therefore, can be used to enrich descriptions of behavioral patterns. In other words, it is not merely the presence or absence of behaviors that is important in qualitative ethology, but the interpretation of behaviors within the context in which they occur. It becomes possible to identify changes in the meaning of any item of behavior according to the relationship it has with other behaviors that occur concurrently, as well as sequentially (Kendon, 1979). Also, because the behavior is analyzed in context, the likelihood of being able to identify possible antecedents and consequences of behavioral or interactional patterns is enhanced. In addition, because a full range of behaviors is captured in VTR, they all can be subject to analysis and reanalysis. It is not only unnecessary to exclude prematurely any aspect of behavior from our analysis of VTR but also unwise to do so. As Scheflen (1966) stated, "We do not decide beforehand what is trivial, what is redundant, or what alters the system. This is a *result* of the research" (p. 270). From this point of view, VTR of behavior are essential to investigate patterns of behavior or interaction.

Despite the advantages of using VTR, this method should not be used to answer all questions involving direct observation. But in situations where informants are unable to report on their behavior (or that of others) reliably, or a large amount of detail is required to answer questions of interest, or observers are unable to record behaviors in sufficient detail, VTR effectively will broaden the possibilities for analysis of behavior. The success of any project using VTR depends on careful planning and the expertise of the researcher. If the researchers have not used VTR in their investigations before, they would be well advised to work closely with others who have been involved in this type of research. Although using VTR in qualitative research is a complex and technically demanding process, the potential this method holds for extending our understanding of behavior and illuminating new problems should not be underestimated.

References

Bateson, P. P. G., & Hinde, R. A. (Eds.). (1976). *Growing points in ethology.* Cambridge, UK: Cambridge University Press.

Bekoff, M., & Jamieson, D. (1991). Reflective ethology, applied philosophy, and the moral status of animals. In P. P. G. Bateson & P. H. Klopher (Eds.), *Perspectives in ethology* (Vol. 9, pp. 1-47). New York: Plenum.

Birdwhistell, R. L. (1970). *Kinesics and context.* Philadelphia: University of Pennsylvania Press.

Blurton Jones, N. (1972). Characteristics of ethological studies of human behavior. In N. Blurton Jones (Ed.), *Ethological studies of child behaviour* (pp. 3-33). Cambridge, UK: Cambridge University Press.

Bottorff, J. L. (1992). *Nurse-patient interaction: Observations of touch.* Unpublished doctoral dissertation, University of Alberta, Edmonton, Alberta, Canada.

Bottorff, J. L. (in press). Caring for cancer patients: The use and meaning of touch. *Oncology Nursing Forum.*

Bottorff, J. L., & Morse, J. M. (in press). Identifying types of attending patterns of nurses' work. *Image: Journal of Nursing Scholarship.*

Drummond, H. (1981). The nature and description of behavioral patterns. In P. P. G. Bateson & P. H. Klopher (Eds.), *Perspectives in ethology. Volume 4: Advantages of diversity* (pp. 1-33). New York: Plenum.

Duncan, S. D., & Fiske, D. W. (1977). *Face-to-face interaction: Research methods and theory.* Hillsdale, NJ: Lawrence Erlbaum.

Duncan, S. D., & Sayre, R. E. (1991). C-QUAL: A system for computer-aided transcription of videotaped action sequences. *Behavior Research Methods, Instruments, and Computers, 23,* 505-512.

Eibl-Eibesfeldt, I. (1989). *Human ethology.* New York: Aldine de Gruyter.

Ekman, P. (1992). Facial expressions of emotion: New findings, new questions. *Psychological Science, 3,* 34-38.

Ekman, P., & Friesen, W. V. (1975). *Unmasking the face: A guide to recognizing emotions from facial cues.* Englewood Cliffs, NJ: Prentice Hall.

Erickson, F. (1992). Ethnographic microanalysis of interaction. In M. D. LeCompte, W. L. Millroy, & J. Preissle (Eds.), *The handbook of qualitative research in education* (pp. 201-225). New York: Academic Press.

Estabrooks, C. A. (1987). *Touching behaviors of intensive care nurses.* Unpublished master's thesis, University of Alberta, Edmonton, Alberta, Canada.

Estabrooks, C. A., & Morse, J. M. (1992). Toward a theory of touch: The touching process and acquiring a touching style. *Journal of Advanced Nursing, 17,* 448-456.

Fisher, J. A. (1991). Disambiguating anthropomorphism: An interdisciplinary review. In P. P. G. Bateson & P. H. Klopher (Eds.), *Perspectives in ethology* (Vol. 9, pp. 49-85). New York: Plenum.

Fourcher, L. A. (1979). Ethology and phenomenology. *Behaviorism, 7,* 23-36.

Grimshaw, A. D. (1982). Sound-image data records for research on social interaction: Some questions and answers. *Sociological Methods and Research, 11,* 121-144.

Gross, D. (1991). Issues related to validity of videotaped observational data. *Western Journal of Nursing Research, 13,* 658-663.

Hartmann, D. P., & Wood, D. D. (1990). Observational methods. In A. S. Bellack, M. Hersen, & A. E. Kazdin (Eds.), *International handbook of behavior modification and therapy* (2nd ed., pp. 107-138). New York: Plenum.

Hood, L., McDermott, R., & Cole, M. (1980). "Let's try to make it a good day"—Some not so simple ways. *Discourse Processes, 3,* 155-168.

Jones, S. E., & Yarbrough, A. E. (1985). A naturalistic study of the meanings of touch. *Communication Monographs, 52,* 19-56.

Jorgensen, D. L. (1989). *Participant observation. A methodology for human studies.* Newbury Park, CA: Sage.

Kendon, A. (1979). Some theoretical and methodological aspects of the use of film in the study of social interaction. In G. P. Ginsburg (Ed.), *Emerging strategies in social psychological research* (pp. 67-91). New York: John Wiley.

Lehner, P. N. (1979). *Handbook of ethological methods.* New York: Garland.

Lucero, M., Hutchinson, S., Leger-Krall, S., & Wilson, H. (1993). Wandering in Alzheimer dementia patients. *Journal of Clinical Nursing Research, 2,* 160-175.

Lytton, H. (1971). Observational studies of parent-child interaction: A methodological review. *Child Development, 43,* 651-684.

Martin, P., & Bateson, P. (1986). *Measuring behaviour. An introductory guide.* Cambridge, UK: Cambridge University Press.

McKay, S., Barrows, T., & Roberts, J. (1990). Women's views of second-stage labor as assessed by interviews and videotapes. *Birth, 17,* 192-198.

Medwar, P. B. (1976). Does ethology throw any light on human behaviour? In P. P. G. Bateson & R. A. Hinde (Eds.), *Growing points in ethology* (pp. 497-506). Cambridge, UK: Cambridge University Press.

Morse, J. M., & Bottorff, J. L. (1990). The use of ethology in clinical nursing research. *Advances in Nursing Science, 12*(3), 53-64.

Morse, J. M., & McHutchion, E. (1991). Releasing restraints: Providing safe care for the elderly. *Research in Nursing and Health, 14,* 187-196.

Pepler, C. J. (1984). Congruence in relational messages communicated to nursing home residents through nurse aid touch behaviors. *Dissertation Abstracts International, 45,* 2106b. (University Microfilms No. 84-22312)

Rosenblum, L. A. (1978). Measurement in observational research. In G. P. Sackett (Ed.), *Observing behavior, Vol. 2: Data collection and analysis methods* (pp. 15-24). Baltimore: University Park Press.

Scaife, M. (1979). Observing infant social development: Theoretical perspectives, natural observation, and video recording. In G. P. Ginsburg (Ed.), *Emerging strategies in social psychological research* (pp. 93-116). New York: John Wiley.

Scheflen, A. (1973). *Communication structure.* Bloomington: Indiana University Press.

Scheflen, A. E. (1966). Natural history method in psychotherapy: Communicational research. In L. A. Goltschalk & A. H. Auerback (Eds.), *Methods of research in psychotherapy* (pp. 263-289). New York: Appleton-Century-Crofts.

Scherer, K. R., & Ekman, P. (1982). *Handbook of methods in nonverbal behavior research.* Cambridge, UK: Cambridge University Press.

Slater, P. J. B. (1978). Data collection. In P. W. Colgan (Ed.), *Quantitative ethology* (pp. 8-24). New York: John Wiley.

Solberg, S., & Morse, J. M. (1991). The comforting behaviors of caregivers toward distressed postoperative neonates. *Issues in Comprehensive Pediatric Nursing, 14,* 77-92.

Tinbergen, N. (1963). On aims and methods of ethology. *Zeitschrift für Tierpsychologie, 20*(3), 410-433.

Weiss, S. J. (1979). The language of touch. *Nursing Research, 28,* 76-80.

Weiss, S. J. (1986). Psychophysiological effects of caregiver touch on incidence of cardiac dysrhythmia. *Heart & Lung, 15,* 495-505.

Wolcott, H. F. (1992). Posturing in qualitative inquiry. In M. D. LeCompte, W. L. Millroy, & J. Preissle (Eds.), *The handbook of qualitative research in education* (pp. 3-52). New York: Academic Press.

Dialogue

On Mentoring

KNAFL One of the problems is that we spend so much time talking about methods, that we never teach people where the good ideas come from. We never teach our students passion—passion for their work.

BOTTORFF Mentorship is really good, but we are still left with this environment that people have to go to work in. How do we as colleagues support each other? Isn't it this environment that creates this problem?

KNAFL I think this is the tension. How do you teach people some skills for succeeding in these environments? Maybe also trying to do things that might alter these environments. It's real tough for pretenure people.

14

Secondary Analysis in Qualitative Research: Issues and Implications

SALLY THORNE

It was fun to take on this topic. It was one that I often had wished somebody had written something about. I could never find the answers to some of the things I would like to have answered. I may not have answered those questions in this chapter, but I at least have tried to list what those questions might be when using secondary analysis with a qualitative data set. I have done some of this secondary analysis, but as I wrote the chapter, I became aware of some interesting dilemmas. I began to realize that some people who did secondary analysis may not have said so when they published it. And sometimes one author does two separate and different pieces from one sample, and it is hard to determine from what they have written how these pieces relate, which came first, and so on. I suspect this is also some sort of secondary analysis. Then I completely sidestepped the issue of meta-analysis, but at some level that is also a type of secondary analysis.

After a decade of enthusiastic methodological advancement in qualitative data construction and interpretation, the position of qualitative research within health and social science scholarship is well established. The volume of existing data, constructed according to the tenets of various qualitative approaches, is expanding rapidly. Scholars in possession of these databases are beginning to address their potential application beyond the original intent and in relation to new and extended inquiries.

However, we have not yet established a tradition or articulated a set of principles from which to generate methodological decisions or evaluation criteria for such research. My purpose in writing this chapter, therefore, is to initiate dialogue regarding the opportunities that secondary analysis affords and to propose some beginning notions of the bases on which a secondary analysis might be considered as effectively representative of qualitative research approaches and procedures.

In its traditional (quantitative) usage, secondary analysis has been considered to be "poor cousin" to primary research because of the limited relationship between the investigator and the original data source and because of the potential errors inherent in coding and counting something that the original research may not have considered as central to the investigation. However, it also has been cited as an interesting option for those who have access to databases that may not have been fully tapped in the original designs (Lobo, 1986; McArt & McDougal, 1985; Woods, 1988). Secondary analysis has appeared in the form of traditional content analyses of qualitative databases. Use of the term *secondary analysis* within the social science and health research literature, however, seems exclusively applied to essentially deductive approaches in answering subsidiary research questions.

In contrast, the objective of this discussion is to consider the possibilities for secondary analytic approaches to qualitative data sets using inductive, interpretive analytic methods. Unlike some scholarly traditions, in which text is considered to be a primary data source, qualitative health research has been limited largely to primary study involving human observation and/or interaction. The text generated from these primary studies rarely has been considered as a data source beyond the original research. Toward this end, the potential contribution of secondary analysis is argued, its limitations are acknowledged, and some suggestions for rigorous implementation are proposed.

Potential Contributions of Secondary Analysis

As the qualitative researcher is well aware, data gathering and construction are intensely time-consuming and exhaustive. Face-to-face interviewing, participant observation, and field research all involve a serious commitment to obtaining access, establishing credibility, developing and maintaining relationships, checking and rechecking interpretations of emerging data, and validating the eventual conclusions. Each of these activities entails considerable skill at human interaction, process negotiation, and patience. Further, qualitative designs typically require verbatim transcription of interview data and field notes, as well as meticulous processual record keeping. The result is that a typical qualitative database may well represent several years worth of researcher investment and many dollars worth of granting agency support. Obviously there are limits to the number of primary databases that a researcher is willing or able to generate, and there would be tremendous advantage to maximizing the extent to which each database can be used to answer important questions (Bernard et al., 1986; Glaser & Strauss, 1967). Further, some research questions may be amenable only to inquiry through examination of databases that extend beyond the scope of a single researcher. Such questions could include the study of events too rare to be observed with any regularity within discrete populations, or events influenced by temporary cycles within a living history (Bernard et al., 1986). Thus the potential for secondary analysis to extend the larger context within which research findings can be appreciated is a powerful argument in its favor.

A related issue is the obvious influence that time and knowledge have on the evolution of any researcher's thinking about a subject in which she or he is immersed. Although we do have traditions that allow us to draw conclusions with some confidence, human experience is sufficiently various that there will never be a completely formed grounded theory, ethnographic description, or phenomenological account. Indeed the impact of new insights, unpredicted angles in thought, and shifts in convention does (or should) make all of our theories somewhat fluid and amenable to modification over time. Therefore a secondary analytic tradition ought to be built into our expectations for managing the continuance of all of our important research findings. Undoubtedly, new data often will be required. The old data sets, however, ought never to be discounted in our efforts to track the progressions within our knowledge and the trends in the way we make sense of what we find. The legacy we leave behind should not be in the form of absolute conclusions, but rather should take the shape of data that can be reexamined in the light of the inevitable new insights that will emerge as others take their turn at considering new questions.

The qualitative research approaches that have become mainstream within the health and social sciences (phenomenology, grounded theory, ethnography, and methods derived from these) all require intense and vigorous encounters between the researcher and the sources of knowledge about the phenomenon of interest (Tesch, 1987). Nurses tend to adapt readily to the rigors of this researcher role, presumably because of inherent similarities in the skills required of expert clinical practice and expert field research (Chenitz, 1986; Lipson, 1989). However, there are undoubtedly nurse researchers and others whose interactional skills make field research difficult, if not impossible, but whose talents may lie in the intellectual power they could bring to interpreting meaning within data (Glaser & Strauss, 1967; May, 1986). In fact, many academic disciplines have well-established traditions in which taking some distance from the source of knowledge is a respected form of inquiry and theory building. Pushing the limits of what qualitative research can contribute to the larger projects of knowledge development surely will require the full range of thinking within our midst. Thus secondary analysis creates one rather powerful opportunity for contributions within the qualitative research tradition by those whose aptitudes are more remote from the data source.

With these potential contributions in mind, one can envision at least five discrete varieties of research involving qualitative secondary analysis:

1. *Analytic expansion,* in which the researcher makes further use of his or her own original database to answer questions at the next level of analysis or to ask new questions as the available theory base expands;
2. *Retrospective interpretation,* in which the database is used to consider new questions that were raised, but not thoroughly examined, in the context of an original study;
3. *Armchair induction,* in which those whose talents lie in theory development, rather than engagement with the phenomenon under study, can apply inductive methods of textual analysis, such as hermeneutical inquiry, to existing data sets;

4. *Amplified sampling,* in which wider theories can be generated through comparison of several distinct and theoretically representative databases; and

5. *Cross-validation,* in which existing data sets are employed to confirm or discount new findings and suggest patterns beyond the scope of the sample in which the researcher personally has been immersed.

Thus the rationale for considering secondary analysis as a serious qualitative approach includes efficiency and effectiveness in the use of data, recognition of our individual strengths and limitations within the research tradition, and appreciation for the inevitable progress of knowledge beyond the time frame of our discrete research endeavors.

Hazards Within Secondary Analysis

Although secondary analysis appears to offer some expedient routes to inquiry, there are important reasons why it has not achieved any real popularity, especially among qualitative researchers. A brief overview of the intellectual hazards inherent in secondary analytic approaches, therefore, will make the need for formal and rigorous principles quite apparent.

Within all of our qualitative research traditions, the potential for researcher bias is well understood, and techniques to reduce and account for it are well established. However, we are all well aware that the findings are never completely free from the perspective of the researcher (Corbin, 1986). Even a brief review of the writings by our prominent scholars clearly reveals their unique interpretive styles and characteristic decision trails, despite evidence of deliberate and methodical attention to their influence on the data. If we recognize that bias will always exist within data sets, as well as within the interpretive methods used to convert them into research findings, secondary analysis undoubtedly holds the potential to intensify or exaggerate the effect of those biases, either positively or negatively (Swanson, 1986). Because the human mind has an established affinity for polarization, this exaggerated effect probably would take the form of either confirming or refuting the original idea. Either stance injects a bias that would be extremely difficult to untangle from the formal account of the original phenomenon of study.

Another predictable hazard is "lazy" research, in which existing data sets used for convenience become overly available and overused for new inquiries. Most qualitative data sets are sufficiently small as to harbor all manner of statistically improbable qualities. For example, in my own first study of cancer families (Thorne, 1985), almost half the sample had surnames starting with the same letter of the alphabet. Although a secondary analyst would probably not be looking for trends in the nomenclature of these families, the case dramatically illustrates the potential for exaggerating the influence of any number of more invisible and, perhaps, more convincing peculiarities within each data set.

A related danger of secondary analysis is that the influence of certain features of the original data set may not be as obvious to the researcher removed from the data. In other words, field researchers continuously employ a sophisticated set of mental devices intended to protect them from predictable interpretive traps (Cicourel, 1982). They make mental notes of the conditions that make a single key informant more vehement, analytical, or articulate than the rest, features of the setting that might shape a particular instance of data, and an infinite number of details that influence direction but that may never become accessible within formal field notes (Scheff, 1986). Further, the immediacy of the researcher role in data construction gives the researcher access to tacit understandings and nuances that may be very difficult to reconstruct at a later date. One would expect, for example, that studies of race relations would reflect qualitative differences before, during, and after an event as significant as the aftermath of the trial involving Rodney King.[1] However, it might prove impossible to reconstruct or even interpret the mental processes of a researcher whose investigation has been influenced by such contextual factors, especially because they inevitably include many more mundane situational and sociopolitical events (Hinds, Chaves, & Cypess, 1992).

Beyond these critical methodological concerns, secondary analysis may raise problematic questions regarding adherence to the ethical principles associated with research using human subjects. Although secondary analysis implies a new research question, there may be especially sensitive instances in which the implied consent of original subjects cannot be presumed. Thus, even though subjects may have volunteered to share their experiences about a phenomenon for an identified purpose, a radical departure from that stated purpose could violate the conditions under which consent for secondary analysis was obtained. Similarly researchers who permit their databases to be studied by others may find themselves in ethical dilemmas if the secondary analyst applies the data to purposes distinct from those that were proposed. In both cases, a professional judgment clearly is required as to the scope of the original consent (because secondary consent would rarely be possible) and the specific conditions under which secondary analysis is appropriate. These ethical challenges may make secondary analysis problematic in some cases; however, where they can be confronted appropriately, secondary analysis offers an important response to another ethical predicament, that of failing to make optimal use of hard-earned, costly, and valuable human data.

Thus the most serious hazards inherent in secondary analysis of qualitative work include the potential to exaggerate the effects of researcher biases, contextual factors, ethical questions, and peculiarities within the data set. Clearly, rigorous secondary analysis within a qualitative tradition requires careful adherence to strategies that will both reduce and account for the influence of each of these factors.

Issues in Secondary Analysis

Having established the opportunities and dangers inherent in secondary analysis, I now discuss some of the issues that seem central to its scholarly application and propose tentative solutions to some of the most glaring potential problems. Obviously the wide range of secondary analytic options addressed earlier alludes to a variety of theoretical issues that will be brought to light. Some of the critical issues that must be addressed in a research design will be specific to the approach selected. For example, where the secondary analyst was involved in primary data construction, the researcher's relationship to the data will be inherently different from that of the researcher looking at the data for the first time. Similarly questions of rigor may be considered quite differently in cases in which secondary analysis is part of or extends research that also includes new primary data construction than in cases in which interpretation relies totally on secondary analysis. Such variations illustrate the complexity intrinsic to any set of principles on which secondary analysis can comfortably proceed. However, certain common themes within the various approaches provide a basis for discussion of some general issues, including the fit between the secondary research question and the data set(s) and the nature of the data themselves.

The Fit Between the Data Sets and the Research Question

The degree to which the secondary research question fits the available data is probably the most pivotal issue in deciding whether secondary analysis is a viable option in any inquiry (McArt & McDougal, 1985; Woods, 1988). In considering this question, there are two levels at which a strong fit is critical. First, the question posed in the secondary analysis must be sufficiently close to that of the original research that the data set will represent uniformly the topic of secondary inquiry. For example, if some informants have addressed a subtheme and others have not, the absence of such data cannot be understood as meaningful unless there is clear evidence of comparable probes in that direction. Even subtle distinctions within research questions could betray strong tendencies toward or away from certain dimensions within the phenomenon under study. The more distant the second question is from the first, the more cautious the researcher must be about the meaning of actual (and missing) data. Thus the first issue of fit is the theme, or topic, that the original research addressed.

The second element of fit is the formal methods by which the original data set was derived. Given research questions within the same general sphere, a phenomenological researcher and a grounded theorist, for example, will generate rather different data sets. Their responses to cues, processes for clarifying meaning, and indeed even their language usage as the data construction progressed probably would become markedly distinct (Knafl & Webster, 1988; Wilson & Hutchinson, 1991). Further, it has been suggested that the substance and form of qualitative research results even may be idiosyncratic to each study (Ammon-Gaberson & Piantanida, 1988). Therefore an apparent match in formal method may not, in and of itself, be sufficient to permit comparison of two sets of data. Thus a serious consideration for the researcher contemplating secondary analysis of a data set would include interpretation of the influence of method on product.

The Nature of the Data

Beyond recognition of the general influence of methodological choices on the data set overall, a complication arises concerning the evolution of meaning within the data set. Inasmuch as qualitative data construction is always interactive, the nature of the data invariably changes as the research progresses (Scheff, 1986). Certainly a theme that arises spontaneously in the early phases of investigation will have a different impact on the data construction from one that is triggered by the increasingly pointed probes as the research enters its final phases. Thus not only the method but also the process within the method must be considered in the examination of fit between the new investigation and the available data.

Where several distinct data sets are being studied for comparative purposes or to expand the theoretical sample on which new interpretations can be generated, the problem of fit is exponentially more complicated. Not only will the secondary analyst have to account for the relationship between the original and secondary research questions, but she or he also will have to consider the implications of explicit and implicit methodological variations between the original pieces of research. For example, predictable differences among units of analysis, such as the perceptions of individuals as compared to families or groups, could make equivalency within the data sets difficult to establish (Miller & Crabtree, 1992). Although identical methods would not be anticipated and perhaps would not be desirable, the onus would lie squarely on the shoulders of the secondary analyst to account for the limitations that the variations could impose on the secondary interpretations. Obviously this accounting would require a solid theoretical grounding in the various methods, as well as an imaginative appreciation for their implications in the practice of research.

Beyond these considerations are the more concrete but inevitable variations that will emerge in comparison of data sets derived by any two individual researchers. Where intimate access to the original researcher is possible, the secondary analyst has the opportunity to make sense of some of these variations in a qualitatively interesting manner (McArt & McDougal, 1985; Woods, 1988). Inquiries into apparent strategy shifts, implicit preconceptions and biases, sources and timing of inductive inspiration, and eventual coding and interpretation may yield sufficient insight to account for the influence of artifacts of the original researcher's process. Where the secondary analyst is at arm's length from one or more of the original researchers, however, more formal methods of estimating the influence of data set variations and accounting for these in the formal report should be considered. Such methods could include formal manifest and latent content analysis for various indications of researcher influence on the evolving data sets, as well as explication of the precise decision trails as they appear within the documented evidence of the data construction process.

Thus, in view of all of the theoretical considerations inherent in this sort of project, secondary analysis might be suited best to the skills of an experienced, rather than a novice, researcher. Making sense of the complex relationships between question and method, between purpose and process could well be the undoing of the researcher bent on clarity and methodological precision!

Implications

The complexity of the issues underlying any secondary analysis within the qualitative tradition makes it apparent that the researcher will need courage and creativity to make a convincing argument about the rigor of the process and the credibility of the product. In this final discussion, specific steps to enhance success at both are considered.

Interaction With Textual Data

Although historians and philosophers have developed rigorous traditions for interactive inquiry into text (Bedola, 1992; Brody, 1992), health and social science researchers tend to favor the immediacy of the human interaction required of the dominant qualitative research traditions. However, the case can be made that interactive interpretation of text is possible if the conditions of engagement are fully met. According to Tesch (1987), these conditions would appear as an act of "imaginative participation" in a dialogue with the textual materials in the sense that, just as the researcher questions the text, the text questions the researcher. As Charmaz (1990) pointed out, the interpretation of data is always dependent on researcher perspective, which includes experiences, values, and priorities. Thus new researchers may "see" within the data an infinite range of patterns and theoretical constructs (Field & Morse, 1985).

The established means for secondary textual analysis is content analysis, which, at either the manifest or latent level, always involves coding and counting in some form (Catanzaro, 1988; Miles & Huberman, 1984). Content analysis has been described as a form of "quasi statistics" (Wilson, 1985) in which various analytic procedures create a measure of confidence that certain frequencies and distributions accurately portray a data set. As such, it typically reflects a deductive form of analysis. In contrast, hermeneutic inquiry, which is concerned primarily with inductive analysis of textual materials (Gadamer, 1988; Reeder, 1988; Ricoeur, 1981), is much less prominent within the applied health and social science scholarship traditions. Whether this reflects our collective general distrust of textual materials or the paucity of adequate text to answer our most pressing research questions, it perhaps has inhibited our creativity in knowledge development.

As Armstrong (1990) reminded us, however, the distinction between primary and secondary sources becomes considerably less relevant if one treats all data sources as primary for the duration of the inquiry. Indeed, immersion in and interaction with text for the purpose of inductive analysis seems both possible and desirable if we look to the traditions within other disciplines for direction. What processual immediacy might be sacrificed could well be balanced by the range of atypical or idiosyncratic cases to which a secondary analyst might have access (Lincoln & Guba, 1985). Thus the development of a qualitative secondary analytic tradition requires tolerance for rethinking some of the tenets within our disciplinary methodological imperatives.

The Traditions of Credibility

Although data collection and analysis would not typically be concurrent in secondary analysis research, there are various means by which the investigator can adapt and apply analytic methods that are used in primary data construction. The constant comparative method of interspersing periods of objectivity and subjectivity, distance and immersion, can be applied to engagement in text as well as to human interaction (Glaser & Strauss, 1967; Patton, 1980). Further, the tasks, techniques, and processes central to inductive analysis (Knafl & Howard, 1984) are generally quite applicable to the conditions of a secondary interpretive process.

Application of accepted principles of establishing and conveying the truth value of qualitative research reveals a number of strategies of interest to the secondary analyst. As Strauss and Corbin (1990) argued, new species of qualitative research require evaluation criteria that fit the nature and circumstances of the research. Rather than propose a fixed set of measures to which newer methods must adapt, these authors proposed a set of general and inclusive criteria relating to the systematic relationships between concepts, the density and development of the conceptual linkages, and the degree to which conditions and processes are accounted for in the theoretical findings. Such a set of criteria, which names the ends rather than the means by which they are established, offers considerable opportunity for secondary analysts to demonstrate credibility within their research products.

Overt adherence to such dimensions as credibility, transferability, confirmability, and dependability creates the major mechanism by which the trustworthiness or "truth value" of the products of qualitative research can be evaluated by the consumer (Lincoln & Guba, 1985). Toward this end, various authors have articulated a range of creative and adaptable procedures by which researchers can make the processes of inductive analysis explicit, leave an auditable decision trail, and create a research report that convincingly portrays an analysis that has not fallen prey to known errors of interpretation (Catanzaro, 1988; Kirk & Miller, 1986; Sandelowski, 1986). With a few relatively minor exceptions, all of these procedures are accessible to the secondary analyst. Procedures that typically rely on further interaction with the primary data source can often be modified for those whose contact with the data is secondary. For example, in lieu of confirmation, elaboration, and clarification with original informants, secondary analysts might consider the original researcher(s), new key informants, additional untapped data sets, or clinical experts as possible sources of validation of an emerging analytic framework. Further, because secondary analysis often involves triangulation of investigator, data source, or unit of analysis, it may even offer some intrinsic benefits to the confirmation of accuracy within qualitative research findings (Brody, 1992; Knafl & Breitmayer, 1986).

The Culture of Research Reporting

A final implication of the issues arising from an analysis of secondary research designs involves examination of the options available for formally reporting such research. Within the scholarly arena, the majority of opportunities to articulate research findings require the extremes of brevity and precision. Further, the mandates of the practice disciplines place an additional burden on researchers to include implications as a central feature of any research presentation. Therefore many qualitative studies are being published currently in the form of a 15-page manuscript or squeezed into a 15-minute oral report.

The outcome of this trend is a serious deficit in the extent of explanation about design and methods that the reader can extract from the product. We have grown accustomed to seeing reports in which evidence of the qualitative method named is not made apparent in the form or analytic level of the findings. The reluctance of some journal editors to accept longer manuscripts and of conference organizers to allot more generous presentation times creates a climate in which we do not expect extensive methodological discussion in our research reporting. Thus the complexities of an approach using secondary analysis are probably not granted the attention they deserve. Indeed there may well be a body of research within our literature that reflects thoughtful but formally unacknowledged secondary analytic approaches!

An examination of some of the theoretical obligations of the secondary analyst within the qualitative tradition makes it apparent that serious attention to methodological implications is essential if the results are to be regarded as credible. At the very least, the reader requires access to the original data collection procedures, the processes involved in categorizing and summarizing the data, the management of threats to credibility in both the primary and secondary analysis, and the processes by which conclusions were derived from the data (Knafl & Howard, 1984). A thorough accounting for these minimum conditions may be beyond the scope of most of our current publication and presentation formats. Therefore it appears that we require alternative forums for reporting our research to allow access to the details of decision making. What we think in the end is only as valid as the process by which we got there.

Conclusion

In conclusion, it appears that much benefit can be gained from a more active exploration of the possibilities afforded by qualitative secondary analysis within our programs of qualitative research. A sufficiently large cadre of health and social science researchers exists whose databases reflect a similar curiosity for subjective experience within health and illness that many of our evolving questions may well be best addressed through application of one or another variant on this method. In much the same way that meta-analysis has expanded our interpretation of the possibilities for applying quantitative research findings, secondary analysis offers great promise for another layer of meaning to the work in which we are engaged. With thoughtful attention to rigor and a careful accounting for methodological reasoning, we can begin confidently to tap the potential of this complementary source of knowledge.

Note

1. On April 29, 1992, a California jury found four white police officers not guilty of assaulting black motorist Rodney King; there was widespread media coverage of an amateur video depicting the vicious beating. Riots in Los Angeles in response to that jury decision caused at least 53 deaths and a billion dollars in property damage.

References

Ammon-Gaberson, K. B., & Piantanida, M. (1988). Generating results from qualitative data. *Image: Journal of Nursing Scholarship, 20*, 159-161.

Armstrong, D. (1990). Use of the genealogical method in the exploration of chronic illness: A research note. *Social Science and Medicine, 30*, 1225-1227.

Bedola, M. (1992). Historical research: A brief introduction. In W. L. Miller & B. F. Crabtree (Eds.), *Doing qualitative research* (pp. 163-173). Newbury Park, CA: Sage.

Bernard, H. R., Pelto, P. J., Werner, O., Boster, J., Romney, A. K., Johnson, A., Ember, C. R., & Kastakoff, A. (1986). The construction of primary data in cultural anthropology. *Current Anthropology, 27*, 382-396.

Brody, H. (1992). Philosophic approaches. In W. L. Miller & B. F. Crabtree (Eds.), *Doing qualitative research* (pp. 174-185). Newbury Park, CA: Sage.

Catanzaro, M. (1988). Using qualitative analytic techniques. In N. F. Woods & M. Catanzaro (Eds.), *Nursing research: Theory and practice* (pp. 437-456). St. Louis: C. V. Mosby.

Charmaz, K. (1990). "Discovering" chronic illness: Using grounded theory. *Social Science and Medicine, 30*, 1161-1172.

Chenitz, W. C. (1986). The informal interview. In W. C. Chenitz & J. M. Swanson (Eds.), *From practice to grounded theory: Qualitative research in nursing* (pp. 79-90). Menlo Park, CA: Addison-Wesley.

Cicourel, A. V. (1982). Interviews, surveys, and the problem of ecological validity. *American Sociologist, 17*, 11-20.

Corbin, J. (1986). Qualitative data analysis for grounded theory. In W. C. Chenitz & J. M. Swanson (Eds.), *From practice to grounded theory: Qualitative research in nursing* (pp. 91-101). Menlo Park, CA: Addison-Wesley.

Field, P. A., & Morse, J. M. (1985). *Nursing research: The application of qualitative approaches.* Rockville, MD: Aspen.

Gadamer, H. G. (1988). On the circle of understanding. In J. M. Connolly & T. Kentner (Eds. & Trans.), *Hermeneutics versus science? Three German essays* (pp. 68-78). Notre Dame, IN: University of Notre Dame Press.

Glaser, B. G., & Strauss, A. L. (1967). *The discovery of grounded theory: Strategies for qualitative research.* Hawthorne, NY: Aldine.

Hinds, P. S., Chaves, D. E., & Cypess, S. M. (1992). Context as a source of meaning and understanding. *Qualitative Health Research, 2*, 61-74.

Kirk, J., & Miller, M. L. (1986). *Reliability and validity in qualitative research.* Beverly Hills, CA: Sage.

Knafl. K. A., & Breitmayer, B. J. (1986). Triangulation in qualitative research: Issues of conceptual clarity and purpose. In J. M. Morse (Ed.), *Qualitative nursing research: A contemporary dialogue* (pp. 209-220). Rockville, MD: Aspen.

Knafl, K. A., & Howard, M. J. (1984). Interpreting and reporting qualitative research. *Research in Nursing and Health, 7,* 17-24.

Knafl, K. A., & Webster, D. C. (1988). Managing and analyzing qualitative data: A description of tasks, techniques, and materials. *Western Journal of Nursing Research, 10,* 195-218.

Lincoln, Y. S., & Guba, E. G. (1985). Processing naturalistically obtained data. In Y. S. Lincoln & E. G. Guba, *Naturalistic inquiry* (pp. 332-356). Beverly Hills, CA: Sage.

Lipson, J. G. (1989). The use of self in ethnographic research. In J. M. Morse (Ed.), *Qualitative nursing research: A contemporary dialogue* (pp. 61-75). Rockville, MD: Aspen.

Lobo, M. L. (1986). Secondary analysis as a strategy for nursing research. In P. L. Chinn (Ed.), *Nursing research methodologies: Issues and implications* (pp. 295-304). Rockville, MD: Aspen.

May, K. A. (1986). Writing and evaluating the grounded theory research report. In W. C. Chenitz & J. M. Swanson (Eds.), *From practice to grounded theory: Qualitative research in nursing* (pp. 146-154). Menlo Park, CA: Addison-Wesley.

McArt, E. W., & McDougal, L. W. (1985). Secondary data analysis: A new approach to nursing research. *Image: Journal of Nursing Scholarship, 17,* 54-57.

Miles, M. B., & Huberman, A. M. (1984). *Qualitative data analysis: A sourcebook of new methods.* Beverly Hills, CA: Sage.

Miller, W. L., & Crabtree, B. F. (1992). Primary care research: A multimethod typology and qualitative road map. In W. L. Miller & B. F. Crabtree (Eds.), *Doing qualitative research* (pp. 3-28). Newbury Park, CA: Sage.

Patton, M. Q. (1980). *Qualitative evaluation methods.* Beverly Hills, CA: Sage.

Reeder, F. (1988). Hermeneutics. In B. Sarter (Ed.), *Paths to knowledge: Innovative research methods for nursing* (pp. 193-238). New York: National League for Nursing Press.

Ricoeur, P. (1981). The task of hermeneutics. In J. B. Thompson (Ed. & Trans.), *Paul Ricoeur: Hermeneutics and the human sciences* (pp. 43-63). Cambridge, UK: Cambridge University Press.

Sandelowski, M. (1986). The problem of rigor in qualitative research. *Advances in Nursing Science, 8*(3), 27-37.

Scheff, T. J. (1986). Toward resolving the controversy over "thick description." *Current Anthropology, 27,* 408-409.

Strauss, A., & Corbin, J. (1990). *Basics of qualitative research: Grounded theory procedures and techniques.* Newbury Park, CA: Sage.

Swanson, J. M. (1986). Analyzing data for categories and description. In W. C. Chenitz & J. M. Swanson (Eds.), *From practice to grounded theory: Qualitative research in nursing* (pp. 121-132). Menlo Park, CA: Addison-Wesley.

Tesch, R. (1987). Emerging themes: The researcher's experience. *Phenomenology + Pedagogy, 5,* 230-241.

Thorne, S. (1985). The family cancer experience. *Cancer Nursing, 8,* 285-291.

Wilson, H. S. (1985). *Research in nursing.* Menlo Park, CA: Addison-Wesley.

Wilson, H. S., & Hutchinson, S. A. (1991). Triangulation of qualitative methods: Heideggerian hermeneutics and grounded theory. *Qualitative Health Research, 1,* 263-276.

Woods, N. F. (1988). Using existing data sources: Primary and secondary analysis. In N. F. Woods & M. Catanzaro, *Nursing research: Theory and practice* (pp. 334-347). St. Louis: C. V. Mosby.

Dialogue

On Writing It Up

SANDELOWSKI I think one of the hallmarks of a good qualitative researcher is someone who writes in a very accessible way for particular audiences.

LIPSON If we can't express the things that we are learning from people, then we'll never get anywhere.

DREHER I keep thinking about faculty who are pursuing this tenure business and looking to publish in peer-reviewed journals. It's the reality that young scholars are facing and I think it inhibits their pursuit of this other type of writing.

SANDELOWSKI Maybe they need to legitimate themselves with the conventional first—and maybe one should do that. In other words, you should show that you know what the rules are, then you can more legitimately break them!

MUECKE I think that the places to publish in nursing have been very constrictive for a lot of us.

SANDELOWSKI I think a lot of us feel the same thing. I do my more, shall we say, conventional pieces for nursing journals.

15

Qualitative Research Methods From the Reviewer's Perspective

MELANIE DREHER

I changed the name from "funding," because sitting on these review committees, we learn not to say the "f" word. Funding is really outside the control of the investigator, the review committees and even the funding agency. Sometimes you get a great proposal that just cannot be funded at that particular time. In this chapter I am focusing on the review process itself. In some ways I believe I am preaching to the choir, as many of you have been funded. . . .

I am a creature of habit and, as an ethnographer, always collect data the same way. Yet I know, as a reviewer, there are many styles. So one of the things I look for is a systematic approach. When you are doing a history and a physical, you do it the same way. You do not start here on one patient and here on another; you work from the general to the specific. We develop the context, and then we place the problem within the context, so you look for those things when evaluating ethnography, or grounded theory, or whatever. So my advice is, if you are not going to adhere to the standards for data collection, then at least say what you are going to do.

Nursing bears much in common with astronomy, zoology, botany, and anthropology in that a large proportion of its body of knowledge is derived from naturalistic observation and categorization, as opposed to experimental testing of generalizations. Assigning a qualitative label to each classification and subclassification (as medicine has done with diseases and zoology has done with animal species) is a critical component of nursing's scientific process. Ultimately it provides a vernacular within the discipline/profession that is heuristic and enhances the capacity for even further development of nursing knowledge. Indeed, whether nursing knowledge reaches maturity will depend on the progress it makes in describing and classifying human responses to health and illness.

To advance its scientific base, nursing research must take at least two directions. First, it must continue to observe, classify, and name the patterns of human behavior surrounding health and illness. Second, and equally fundamental, it must focus on the development of nursing technology, including a description of clinical decision making and the nature of the nurse-patient relationship. A better understanding of clinical techniques and strategies will assist nurses not only to be better clinicians but also to teach and transmit nursing theory and practice.

At least part of the reason that nursing has not achieved the same sophistication as medicine in classifying its relevant phenomena is that, for several years, nursing relied almost solely on research methods that could not capture the breadth and complexity of human responses to health and illness. Likewise it has been difficult to describe and analyze nursing practice because the holistic presence that constitutes nursing cannot be reduced to a series of acts and procedures.

To develop a system of classification for human responses and to understand nursing technology, it is essential to employ research methods consistent with the profession's proclaimed affinity for a practice that is comprehensive and holistic and that includes the total human experience. Such methods must be able to capture the meaning of health events for patients and families and communities, and not just the events themselves. There is a need to use research methods that specifically embrace the concept that both the experience of health and illness and the practice of nursing are more than the sum of their parts.

The salience of what are termed "qualitative methods" for the development of nursing knowledge has been increasingly acknowledged (Field & Morse 1985; Germain, 1979; Leininger, 1985; Morse, 1991). Such methods are particularly well suited for documenting and analyzing human responses and clinical decision making because the complexity and elusiveness of these phenomena often make it difficult even to formulate the appropriate questions or to identify the relevant variables. Although this shift in paradigms has been heralded as appropriate and necessary, the expansion of research methods available to nursing has not been without problems and misunderstandings that have impeded their usefulness. Investigators from many disciplines, in attempting to use inductive, naturalistic methods, have expressed concern that the scientific establishment, apparently embodied in the reviewers of grant proposals, is not sensitive to the nuances of research that is qualitative in nature (Morse, 1991; Price, 1992; Tripp-Reimer, 1986). Reviewers, however, charge that some investigators using qualitative methods appear to think they should be exempted from the rigors of scientific inquiry.

After serving for several years as a reviewer on study sections in the National Institutes of Health and for various private foundations, I am inclined to suggest that often the disagreements between investigator and reviewer that emerge in the course of a proposal review are related more to problems in presentation than to fundamental epistemological disparity. It is important to acknowledge that most funding agencies are committed to the goals and standards of science. This is not to say that there are not other kinds of knowledge and other ways of knowing, nor is it intended to diminish their value. Whether adherence to the canons of science is considered to be vital for the development of nursing knowledge or an unfortunate bias, it is nevertheless the reality that is reflected in the comments that follow. These comments do not reflect any particular order of importance. They are offered, instead, simply as ruminations about some of the most common methodological problems associated with research proposals identified as "qualitative." Most of these problems encountered in the review process can be found under one of the following categories: inappropriate use of qualitative and quantitative paradigms, inadequate plans for analysis, excessive reliance on verbal data, insufficient description of the research design, or inadequate justification for the use of qualitative research strategies.

Inappropriate Use of
Qualitative and Quantitative Paradigms

Notwithstanding the undeniable significance of so-called "qualitative" methods, I now risk accusations of heresy from my colleagues who join me in using methods such as ethnography, grounded theory, life histories and phenomenology, by stating that most research proposals would be vastly improved by omitting the terms *qualitative* or *quantitative* altogether. Although I employ the terms here for the sake of convenience, their use in research proposals seldom, if ever, adds either insight or credibility to the design and more frequently raises questions in the review process that need not have occurred.

First, the very nature of nursing phenomena limits the number of research designs that are exclusively qualitative or quantitative. Even proposals that are predominantly in the grounded theory, phenomenological, or ethnographic traditions usually involve some attention to frequencies of occurrence. Often, when investigators refer to qualitative methods as opposed to quantitative methods, they really mean that data are derived from unstructured observations and/or interviews instead of from questionnaires, structured observations, or standardized interview schedules. References in a proposal to "qualitative data" and "quantitative data" are clarified greatly for the reviewer when replaced, for example, with references to "data derived from direct observations or interviews" and "data derived from questionnaires or standardized instruments."

Moreover, the gathering of these supposedly qualitative data does not ensure or even require that they be analyzed qualitatively. For example, the analysis of open-ended interviews by counting the number of times particular themes occur can hardly be called qualitative, especially if the themes are assigned a significance based on the frequency of occurrence. Actually a more qualitative approach might be to assign greater importance to topics that did *not* surface in the interviews—especially when contextual observations may have predicted their occurrence. For instance, if an investigator were exploring the experiences of women who have had spontaneous abortions and an informant never mentioned her partner as she relayed her feelings and reactions, it would be unwise to assume by this omission that her partner's response was unimportant simply because it did not emerge several times in her discourse. A truly qualitative approach would demand that the interview be interpreted in relation to the context that would include the woman's household and family. At the very least, the investigator should wonder why the informant failed to mention her partner in the course of the interview and explore it both in data collection and analysis. Indeed it is often the things that are *not* talked about that are the most critical and the most revealing.

Even "saturation," so central to grounded theory research, is as much quantitative as qualitative in the sense that new participants are interviewed until no new themes are reported. We then assume that we have captured the *quantity* of themes that adequately describe the phenomenon being studied. But while we are waiting for nothing new to appear, the themes that are so profoundly important yet so sensitive that they are not talked about may elude us entirely.

Despite the proclamations of many investigators that the proposed research is qualitative, the tendency is to apply experimental and survey design criteria to observational, naturalistic research. It is difficult to say whether this application is merely an attempt to appease what investigators assume is the reviewers' quantitative bias or whether it reflects the difficulty in shifting from one research paradigm to another. It is not unusual, however, for investigators to claim that they are doing an ethnographic study and then refer to study participants as "subjects" rather than as "informants." Because the two have very different methodological roles, using the correct term is not a trivial issue.

Similarly it is common for researchers to state that their ethnographic or phenomenological sample will be "randomly" selected even though the use of random samples may be irrelevant or even counterproductive to the ethnography. The criterion of randomness is not necessary or appropriate for all research designs, and if used in an ethnographic or grounded theory study, for example, it should be justified carefully. Even the notion of "selecting a sample," rather than using a naturally occurring population, may be inappropriate for some naturalistic studies and thus require some explanation.

Another example of the misapplication of the quantitative paradigm is the attempt to reduce or eliminate investigator bias, rather than to account for it. For example, some research designs call for the informants to be interviewed by more than one investigator or even a number of research assistants to ensure that the data do not reflect the idiosyncrasies of a particular investigator. A fundamental dimension of contextual, naturalistic research, however, is the quality of the relationship between the observer and the observed. Indeed the quantity, validity, and reliability of the data are grounded in the skill of the investigator to establish relationships with informants. In contrast to experimental studies or large sample surveys, bias is reduced, not by standardizing observations or observers, but by integrating the investigator into the social field so that his or her presence no longer generates special behavior. The use of naturalistic, inductive research designs usually implies working with a smaller number of participants for a longer period of time. Validity and reliability in such studies are enhanced by the manageability (smallness) of the sample, which permits greater participation and observation on the part of the investigator. Reports can be confirmed through repeated contacts and direct observations in the small study population with which the investigator has established rapport and trust.

Thus validity and reliability are not irrelevant in interpretive research, as so many proposals claim. They are achieved through an extended, trusting, and confidential relationship between investigator and informants, rather than through the establishment of the psychometric properties of research instruments. This relationship may be difficult to explain to those who are used to eliminating or at least reducing "observer bias." Reviewers, however, are more likely to be persuaded by explicit acknowledgment of the investigator's integration and its importance for the study than by strategies derived from and only appropriate to quantitative paradigms. Particularly convincing in this regard are demonstrated knowledge of the field site and some indication that the investigator is known and trusted by the study population. If such a relationship has not been established already, the proposal should provide evidence that this period of "entry" and establishment of rapport are built into the research design (Cohen, Langness, Middleton, Uchendu, & Van Stone, 1973). It is advantageous to include examples of data derived from preliminary work that demonstrate the significance of investigator integration. This is especially true if the research question is sensitive in nature and requires an indirect, circuitous approach.

Inadequate Plans for Analysis

Perhaps most indicative of the reluctance to relinquish quantitative research paradigms are the plans for analysis in qualitative research proposals. In most such proposals, the analysis section seldom goes beyond the identification and counting of concepts and themes derived from literal transcriptions of recorded interviews, perhaps aided with a software package such as Ethnograph (Seidel & Clark, 1984). This procedure may constitute the management and organization of data, but it does not constitute analysis.

A quantitative analysis is one in which numerical values can be assigned to a variable and then manipulated with various statistical procedures. Such techniques are highly convenient and should be used whenever possible. Qualitative analysis, however, is most applicable when using variables that defy quantification or in which quantification would have no significance. For example, if we were attempting to determine how a school-age child responds to the hospitalization of a sibling, it would be meaningless (both theoretically and clinically) to say that the impact is a 4 or a 7.2 or a 1.3. Rather the impact has to be described, with words, in a narrative embracing the range of variation. This range may yield a typology of responses and ultimately bring us closer to an explanation linking the variation in responses to other phenomena.

Although it is true that, in inductive studies, the strategy for analysis will, to a great extent, depend on the nature of the findings, there are features of such research that should find their way into practically every analysis. For one, it is almost always contextual, yet only seldom do analysis plans include reporting the context and linking the phenomenon under study to that context. For example, in what setting were certain statements made? Who made them? To whom? In relation to what other statements? How do the responses of informants vary in relation to contextual variables? Without reference to the context, it is impossible to determine the meaning of informants' reports or to develop explanations for the responses.

Another almost standard feature of ethnography, phenomenology, and grounded theory research is comparison, yet it is rare to find a comparative analytic strategy included in the proposal. While recognizing that it may be difficult to identify in advance the exact nature of comparisons, it is almost a given that the research will reveal a range of responses across informants. Comparison according to variables identified within the research process is the main strategy used to account for that variation.

The search for patterns in human responses is the essential goal for nursing science, but it is often the exception to patterns that will generate the most theoretical interest and be heuristically most fruitful. For example, the fact that a pattern occurs in the way nurses respond to a patient's request is only of modest interest. If, however, a nurse responds differently, it causes us to ask why. What factors made the nurse deviate either from a statistical or cultural norm? Unfortunately the analyses for most "qualitative" proposals are limited to the identification and classification of patterns, usually through a determination of frequency. Very few build in an exploration of exceptions. In addition to creating assumptions of uniformity among the sample and, ultimately, its application to the entire population, ignoring negative cases or exceptions may leave the reviewers with the impression that negative cases will not be considered in the analysis, thus compromising the scientific objectivity of the research.

Description and classification thus comprise only the beginning steps. The analysis must be pushed further because the ultimate goal of science is explanation. The nursing community will want to know not only the range of response but also how the variation in response is linked with other variables. This information requires identifying the exceptions, as well as the patterns. One of the primary advantages of having a large amount of data on a small sample is that exceptions can be explored to reveal the underlying variables and truly explain the observed behavior. In many proposals, however, the plans for analysis do not take advantage of the richness of this type of data set and the ability to confirm statistical procedures with case analyses.

Finally, in those countless studies that combine quantitative and qualitative techniques in a triangulated design, only rarely is an attempt made to integrate the two components of the study. Rather they are treated like two separate studies in one project. *This treatment is unfortunate because even a simple comparison of the results of the two components could lend confirmation to and thus strengthen the argument.*

Insufficient Description of Research Protocol

In general, terms such as *ethnography, participant observation, grounded theory,* and *fieldwork* are not useful to a reviewer unless they are described procedurally, in relation to the specific proposal. For example, participant observation is perhaps the most pervasive technique used in ethnographic designs, yet we know that the investigator cannot participate and observe everywhere at the same time. Methodological choices must be made about where and when observations take place. Although some of these decisions necessarily are made in the actual process of the research, from the emerging data, the investigator should be able to provide reviewers with a general outline of observations that is consistent with the problem being researched.

Because nursing phenomena often require a multiplicity of methods, they frequently and necessarily deviate from the classic descriptions of specific strategies. Many investigators, for example, who have labeled their designs "ethnography," actually are conducting ethnographic interviews (see Spradley, 1979) with a randomly selected sample. This strategy may be entirely appropriate for answering the research question. For the reviewer, however, certain expectations may attend the term *ethnography* that the research design does not fulfill. It implies, for example, an extensive physical and temporal immersion in a carefully selected but naturally occurring field site. In addition to providing the context in which the question is being investigated and analyzed, this strategy reduces bias and helps ensure that the data are not only bountiful but also valid and reliable. In conducting an ethnography of a hospital, for example, it would be essential that observations include all three shifts, all days of the week, and any seasonal changes in organization and activity. It is only in this way that the investigator can determine that observed behavior is not simply a product of a particular time period. Investigators who claim to be using ethnography but actually are only conducting ethnographic interviews often are criticized for not adhering to the conventions of the designated method. This criticism is especially true if the investigators have failed to compensate for the absence of ethnography's intrinsic methodological advantages by building in alternative methods for achieving validity and reliability.

Finally the terminology may be unfamiliar to those who do not employ these research strategies. *Etic* and *emic*, for example, are a source of confusion for reviewers, a confusion that is reinforced by the multiplicity of definitions offered by investigators. Regarding data, *emic* refers to those that are derived from the informants and address the "meaning" that informants ascribe to phenomena. *Etic* refers to those data derived from the observations of the investigators that describe the actual "behavior" associated with phenomena (Pelto & Pelto, 1986). The emic/etic distinction may be described best as the difference between "what people say" and "what people do," respectively. Many proposals, however, erroneously treat *emic* and *etic* as synonymous for *qualitative* and *quantitative* or *inductive* and *deductive*. The problems associated with the interpretation of terminology could be avoided simply by describing the design in as much detail as possible, without reference to qualitative jargon, and then explaining why that method is better than any other for this particular problem and these particular research questions.

Excessive Reliance on Verbal Reports

Some of the methodological problems described thus far could be avoided if it were not for the excessive, and sometimes exclusive, reliance on verbal data. Data pertaining to human behavior and events are derived basically from three sources:

what people tell us, what we observe, and the products of human activity, such as documents, records, buildings, television programs, and literature. On the basis of the techniques used to collect data, each of these sources yields information that can be analyzed qualitatively, as well as quantitatively. Most qualitative proposals, however, limit the data source to verbal reports derived in unstructured interviews. The "emic" search for the sociocultural meanings that attend events and behavior is a legitimate concern and a valid pursuit for nursing. Understanding the cultural meanings of nursing phenomena from the patient's perspective has both theoretical and clinical significance. The meaning of hospitalization for individuals and families, for example, influences the way they behave when hospitalized and the relationships they have with the health care team. The differences between patients and providers in the meanings they assign to an illness have the potential to impede care and recovery. It would be misguided, however, to suggest that the expression of meaning can be found only in conscious discourse, while neglecting direct observations of behavior or examination of social products and institutions.

Paradoxically, the phenomena most difficult to articulate verbally often are those that may be the most critical for understanding both human responses and nursing technologies. Nurses, for example, always have made clinical decisions in the management of patient care. The decision-making process, however, frequently is so internalized and so out of awareness that it is almost impossible for them to explain why they pursued a particular course of action, other than attributing it to intuition or "gut feelings." Although not trivializing intuition, it is highly important for the development of nursing knowledge to truly understand clinical decision making. It may not be possible, however, to capture that process through interview alone. For instance, nurses are supposed to provide care to all patients and families with equal expertise and commitment. In reality, however, we know that that does not happen. What variables explain why some patients get more and better care than others? These departures from professionally prescribed behavior are of great interest because they tell us the difference between ideal and real behavior. Very few nurses could acknowledge, much less articulate, that they tend to medicate men more frequently than women or to provide more care to younger than older patients or to link the quality of their patient care with the organizational context in which they are working (Caudill, 1958; Goffman, 1961). Indeed, so many of the phenomena that we study are as fundamental as the air that we breathe but, also like the air we breathe, exist outside of our consciousness and therefore cannot be obtained through verbal reports alone.

There is nothing inherently wrong in using interviews to help us understand nursing phenomena, but investigators must recognize that when research participants are not responding to a standardized set of questions to which there is a limited range of responses, their discourse necessarily reflects not only their perceptions but also their facility in articulating those perceptions. When investigators use verbal reports to identify, for example, the "lived experience of coronary by-pass surgery" or the "perceptions of women undergoing a mastectomy," it is actually the *reports* of lived experiences and perceptions that they are capturing. These reports are limited, of course, by the informants' vocabulary and the ability to describe and conceptualize. Given that verbal expression is subject to individual variation, it is important that the investigator take precautions to ensure that the interpretation is truly a reflection of differences in experience and not simply differences in the capacity to use language and discourse. The analysis plan should address the differences in the verbal abilities of informants, or at the very least, investigators should identify the exclusive use of verbal reports as a weakness of the study so that the reviewers know that they are aware of the problem.

Excessive or exclusive reliance on verbal reports also may compromise the clinical utility of the results. If, for instance, we were conducting a study of pregnancy and social support, it is important to know not only how much support a woman *believes* she is getting but also how much support she *actually* is getting. This distinction ultimately affects the nursing interventions generated from the research. For the woman who claims that her social support is insufficient and who, in fact, receives little measurable support, the nursing intervention would be to find a way to provide more support. In contrast, if a woman claims that she has insufficient support but actually is receiving observably substantial support, the nursing intervention would be to find out why the woman perceives her support to be insufficient and to help her work through her perceptions.

Inadequate Justification
for Qualitative Design

Because the emphasis on nonexperimental, inductive designs is relatively recent in nursing research, it is incumbent on the investigator to explain why this particular design optimizes the study of an identified problem. Why, for example, is monitoring the behavior of 30 women over a period of 2 years more useful than interviewing 300 women once by telephone? Unfortunately, many researchers respond to this mandate with a zealous "quantitative-is-bad-qualitative-is-good" defense that bears little relationship to the problem being studied. At best, such defenses are abstract, textbook descriptions of specific methods. At worst, they arraign the shortcomings and inferiority of methods endorsed and used by the majority of reviewers.

The single most important element in constructing a research design is the consistency of the method with the research questions being asked. Providing a rationale for using a specific method should not be a treatise on the relative merits of phenomenology and logical positivism, but rather the clearest explanation possible for why the proposed strategy has the most potential for answering the specific research question and ultimately improving the clinical practice on which that research question bears. This explanation must be grounded in an analysis of the existing research literature that describes the gaps and deficiencies that the proposed method intends to correct. For example, suppose the research on social networks of the elderly were dominated by large-scale surveys using statistical correlations, the question may remain as to how and why those variables are related in actual human behavior. The best way to answer that question may be extensive and intensive, naturalistic monitoring of a small number of elderly in order to observe the deployment of networks in everyday life.

Interestingly, there appears to be a misconception that qualitative is necessarily exploratory, inductive research and therefore should precede large-scale, quantitative research. In fact, naturalistic, interpretive studies have functions that range from exploratory identification of variables to the actual testing of hypotheses through naturally occurring "experiments," depending on the nature of the question and the existing literature (Sechrest, 1973). For example, many of the studies proposed by researchers who identify themselves as "qualitative" employ a cross-cultural comparative design. Yet we know that crosscultural studies can be used to scrutinize (or even test) some commonly held assumptions or theories about human development, health, illness, crisis, patient care, and nursing practice in general. Indeed classic examples of early cross-cultural research that tested ethnocentric assumptions such as the universality of child development and child-rearing methods (Mead, 1928, 1935; Minturn & Lambert, 1964; Whiting & Whiting, 1975) have been extremely useful to nursing practice. More recently, cross-cultural designs have been used by nurse researchers to explore health and illness in specific cultural groups. If, however, there already is a substantial body of knowledge regarding a particular health problem, the investigator must justify exploration of the problem in the selected cultural or ethnic group. It is not enough, for example, to rationalize conducting a study on the management of diabetes in Native American populations only by citing the extent and severity of the problem in that population. The investigator must explain also why he or she thinks Native Americans will respond differently to the problem from the populations on whom research already has been conducted—that is, why the existing literature is not applicable to Native American populations.

Conclusion

In my experience I have found that reviewers do not object to the use of qualitative methods in the service of scientific explanation, provided they are appropriately justified and described. The concern expressed by many reviewers is that the methods employed always will be able to produce exactly what the investigator is looking for; that is, the evidence is carefully selected to *illustrate* the researcher's arguments, and there is no opportunity for the introduction of contrary evidence.

This apparent desire to prove, rather than test, an argument is pervasive, and the problem of validation is a central difficulty that often is unrecognized by investigators. In the end, however, reviewers seldom are willing to suspend their skepticism and, because of the lack of attention to validation, refuse to take seriously a great proportion of what is proposed. This refusal does not mean that reviewers are not sensitive to and accepting of different ways for answering research questions. It means that all methods must conform to basic scientific principles and that the explanations generated must be open to refutation.

All theory, whether derived from experimentation or from categorization of natural phenomena, involves an imaginative and creative leap from observed data to synthesis, hypothesis, and generalization. Unfortunately, with much of the qualitative research being proposed, it is impossible to follow the logic of the leap because it exists only inside the investigator's head. The search for explanation is confounded further by a democracy of interpretations. This notion that any explanation is as good as any other renders refutation of interpretation impossible, for no evidence exists that could counter the arguments offered. Ultimately reviewers want to know how explanation gets from evidence to premises to hypotheses and conclusions. As stated in the beginning of this discussion, an endorsement of scientific methods in the search for explanation does not mean to suggest that knowledge derived in other traditions does not make an epistemological contribution. We have learned much from non-scientific knowledge such as religion and other unassailable theories. It simply means that such knowledge it is not scientific (Manners, 1989; Naroll & Cohen, 1973).

The most essential point to be made in this contribution is that it does not matter whether the proposal is announced as qualitative or quantitative; it will receive the same level of scrutiny and be subjected to the same scientific standards. Essentially, too much is made of the split between qualitative and quantitative approaches. It is a spurious distinction, but, unfortunately, it is one that is reinforced in nursing doctoral research courses throughout the country. In the end, the merits of a research proposal are derived from its clinical significance, from the appropriateness of the method to the question being asked, from the clarity with which it is presented, and from the openness of the findings to refutation.

References

Caudill, W. (1958). *The psychiatric hospital as a small society.* Cambridge, MA: Harvard University Press.

Cohen, R., Langness, L. L., Middleton, J., Uchendu, V. C., & Van Stone, J. W. (1973). Entrée into the field. In R. Naroll & R. Cohen (Eds.), *A handbook of cultural method* (pp. 220-245). New York: Cambridge University Press.

Field, P. A., & Morse, J. (1985). *Nursing research: The application of qualitative approaches.* Rockville, MD: Aspen.

Germain, C. (1979). *The cancer unit: An ethnography.* Wakefield, MA: Nursing Resources.

Goffman, E. (1961). *Asylums: Essays on the social situation of mental patients and other inmates.* New York: Anchor.

Leininger, M. (1985). *Qualitative research methods in nursing.* New York: Grune & Stratton.

Manners, R. (1989). Confronting Emerson's hobgoblin: A self-indulgent exercise in explanation. *Anthropology and Humanism Quarterly, 13,* 30-36.

Mead, M. (1928). *Coming of age in Samoa.* New York: William Morrow.

Mead, M. (1935). *Sex and temperament in three primitive societies.* New York: William Morrow.

Minturn, L., & Lambert, W. (1964). *Mothers of six cultures.* New York: John Wiley.

Morse, J. (1991). *Qualitative nursing research: A contemporary dialogue.* Newbury Park, CA: Sage.

Naroll, R., & Cohen, R. (1973). *A handbook of method in cultural anthropology.* New York: Columbia University Press.

Pelto, P., & Pelto, G. (1986). *Anthropological research: The structure of inquiry.* New York: Cambridge University Press.

Price, L. (1992). A medical anthropologist's ruminations on NIH funding. *Medical Anthropology Quarterly, 6,* 128-146.

Sechrest. L. (1973). Experiments in the field. In R. Naroll & R. Cohen (Eds.), *Handbook of method in cultural anthropology* (pp. 196-197). New York: Columbia University Press.

Seidel, J. V., & Clark, J. A. (1984). The Ethnograph: A computer program for the analysis of qualitative data. *Qualitative Sociology, 7,* 110-115.

Spradley, J. P. (1979). *The ethnographic interview.* New York: Holt, Rinehart & Winston.

Tripp-Reimer, T. (1986). The Health Heritage Project. *Western Journal of Nursing Research, 8,* 207-228.

Whiting, B., & Whiting, J. (1975). *Children of six cultures.* Cambridge, MA: Harvard University Press.

Dialogue

Researcher-Participant Relationships

BOYLE It may be that one question [as used in one type of qualitative research] is more therapeutic than another. Is that possible?

MORSE It might be helpful to ask where the therapeutic-ness comes from. I don't think it comes from the question [asked]. I think it comes from the person being given the opportunity to have a listener and then to reflect on themselves.

MUECKE What is therapeutic? It's very problematic. I think of ethnographic interviewing, and you can get people who just finally have a chance to talk about themselves. Now they have finally had an opportunity to reflect back and see things. Now, is that therapeutic?

HUTCHINSON We have been trying to figure that out, and finally decided that it is when anyone feels helped in some way, or if the interview is useful. For instance, we found people who said it was a wonderful catharsis. We had people—these were cancer patients who were dying—who said "At least I've gotten to tell my story." Or, "By telling my story, my life has not been in vain." Interviewing Vietnam vets—those people were sort of a marginal group—and they were never heard, so it is this idea of having a "voice."

WILSON We have mothers who use crack, where when they are on a binge they do it every few minutes. And what these mothers said was that the benefit of participating in the research was that for the hour and a half or two hours, when she was talking to the interviewer, she wasn't doing crack.

MORSE Another example is that it gives the participant a chance to give something back to nursing.

HUTCHINSON Another one was self-awareness. I have heard people say, "I have not thought it through that way until I heard myself say it. Then I saw things differently, and then I could go and do it."

BOYLE And there is validation. I have a student who is interviewing young women, and they are always saying, "Do other women go through this?"

STERN It is really the intentional versus the serendipitous therapy that makes the difference.

MAY   In my project now we are encountering women who are really at risk, but the regimen was going to get them if somebody didn't watch carefully. And I wasn't doing all the interviews. I had my research team doing most of them until I had to coach them very carefully to say, "Whoa! We are not intervening here, we are gathering data." Then at some point we had to have a meeting—we called them "pull the plug meetings,"—in which we said, "All right, now we cross the line. Now we interview to provide us with information that we are doing everything we can, or asking the woman if she is safe, if we were concerned that she wasn't." I know that what we were doing was no longer science, but we couldn't stay in that relationship and not do it, and we couldn't exit stage left, saying, "Sorry your family is crazy, and we are going to refer you to social workers." So these interventions were not at the level of the interview. . . . Now it's playing real fast and loose with the researcher versus clinical relationship, but I think that with some of the work that we do to make those judgments, we have to make them fast.

DREHER   It's like a role. I have been in my community for over a year. Now, even if I am not doing a therapeutic interview, when I come back they have a series of questions to ask me. Generally these prostitutes live together in a crack yard, and they will say, "Now tell her, Ms. Mel. Tell her that she shouldn't be out on the street tonight because she just got out of the hospital." And they have put me into this role of an authority, or a therapeutic person.

MORSE   Or as some people call it, "mother"!

DREHER   Yes! It is. Only just recently, someone called me long distance from Kingston, Jamaica, to Massachusetts. She said, "The police took my baby away, and I don't know where my baby is. How am I going to get my baby back?" And I was on the phone with authorities, trying to figure out how this baby could get back to her. I mean that's not directly what you mean by therapeutic. . . . But if you want the data that is the most intimate aspects of their lives, you have to have that kind of relationship.

16

Research and Therapeutic Interviews: A Poststructuralist Perspective

SALLY HUTCHINSON
HOLLY WILSON

HUTCHINSON Several years ago, Florence Downs suggested this topic. She said, "I don't see any difference between therapeutic and qualitative research interviews." So I began to think about it for a while. Over a period of 3 years, I started going to Nancy Diekelmann's hermeneutic seminars, and I started hearing the differences between hermeneutic and grounded theory interviews. I became aware that qualitative researchers had different "models" in their heads, and that became the beginning of this chapter.

WILSON One idea that we wanted to bring to the table was to see whether we could deconstruct some of the themes that are implicit in this discussion. For instance, "a qualitative interview is a qualitative interview is a qualitative interview" . . . so that's one myth we would like to deconstruct. We also want to deconstruct the notion that "a research interview is a research interview" always, and never has any therapeutic benefits in the health care sciences, because we have lots of data in which patients say that they participated in the study because they needed someone to talk to or that they were guided to other resources by virtue of having participated in the study. So we also wanted to take apart the idea that the two types of interviews were so neat and separate.

Interviews, the foremost method used both in qualitative research and in psychotherapy, provide forums for the exchange of verbal and nonverbal information. The researcher/therapist and participant/client respond to and influence each other

(Ramhoj & de Oliveira, 1991). The interviews in both contexts involve a process of unveiling personal feelings, beliefs, wishes, problems, experiences, and behaviors. Yet confusing the research interview with the psychotherapeutic interview has been known to derail the objectives of each enterprise. Although in therapeutic interviews therapy is the object and in research interviews therapy may be a by-product (Lipson, 1984), in some instances the objectives of the two overlap. The research interview benefits the participant, and the psychotherapeutic interview yields valuable scientific insights.

Previous work has addressed the therapeutic nature of research interviews (Boss, 1987; Hutchinson & Wilson, 1993) and the therapist as researcher (Hutchinson, 1986; Lipson, 1984). In this chapter we deconstruct two prevailing assumptions about research and therapeutic interviews. The first assumption suggests that all research interviews are similar and, likewise, all therapeutic interviews are alike. The second assumption suggests that the differences between research interviews and therapeutic interviews overshadow any similarities.

Research and Therapeutic Interviews Defined

Research aims to develop knowledge. The predominant qualitative methods in nursing research—grounded theory, ethnography, Heideggerian hermeneutics, and phenomenology—rely on interviews as a source of data. Interview data are analyzed according to a chosen method that illuminates the central themes in the experiences and feelings of a selected person or group of people about a specific issue or situation. Interview data, when interpreted, provide valuable information for the development of nursing practice and theory. When we listen to others' stories about the pain of incest, mothering on crack, caring for a demented loved one, or living with a bipolar disorder, we learn about people's lives in their own terms. We do not anticipate the categories into which experience and meanings will somehow neatly fit.

Therapeutic interviews aim to facilitate growth and therapeutic change. Interviews are central to the therapeutic process that transpires between therapist and client. Effective therapeutic interviews not only benefit the client who admits to having problems in living but also focus on painful topics that may be quite similar to those mentioned above. Zinberg (1987) noted that the generic psychotherapeutic situation is "highly stylized" in that it focuses on "the study of itself and one of its participants" (p. 1528). Over time, language and gestures reveal the client's intrapsychic patterns. The therapist's role encourages self-disclosure, the expression of feelings, emotions, and attitudes. Such personal information is indispensable to the therapist in making decisions designed to help the client learn new ways of seeing and new ways of behaving. The therapist first seeks to understand, moves on to diagnose/assess, and then provides interventions designed to encourage therapeutic change.

A Poststructuralist Perspective

Most existing literature stops after distinguishing between what is assumed to be the "core identity" of a research interview and the "core identity" of a therapeutic interview. In fact, much more refined distinctions about differences within these types and similarities between them are revealed when a poststructuralist perspective is brought to bear on this discussion. *Poststructuralism, also called postmodernism,* refers to specific forms of cultural critique that have emerged in intellectual circles since the mid-1970s. These critiques refuse the appeals of epistemological absolutes and embrace the wisdom of a multiplicity of positions acknowledging the contradictions implicit in them and accommodating ambiguity.

Dissimilarities Between Research and Therapeutic Interviews

Theoretical Models

One of the sources of differences in the style and form of research and therapeutic interviews is rooted in theoretical models that underpin the interview process in each endeavor.

In the case of qualitative research interviews, grounded theory is based on symbolic interactionism, ethnography is based on cultural theory, hermeneutics is based on the philosophy of Heidegger, and phenomenology is based on the philosophy of Husserl. These theories undergird the entire research endeavor, guide and delimit the interviews, including the kinds of questions asked, the interview process itself, and data analysis.

In the Research Interview. Because grounded theory is based on symbolic interactionism, the researcher focuses on interaction and social problems and processes. The grounded theorist begins with open-ended, general questions and advances to more specific questions about strategies, processes, and consequences—concepts central to generating a grounded theory—for example, "What is the hardest part of taking care of your relative with Alzheimer's dementia (AD)? Describe the major problems you face every day. What has worked for you in managing those problems?"

The ethnographic method (Spradley, 1979) facilitates the study of cultures and subcultures found on a cancer ward (Germain, 1979), in the nursing profession (Wolf, 1988), or in folk healing practices among Greek immigrants (Tripp-Reimer, 1983). Researchers look for domains or categories of meaning/behavior, generate taxonomies or classification schemata, and ultimately discover cultural themes such as "neighboring" among Swedish immigrants in the Midwest (Aamodt, 1981). Interview questions are designed to elicit information that will enable the researcher to understand, for example, all *kinds* of AD caregivers, the *organizational structure,* the *interactional styles,* the *types* of patient management problems, the *interrelationship of factors* that shape a day care or nursing home culture, and the themes that describe the culture.

A researcher engaged in Heideggerian hermeneutics focuses on the ontological (modes of being) (Ray, Chapter 7). The search is for "the lived experience" of others. Consequently this researcher is likely to listen to participants' stories without asking questions except to clarify. The hermeneutic researcher may ask only one general question at the beginning of the interview—for example, "Tell me about your most unforgettable experience as a family caregiver for a relative with AD."

Some researchers engaged in phenomenological research that also probes the lived experience have expertise in the philosophy of Husserl. They focus on the epistomological (modes of awareness) (Ray, Chap. 7). Only by understanding Husserl's philosophy will researchers interview correctly—that is, in keeping with phenomenological traditions. In this case the researcher also encourages interviewees to tell their stories about the subject at hand, and the data are recorded verbatim. However, when presenting study outcomes, the final product should "speak simply for itself" (Oiler, 1982, p. 179). Unlike hermeneutics, with its emphasis on interpretation by the researcher, Husserlian phenomenology emphasizes rich, detailed description. Phenomenology that results in structural definitions is based on the methods of Colaizzi (1978) or vanKaam (1969).

In the Therapeutic Interview. As in the research interview, therapeutic theoretical orientations and models guide the interview process. A therapist who embraces psychoanalytic theory says little and appears impassive during the therapeutic session. Interview questions focus on a client's history, beginning with early childhood. Clients are encouraged to "free associate," or to verbalize whatever enters their minds, and the therapist's task is "to find the center from which the [client's] thoughts radiate" (Kepecs, 1977, p. 384). This center is also called the "focal conflict." The therapeutic relationship is the therapy; energy is focused on unraveling the "transference" between analyst and client as a "faithful replication of critical past experience" (Spence, 1987, p. 4). Questions are few and open ended. They might include, "What brings you to analysis? What do you remember about your childhood?"

In contrast, a therapist who adopts a Bowenian family systems approach asks systemic questions or makes statements that relate to multigenerational family processes. For example:

THERAPIST You said your father and Tom (boyfriend) have similar ways. Remember when you were a little kid. You went into your fantasy. You went into making your world the way you wanted it, not the way it was. So, therefore, you were never able to see your father for who he really is. You wanted him to be this way. You didn't want him to be the way he was. So the relationship between your father and Tom is that. It's the theme that you imagined your father more what he was not than what he is. You imagined with Tom more of what he is not than what he is. That's the similarity.

In a family systems approach, the energy is on the family relationship. The therapist assumes the role of coach and views the therapist-client relationship as a therapeutic alliance. Changes are made in relationships under daily living conditions, rather than within the therapeutic dyad.

A therapist with a behaviorist approach is concerned with using positive reinforcement to encourage healthy behaviors and with shaping or extinguishing those unhealthy or destructive behaviors, both during the therapeutic hour and in the client's broader life. Questions might include, "What does your fear feel like? When does it occur? What do you do to feel better?"

Other health care professionals who engage in therapeutic interviews draw on their own conceptual orientations (e.g., feminism, critical theory). Their interviews are continually focused and refocused by the assumptions about people that underlie that orientation. These therapists derive direction from the framework, as well as from the client and the data.

Interview Agendas and Interviewer Roles

Differences between interview agendas and interviewer roles abound in existing literature that contrasts research and therapeutic interviews. The research interviewer is, first and foremost, an investigator interested in gaining understanding of a particular phenomenon. Although a researcher may provide information, reassurance, and/or emotional support at some time during an interview, the major role is that of scientist. The researcher chooses participants who possess knowledge of the subject because of their life experiences. Research interviews are used to collect data that will be analyzed according to a variety of methods in order to make explicit the participants' views regarding the research question. Interview questions are linked to an overriding research question (e.g., "What is it like for daughters to care for a demented parent?"). The aim of the interviewer is to understand the participant's perspective and ways of making meaning. Data analysis involves interpretation of masses of narrative data.

Therapeutic interviews move beyond understanding and interpretation to intervention. On the basis of the chosen theoretical model or conceptual posture (Tomm, 1987), a therapist makes decisions about interventions aimed at accomplishing therapeutic change.

Temporal Issues

Research interviews typically last 1 or 2 hours. A particular person may be interviewed only once or repeatedly. In therapy, except for consultation interviews, interviews are usually not one-shot occasions, but rather continue over time; this "ongoingness" is embedded in the relationship from the beginning. In each session, groundwork is laid for the next session; threads of continuity link past, present, and future sessions. The longitudinal nature of the therapeutic process results in certain rhythms developing between therapist and client (Zinberg, 1987). Such personal and dyadic rhythms rarely develop with short-term research interviews. Likewise intimacy generally varies in degree in short- and long-term interviews, with the long-term interviews being more likely to encourage intimate interpersonal experiences.

Participant/Client Motivation

Participants in research and therapeutic interviews are volunteers. For a variety of reasons, such as to achieve self-acknowledgment, self-awareness, catharsis, empowerment, a sense of purpose (Hutchinson, Wilson, & Wilson, 1993), social status, and looking good (Hosie, 1986), *participants* agree to help the researcher by sharing personal information. *Clients,* however, want help, and so they seek out a therapist, much in the same way that a researcher may seek out participants, either by word of mouth, advertisement, or serendipity.

Interview Focus

Research participants tell stories about certain actions or situations, about critical events such as the loss of a loved one or a particular illness, or about unique or even routine experience. People in therapy focus on phenomena that result in feelings of dysphoria and problems in living. The focus and content create a different kind of interview. In therapeutic interviews, clients are more likely to be tense, self-conscious, and concerned about the therapist's evaluation of their responses. Depending on the topic of study, research participants may be somewhat hesitant, fearful, or emotional, but they are less likely to experience strong feelings or concerns about the interviewer. Despite the preponderance of emphasis on differentiating between research and therapeutic interviews, close scrutiny begins to reveal similarities as well.

Similarities Between Research and Therapeutic Interviews

Rapport/Reflexivity/Ethical Decisions

For both research and therapeutic interviews to be effective, the two parties must establish rapport. Good interviewers must "be present" in the situation (Ramhoj & de Oliveira, 1991), attentive, and responsive to the verbal and nonverbal communication of the participant/client. In addition, interviewers must transcend the interview process and observe reflexively themselves and the interview dynamics. Ramhoj and de Oliveira (1991) noted that, at times, interviews may superficially resemble conversation, but at their hearts they are different because of "1) A methodic consciousness of the form of questioning; 2) A dynamic consciousness of interaction; and 3) A critical consciousness of what is said, as well as of one's own interpretations of what is said" (p. 127).

Both research and therapeutic interviews are reflexive in that they encourage self-exploration and attention to what the researcher/therapist is asking, feeling, and thinking. *Reflexivity* is "a self-awareness and an awareness of the relationship between the investigator and the research environment" (Lamb & Huttlinger, 1989, p. 766). Likewise, in therapy, a "critical consciousness of prejudice" (Ramhoj & de Oliveira, 1991, p. 124) is required. In both the therapeutic and research arena, the therapist and the researcher are part of the interaction and thereby influence and are influenced by the interaction. However, how this influence is felt and/or made known is not often clear. Such reactive effects may alter the process and outcome of a study (Raudonis, 1992) or, in a therapeutic situation, the treatment process and goals. Raudonis (1992) noted that health care research focuses on the ends, rather than on the investigative process, but she emphasized their intimate connection. The therapeutic process, however, is far more open to scrutiny by the therapist and the client.

Both researchers and therapists are "juggling levels of thought" (Zinberg, 1987, p. 1530). They pay attention to the content of the interview, yet simultaneously observe affect and think about language while listening for patterns. In the case of the researcher, the patterns are transpersonal across the studied group; for the therapist the pattern is within the client/family. In both cases, content is not useful in and of itself, but only as it fits with the emerging sense of pattern, structure, and themes.

Reflexivity in the therapeutic process involves self-examination via analysis of transference, countertransference, and familial issues. Although therapists are taught to focus on the client and his or her identified problem, to keep their personal issues and personal lives out of the therapeutic arena, understanding one's own family and personal patterns is considered to be essential to working constructively with clients. Karshmer (1982) suggested that therapists "critically analyze the reasons and conceptual underpinnings for each encounter" (p. 28). Informal discussions with colleagues and participation in a supervisory group or in one's own therapy also work toward the therapist's goal of becoming clear about his or her intrapsychic and familial issues and their effects in therapy.

For ethical reasons, researchers occasionally may step out of the research role and provide information or assistance to participants. For example, Hutchinson (1992) found that some nurses she interviewed who were accused of violating the Nurse Practice Act were extremely upset and that they had erroneous information about their hearings with the Board of Nursing. She provided corrective information and suggested resources, believing that this was the only possible moral decision. Likewise therapists make ethical decisions (e.g., supporting a bipolar client's choice to not voluntarily disclose his or her illness to a potential employer) because that disclosure would result in not being hired.

Interviewer Self-Dialogue/
The Nature of Questions

For researchers and therapists, an internal self-dialogue occurs throughout the interview process. A researcher is not only listening but also thinking about what question to ask next and how to ask it. Often he or she will write a few notes as a prompt to revisit a topic of interest. Tomm (1987) noted that therapists make decisions on a moment-to-moment basis when it comes to what to ask. They wonder what will happen if a question is asked or is not asked. How should the question be asked? What will the effects be? What effects are desired?

Other strategies common to research and therapeutic interviews include the use of open-ended questions that elicit an extended reply and free expression of feelings and description of experiences. All questions "embody some intent and arise from certain assumptions" (Tomm, 1988, p. 1). Both researchers and therapists agree that the style and content of the questions affect the interview process. Questions are focused on certain themes in the world of the participant/client.

In a study's initial interviews, researchers generally begin with semistructured questions that allow participants to guide the interviews and to illuminate their own perspectives on the topic under study (May, 1991). Over time, researchers shift to more focused questions after they have analyzed some data and have caught sight of patterns among participants (May, 1991). These focused interviews permit researchers to check their hunches or initial hypotheses. Likewise, over time, therapeutic interviews become more focused on the person's patterned responses to life experiences.

Other strategies used in research interviews include posing a hypothetical question, asking for the ideal situation, and playing the devil's advocate. Different therapeutic models also suggest different kinds of questions (e.g., reflexive, circular, strategic, lineal) (Tomm, 1988). Interviewers also learn strategies for refocusing an interview and for dealing with angry, silent, resistive, and emotionally distraught participants/clients.

Although questions make up the majority of researcher/therapist "talk," statements are used on occasion. Researchers/therapists may provide information. Also, different therapeutic models call for different comments at different times in the therapeutic process.

May (1991) pointed out that the difficulties in research interviewing involve "the delicate balance between flexibility and consistency, depth and breadth, and how to get the story and attend to the needs of the storytellers themselves" (p. 200). In therapy the difficulty lies in discovering those verbal interventions that enhance therapeutic change. Both types of interviews require awareness, sensitivity, and careful scrutiny.

Description/Interpretation

In recording and analyzing interviews, both researchers and therapists strive for "precision in the description and stringency in the interpretation of meaning" (Ramhoj & de Oliveira, 1991, p. 123). Therapy tends to be more deductive because meaning is interpreted from a specific theoretical framework, although Spence (1987) advocated for a new hermeneutic discipline that avoids standard theory in favor of new interpretive formulations. Research relies on induction because the philosophical roots of most of the varied qualitative methods encourage conceptualizing participants' perspectives, rather than interpreting based on predetermined theoretical frameworks (Boss, 1987).

Sensitivity/Judgment/Legal-Ethical Standards

Both researchers and therapists want to conduct interviews with sensitivity and judgment (Smith, 1992) and in accordance with relevant legal and ethical standards. Research interviews often involve questions about "highly personal, emotionally charged and, in some cases, unresolved" (Smith, 1992, p. 102) issues such as rape, child abuse, violence, drug abuse, and homosexuality. Therapeutic interviews, likewise, deal with the entire range of human behavior. Both types of interviews have the potential for further traumatizing the participant/client.

Research participants enter a study after signing an informed consent statement that describes the research study, including the topic of the interview and the anticipated risks and benefits. Munhall (1989) suggested that "process consenting" is more appropriate for qualitative research because the risks never can be predicted fully, and unforeseen issues inevitably arise. Process consenting allows the researcher/participant to assess consent throughout the research process, providing more protection and freedom of choice for participants. Participants are always free to withdraw from the interview/study at any time.

In a therapeutic relationship, clients should be able to have complete trust in the therapist who is responsible for protecting their interests. Clients are protected by state practice acts and the legal notion of "the acceptable" that describes the standard of care. Violation of the act or of the reasonable standard of care constitutes malpractice, which becomes grounds for litigation. In addition, ethical codes for both practice and research exist for nurses, physicians, social workers, and psychologists.

Management of Privacy/ Anonymity/Confidentiality

Privacy, including maintaining the confidentiality and ano-nymity of data, is critical to both researchers and therapists. Interview transcriptions are anonymous; a code number or a name usually is assigned to each participant. Confidentiality concerns the matter of who has access to the data. The informed consent agreement should specify who has access to the data (e.g., a research team, research class) and the use of the data (will it be used only for a given study, or might it be used later for a secondary analysis or for another research study? Will it be used in publications and presentations?). Because researchers often tape-record interviews, the storage and disposition of the tapes are also key issues. Tapes usually are erased after they are transcribed; they and the interview transcripts are stored in locked file cabinets.

In therapy, clients' names are on files kept in locked file cabinets. Interview sessions occasionally are tape-recorded and transcribed for educational and/or research purposes, but usually therapists make notes in their clients' charts at the end of each session and request formal releases for the use of audio- or videotaped sessions.

Neutrality/Reliability/Validity

Interviews aim for a balance that facilitates interaction but maintains objectivity (Smith, 1992), also called *neutrality* (Lincoln & Guba, 1985; Tomm, 1987). The aim in research is to remain relatively objective. We say "relatively" because "the interpretation of interview data is never wholly objective and dispassionate despite any effort made to be so. Data interpretation is influenced by life experience and intellectual ability" (Smith, 1992, p. 99). Qualitative research findings meet the test of objectivity or neutrality to "the degree . . . [that they] are determined by the [participants] and conditions of the inquiry and not by the biases, motivations, interests, or perspectives of the inquirer" (Lincoln & Guba, 1985, p. 290). In therapy, *neutrality* refers to being noncommittal, meaning that the therapist refuses to take sides with any person or on any issue. The therapist gives up his or her own intentions/preconceptions and remains flexible and open to the present situation. The stance of neutrality, "what is," alternates with strategizing "what ought to be" (Tomm, 1987) throughout the therapeutic process.

Researchers make preconceived ideas explicit, monitor themselves by keeping a research journal of ongoing thoughts and feelings, and discuss their concerns with a research team. By using such strategies, they aim to enhance objectivity and decrease bias, thus making the research product valid and reliable for practice. We addressed particular threats to validity in research interviews in a prior publication (Hutchinson & Wilson,

1992). As is true with some models of therapy, some contemporary researchers (Lamb & Huttlinger, 1989; Watson, Irwin, & Michalske, 1991) advocate for engagement and partiality, rather than objectivity and detachment.

Summary

In this chapter we explored similarities and dissimilarities between research and therapeutic interviews. We have challenged two pervading foundational ideas by subjecting them to closer scrutiny. Clearly, theoretical frameworks, conversational patterns, interviewer roles, and the interview focus vary considerably within both research and therapeutic interviews. Interviews are not best understood as essential core identities, but rather as processes situated in culture and context and socially constructed by the participants involved. Furthermore, despite conventional claims regarding fundamental differences between research and therapeutic interviews, at least as many commonalties are identifiable. Interviewing in research and in therapy is challenging, requiring the interviewer to be aware of the interview purpose, the theoretical model that undergirds the interview process, and the relevant methodological issues. Only with such awareness can health care professionals and researchers be astute when relying on this widely used strategy.

References

Aamodt, A. (1981). Neighboring: Discovering support systems among Norwegian-American women. In D. A. Messerschmidt (Ed.), *Anthropologists at home: Methods and issues in the study of one's own society* (pp. 133-152). New York: Cambridge University Press.

Boss, P. (1987). The role of intuition in family research: Three issues of ethics. *Contemporary Family Therapy, 9*(1-2), 146-159.

Colaizzi, P. (1978). Psychological research as the phenomenologist views it. In R. Vaile & M. King (Eds.), *Existential phenomenological alternatives for psychology* (pp. 48-71). New York: Oxford University Press.

Germain, C. (1979). *The cancer unit: An ethnography.* Wakefield, MA: Nursing Resources.

Hosie, P. (1986). Some theoretical and methodological issues to consider when using interviews for naturalistic research. *Australian Journal of Education, 30*(2), 200-211.

Hutchinson, S. (1986). Research issues in nursing psychotherapy practice. In J. Durham & S. Hardin (Eds.), *The nurse psychotherapist in private practice* (pp. 39-49). New York: Springer.

Hutchinson, S. (1992). Nurses who violate the Nurse Practice Act: Transformation of professional identity. *Image: Journal of Nursing Scholarship, 24*(2), 133-139.

Hutchinson, S., & Wilson, H. (1992). Validity threats in scheduled semistructured research interviews. *Nursing Research, 41*(2), 117-119.

Hutchinson, S., Wilson, M., & Wilson, H. (1993). *Participant benefits of in-depth interviews*. Manuscript submitted for publication.

Karshmer, J. (1982). Rules of thumb: Hints for the psychiatric nursing student. *Journal of Psychosocial Nursing and Mental Health Services, 20*(3), 25-28.

Kepecs, J. (1977). Teaching psychotherapy by use of brief typescripts. *American Journal of Psychotherapy, 31*(3), 383-393.

Lamb, B., & Huttlinger, K. (1989). Reflexivity in nursing research. *Western Journal of Nursing Research, 11*(6), 765-772.

Lincoln, Y., & Guba, E. (1985). *Naturalistic inquiry*. Beverly Hills, CA: Sage.

Lipson, J. (1984). Combining researcher, clinical and personal roles: Enrichment or confusion. *Human Organization, 43*(4), 348-352.

May, K. (1991). Interviewing techniques: Concerns and challenges. In J. Morse (Ed.), *Qualitative nursing research* (pp. 188-201). Newbury Park, CA: Sage.

Munhall, P. (1989). Ethical considerations in qualitative research. *Western Journal of Nursing Research, 10*(2), 150-162.

Oiler, C. (1982). The phenomenological approach in nursing research. *Nursing Research, 31*(3), 178-181.

Ramhoj, P., & de Oliveira, E. (1991). A phenomenological hermeneutic access to research of the old age area. *Scandinavian Journal of Caring Science, 5*(3), 121-127.

Raudonis, B. (1992). Ethical considerations in qualitative research with hospice patients. *Western Journal of Nursing Research, 2*(2), 238-249.

Smith, L. (1992). Ethical issues in interviewing. *Journal of Advanced Nursing, 17,* 98-103.

Spence, D. (1987). *The Freudian metaphor*. New York: Norton.

Spradley, J. (1979). *The ethnographic interview*. New York: Holt, Rinehart & Winston.

Tomm, K. (1987). Interventive interviewing: Part 1. Strategizing as a fourth guideline for the therapist. *Family Process, 26,* 3-13.

Tomm, K. (1988). Interventive interviewing: Part 3. Intending to ask lineal, circular, strategic, or reflexive questions? *Family Process, 27*(1), 1-13.

Tripp-Reimer, T. (1983). Retention of a folk healing practice (matiasma) among four generations of urban Greek immigrants. *Nursing Research, 32,* 97-101.

vanKaam, A. (1969). *Existential foundations of psychology.* Garden City, NY: Doubleday.

Watson, L., Irwin, J., & Michalske, S. (1991). Researcher as friend: Methods of the interviewer in a longitudinal study. *Qualitative Health Research, 1*(4), 497-514.

Wolf, Z. (1988). *Nurses' work, the sacred and the profane.* Philadelphia: University of Pennsylvania Press.

Zinberg, N. (1987). Elements of the private therapeutic interview. *American Journal of Psychiatry, 144*(12), 1527-1533.

Dialogue

On Being a Stranger in the Field

SANDELOWSKI I know we have to "make the familiar strange and make the strange familiar." Especially when you are dealing with your own culture. One of the things you really have to do is step back and not make assumptions that you think you know something. That you are actually going through a process of estranging yourself from the setting in order to understand it better. None of us are likely to go into an area that we know little about.

MORSE The problems we are having is with the word *know*. I think the problem areas that are disastrous are the ones you already work in and where you already have a role.

LIPSON I have a student who is an experienced ICN nurse, and she is doing an ethnographic study in the setting where she works—she is following the role of the moms—and she said, "I'm seeing things about this place that just shatter me!"

MORSE Yes, but aren't her co-workers saying, "Come on. Roll up your sleeves and get to work"?

LIPSON Oh yes, she is having to negotiate all the time.

MORSE Oh, how terrible for her. She doesn't need that! How terrible for a new researcher to have to handle all that political flack.

DREHER But I am concerned about some novice researcher taking this [advice about being a stranger] very literally, saying "I shouldn't know anything about this place. I shouldn't have read anything."—

KNAFL What about clinical nurse researchers? Does this give the impression that they should not do qualitative research?

BOYLE Just cite Agar and go on.

DREHER The other thing is, I think you see a contradiction in proposals. Many researchers write that they should "not be known in the area." Then they hire research assistants: a black one for the black community because they are known in the area, an oriental one for the oriental area because they are known by the population, and so on. There has to be some way of working this out.

MUECKE It works both ways. There is some information that you will only get because you are an insider.

LIPSON This being a stranger thing is necessary, but you can be a stranger without being a stranger—by shifting your consciousness to a different place.

17

Research Teams:
Possibilities and Pitfalls
in Collaborative Qualitative Research

TONI TRIPP-REIMER
BERNARD SOROFMAN
JENNIFER PETERS
JAMES E. WATERMAN

The issue we have been struggling with in this chapter concerns the dialectic of qualitative research. The dialectic of collaborative research is that it is at once the most exciting and most difficult scientific path one can walk. On one side, uniquely innovative ideas are synthesized and fresh insights into the world emerge. On the other side, conflict and frustration result from the clash of strong wills, competing ideologies (philosophies), and imperfect theoretical frameworks for the problems at hand. The realization that personal biases and scientific limitations eventually will be supplanted with a more complex understanding for science holds a true collaborative team together. The challenge is for the teams to stay together long enough for the team to grow.

Qualitative research is almost invariably a collaborative endeavor. A basic tenet of the naturalistic approach to inquiry is that persons who are the focus of investigation are considered to be participating informants, rather than objectified subjects. From this perspective, investigators and informants are colleagues who can be considered as a type of research team. Ethical and logistical issues for the field teams of investigators-informants have received considerably attention (Adler & Adler, 1987; Byerly, 1969; Shaffir & Stebbins, 1991). However, there is a surprising dearth of information regarding issues that confront larger teams of investigators and research staff working together to conduct qualitative research. In this chapter we provide an overview of models of collaboration and address methodological issues that arise during specific research phases.

Models of Collaboration

The most common form of collaboration is that of investigator and staff. Although staff assistants may be used during any phase of research, they are recruited most commonly for data collection and management. An investigator may employ field interviewers to assist in gathering data to overcome numerous barriers, including linguistic fluency, gender or age normative roles, or time constraints. During the data management phase, staff also may be employed to transcribe taped interviews or to code data (particularly if the coding structure fits either the codebook or template style described by Miller and Crabtree, 1992).

A more complex form of collaboration occurs when a group of investigators forms a team to undertake research of mutual interest. This investigator-team model is the norm for research that combines the expertise of investigators from different disciplines or with different methodological expertise. For example, several nurse investigators teamed over a decade to develop a classification system for nursing interventions (Iowa Intervention Project, 1992). This group differed considerably in methodological expertise and, depending on the phase of the research, relied more heavily on the expertise of particular persons during various phases of the study. In the earlier phases of the taxonomic development, when qualitative methods (e.g., Q- or pile sorts) were most prominent, investigators with expertise in these methods assumed more responsibility (Cohen et al., 1991). In the later phases, when techniques of multidimensional scaling and factor analysis were most prominent, the role of the qualitative investigators shifted to a more consultative role (e.g., naming or interpreting the factors and dimensions).

A third model of collaboration, a team of investigators with staff assistants, is a combination of the first two models. This model has greatest utility when multiple disciplines are needed to comprehensively approach a research topic and when the size of the project requires staff assistance at a variety of phases. The Health Heritage Project (Tripp-Reimer, 1985a) is an example of a project that drew on the expertise of investigators from a number of disciplines (nursing, anthropology, pharmacy). The mutual efforts of co-investigators and a large research staff were necessary to complete data collection, coding, and analysis.

The wide variety of issues surrounding all of these models of collaborative qualitative research can be most logically approached by addressing topics that are most salient during particular phases of the research process. Although most of these issues are not isolated to a particular phase of research, the key dimensions may be most identified prominently in this way. In the remainder of this chapter we identify issues during each phase of research and employ examples from the Health Heritage Project.

Methodological Issues
in Qualitative Collaboration

Project Conceptualization and Design

One of the most positive characteristics of collaborative research is its dynamic character. Because of the inherent stolid nature of scientific disciplines, research at the margins between disciplines is often the most exciting and innovative. However, disciplinary differences in philosophical or theoretical orientations and design preference merit considerable discussion and negotiation prior to the establishment of an interdisciplinary team.

For ongoing teams, subsequent areas of research become natural outgrowths of results of prior studies. The Health Heritage Project was the sixth in a series of studies of health behaviors of four groups of ethnic elderly (Old Order Amish, Czech, Greek, and Norwegian). Previous work of the team had established that patterns of practitioner use, and knowledge and use of folk remedies varied significantly among the four ethnic groups. Because of limited resources, however, a broader understanding of the multiple lay responses to symptoms was not possible. The Health Heritage Project was a comparative descriptive field study that combined quantitative and qualitative methods to investigate illness-related self-care responses among middle-aged and elderly persons in the four ethnic groups. Illness-related self-care was conceptualized as a continuum of responses in which home treatment and lay, folk, and professional consultation were all options. This conceptualization of self-care went beyond what was found typically in either nursing or pharmacy and was more congruent with literature from medical anthropology.

Membership Roles

Membership and member roles may need to remain fluid if the team is to continue functioning past an initial project. Effective interdisciplinary teams often have a core of key investigators who have common or similar research interests. This core is augmented by other investigators for particular projects for which they have special expertise. These additional investigators often collaborate only during the life of a specific project. Similarly the leadership position may be filled by different investigators, depending on the specific expertise called for in any given project.

The articulation of membership roles is both important and difficult. Although the roles may be fluid, some considerations may warrant structure. Expectations for role performance, privileges of team membership, and length of association need to be addressed a priori to decrease potential conflict.

In the Health Heritage Project, the following constituted the research team: an administrative core (the principal investigator [PI], a co-principal investigator [Co-PI], and a project director [PD]; 8 interviewers, some of whom were also co-investigators; a content analysis core (3 anthropologists trained in use of Ethnograph); a statistical analysis core (programmer, statistician, and analyst), coding staff (15 individuals), and secretarial and clerical (4) staff.

Field Entry

It is generally important for the principal investigator to establish and maintain field contacts with key individuals in the community. In the Health Heritage Project, the PI personally had conducted field entry with three of the four targeted communities. These relationships were maintained over a period of about a decade. As a consequence, the PI was much better able to understand interviewer issues and to manage data interpretation in the three initial communities. Although the PI visited the fourth community on several occasions, she did not establish any true informant relationships there. Consequently contextual issues for that community were considerably more difficult to interpret than for the original three communities.

Strategies for Data Collection

When observation and interviews are not collected by a single investigator, considerable attention must be given to mechanisms to help the PI maintain contact with the field context and the data. Not only do the collaborators need the research skill and cultural knowledge of the investigator, but they also need to communicate, in an organized form, the information they obtain.

Methods for data collection during the course of the project included structured interviews, family health diaries (28 days), unstructured (guided) interviews, life histories, and participant observation. Instrument development and training for process recording took 3 months and included up to four revisions of data collection tools. Data were gathered from 586 individuals residing in 200 family units (50 per ethnic group).

The family health diary was similar in form to that of most other health diary studies. The diary provided space for a designated family informant to note each day symptoms reported by all family members and any action taken in response to these symptoms. Additional information (regarding regular and preventive care, patterns of consultation, and practitioner use) also was noted. A sample diary was developed for each ethnic group, and examples of items were provided for each informant. Culturally specific examples were devised to serve as models to the family informant completing the diary. Additionally a set of probes was devised for interviewers to use to elicit more detailed descriptions of the symptoms, their meaning to the subject, and treatment decisions. During this formative period, the core research team and all interviewers met weekly to make group decisions regarding strategies for data collection.

Interviewer Selection and Training

Three research associates (one each for Amish, Czech, and Norwegian communities) had been trained previously by the PI and had participated in prior investigations in their respective communities. New interviewers were added for the Greek community, and additional interviewers were added for the Norwegian and Amish communities to complete data collection. Each interviewer was affiliated personally with his or her respective ethnic group (usually by heritage, occasionally by marriage or course work). Each interviewer was also at least master's prepared in health or a social science discipline and had prior interviewing experience.

Because of the diversity of interviewers, considerable effort was made in their training. Variation in interviewer style for guided and semistructured-structured interviews created a high possibility of introducing observer error. Because the symptom response data had to be comparable across the four ethnic groups, the types of probes and styles of interviewers had to have as much regularity and structure as possible. However, after the core data had been obtained, interviewers needed to be able to follow up important leads in order to more fully understand the cultural context in which the symptom response occurred. Thus the interviewers were confronted with two distinct, but not contradictory, goals: to obtain data that would be comparable across the four ethnic groups, and to obtain data that elaborated each specific cultural context.

Initial training of the interviewers has been described elsewhere (Tripp-Reimer, 1985b) but is reviewed briefly here. The PI videotaped model interviews with informants. These tapes subsequently were shown to the interviewers until they were familiar with the base protocol. Interviewers then were videotaped and their styles critiqued by the research team. When their styles warranted refinement, further practice sessions were held until the interviewers' styles were deemed equivalent to that of the PI. These procedures gave confidence that the interviewer styles would be comparable for the base data and that differences among the groups were not merely artifacts of interview style. Additionally, for the Greek and Czech ethnic groups, tape recordings of the interviews were made and checked by the PI and a research assistant. The Norwegian and Amish interviewers dictated their interviews and field notes immediately after interviews occurred. After the interviews were transcribed, they were checked for accuracy by the interviewer. Approximately 10% of the total interviews were checked by the PI to assess for "drift" in interview style and overcueing by the interviewers. In no cases was it necessary to retrain interviewers; however, occasionally, recommendations for additional probes were suggested.

In the second year of the project, during which most data collection occurred, coordinating meetings of the research team were held every other week. The format for these meetings generally took the form of a set of initial topics formulated by the administrative core for which information needed to be shared or decisions made by the team. Subsequently a lengthy period was provided for individuals to discuss issues and progress in the field. Issues emerging during this phase included logistical problems (problems scheduling interviews during holiday seasons for all groups, during planting and harvesting seasons for Amish), ethical problems (whether to report health problems stemming from polypharmacy to an informant's primary physician; whether to continue interviewing a reluctant family), and technical (whether to count a family residing in adjacent apartments as one or two households; informant selection in the four communities). Because data coding occurred concurrently with data collection, considerable time was given to clarification of data codes and the continuing identification of new codes (for open-coded topics). This regularized period of sharing and working through field and data management problems proved crucial to the completion of the project. The biweekly team meetings also included noting and celebrating project achievements (end of a phase of the project, publication, and presentations), as well as special personal events (birthdays). These meetings were extremely helpful for problem solving, for aiding others who were dealing with similar issues, and for increasing cohesion of the research team.

Data Management

Tracking Procedures

When a team is conducting a project using multiple methods of data collection by several team members in several communities, data management strategies are crucial to the successful completion of the project. Data flow sheets are a useful device for determining progress toward research goals, identifying potential bottlenecks in the stages of research, and aiding team communication. The data flow sheets tracked the number of informant families contacted and initiated into the study, and the progress (according to the type of data collected: e.g., structured interview, family diary, guided interview). It also identified the stage of data processing (data collection, transcription, coding, or analysis). As a result of maintaining this tracking record, areas of bottlenecks could be identified and resources reallocated according to project need.

Health Diary Coding

All data from the health diaries initially were dictated onto audiotapes and then transcribed onto a word processing system (Volkswriter). The data totaled 15,902 diary days representing more than 47 years of data. A 6-inch thick codebook containing more than 14,000 codes was constructed to assist in coding the diary data. The project stalled at this point, as nearly 2 years were devoted to the coding of the data from the health diaries. The enormity of data on the diaries necessitated a coding crew that, at times, numbered more than 15 persons.

Because of the number of persons coding data and the amount of data being coded, concerns about the accuracy of the data became paramount. Consequently the following procedures were initiated, which slowed data coding and subsequent analysis but served to maintain the integrity of the data. To minimize error, a limited number (three) of senior persons were responsible for "precoding" the transcriptions. This process involved both flagging salient variables and preassigning codes for certain designated items requiring specialized knowledge. When all 28 days of the diaries for a family had been precoded, they were exchanged with another precoder for verification. Incongruities were identified, and evaluative decisions regarding coding were referred to the PI or Co-PI.

Following precoding, the transcriptions were given to one of a number of coders who had received extensive training by the project director. Coders then categorized information from the transcriptions onto three varieties of data flow cards. The first card was completed for every diary day for each family member. The first card included the following information: subject code, data, diary day, number of symptoms experienced, and number of treatments used.

For each symptom indicated on Card 1, a second card was completed. The symptom card (Card 2) provided the following information: subject code, data, diary day, physical system involved, anatomical location of symptom, symptom label, subject's diagnosis, other diagnosis, reported cause, duration of symptom, and symptom details. Additionally information regarding whether behaviors were altered, persons first noticing symptoms, persons with whom the symptom was discussed, and whether treatments were performed or considered were coded.

For each treatment indicated on Card 1, a third card was completed. The treatment card (Card 3) documented the following information: treatment type, treatment label, class, category, whether the treatment was performed or only considered, dosage, number of symptoms associated with this treatment, number of associated treatments, symptom label, diagnosis, and further treatment detail.

The coders entered the information directly on to one of the coding cards, which subsequently were checked against the precoded transcript for errors (a process designated as "sweeping"). Any errors detected by the precoders were corrected. Keypunched data were entered on the mainframe computer. All fields were examined for unexpected codes, verified, and where necessary, corrected. A systematic random sample of 10% of the families verified online data with original records. This verification demonstrated a 0.0005% error rate for each data unit. Each interviewer entered field notes on audiotapes with a specified format that included the following content areas: (a) interviewer identification, informant identification, and date, (b) description of the place, (c) description of the circumstances (e.g., purpose of a group), and (d) content (observations, interpretations, and personal memos).

Narrative Qualitative Data Coding

All interview and field note data were analyzed with a considerably different procedure. The computer program ZY-Index was used initially to organize coded field notes and interviews and had been considered for use for all interview data. However, ZY-Index soon proved to be insufficiently flexible to meet the needs of the project. Consequently a second program, Ethnograph, was employed for overlaying a topical coding system on a large set of qualitative data.

The central problem was managing a large qualitative database in a way that would allow access to all needed information accurately and efficiently for the purposes of analysis. To address that problem, it was necessary to devise a system for the storage of data and correlated topical codes, as well as a system for retrieving related relevant data. Unfortunately the initial release of the Ethnograph software package contained a series of computer problems that slowed the process of coding the transcripts. These problems with the Ethnograph software were worked out through collaboration of the project director, the primary Ethnograph coder, and the software author (John Siedel). In all, the Health Heritage Project worked with more than 15 different versions of Ethnograph.

Two separate Ethnograph coding systems were devised for this project, each with a different purpose and history, The first, the "discrete coding system," was based on the Human Area Relations File codes, with numerous additional code numbers and words created to meet the specific needs of this project. This coding scheme was designed to be detailed, specific, and comprehensive. Codes for health and other related activities were created. All responses to the special events section of the diaries were coded by using this system. However, the magnitude of entering all qualitative data through this detailed system soon proved impossible due to time and personnel constraints.

As a consequence, a second, smaller and less comprehensive coding system was devised. The "truncated coding system" contained 17 codes. These codes were designed to (a) tag specific basic information needed (e.g., data on ethnicity, health, aging) and (b) block out broad subject areas while still reducing the amount of text involved (e.g., for treatments, consultations, symptoms, diagnoses). The purpose of this coding was to allow data sorting only and used topical area coding (rather than line-by-line categoric coding, which is performed more commonly prior to thematic analysis).

Data Analysis

Because of the complexity and the variety of data sets, a team was established to monitor data analysis. Several analytic methods were employed. The family health diary data were analyzed by using two primary methods. The first was the statistical comparison of the number and types of symptoms, treatments, and consultations across the four ethnic groups and between the two age cohorts (Tripp-Reimer, Sorofman, & the Health Heritage Team, 1989), which fulfilled a requirement to the granting agency. The second consisted of qualitative analysis of topical areas. For example, sorting the cases of whole symptom-treatment episodes allowed for analysis of the natural history of symptom experiences (Sorofman, Tripp-Reimer, Lauer, & Martin, 1990). Specific content areas (e.g., medication sharing) were sorted by Ethnograph, and subsequent categoric and thematic analysis of each sharing incident was performed (Sorofman, Tripp-Reimer, Haas, & Lauer, in press). Analyses of other topical areas (pain response and alcohol use) have been analyzed more recently, first by Ethnograph sorting, and subsequently employing Matrix analysis (Miles & Huberman, 1984). More interpretive analysis, such as community health ethnographies (Tripp-Reimer, Sorofman, Martin, & Afifi, 1988), will be conducted for the other three ethnic communities, as well as for individual life health histories, to understand the social context and meaning of alcohol consumption within and across the four ethnic groups.

Publication Issues

A prominent issue for all collaborative research concerns credit related to publication and publicity. With an interdisciplinary research team, it is important that all academic departments receive credit and recognition. News service reporters often exclude the names or departments of collaborating individuals other than that of the PI. To encourage more inclusive news releases, the Health Heritage Team used several strategies: (a) meeting as a group with reporters, (b) identifying the important contributions of the different members that derived, in part, from their disciplinary expertise, and (c) requesting (albeit not always receiving) authority to review an advance copy of the news article.

With regard to publications and presentations, it is advisable to establish at least preliminary guidelines during the formative stages of collaboration. Although these guidelines must remain somewhat flexible (depending on changing composition and contribution of team members), they serve to decrease fears and conflicts regarding credit for research effort.

In the Health Heritage Project, several guidelines were established with the research team. First, the members of the administrative core (PI, Co-PI, and PD) had primary responsibility for writing manuscripts emanating from this project. To this end, each member of the administrative core identified specific topics for which he or she would prepare the initial draft. Other core members then reviewed and refined each draft. Second, whenever ethnic-specific content was addressed at length in a manuscript, interviewers would be identified as authors after they provided contextual verification. This approach was taken because of the authors' importance in establishing the data set and their creative contributions related to culturally specific phenomena. Third, any team member could, with assent of the administrative core group, analyze and publish data on a specific topic. In these instances, the initiating team member would be designated first author, with members of the administrative core who provided editorial and analytic assistance as secondary authors.

These same guidelines also generally applied to presentations at various research conferences, such as the American Anthropological Association, the Council of Nurse Researchers, and the Midwest Nursing Research Society. As new doctoral students have engaged in research practica with the team, they have assumed the role of general team members, with the capability of identifying and drafting manuscripts in their areas of interest. Clearly the data sets are sufficiently numerous and complex to accommodate work for a considerable time.

Summary

Collaboration of a large research team brings inherent benefits and problems. These can be viewed as a series of trade-offs, with no one single approach being inherently "better." The determination to work in a research team largely depends on the nature of the research problem, the variety in expertise required, the degree of cooperation and commitment among members of ongoing teams, and the willingness to trust the information and interpretation provided by others.

When the research questions can be answered only by large-scale comparative ethnographically based work, a team approach is demanded. The key issue for comparative ethnographic research, however, is obtaining a core data set that is common among the participating communities while still obtaining sufficient cultural depth so that the contextual information is not stripped from the data.

The degree to which the PI or other investigators are distanced from the field informants is balanced, to some extent, by the closeness of members of the team. Indeed considerable knowledge of the particular communities is obtained through the experiences of the separate interviewers. However, the sense of knowing that comes from the personal experience of fieldwork cannot be matched through the vicarious accounts of the co-investigators. Maintenance of rigor and accuracy are perhaps of less issue than the personal sense of loss that results from lack of contact with each informant.

Further, whereas all levels of analytic depth are possible by using text provided by others, large comparative studies most often result in a more superficial level of analysis than is accomplished by a single veteran ethnographer. This issue can be obviated through the analytic assistance of the actual interviewers, but it remains perhaps the most problematic of all the dilemmas in qualitative team research.

References

Adler, P. A., & Adler, P. (1987). *Membership roles in field research.* Newbury Park, CA: Sage.

Byerly, E. L. (1969). The nurse-researcher as participant observer in a nursing setting. *Nursing Research, 18,* 230-236.

Cohen, M., Kruckeberg, T., McCloskey, J., Bulechek, G., Craft, M., Crossley, J., Denehy, J., Glick, O., Maas, M., Prophet, C., Tripp-Reimer, T., Nelson, D., Wyman, M., & Titler, M. (1991). Inductive methodology and a research team. *Nursing Outlook, 39,* 162-165.

Iowa Intervention Project. (1992). *Nursing intervention classification (NIC).* St. Louis: C. V. Mosby.

Miles, M. B., & Huberman, A. M. (1984). *Qualitative data analysis.* Beverly Hills, CA: Sage.

Miller W. L., & Crabtree, B. F. (1992). Primary care research: A multimethod typology and qualitative roadmap. In B. F. Crabtree & W. L. Miller (Eds.), *Doing qualitative research* (pp. 3-30). Newbury Park, CA: Sage.

Shaffir, W. B., & Stebbins, R. A. (Eds.). (1991). *Experiencing fieldwork: An inside view of qualitative research.* Newbury Park, CA: Sage.

Sorofman, B., Tripp-Reimer, T., Haas, S., & Lauer, G. (in press). Sharing medications: Lay networks of prescription drug distribution. *Medical Care.*

Sorofman, B., Tripp-Reimer, T., Lauer, G., & Martin, M. (1990). Symptom self-care. *Holistic Nursing Practice, 4*(2), 45-55.

Tripp-Reimer, T. (1985a). The Health Heritage Project. *Western Journal of Nursing Research, 8,* 207-224.

Tripp-Reimer, T. (1985b). Reliability issues in cross-cultural research. *Western Journal of Nursing Research, 7*(3), 391-392.

Tripp-Reimer, T., Sorofman, B., & the Health Heritage Team. (1989). *Illness-related self-care responses in four ethnic groups. Final Report* (NU01101). Washington, DC: Department of Health and Human Services, National Institutes of Health, National Center for Nursing Research.

Tripp-Reimer, T., Sorofman, B., Martin, M., & Afifi, L. (1988). To be different from the world: Patterns of elder care among Old Order Amish. *Journal of Cross-Cultural Gerontology, 3*(3), 185-195.

Dialogue

The Politics of Writing

MUECKE   When I read your chapter and the chapters here, I notice that something is missing, and that is the notion that we are political as nurses, and researchers, and whatever we do is political. By what we study, by how we study, these are not just ethical decisions, not just theoretical decisions—they are inextricably political decisions.

CAREY   A part of construct validity—and this is the qualitative analog—is the impact that the research will have on the research participants. You shouldn't do research unless you think through the impact that it will have on the people you are studying. And that's part ethical, but it's also a part of the meaning of the measure.

MUECKE   It's ethical, moral, and political. I must confess that in the past year my definition of myself as a professional nurse-as-a-researcher is moving much more to seeing that. Whereas before I thought I had to be politically neutral, objective, now I realize not only that I cannot be objective or neutral, but I should not be, that I am sufficiently privileged with the resources that have brought me to where I am, and to work with the people with who I am, that it's kind of a moral obligation to try to expose some of the things that are going on politically.

HUTCHINSON   But be real careful of the consequences for the research participants.

MUECKE   Oh yes, of course!

18

Ethical Issues in Ethnography

JULIENE G. LIPSON

I work with people who have been through very traumatic experiences, and I felt there was a need to address ethical issues for the kind of work we do. With vulnerable populations, our IRB requires that we have someone to call on for help, and I do have online someone who deals with posttraumatic stress disorder. I feel fairly comfortable handling some of the dynamics in the interview in terms of people getting quite distressed. I make myself available. But that moves into an intervention issue. And when the researcher gets upset, what do you do? Anyway, those are the issues I tried to address. There are all sorts of ethical, legal, and moral issues here, and I have only 23 pages.

Ethical issues in qualitative research are often less visible and more subtle than issues in survey or experimental research. These issues are related to the characteristics of qualitative methodologies, which usually include long-term and close personal involvement, interviewing, and/or participant observation. Cassell's (1980) overview of ethical issues specific to different research designs noted that the two principles that differentiate participant observation from other varieties of research have ethical consequences for the behavior of the researcher: Field research is a paradigm based on human interaction, rather than one seen as outside of human interaction, and field researchers are themselves the measuring instruments. Although the focus of this chapter is on ethnography, the ethical issues are similar to those faced by researchers who use other qualitative research methods. Thus ethnography can serve as an exemplar.

I begin this chapter with sources of guidance for ethical research in social science and biomedical research and then briefly describe ethnography. In the remainder of the chapter, I outline several ethical issues in ethnography—informed consent and its application to different populations, relationship issues and covert research, risk, and reciprocity. Because ethnography depends on interaction between investigator and informant, relationships between researcher and researched become close and multifocal, and the roles become much fuzzier than positivistic models that discourage interaction between researcher and subjects. In fact, the mandates of qualitative research itself, to form relationships and become close enough to informants to see the world through their perspective, create ethical issues, such as those coming from conflict or porous boundaries between the roles of researcher, friend, and clinician (Lipson, 1984).

As a nurse-anthropologist, I have done all my research in the urban United States, which is more similar to work of American nurse researchers than anthropological researchers (who study outside the U.S.). Examples from my current research with Afghan refugees are used to elucidate issues that are often subtler than in populations that understand and willingly volunteer for research studies.

Many immigrant or refugee populations have little understanding of or sympathy for research. Afghan refugees in California, who come from a poor and mostly rural country devastated by 12 years of war and political strife, demonstrate well-founded paranoia when asked to participate in research or, indeed, have any contact with "public agencies" or even a university faculty member. In this sense they are similar to other stigmatized, powerless, or vulnerable populations. Researchers should be particularly careful to protect anonymity and confidentiality of informants and to advise them of other risks.

Professional and Institutional Guidelines

Nurse ethnographers can consult several relevant codes of ethics to guide their research. These include codes published by social and behavioral science organizations and institutional review boards (IRBs) of universities and health care institutions.

Social Sciences

The "Code of Ethics of the American Anthropological Association" has gone through several versions (1973, 1983, amended 1990). This code emphasizes professional responsibility to the public, to the discipline, to students, to sponsors, and to one's own and host governments. In particular, it focuses on anthropologists' paramount responsibility to the people whose lives are studied. The guidelines state that, in cases of conflict of interest, these individuals must come first. Anthropologists should do everything in their power to "protect the physical, social and psychological welfare of informants and to honor their dignity and privacy." However, informants can choose to either remain anonymous or be publicly recognized. In addition, the aims of the anthropologist's professional activities should be communicated clearly to informants, and the anthropologist has an ongoing obligation to assess the potential or actual positive and negative consequences of the research and publications resulting from this research.

The American Sociological Association's (1989) code of ethics includes sections on the objectivity and integrity of the conduct of sociological research (including disclosure and the rights of the research populations); the publication and review processes; teaching and supervision; ethical obligations of employers, employees, and sponsors; and ethics committee policies and procedures. With regard to participants, the ASA code mentions protection of confidentiality and anonymity, informed consent where the risks of research are greater than the risks of everyday life, and taking "special actions" to protect individuals who are of very low social status, illiterate, or unfamiliar with social research.

Nursing Organizations

Nursing offers little guidance specifically directed to qualitative nurse researchers. However, nurses who do participate in clinical research can consult the American Nurses' Association

"Human Rights Guidelines for Nurses in Clinical and Other Research" (1975), summarized in Wilson (1989). These guidelines cover the importance of nurses knowing the conditions of employment in which clinical research is in progress; types of potential risks and how to recognize when risk is present; nurses' responsibility for vigilant protection of human subjects' rights of patients, informants, normal volunteers, and vulnerable populations; principles of informed consent and what information subjects must be given; and inclusion of nurses on institutional review committees (pp. 246-247).

In addition, nursing is primarily a human service profession with a "socially sanctioned (and therefore morally experienced) clinical or service mandate" (Chrisman, 1982, p. 117). Qualitative nurse researchers, because of the interactional dimension of their approach, often are pulled into clinical situations in which they must decide whether or not to intervene. For example, a doctoral student in nursing who has considerable neonatal intensive care experience is doing an ethnographic study of an NICU. While she is chatting with one mother, she hears an alarm and looks over to see another baby in respiratory distress. Seeing no nurse nearby, she resuscitates the baby.

The ANA Code for Nurses (1985), similar to nurses' codes of ethics in several other countries, addresses professional issues, patient issues, and societal issues (Sawyer, 1989). Two patient responsibility guidelines related to research ethics principles are (a) safeguarding the client's right to privacy by protecting information of a confidential nature and (b) safeguarding the client and the public when health care and safety are threatened by incompetent or illegal practices (e.g., being an advocate or whistle-blowing).

Institutional Review Boards

Finally ethnographers must conform with the guidelines of institutional research review boards for the protection of human subjects. Davis (1980) noted that at least 33 different formalized guidelines and codes of ethics for researchers have been issued since World War II. Five basic principles generally are accepted in research with human subjects: (a) Research subjects have sufficient information to make an informed decision to volunteer, (b) subjects should be allowed to withdraw from the study at any point, (c) all unnecessary risks should be eliminated, (d) the benefits to society or the individual, preferably both, should outweigh the risks, and (e) experiments should be conducted only by qualified investigators. Davis pointed out the conflict between individual rights and dignity and increased knowledge from research, both of which are strongly held values in our society.

Institutional bioethics and research committees are recent developments; previously, field researchers handled ethical issues on a disciplinary or individual basis. In 1974, under Public Law 93-348, the federal government mandated the establishment of institutional review boards (IRBs) at all universities that accept federal funding from the Department of Health and Human Services for biomedical or behavioral research involving human subjects. There was no IRB when I embarked on my 1972 dissertation research on Jews for Jesus. When an ethical issue came up (e.g., being asked to "spy" on a local chapter of the Jewish Defense League; the group's concern about publication of what they considered to be sensitive material), I based my decisions on my own ethical principles informed by discussion with my dissertation advisor and the American Anthropological Association guidelines.

IRBs interpret federal guidelines on protection of human subjects in varying ways, but most rely on a research subject's bill of rights, at least in spirit. These rights are having the study, including risks and benefits, explained; having the opportunity to drop out or refuse to answer certain questions; and protection of anonymity and confidentiality. Some IRBs attempt to apply the same standards of protecting "human subjects" to all research designs, insisting that all research subjects be given a copy of the bill of rights (see Figure 18.1) and expecting everyone to sign consent forms.

With an experimental design, the researcher can describe clearly the research process and procedures to a specific sample of subjects, but an ethnographer can predict only partially the research direction or may even end up with a population different from what he or she initially intended to study (Wax, 1977). Although ethnographers are responsible for attempting to anticipate and deal with ethical problems during a study, Cassell (1980)

UNIVERSITY OF CALIFORNIA, SAN FRANCISCO
EXPERIMENTAL SUBJECT'S BILL OF RIGHTS

The rights below are the rights of every person who is asked to be in a research study. As an experimental subject, I have the following rights:

1. To be told what the study is trying to find out,
2. To be told what will happen to me and whether any of the procedures, drugs, or devices are different from what would be used in standard practice,
3. To be told about the frequent and/or important risks, side effects, or discomforts of the things that will happen to me for research purposes,
4. To be told if I can expect any benefit from participating, and, if so, what the benefit might be,
5. To be told of the other choices I have and how they may be better or worse than being in the study,
6. To be allowed to ask any questions concerning the study both before agreeing to be involved and during the course of the study,
7. To be told what sort of medical treatment is available if any complications arise,
8. To refuse to participate at all or to change my mind about participation after the study is started. This decision will not affect my right to receive the care I would receive if I were not in the study,
9. To receive a copy of the signed and dated consent form,
10. To be free of pressure when considering whether I wish to agree to be in the study.

If I have other questions, I should ask the researcher or the research assistant. In addition, I may contact the Committee on Human Research, which is concerned with protection of volunteers in research projects. I may reach the committee office by calling (415) 476-1814 from 8:00 a.m. to 5:00 p.m., Monday to Friday, or by writing to the Committee on Human Research, Box 0962, University of California, San Francisco, CA 94143. Call 476-1814 for information on translations.

Figure 18.1. An Example of a Bill of Rights

suggested that attempting to weigh potential harms against benefits before research is carried out may be an exercise in creativity, with little relevance to the ethical dilemmas and problems that might emerge during the study. Further, she said that "the majority of harms and benefits of fieldwork are less immediate, measurable, and serious than the harms associated with other research modes" (p. 54).

Ethnography

Purposes and Characteristics

The essential purpose of *ethnography*, which literally means "a portrait of a people," is to understand a cultural group's way of life from the "native's" point of view. Ethnography is used to describe and explain the regularities and variations of social behavior. One particular contribution is ethnography's ability to inform culture-bound theories from other disciplines. Our theories reflect that we are human beings conditioned by our own cultures; ethnography shows the existence of alternative realities.

Ethnographers use prolonged observation, participation in the daily life of a group, flexible and sensitive questioning, and the skilled use of a wide range of techniques. Teaching ethnographic techniques is difficult because conditions of fieldwork are so varied that what works well in one situation may be impractical or even dangerous in another. Being a good fieldworker depends on qualities of sensitivity, adaptability, and insight that are difficult to train for or identify in advance.

The type of ethnography, the settings, and the population each raise slightly different ethical issues (e.g., see Boyle [Chapter 9] and Muecke [Chapter 10] for types of ethnography). Nurses usually do focused or problem-oriented ethnographies, rather than holistic community, village, or group studies. We often use the ethnographic method to study cultural variations in response to health and illness or to focus on a patient subculture within a larger social context. Because nurse researchers often focus on vulnerable populations for whom ethical issues are especially salient, we must remain constantly aware of risk and intervention issues.

Culture and Ethics

Two of ethnography's characteristics suggest ethical issues that should be considered: (a) its basis in the concept of culture and (b) the perspective of cultural relativism. Although ethnography relies on the concept of *culture,* there are numerous definitions of culture. These include positions on whether ethnography's distinctive feature is the elicitation of cultural knowledge, patterns of social interaction, descriptive storytelling, or the discovery of grounded theory. Different perspectives yield different research questions, methodological variations, and ethical issues. For example, using ethnosemantic interviews to elicit cognitive categories of illness among "normal" immigrant adults poses quite different risks to informants than doing participant observation in a drug subculture.

Cultural relativism has lost favor in recent years. *Cultural relativism* means studying other cultures on their own terms and avoiding ethnocentric value judgments about them. But Lieban (1990) noted a tendency to view ethical aspects of health care in other societies as cultural givens and to neglect ways they relate to moral questions and ambiguities. Other anthropologists argue that cultural relativism has been used as an excuse for doing nothing in situations in which people are oppressed or in danger or for not improving the situation of their informants. Respect for the uniqueness of a particular culture may be a cop-out for not dealing directly with ethical issues (e.g., accepting men's violence toward women as a cultural phenomenon).

Although rejecting cultural relativism as a formal theory, Washburn (1987) asserted that anthropologists have retained their moral and emotional commitment to those whom they perceive as victims of Western civilization, as seen in "action anthropology" based on a theory of advocacy or applied anthropology. For this reason and others, cultural sensitivity should inform the discussion of ethics. Lieban (1990) suggested the need to learn more about "ethnoethnics" to explain not only cross-cultural variations in ethical principles of medicine but also what different groups define as morally relevant or problematic.

Ethical Relativism

Davis (1990) described the dilemma of trying to reconcile attempts to discover ethical principles that can be endorsed as true for all people, with awareness of the world's great cultural and social diversity. Fowler (1988) found that nurse researchers from 33 countries, meeting in Edinburgh in 1987, were grappling with many of the same issues, such as protecting human subjects (e.g., safeguards for human subjects that were either inadequate or so stringent that research on such large populations as the institutionalized elderly was prohibited). Christakis and Panner (1991) argued that international guidelines are problematic because, in asserting their universality, they obscure cross-cultural differences and often suggest a normative function, providing a set of standards by which to sanction a researcher's conduct.

Davis (1990) noted it has been claimed that all cultures endorse ethical principles (e.g., stealing is wrong) but that differences appear in the application of these principles (e.g., what is stealing in one society may not be stealing in another). Davis (1990) stated:

> Perhaps we tend to adopt ethical relativism because we wish to show respect and tolerance for the moral beliefs of others. Ethical relativism makes tolerance a virtue and in doing so, contradicts the claim that any set of moral beliefs is as legitimate as any other. This claim says that tolerance as a moral rule is not relative but is binding on everyone. (pp. 413-414)

In the context of this dilemma, the question to ask is this: To what extent are we facing conflicting ethical standards in our research? As researchers, we need to acknowledge our own cultural baggage and how it affects our ethical values and decision making. Most bioethical discussions are based on North American or European ethical standards of individual rights, self-determination, autonomy, beneficence, veracity, and utilitarianism, which are assumed to be universal.

A basic theme in Western bioethics is the idea of respect for persons—that each individual is seen as equal to others and should be treated in consideration of his or her uniqueness. Most IRBs focus on the individual as the unit of concern, particularly with reference to individual "rights." However, we must remind ourselves that the individual as a unit of focus is rare outside North America and Northern Europe (Davis, 1990); in many other cultures, "personhood" is defined in terms of one's tribe, social group, or village.

This conflict comes up in my research; I am caught between my own Euro-American ethical values and Afghan worldview and ethics. Afghans do not think of themselves as individuals who have their own rights or autonomy, but as members of families. When considering protection of human subjects, I have to think in terms of family privacy or risks to the family. This notion is not easy for an individually oriented researcher, and, as noted by Larossa, Bennett, and Gelles (1981), there is no literature to guide qualitative researchers on ethical issues in studying families. One issue is that an individual has less opportunity to exercise "informed consent" about what is covered in a family interview because of having less control over what will be said. In essence, ethics uninformed by cultural knowledge can miss the point.

Which set of ethics should the researcher use? We have "official" guidance, our own personal ethics, and the ethics of the group being studied. I am strict about keeping interview data confidential and anonymous. If I am interviewing an Afghan refugee in his or her home and if family members and even neighbors come in and join the interview, I change the agenda to more of a social visit and limit my questions to general, rather than personal, ones. I want to preserve confidentiality, and the others have not consented to be interviewed. Some Afghans, however, might be quite willing to continue the interview as originally intended, family members included, because such information is family, rather than individual, information. Am I being overprotective? Locked into my own values to the detriment of my research?

In another example, American norms regarding dealing with public agencies differ from those of many Afghan refugees, whose experience with the government of Afghanistan was quite different (e.g., as one informant explained, Afghans are "honest with each other, but not with the government" [Lipson & Omidian, 1993]). I face a dilemma when I observe people "working the system" (e.g., taking written driver's tests for each other), although I consider this to be useful data. My Afghan friends accept my American tendency to refuse to "push the truth" in the "official" letters they ask me to write for them. Other ethical issues inherent in the researcher-informant partnership are described later in the chapter.

Types of Ethical Issues

The ethical issues mentioned most commonly in the field research literature include informed consent; deception or covert research; the researcher's responsibility to informants, sponsors, and colleagues; risks versus benefits; and, to a lesser extent, reciprocity and intervention.

Informed Consent

The principle of informed consent is important in any type of human research. The question to be answered is, Do subjects/respondents/informants fully understand what it means for them to participate in the study, and have they consented to do so? In essence, informants need to have enough information about risks and benefits, the character of their potential involvement, and the purpose of the study to make a decision about whether or not they will participate.

Consent may be obtained in several ways. Some IRBs inflexibly expect signed consents, which expectation often is based on inadequate knowledge of qualitative methods and the realities of community-based research. The bill of rights and the signed consent may worry potential informants unnecessarily or discourage them from participating in a study altogether. Some examples of those who may be concerned about signed consent are undocumented entrants afraid of discovery and deportation, those who are illiterate and embarrassed to admit it, and members of a stigmatized group who do not want their names recorded anywhere. More flexible IRBs allow verbal consent with an information sheet or posting a notice describing the study and informing those present that a researcher will be on the premises.

Language and cultural factors are frequent barriers to an informant's real understanding of what it means to participate in a study and who can consent for whom. At the beginning of my Afghan study, I attempted to interview a 16-year-old (who told me she was 18) who had been in the United States only 8 months and who spoke much better English than she understood. I had explained that we would take a walk and that we could have a conversation about her experiences in the United

States and her health, and she agreed. However, once I began asking questions, she answered the majority with, "You have to ask my father about that." I not only overestimated her language capabilities and status as an adult but also learned that only her father could consent to her being interviewed, no matter how informally. I subsequently learned that, to interview any woman or child (a category that includes unmarried adults), the father's consent is necessary.

In biomedical or survey research, it is relatively straightforward (if not always attainable) to explain what participating might entail because the hypotheses or research questions and protocol are spelled out in advance and "subjects" usually will be involved on a time-limited basis. Where biomedical researchers fall short, however, is in recognizing that their potential subjects may not have a real understanding of possible side effects or risks. For vulnerable populations, we must ask, How informed can informed consent be?

Qualitative studies evolve over time; seldom does the investigator know in advance exactly what kinds of questions he or she might ask an informant or what potential risks might be involved in the future. Munhall (1988) addressed this issue through the idea of "process consent," which offers the opportunity to negotiate and change arrangements. She suggested a consent form that is developed with the input of participants and reviewed and changed at specific times, as necessary.

In the same way, ethical issues evolve over time; they are ever-changing with the researcher's changing relationships with informants. A subtler aspect of the consent process is the probability of participants' "forgetting" they are being observed once the researcher becomes more a part of the social scenery and less a novelty (Cassell, 1980). Ethnographers expend a lot of energy learning to behave appropriately enough to function in a social situation or group and forming friendships close enough to allow informants to relax and tell "the real story." Thus it is common for participants to forget that the ethnographer is still a researcher whose main purpose is gathering data. For example, a close friend and chief informant who has worked as my research assistant acts as if she does not really understand that ethnographic data collection is ongoing and constant, including my recording of notes on what she says about herself and her family. In part, this behavior is due to my alternating between periods of concentrated data gathering and months when I visit her mostly to maintain our relationship. However, I also interpret this "misunderstanding" as her preference, despite my ongoing cultural questions, to forget my researcher role in order to think of me as a friend first. She knows that I value both her friendship and her role as my teacher about Afghan culture, and she relishes this teacher role. But even though she sees me take notes about something from our conversation, she minimizes the research aspect of our relationship.

Porous role boundaries in ethnographic research pose a dilemma. How frequently and under what circumstances should the ethnographer remind informants that he or she is conducting research? Some chance telephone conversations have provided enormous insights in my attempts to understand Afghan culture, and it would be irresponsible as a researcher not to record them in field notes. For example, my friend and chief informant complained that her sister demanded a visit "right now" when she had another important obligation. When I asked whether she could not just tell her sister that she would visit after the obligation, she replied, "Because she is older, I must obey." This statement brought home my understanding of the sheer power of the Afghan family to control the behavior and time of its members, and how family obligations can result in work or school absences or even breaking a law. I could not tell her I was writing notes as we talked on the phone; it probably would have hurt her feelings. However, I did tell her that this conversation really helped me understand Afghan culture better. This example introduces the topic of covert observation in research.

Deception or Covert Research

One of the issues discussed earlier in the social science research literature has been the ethics of covert fieldwork. Bulmer (1982) collected case examples and discussed the various ethical issues involved in collecting data unobtrusively when the population did not know that the researcher was a researcher. Humphreys's (1970) disguised observation of gay men in homosexual encounters by acting as a "tearoom watch queen" has been the subject of numerous debates.

The argument in favor of covert research is that it may not be possible to obtain data if a specific population knows of the existence of the researcher, because the behavior to be observed may be stigmatized, illegal, or embarrassing. Such data may not be obtainable in any other way. In recent years, however, most social scientists have tended to discourage covert observation. Whether engaged in academic or nonacademic research, the American Anthropological Association's code of ethics states that researchers must be candid about their professional identities.

However, it is useful to view the stance toward covert research on a continuum along which the ethnographer moves back and forth, from somewhat covert to completely open, depending on the situation. Because ethnographic research is conducted over a prolonged period, the context of the research can change dramatically or more subtly. Like process consent, the ethnographer's stance should not be static, but should respond sensitively to the changing situation. In some situations, it is more appropriate simply to interact and observe than to make an announcement that essentially says, "Attention! You are all being observed as part of a research study."

It is important to consider culture in the issue of openness about one's researcher role. Among people to whom research is foreign or frightening, such as undocumented people (those without legal immigration papers) or those whose behavior is potentially stigmatizing, one must build trust gradually through becoming familiar. Only later, when people get to know the researcher, is it appropriate to mention the research and to ask for an interview, no matter how informal. Even when an interview is scheduled, jumping into the "business" of an interview before having tea and beginning to get to know each other is considered to be rude in many cultural groups (Lipson & Meleis, 1989).

In our studies of Afghan refugees, Pat Omidian (1992) and I were strongly advised by our chief informants not to divulge our research purposes to most of those with whom we talked. They also advised us not to conduct scheduled interviews because people would be nervous about "what would happen to the information." We were told not to make appointments (because Afghans are not used to appointments) but simply to call and ask, "Are you home?" before dropping in casually and to act like guests; if invited for tea, we should just visit and talk informally. In essence, our informants were telling us to be covert both to enhance our data gathering and to avoid insulting or worrying our informants. We each recorded field notes after leaving peoples' houses, but we used them mainly as a rich context in which to situate later interviews.

With growing trust, however, came growing mistrust. Because the Afghan community is divided politically and ethnically, becoming trusted by people of one faction created mistrust by others. Because Pat wore Afghan clothes when she visited elderly people of one ethnic group, and as her Dari language skills improved, those from another group circulated a rumor that she was a spy. Some people feared that answers to her "personal" questions would be revealed to welfare officials. This reaction is understandable because Afghanistan under former soviet occupation was a police state in which nothing controversial or even personal could be said openly; it might be reported, and, as a result, the person could be imprisoned and/or tortured.

Indeed, ethnographers may need to judge each instance situationally along a range of the most public to the most private with regard to how open they are about their purposes. For example, Carole Chenitz announced her presence and research intentions through a small poster in a methadone clinic (J. M. Swanson, personal communication, November, 1992). With an undocumented or highly suspicious population in a public place, it is probably most expedient simply to be an observer, recording field notes in private afterward. Anonymous observation is ethically appropriate and defensible in public situations open to anyone, such as journalists. For example, I attended an Afghan demonstration in front of the former Soviet embassy to protest the occupation of Afghanistan. When Afghan friends wanted me to see a wedding, I attended as part of their family and later recorded field notes, with their full knowledge, but no one else's.

At the more private end of the continuum is observing behaviors that are considered to be private or participating in an organization in which secret rituals are involved (Chrisman, 1976). In this case, the ethnographer must consider carefully the consequences of his or her stance. I think it is important to be open about my researcher role, and I check carefully with informants about what information can be made public and what information needs to remain strictly within the group. In general, I ask myself whether an open or more covert stance is more likely to result in harm to a family or group in a specific situation. This question brings us to a discussion of issues related to risks to informants.

Responsibility to Informants: Handling Risks

Risks to informants can occur in (a) not fulfilling obligations or responsibilities to informants during actual research and (b) subsequent publication about informants and their culture. All of the codes of ethics described earlier include rules regarding the rights of informants to privacy, dignity, keeping information confidential, and care to avoid causing personal harm. Sieber (1992) identified eight risk-related issues in social research: privacy and confidentiality, personal safety and well-being, lack of validity, deception and debriefing, informed consent (and respectful communication), justice and equitable treatment, ownership of data, and gatekeepers and opinion leaders.

Some populations are particularly vulnerable to possible harm from participating in research, such as those who have "secrets" that could hurt them or those who "break the law" in major or minor ways (e.g., Muslim co-wives [polygyny], those who cheat on welfare, users of illegal substances), those with stigmatized identities, (e.g., gays or lesbians, HIV-positive people), or those who lack resources or autonomy (e.g., children, the mentally ill, the retarded).

DeSantis (1990) pointed out that a major concern in conducting research with undocumented aliens is confidentiality and anonymity; these groups are similar to other populations at risk for social, legal, political, and economic repercussions resulting from study participation or publication of results. Despite her precautions of number coding of names, reporting results in the aggregate, securing records, and limiting access to research data, DeSantis feared that there was nothing to keep the Immigration and Naturalization Service (INS) from issuing a subpoena of her records to seek the names and addresses of undocumented aliens.

Can we really protect potentially vulnerable informants? DeSantis (1990) stated that she could not promise absolute anonymity to her Haitian informants, despite her precautions—not asking for immigrant status, number coding, reporting results in aggregate, securing records, and limiting access to data. A frightening article in *Science* (Barinaga, 1992) describes a Massachusetts court giving R. J. Reynolds, the maker of Camel cigarettes, access to a researcher's files on a study of children's responses to "Old Joe Camel" advertising, including the data, the researcher's notes and correspondence, and the names of the children who were interviewed. The tobacco company subsequently withdrew its request for names but claimed that it had a right to see whether the study was biased; it then released the data, notes, and correspondence to the mass media.

The assistant secretary for health in the Department of Health and Human Services now is granting protection of confidentiality through a certificate of confidentiality issued under Section 301(d) of the Public Health Service Act. The purpose is to protect those who participate in sensitive research. Categories of sensitive information are sexual attitudes, preferences, or practices; use of addictive substances; illegal conduct; information that could damage an individual's financial standing, employability, or reputation; medical record information that could lead to stigma or discrimination; and information pertaining to an individual's psychological well-being or mental health. It is worth applying for such a certificate, although the process has not yet been shown to protect the data elicited from informants in court.

One of the safest ways to ensure anonymity is not to record the names of informants at all and provide an information sheet that asks for verbal rather than signed consent. Another way of protecting information that the researcher perceives as potentially damaging to informants is to omit such information from one's field notes, or certainly from one's published reports. If the researcher receives information about illegal activities, it can be handled anonymously or in the third person: "Don't tell me your name." I try to protect individuals by recording very few names of my Afghan informants and no addresses because their identities are less important than their perceptions or experiences. In addition, in writing an article, I change unimportant details in illustrating a theme (e.g., does it matter whether the person who asks a relative to write a letter fabricating employment is a man or a woman?).

An issue separate from identifying a vulnerable individual or family is how one writes about a stigmatized or vulnerable population in general. I constantly am warning my graduate students who study immigrant or refugee health to balance their reports. They tend to leave the impression (by omission and by focusing on people's difficulties) that, for example, "the whole Ethiopian immigrant population is mentally ill." The furor following Humphreys's (1970) tearoom study was not just about his use of covert observation; his portrayal of anonymous sex among homosexual men also conveyed a one-sided view. He was apparently careful in data collection and unbiased reporting, but some have argued that the larger issue of doing the study and publishing the monograph was damaging to the gay population.

Finally I should touch briefly on potential harm to informants during data collection itself, which is important in vulnerable populations. Cowles (1988) described how qualitative interviews on sensitive topics can stimulate powerful emotional responses on the part of informants, such as uncontrollable crying and struggling to regain control both during and after data collection. She suggested offering to stop interviewing, at least temporarily, but also noted the potential need for immediate therapeutic intervention because interviewees' emotional responses may put them in jeopardy. Interviewers should be prepared to act promptly. For example, Joanne Hall, a postdoctoral fellow at the University of California, San Francisco, is interviewing lesbians who experienced childhood sexual abuse and is finding that some women become aware of long-repressed details of their experiences during the interviews. Although she is a skilled and sensitive interviewer, and as yet there have been no ill effects for informants, she has appropriate referral sources ready that include gender- and issue-sensitive professionals, should referral be necessary.

Reciprocity

What obligations do ethnographers have to people who bare their souls so that researchers can write an article or a book or get a promotion? However one answers this question, fieldwork poses a dilemma. To whom is this obligation owed—the individuals in a community where one worked? The ethnic group as a whole? The local government? The funding agency? These obligations often are in conflict. To help one segment may hurt another.

A letter in the *Anthropology Newsletter* illustrates the feelings of a villager in North India, who wrote:

> As far as I know we gave the PhD to three American scholars. I don't know how many papers have been written about us because we don't usually get copies. Day by day, we talked to these new anthropologists in friendship; we didn't know this information would go into books and disclose our privacy. . . . I fear your writings would hurt the feelings of village people if they could read; they will certainly hurt our great-great grandchildren who will read. . . . As you have made a path into our private worlds, will you make for us, the people you study—a path into your private circle? Would you like to listen or not? (Pandey, 1992, p. 3)

This quote illustrates the long-range view of reciprocity, which most ethnographers have difficulty considering. In the short range, reciprocity usually is expected and intervention of some kind is inevitable, but their degree and type are influenced by the population being studied. The dilemma is not whether to reciprocate or intervene, but what to do and how to do it responsibly. In traditional ethnographies, the researcher went into the field to observe the full seasonal round of activity, living in the native style and observing life firsthand, disturbing it as little as possible. This ethnographer was the culturally incompetent person, dependent on informants to teach him or her how to function and behave appropriately. In urban research, particularly with vulnerable groups such as patients or refugees, the roles may be switched, and the researcher may be viewed as a valuable and coveted asset who can act as an advocate on behalf of the informant. Some informants expect money or health services. Certainly informants have more rights and privileges than do "subjects" in experimental studies, such as the right to approve a manuscript before it is submitted or to suppress certain data.

Like process consent and movement between covert and open observation, it seems most useful to be flexible on the continuum between pure observation and full participation, including acting on behalf of informants. Pure observation assumes "objectivity," which is not really possible in qualitative research, although novice researchers assume they can be a "fly on the wall." I reciprocate with favors that are not central to the topic of study (e.g., for refugees and immigrants, my actions have included being an advocate, driving people around, and helping them fill out forms in English).

In actuality, acting on behalf of informants while collecting data gives the ethnographer firsthand experience with informants' day-to-day frustrations in what they may consider a hostile culture. For example, I spent an hour trying to get an answer for an Afghan who needed visa information via the complicated taped telephone messages of the INS. I did not succeed in getting the information until I called someone in another office and bullied him into giving me the telephone number of a human being. I also drove an informant to the Department of Motor Vehicles (DMV) for her third attempt to get an identification card. She wanted an American to help her because "all the public agencies don't like us." Following our not-too-pleasant experience, I assured her that although some agencies do not treat people with accents with respect, "the DMV treats everyone this way."

The basis of applied research, which can be conducted with an ethnographic focus, is helping empower or assist the group to make changes in a desired direction. However, planning and implementing an intervention is also an excellent source of data. For example, Pat Omidian, after interviewing a number of elderly depressed and lonely Afghan women, wanted to do something to help them. She and her interpreter drove seven women to the park, where they shared a picnic lunch and got acquainted. This became a weekly outing that continued for several months. Within several weeks, Pat began to observe remarkable changes in the affect and energy levels of these women (e.g., one woman, previously too weak to lift a teacup to her mouth, walked 3 miles around a lake) (Omidian & Lipson, 1992). After Pat stopped driving the women, they learned to walk to meet each other at a prearranged place and have continued their weekly outings. Thus this "intervention" yielded a crucial connection between elderly Afghan women's isolation and depression.

Conclusion

How does an ethnographer make decisions regarding the ethics of his or her research in light of the issues mentioned here? These issues are only a taste of many that arise in qualitative research. We can use the guidelines of the anthropology and sociology associations, which are useful, if general. We must comply with IRBs to be allowed to conduct our research, and we often must be fairly creative to be approved by more inflexible human subjects' committees. Sieber's (1992) book is a useful guide to planning ethically responsible research for students and internal review boards.

For the myriad ethical issues that require on-the-spot decisions and are not covered in any of the more general guidelines, Cassell's (1980) advice is sound. She stated, "The principle of respect for human autonomy—regarding people primarily as ends rather than means—may sound soft and indefinite when compared with utilitarian calculations" (p. 37), but it may be the best principle when considering the variety of issues that arise in different kinds of field work. I also suggest that we inform ethical decisions with cultural sensitivity, awareness of our own ethical values and how strongly we need to impose them, and trust in our own gut feelings about what is right in the immediate situation and whether there will be later repercussions.

References

American Anthropological Association. (1973). *Professional ethics: Statements and procedures of the American Anthropological Association.* Washington, DC: Author.

American Nurses Association. (1985). *Code for nurses with interpretive statements.* Washington, DC: Author.

American Sociological Association. (1989). *Code of ethics.* Washington, DC: Author.

Barinaga, M. (1992). Who controls a researcher's files? *Science, 256,* 1620-1621.

Bulmer, M. (1982). Ethical problems in social research: The case of covert participant observation. In M. Bulmer (Ed.), *Social research ethics* (pp. 3-15). New York: Macmillan.

Cassell, J. (1980). Ethical principles for conducting fieldwork. *American Anthropologist, 82,* 28-41.

Chrisman, N. (1976). Secret societies and the ethics of urban fieldwork. In M. Rynkiewich & J. Spradley (Eds.), *Ethics and anthropology* (pp. 135-147). New York: John Wiley.

Chrisman, N. J. (1982). Anthropology in nursing: An exploration of adaptation. In N. J. Chrisman & T. W. Maretsky (Eds.), *Clinically applied anthropology* (pp. 117-140). Dordrecht, The Netherlands: D. Reidel.

Christakis, N., & Panner, M. (1991). Existing international ethical guidelines for human subjects research: Some open questions. *Law, Medicine and Health Care, 19,* 214-221.

Cowles, K. V. (1988). Issues in qualitative research on sensitive topics. *Western Journal of Nursing Research, 10,* 163-179.

Davis, A. J. (1980). Ethical principles of research. In A. Davis & J. Krueger, *Patients, nurses, ethics* (pp. 3-8). New York: American Journal of Nursing.

Davis, A. J. (1990). Ethical issues in nursing research. *Western Journal of Nursing Research, 12,* 413-416.

DeSantis, L. (1990). Fieldwork with undocumented aliens and other populations at risk. *Western Journal of Nursing Research, 12,* 359-372.

Fowler, M. (1988). Ethical issues in nursing research: A call for an international code of ethics for nursing research. *Western Journal of Nursing Research, 10,* 352-355.

Humphreys, L. (1970). *The tearoom trade: Impersonal sex in public places.* Hawthorne, NY: Aldine.

Larossa, R., Bennett, L., & Gelles, R. (1981). Ethical dilemmas in qualitative family research. *Journal of Marriage and the Family, 43,* 303-313.

Lieban, R. (1990). Medical anthropology and the comparative study of medical ethics. In G. Weisz (Ed.), *Social science perspectives on medical ethics* (pp. 221-239). Philadelphia: University of Pennsylvania Press.

Lipson, J. (1984). Combining researcher, clinical and personal roles: Enrichment or confusion? *Human Organization, 43,* 348-352.

Lipson, J., & Meleis, A. (1989). Methodological issues in research with immigrants. *Medical Anthropology, 12,* 103-115.

Lipson, J., & Omidian, P. (1993). *We don't know the rules: Afghan refugees' interactions with public institutions.* Manuscript submitted for publication.

Munhall, P. (1988). Ethical considerations in qualitative research. *Western Journal of Nursing Research, 10,* 150-161.

Omidian, P. (1992). *Aging and intergenerational conflict in Afghan refugee families in transition.* Unpublished doctoral dissertation, University of California, San Francisco.

Omidian, P., & Lipson, J. (1992). Elderly Afghan refugees: Tradition and transition in Northern California. In P. DeVoe (Ed.), *Selected papers on refugee issues* (pp. 27-39). Washington, DC: American Anthropological Association.

Pandey, U. (1992, May). "Would you like to listen or not?" [Letter in the Correspondence section]. *Anthropology Newsletter,* p. 3.

Sawyer, L. (1989). Nursing code of ethics: An international comparison. *International Nursing Review, 36,* 145-148.

Sieber, J. (1992). *Planning ethically responsible research.* Newbury Park, CA: Sage.

Washburn, W. E. (1987). Cultural relativism, human rights and the AAA. *American Anthropologist, 89,* 939-943.

Wax, M. (1977). On fieldworkers and those exposed to fieldwork: Federal regulations and moral issues. *Human Organization, 36,* 321-328.

Wilson, H. (1989). *Introducing research in nursing* (2nd ed.). Menlo Park, CA: Addison-Wesley.

Dialogue

Sloppy Science

MAY   You know, it's really fairly shocking, but when we come to a really interesting point and we get all passionate about it, it usually boils down to sloppy science.

KNAFL   Maybe the distinction between bad science and scientific misconduct is more elusive with qualitative . . .

MAY   Yes. Supposing I'm the person who employed Sue [to do a qualitative study], and I'm mad because I don't like what she said [in her analysis]. So I take her raw data, and I hand it to someone else to analyze. And if you do that often enough, you are going to find someone to conclude what you want them to conclude. Does that make Sue wrong, or does that make her a sloppy scientist?

KNAFL   Cooking and trimming the data around the expectations of the sponsor, or giving in to pressures to do that. Conflict of interest . . . It's really interesting how universities take a global concept like morality or ethics and really divide it into these little pieces. So somebody does harassment, and somebody does "human subjects," and somebody else does animal subjects, and somebody else does scientific misconduct. But when you are involved in these cases, most of them involve some issues across these divisions.

19

Promoting Academic Integrity in Qualitative Research

KATHLEEN A. KNAFL

Well, I think I found the answer to all this. I was reading through the newspaper a couple of weeks ago, and (because I don't learn by my mistakes—my mistakes being two large dogs) I continue to read through the pet section. And I came across this: "Golden retriever. Bred for integrity, temperament and ability." And I thought, "That's it! If we could breed for integrity and ability, we would have it!" Probably there are people working on it. More seriously, I was trying to do two things in this chapter. The first was to give an introduction to the focus of much of the literature that addresses scientific misconduct and academic integrity from an institutional point of view—which makes it very procedural—and the second was to cover some literature speculating on the reasons for misconduct, such as extreme pressures to produce or misguided self-interest. The purpose was to link academic integrity with the mentoring role, setting the stage for our students to want to do "good stuff," to inspire excellence in our students.

In recent years there has been a growing concern in both the public and the scientific community about fraud and misconduct in science. Although recent concerns about academic integrity and scientific misconduct grew out of a series of highly publicized cases, questions of integrity and misconduct have been raised about individual investigators throughout the history of science (Klotz, 1985). For example, in the 1930s, renowned statistician R. A. Fisher argued that Mendel's results were too good to be true and concluded that Mendel's gardener, who apparently counted the peas, had reported results that conformed to his superior's expectations (Kohn, 1986). Stories of the Piltdown hoax and Blondlot's infamous N-rays are other historical examples of scientific fraud and deception. The Piltdown hoax involved a fabricated archeological find consisting of a human cranium fused with an orangutan's jaw. Found in 1912, the Piltdown Man was regarded as the missing evolutionary link between apes and humans until more sophisticated dating methods proved it to be a forgery. In contrast, Blondlot's discovery of a new kind of radiation, which he named "N-rays," probably was an instance of self-deception (seeing what he wanted to see) that grew out of Blondlot's enthusiasm for what he thought was a significant new discovery (Kohn, 1986). By and large, these early occurrences of misconduct were viewed as individual aberrations that did not threaten the fundamental underpinnings of the scientific enterprise. In contrast to these earlier instances, recent cases of misconduct have raised serious questions about the ability of the scientific community to police itself and have led to the development of federal policies and procedures specifically designed to provide guidelines for dealing with allegations of misconduct.

My intent in this chapter is to provide an overview of key issues and events leading to the development of the federally mandated regulations and then to redirect our attention to the promotion of scientific integrity and responsibility, especially as it relates to the conduct of qualitative research. My own interest in scientific misconduct grows out of my position for the past 2 years as research standards officer (RSO) for the University of Illinois at Chicago. As campus RSO, or "Captain Integrity" as several colleagues now call me, I have become increasingly aware of the complexity of the issues related to scientific misconduct and academic integrity and how little the formal policies and procedures contribute to the clarification of these issues.

The Norms of Science

Discussions of scientific integrity and misconduct direct our attention to the investigator's relationship to the scientific community in general and to her or his immediate colleagues in particular. Although often unstated, several widely accepted norms shape the nature of these relationships. In a discussion of the normative structure of science, Robert Merton (1973), a sociologist, identified universalism, disinterestedness, skepticism, and communalism as the underlying norms of science. *Universalism* means that intellectual criteria, not the attributes of the scientist, should be the basis for judging the merits of scholarly endeavors. *Disinterestedness* directs the scientist to focus on the advancement of science, as opposed to personal gain. *Skepticism* suggests that the acceptance of ideas or results is based on critical evaluation, as opposed to reliance on authority or tradition. *Communalism* calls for the sharing of information to benefit not only the scientific community but also society as a whole. Other authors have identified similar or related norms. Cournand and Zuckerman (1975) mentioned honesty, objectivity, tolerance, doubt of certitude, and unselfish engagement and spoke to the importance of rationality and emotional neutrality. Speaking on the television series *NOVA* in a program entitled "Do Scientists Cheat?" Benjamin Lewin (*NOVA Teacher's Guide,* 1988) summarized the fundamental underpinnings of science, noting:

> Science works on an assumption. The assumption is that everyone is being truthful. It's assumed if somebody says we did an experiment and they show how they did it, what they say is accurate. . . . That's the whole foundation of science. If that foundation is breached, well then you really have nothing left because everything you build upon it is building on sand—it's meaningless. (p. 1)

Similarly, when qualitative researchers claim, as we so often do, that our results "emerged from data," we are implying a systematic, thorough, and communicable process of data generation and analysis.

As Lipson noted (Chapter 18, on ethical issues in ethnography), several disciplines, including nursing, have developed formalized codes of ethics that address, among other things, integrity in the conduct of research. However, despite such codes and the generally accepted importance of underlying scientific norms such as honesty, objectivity, skepticism, and disinterestedness in undergirding the scientific enterprise as a whole, little is known about the way and extent to which these norms guide the behaviors of individual scientists. In part, this paucity stems from the relatively little attention given to explicitly incorporating the teaching of such norms into research training programs. The Panel on Scientific Responsibility and the Conduct of Research (1992) noted: "The basic and particular principles that guide scientific research practices exist primarily in an unwritten code of ethics . . . the principles and traditions of science are, for the most part, conveyed to successive generations of scientists through example, discussion, and informal education" (p. 36). Most graduate research programs are directed to mastering the substantive content and methods of the discipline, and minimal time is devoted to explicating the values and norms underlying the scientific process.

Nature and Extent
of Scientific Misconduct

Violations of the underlying norms and assumptions of science constitute scientific misconduct. The following definition of misconduct was formulated by the Public Health Service (PHS) (U.S. Department of Health and Human Services, 1989) with input from the scientific community and remains the basis for most university policies and procedures regarding scientific misconduct: "Misconduct or misconduct in science means fabrication, falsification, plagiarism, or other practices that seriously deviate from those that are commonly accepted in the scientific community for proposing, conducting, or reporting research. It does not include honest error or honest differences in interpretations or judgments of data" (p. 6). The definition invites differing interpretations because it is frequently difficult to decide what constitutes a serious deviation from generally accepted practice. Some might even argue that all of qualitative research constitutes a serious deviation from how science "should" be conducted! In addition, it can be virtually impossible to distinguish between honest error and deliberate deception.

Because of the ambiguities inherent in the PHS definition of misconduct, the Panel on Scientific Responsibility and the Conduct of Research (hereafter referred to as the Panel), a 22-member committee jointly convened by the National Academy of the Sciences, the National Academy of Engineering, and the Institute of Medicine, argued in favor of distinguishing between scientific misconduct, questionable research practices, and other misconduct. The Panel defined *scientific misconduct* as "fabrication, falsification, or plagiarism in proposing, performing, or reporting research" (p. 27). Unlike the PHS definition, the one proposed by the Panel omitted "other practices that seriously deviate from those that are commonly accepted in the scientific community" as a form of scientific misconduct because panel members found the language highly ambiguous and feared it would set the stage for an "overexpansive interpretation" of misconduct (Panel on Scientific Responsibility and the Conduct of Research, 1992). In particular, the Panel argued that the inclusion of deviant practices as a form of misconduct could stifle creativity by setting the stage for allegations of misconduct to be brought against researchers who used unorthodox research methods. Thus the Panel clearly recognized the potential contribution of innovative methods in advancing science and the danger of confusing innovation with misconduct.

Unlike the PHS guidelines, the Panel (1992) explicitly defined the three types of misconduct identified: "Fabrication is making up data or results, falsification is changing data or results, and plagiarism is using the ideas and/or words of another person without giving appropriate credit" (p. 5). These three behaviors were deemed misconduct because they most seriously undermine the integrity of the research process, which the Panel explicitly defined as "the adherence by scientists and their institutions to honest and verifiable methods in proposing, performing, evaluating, and reporting research activities" (p. 17).

At the same time, the Panel (1992) recognized that other types of behaviors, though not directly undermining the integrity of the research process, can "erode confidence in the integrity of the research process, violate traditions associated with science, affect scientific conclusions, waste time and resources, and weaken the education of new scientists" (p. 28). The Panel termed behaviors such as these "questionable research practices" and gave as examples inadequately supervising research subordinates, using inappropriate statistical techniques to increase the significance of findings, and maintaining inadequate research records. Finally the Panel noted that other forms of misconduct, such as misuse of funds and sexual harassment, may occur in the context of scientific research but are not unique to it. These behaviors they termed "other misconduct." Although all forms of misconduct and questionable research practices need to be addressed and sanctioned, there is considerable merit in clearly distinguishing scientific misconduct from other types of problematic behavior because such distinctions constitute an essential basis for recognizing and addressing scientific misconduct.

Much of the growing body of scholarly literature on scientific misconduct addresses either the extent of such behavior or factors that contribute to its occurrence. On the one hand, most authors (Hawley & Jeffers, 1992; Teich & Frankel, 1992) agreed that it is impossible to know the true prevalence of misconduct because an indeterminate number of cases go unrevealed. On the other hand, both the National Institutes of Health (NIH) and the National Science Foundation (NSF) reported relatively few allegations of misconduct, given the large number of projects these agencies fund (19,000 for the NSF and 25,000 for the NIH in 1990). The NSF received 99 allegations of misconduct between October 1988 and January 1992; the NIH reviewed 192 cases between April 1989 and January 1992 (Teich & Frankel, 1992). Woolf (1988) identified 26 publicly reported cases of scientific misconduct between 1980 and 1987. Despite relatively few confirmed cases, scientific misconduct remains a serious matter that merits the attention of the scientific community. The Panel noted that, in addition to being wrong, scientific misconduct threatens the scientific enterprise by wasting time and resources, leading to injury and harmful consequences, contributing to counterproductive regulation and control, and undermining public support for science (Panel on Scientific Responsibility and the Conduct of Research, 1992, pp. 31-32).

The PHS guidelines for dealing with misconduct were predicated on the assumption that it is a rare, but nonetheless serious, occurrence. These guidelines stated:

> Reported instances of scientific misconduct appear to represent only a small fraction of the total number of research and research training awards funded by PHS. Nevertheless, even such a small number of instances of scientific misconduct is unacceptable and could threaten the continued public confidence in the integrity of the scientific process and in the stewardship of federal funds. (U.S. Department of Health and Human Services, 1989, p. 1)

However, as public awareness of the occurrence of scientific misconduct heightens and procedures for bringing forth allegations of misconduct become more formalized, it is reasonable to expect that the number of reported cases will grow.

Efforts to understand why misconduct occurs and how it might be prevented have focused on the analysis of some of the more widely publicized cases of misconduct, most of which have been related to clinical or basic biomedical research. For example, instances of misconduct such as the one involving John Darsee point to the intense pressures to produce often felt by young scientists and the occasional failure of senior scientists to carry out their mentoring responsibilities (Kohn, 1986). Darsee, who worked at Harvard in the laboratory of a well-established senior scientist, Eugene Braunwald, was discovered fabricating data for the cardiac studies in which he was engaged. Further investigation revealed a long history of such behavior. The panel investigating the case cited the lack of direct supervision by Darsee's mentor in the laboratory as creating an environment in which misconduct was possible (Culliton, 1983). At the same time, Darsee himself attempted to explain his behavior as a function of the extreme pressures under which he was working and the resulting mental fatigue and emotional instability (Kohn, 1986).

Such explanations do not excuse scientific misconduct, but they provide useful insights into the kinds of situations that may spawn such behavior. Explanations for the occurrence of scientific misconduct tend to focus on flaws in the individual scientist or the work environment. In a detailed analysis of 12 cases of misconduct, Bechtel and Pearson (1985) found that most instances of misconduct involved the fabrication of data by individuals who acted alone and engaged in elaborate efforts to hide their behavior. Much attention has focused on situational and organizational factors such as funding and career pressures, poor training, and erosion of the peer review system as contributing to the occurrence of scientific misconduct (Panel on Scientific Responsibility and the Conduct of Research, 1992). In a similar vein, articles exploring the relevance of scientific misconduct for nursing (Chop & Silva, 1991; Hawley & Jeffers, 1992) identified limited guidance and supervision of young scientists and pressures inherent in the tenure and promotion process as creating work environments that may provide opportunities for misconduct.

Mechanisms for Dealing With Misconduct

In addition to highlighting some of the underlying reasons for misconduct, cases such as the one involving John Darsee and others arising in the early 1980s also made evident how ill-prepared most academic institutions were to deal with the problem. As Teich and Frankel (1992) noted: "Because incidents were rare, most institutions did not have formal policies or procedures, and those that had such policies and procedures did not use them often enough to develop any kind of experience base and capacity for handling cases" (p. 10). The situation was highlighted further in 1988 through a series of congressional hearings conducted by Representative John Dingell and the Subcommittee on Oversight and Investigation of the Energy and Commerce Committee, which has jurisdiction over NIH. In 1989, in response to political pressure exerted by Congress, the Department of Health and Human Services established the Office of Scientific Integrity (OSI) within the NIH and the Office of Scientific Integrity Review (OSIR) within the Office of the Assistant Secretary of Health to manage problems of scientific misconduct in federally funded projects. The OSIR was responsible for establishing overall PHS policies and procedures for dealing with misconduct; OSI oversaw the implementation of these policies and procedures. In June 1992, PHS abolished OSI and OSIR and transferred their functions to the newly established Office of Research Integrity (ORI). As of this writing, ORI resides in the Office of the Assistant Secretary for Health and no longer is within the NIH organizationally. As a direct result of federally mandated policies, universities have been forced to develop their own formalized policies and procedures to ensure compliance with federal regulations. The focus of such policies invariably is on scientific misconduct and institutional responsibility for managing allegations of misconduct (Mishkin, 1988). Less attention has been paid to the active promotion of the responsible conduct of research.

Promoting Academic Integrity

Although few would argue with the necessity of having mechanisms in place to deal with misconduct, it is equally, if not more, important to identify strategies for fostering scientific integrity and excellence in research. An editorial in the *Journal of the American Medical Association* supported this view (Rennie & Gusalus, 1993). In it, the authors contended that the scientific community should stop arguing over definitions of scientific misconduct and direct attention to the "task of articulating and defining precisely what constitutes good scientific practices and desirable behavior in specific areas" (p. 917). Teich and Frankel (1992) pointed out that "maintaining the quality and integrity of scientific research is one of the primary responsibilities of scientists. . . . This responsibility makes it incumbent upon the scientific community to find ways to ensure that individual scientists are competent and perform according to high ethical standards" (p. 15). Among the recommendations made by the Panel (1992) regarding the promotion of scientific integrity were the following two, which are especially salient to this discussion of promoting scientific integrity in qualitative research:

1. Individual scientists have a fundamental responsibility to ensure that their results are reproducible, that their research is reported thoroughly enough so that the results are reproducible, and that significant errors are corrected when they are recognized.
2. Research mentors, laboratory directors, department heads, and senior faculty are responsible for defining, explaining, exemplifying, and requiring adherence to the value systems of their institutions. (p. 7)

The Reproducibility of Findings

The first recommendation addresses the importance of generating reproducible findings and reporting the process by which results and conclusions were derived from the data. Most qualitative researchers would argue against the notion of strict reproducibility as a standard for judging qualitative research because this notion contradicts their epistemological stance that the relationship between the researcher and those being studied is interactive and unique and that all data are influenced by contextual, time-bound factors. Given this stance, qualitative researchers might expect two investigators addressing identical questions from identical points of view to produce noncontradictory or complementary findings; they would not expect them to replicate one another's results (Field & Morse, 1985; Lincoln & Guba, 1985; Sandelowski, 1986). At the same time, qualitative researchers recognize the need to address explicitly the nature of the relationship between the investigator and those being studied and to describe how contextual factors may have influenced one's data set and subsequent results and conclusions (Douglas, 1976; Field, 1991; Fine & Sandstrom, 1988; Warren, 1988). Moreover, there has been a long-standing recognition among qualitative researchers of the need to document the process by which results and conclusions have been generated from the data set (Glaser & Strauss, 1967; Guba, 1981; Leininger, 1990; Sandelowski, 1986).

In the light of scientific misconduct concerns related to the fabrication and falsification of data, it is important for investigators to verify that research assistants are collecting data as instructed and that recorded interviews and field notes are being transcribed accurately. Gift, Creasia, and Parker (1991) provided an excellent discussion of integrity issues related to the use of research assistants. Qualitative researchers also should be aware of the need to maintain their original data because "in some cases of alleged misconduct, the inability or unwillingness of an investigator to provide primary data or witnesses to support published reports sometimes has constituted a presumption that the experiments were not conducted as reported" (Panel on Scientific Responsibility and the Conduct of Research, 1992, p. 7).

Despite the importance of retaining primary data, few institutions have formalized guidelines regarding data retention, although one survey indicated that 5 to 10 years was the norm (Thomas, 1992). Scientific integrity issues related to the verification, storage, and retention of data have received little attention by qualitative researchers and merit further discussion.

The Mentoring Relationship

As indicated in the second recommendation cited above, the mentoring relationship remains a primary vehicle for transmitting standards of excellence in research. The focus of this relationship is on the pursuit of academic excellence, not on the avoidance of misconduct. This pursuit directs our attention to specifying the characteristics of both exemplary research and mentoring relationships. Good mentors both communicate and model standards of scientific excellence for their students and in so doing promote the development of scientific integrity in the next generation of researchers.

In *Doing Exemplary Research,* Frost and Stablein (1992) identified themes that characterized the process of doing such studies. The authors presented "the journeys taken on seven different investigations by researchers who were interested in understanding phenomena relevant to organizational life" (p. xi). The book included extensive discussion by the investigator(s) of various aspects of their research (e.g., genesis, process, production of the research outcome, aftermath, reflection), as well as thoughtful appraisals by outside commentators. A panel of experts in organizational research helped identify exemplary studies, and Frost and Stablein (1992) included variation in their exemplars regarding such things as methodology, status and gender of the researcher, single versus multiple authorship, and whether the research unfolded in an orderly or serendipitous manner. Frost and Stablein emphasized, "Our seven articles are not the best seven articles published in the 1980s. . . . They are seven very good articles that may serve as templates or models for other good research" (p. 7).

Characteristics of Exemplary Research. As a result of their analysis of the research processes underlying the seven investigations, Frost and Stablein (1992) identified common themes that characterized the studies. These themes are presented here as useful principles to emphasize and model in our research and mentoring relationships. The themes include persistence, "handling your own rat," the emotional side of research, collaboration, conferences as catalysts, and getting published. Persistence, handling your own rat, and the emotional side of research focus on individual qualities of investigators, whereas the other characteristics address investigators' relationship to the wider scientific community.

The individual quality of *persistence,* as reflected in the exemplary studies, relates to the investigator's willingness to take time to address problems thoughtfully, to pursue unexpected leads, and to rectify flaws in the initial design of the study. *Handling your own rat,* on the other hand, refers to the researcher's immersion in the study, the attention paid to the details of the design, and the finer nuances of meaning of the results. Speaking to the importance of immersion, Frost and Stablein (1992) stated:

> We think that in all these cases, "getting their hands dirty" served to draw the researchers closer to the phenomena they were studying. It served to create as well as stimulate patterns of thinking in the minds of the researchers that in turn may have triggered understandings and insights grounded in deep familiarity with the matter of interest. (p. 249)

Recognition of the intense emotions that characterized the research experiences described in the book points to the importance of understanding the inherently human side of research. Research endeavors as human experiences are characterized by breakthroughs and setbacks, celebrations and disappointments, and an intense sense of commitment to the success of the project. This observation is particularly insightful in view of the previously mentioned norm of disinterestedness, which sometimes is interpreted to mean that researchers should remain emotionally detached from their research. In reality, exemplary researchers care deeply about their work. At the same time, however, they are obliged to guard against becoming so invested in a particular outcome or finding that they manipulate the data to ensure a specific result or misinterpret their data. Accounts by the exemplary researchers demonstrated that feelings are not out of place in science; rather, they can be a source of insight and persistence.

As a social endeavor, research involves a variety of interactions with others, including collaborating directly with co-investigators, networking with colleagues through conferences, and negotiating with journal editors. Analysis of the exemplary studies highlighted the importance of collegial input in generating and shaping research ideas and project designs. These researchers, whose work was judged to be excellent by their peers, actively sought outside input on everything from the conceptual underpinnings of their work to the written clarity of their final reports. They cultivated and took seriously, critical input whether it came from their immediate co-investigators or other colleagues. They used professional conferences as opportunities to discuss new ideas, and most presented their emergent manuscripts at conferences for collegial feedback before submitting them for publication. As such, conferences were seen as an important source of tangible guidance, as well as emotional support.

Interestingly, all of the authors of exemplary research had difficulty getting their work published, and they described the manuscript review process as a negative experience. All were required by journal editors to complete revisions of their work, and some experienced initial rejection of a manuscript. The importance of not being overwhelmed or immobilized by negative feedback and using such feedback to improve the quality of their work was a major theme of investigators' comments about publication. Their experiences indicated that learning to accept and use negative, as well as positive, feedback was an essential skill for both neophyte and established researchers.

Frost and Stablein's (1992) book made visible a dimension of the research process neglected by authors of research texts and articles who typically focused on the philosophical and/or methodological aspects of research, while ignoring the "lived experience" of being a researcher. The analysis of the seven case studies directs our attention to the kinds of human qualities and collegial exchanges that support exemplary research. The authors made evident that even researchers who produced exemplary studies encountered unanticipated setbacks, unexpected results, and unappreciative reviewers and journal editors. They, too, were dependent on critical feedback and supportive encouragement, as well as an occasional bit of good luck, to ensure the success of their studies. They, too, experienced emotional highs and lows during the course of an investigation.

Mentoring and Exemplary Research. As mentors, it is important that we take an active role in developing realistic expectations on the part of students for what the research experience is like. The need to communicate realistic expectations of the research experience seems to be especially important in qualitative research, where students often are unprepared for the intensive time commitment required to collect and analyze qualitative data or lack the conceptual and synthesizing abilities necessary to complete a qualitative analysis.

It is also important that we help students recognize and overcome some of the major barriers to conducting exemplary research. The qualities of persistence and immersion are nurtured by large blocks of uninterrupted time to think about one's design, address methodological problems, pursue serendipitous leads, and ponder the meaning of one's data. Students, like faculty, often have multiple family and professional commitments that hinder their ability to fully immerse themselves in their research. In addition to emphasizing the need for immersion in one's work, mentors can work with students to devise strategies for building large blocks of research time into their busy days. For example, helping students secure fellowship awards or small research grants may make it possible for them to decrease work time. Passing on one's own hard-earned "secrets" about how to hide out for extended time periods from family members and colleagues may give students insights into how to structure their lives to make sufficient room for research. My own students often are surprised that, despite multiple teaching, administrative, and professional obligations, I still insist on disappearing one day a week to pursue strictly scholarly interests. They have learned not to call me on those days! At times, our mentoring role even may include advising a student against doing a qualitative study if we recognize the student will not be able to restructure her or his life to accommodate the rigors and demands of qualitative inquiry.

Mentors also can share with students their own successes and failures and strategies for dealing with negative feedback. It is important for students to know that a good deal of agonizing and revising goes into most of our publications. They need to know that success as a scholar does not mean that scholarship comes easily. Initial reviews of some of my "best work" have been less than flattering, and I make a point of sharing these reviews with students both individually and in classroom settings. Knowing that the editors of major nursing journals have, at various times, described my submissions as "unrelentingly dull," "methodologically flawed," "without substantive import," and "conceptually ambiguous" seems to help students put their own scholarly struggles into perspective, especially when I point out that all of these imperfect manuscripts subsequently were revised, resubmitted, and published. Frost and Stablein (1992) suggested that those of us who teach research design should consider including a written assignment that requires revision of a manuscript on the basis of the instructor's editorial comments. In a doctoral level course, such an assignment could include review comments from fellow students as well.

As mentors we can help our students to distinguish between appropriate and inappropriate feedback and to remember that the peer review process guarantees only the chance of a fair review. The latter is especially important in qualitative research, where reviewers may not apply appropriate evaluative criteria and often fail to understand differences across varying qualitative approaches. At the same time, it is important that qualitative researchers, especially those who have been successful in publishing their work and getting it funded, continue to lobby both journal editors and funding agencies for appropriate reviewers who are knowledgeable of qualitative approaches and methods.

Finally, through advisement and example, mentors can teach students about colleagueship and the essential role played by colleagues in developing a program of research. Ongoing discussions about the student's research serve as "living examples" of the importance of collegial dialogue in shaping one's research ideas and moving them forward. They also serve to reinforce the vigorous, labor-intensive nature of qualitative approaches as both student and mentor become immersed in the processes of data collection and analysis.

Ideally the student's dissertation is not her or his first experience with qualitative data collection and analysis. Through the mentors' own research or that of colleagues, they can provide invaluable hands-on research experiences for their students. Mentors also can put students in touch with other qualitative researchers or substantive experts whose backgrounds and knowledge may contribute to the students' research. In particular, a mentor can work with a student to identify persons with the particular kinds of qualitative expertise needed to guide the research. Mentors can help students to recognize the differences across qualitative approaches and to select research committee members whose expertise supports the particular qualitative approach being used. By providing students with insights into the experience of doing research and the qualities associated with exemplary research, mentors serve a key role in promoting academic integrity; they set the stage for the lifetime pursuit of scholarly excellence.

Qualitative researchers need to be aware of current social and disciplinary issues related to scientific misconduct because, as members of the larger academic community, they are in a position both to shape and be affected by policies and procedures related to these issues.

The intent of this chapter has been to introduce the reader to these issues and to stimulate further dialogue on how they relate to the conduct of qualitative research. In addition, I explored processes underlying exemplary research and characteristics of the mentoring relationship in an effort to stimulate further thinking and discussion on strategies for promoting research integrity. In recent years qualitative researchers have directed considerable attention to developing strategies for increasing their chances of getting their research funded and published. Having achieved considerable success in these arenas, we should, perhaps, now direct our attention and efforts to better understanding and promulgating the values and practices that ensure scientific integrity and research excellence. In particular, we need to continue to articulate standards of integrity and excellence relevant to qualitative research in all of its various forms.

References

Bechtel, H., & Pearson, W. (1985). Deviant scientists and scientific deviance. *Deviant Behavior, 6,* 237-252.

Chop, R., & Silva, M. (1991). Scientific fraud: Definitions, policies, and implications for nursing research. *Journal of Professional Nursing, 7*, 166-171.

Cournand, A., & Zuckerman, H. (1975). The code of science. In P. Weiss (Ed.), *Knowledge in search of understanding: The Frensham papers* (pp. 126-147). Mt. Kisco, NY: Futura.

Culliton, B. J. (1983). Emory reports on Darsee's fraud. *Science, 220*, 936.

Douglas, J. (1976). *Investigative social research.* Beverly Hills, CA: Sage.

Field, P. (1991). Doing fieldwork in your own culture. In J. Morse (Ed.), *Qualitative nursing research: A contemporary dialogue* (rev. ed., pp. 91-104). Newbury Park, CA: Sage.

Field, P., & Morse, J. (1985). *Nursing research: The application of qualitative approaches.* Rockville, MD: Aspen.

Fine, G. A., & Sandstrom, K. L. (1988). *Knowing children: Participant observation with minors.* Newbury Park, CA: Sage.

Frost, P., & Stablein, R. (Eds.). (1992). *Doing exemplary research.* Newbury Park, CA: Sage.

Gift, A., Creasia, J., & Parker, B. (1991). Utilizing research assistants and maintaining research integrity. *Research in Nursing and Health, 14*, 229-233.

Glaser, B., & Strauss, A. (1967). The purpose and credibility of qualitative research. *Nursing Research, 15*, 56-61.

Guba, E. (1981). Criteria for assessing the trustworthiness of naturalistic inquiries. *Educational Communication and Technology Journal, 29*, 75-92.

Hawley, D., & Jeffers, J. (1992). Scientific misconduct as a dilemma for nursing. *Image: Journal of Nursing Scholarship, 24*, 51-55.

Klotz, I. (1985). *Diamond dealers and feather merchants: Tales from the sciences.* Boston: Birkhäuser.

Kohn, A. (1986). *False prophets: Fraud and error in science and medicine.* Cambridge, MA: Blackwell.

Leininger, M. (1990). The philosophic and epistemic bases to explicate transcultural nursing knowledge. *Journal of Transcultural Nursing, 1*, 40-51.

Lincoln, Y., & Guba, E. (1985). *Naturalistic inquiry.* Beverly Hills, CA: Sage.

Merton, R. (1973). The normative structure of science. In N. Storer (Ed.), *The sociology of science: Theoretical and empirical investigations* (pp. 267-278). Chicago: University of Chicago Press.

Mishkin, B. (1988). Responding to scientific misconduct: Due process and prevention. *Journal of the American Medical Association, 260*, 1932-1936.

NOVA Teacher's Guide. (1988). Do scientists cheat? [Teacher's guide for television program #1517, originally broadcast on PBS on October 25, 1988]. Boston: WGBH Educational Foundation.

Panel on Scientific Responsibility and the Conduct of Research. (1992). *Responsible choice: Ensuring the integrity of the research process.* Washington, DC: National Academy Press.

Rennie, D., & Gusalus, K. (1993). Scientific misconduct: New definition, procedures, and office—Perhaps a new leaf. *Journal of the American Medical Association, 269*, 915-917.

Sandelowski, M. (1986). The problem of rigor in qualitative research. *Advances in Nursing Science, 8*(3), 27-37.

Teich, A., & Frankel, M. (1992). *Good science and responsible scientists: Meeting the challenge of fraud and misconduct in science.* Washington, DC: American Association for the Advancement of Science.

Thomas, S. (1992). Storage of research data: Why, how, where? *Nursing Research, 41,* 309-311.

U.S. Department of Health and Human Services. (1989). *Responsibilities of awardee and applicant institutions for dealing with reporting possible misconduct in science* (NIH Guide, 18[30]). Washington, DC: Government Printing Office.

Warren, C. (1988). *Gender issues in field research.* Newbury Park, CA: Sage.

Woolf, P. (1988). Project on scientific fraud and misconduct: Report on Workshop Number One. *Jurimetrics, 29,* 67-95.

Author Index

Aamodt, A., 97, 113, 178, 183, 190, 205, 303, 313
Ablamowicz, H., 151, 153
Adams, R., 204, 205
Adler, P. A., 319, 331
Agar, M. A., 42, 161, 162, 163, 167, 176, 182, 183, 189, 191, 205
Allen, D., see Diekelmann, N.
Allen, L. M., see Stern, P. N.
American Anthropological Association, 335, 353
American Nurses Association, 335, 336, 353
American Sociological Association, 335, 353
Ammom-Gaberson, K. B., 271, 277.
Anderson, G., see Morse, J. M.
Anderson, J., 199, 206
Angus, N. M., 151, 153
Aral, S. O., 72, 90
Armstrong, D., 273, 277
Aronson, N., 53, 61
Asch, J. E., 237, 240
Atkinson, P., 29, 31, 37, 40, 41, 42, 162, 165, 182, 183

Bachman, M., see Magilvy, J.

Bailey, S., see Beldecos, A.
Bailyn, L., 42
Baker, C., 214, 221
Barinaga, M., 349, 353
Barritt, L., 139, 150, 153
Barrows, T., see McKay, S.
Bateson, M. C., 54, 61
Bateson, P. P. G., 254, 258
Bechtel, H., 363, 372
Beck, C. T., 151, 153, 219, 221
Becker, C. S., 151, 153
Becker, M. H., 72, 90
Bedola, M., 277
Beekman, T., see Barritt, L.
Bekoff, M., 254, 258
Beldecos, A., 49, 61
Benedict, R., 179, 183
Benner, P., 151, 153
Bennett, L., see Larossa, R.
Bennett, M. J., 151, 153
Bentley, M., 198, 206
Berger, P. L., 70, 90
Bergum, V., 57, 61, 130, 132
Bernard, H. R., 164, 174, 176, 177, 178, 179, 181, 183, 264, 265, 277
Berscheid, E., see Dion, K.
Bertrand, J., see Irwin, K.

Birdwhistle, R. L., 253, 258
Bishop, A., 118, 122, 132
Bleeker, H., see Barritt, L.
Blumer, H., 73, 90, 215, 222, 353
Blurton Jones, N., 254, 258
Boas, F., 160, 171, 183
Bohay, I., 107, 113
Bohm, D., 15, 16, 20
Boland, D. L., see Sims, S. L.
Bollnow, O., 130, 132
Bolton, N., 139, 143, 148, 149, 153
Borgeson, D. S., see Frenn, M. D.
Boss, P., 301, 310, 313
Bottorff, J. L., 7, 244, 245, 254, 255, 257, 258, 260
Bowman, J. M., 151, 153
Boxer, A. M., 91
Boyle, J., 159, 339
Breault, A. J., 151, 153
Breitmayer, B. J., see Knafl, K. A.
Brice, C. W., 151, 153
Briggs, J., 124, 132
Brink, P., 202, 206
Broadhead, R. S., 67, 71, 78, 84, 86, 88, 90
Brockman, J., 110, 113
Brody, H., 275, 277
Brown, R. H., 48, 51, 57, 61
Bruner, E. M., 37, 42
Bruner, J. S., 50, 54, 61
Bruyn, S., 190, 206
Buchanan, D. R., 74, 81, 90
Bulmer, M., 345, 353
Burch, R., 142, 148, 153
Burns, N., 188, 197, 206
Burnside, I. M., 71, 83, 90
Burton, D., see Sussman, S.
Byerly, E. L., 319, 331

Calvillo, E., see Flaskerud, J.
Cameron, C., 107, 113
Capps, L. L., 202, 204, 206
Carballo, M., see Scrimshaw, S.
Carey, M. A., 6, 225, 228, 237, 239, 240
Carrere, R. A., 151, 153
Cassell, J., 333, 344, 353, 354

Casti, J., 16, 20
Catanzaro, M., 275, 277, 296
Caudill, W., 172, 183
Chapman, L., see Swanson, J.
Charmaz, K., 273, 277
Chaves, D. E., see Hinds, P. S.
Chen, H. T., 91
Chenitz, W. C., 24, 42, 70, 91, 266, 277
Chesla, C., see Benner, P., 153
Chisholm, R., 11, 20
Chop, R., 364, 373
Chrisman, N., 336, 347, 354
Christakis, N., 341, 354
Churchill, S., 152, 153
Cicourel, A. V., 268, 277
Clark, J. A., see Seidel, J. V.
Clark, M., 192, 206
Claspell, E., see Cochran, L.
Clifford, J., 189, 195, 197, 205, 206
Cobb, A. K., see Kirkpatrick, S.
Cochran, L., 49, 61,
Cohen, J. B., see Dorfman, L. E.
Cohen, M. H., 221, 222, 319, 331
Cohen, M. Z., 7, 24, 30, 42, 136, 137, 151, 153
Cohen, R., 286, 296
Colaizzi, P., 304, 313
Cole, M. see Hood, L.
Collins, H., 16, 20
Columbus, P. J., 151, 154
Connolly, M., 151, 154
Cook, T. S., see Reichardt, C. S.
Corbin, J., 42, 212, 213, 220, 21, 222, 267, 277, 274, 278
Corey, L., 72, 91
Council of Nursing and Anthropology, 199, 206
Cournand, A., 359, 373
Cowles, K. V., 354
Crabtree, B. F., see Miller, W. L.
Craft, M. J., see Cohen, M. Z.
Crassweller, J., 199, 202, 206
Creasia, J., see Gift, A.
Crick, F., 16, 20
Cronbach, L. J., 68, 89, 91
Cross, A., 56, 61
Crosse, S., see Lipsey, M. W.

Culliton, B. J., 363, 373
Cypess, S. M., see Hinds, P. S.

Davidson, L., 151, 154
Davis, A. J., 336, 340, 341, 354
Davis, D. L., 166, 176, 183
De Groot, H. A., 103, 113
Denne, J. M., 151, 154
de Oliveira, E., see Ramhoj, P.
Derish, P. A., see Dorfman, L. E.
DeSantis, L., 202, 206, 354
Diamond, J., 3, 7
Diekelmann, N., 150, 151, 154
Diesing, P., 29, 31, 33, 42
Dillard, A., 47, 52, 53, 61
Dion, K., 236, 240
Dorfman, L. E., 83, 91
Douglas, M., 194, 206
Downe-Wamboldt, B., 180, 183, 214, 222
Downs, F., 3, 7
Dreher, M., 6, 202, 206, 281
Drew, N., 151, 154
Dreyfus, H. 146, 154
Drummond, H., 254, 256, 257, 258
Duffy, M. E., 113
Duncan, S. D., 253, 258
Dunkle, J., see Lipsey, M. W.

Eibl-Eibesfeld, I., 253, 254, 255, 259
Eisner, E. W., 48, 62
Ekman, P., 247, 259, 260
Emmons, C., see Joseph, J. G.
Erickson, E., 73, 74, 91
Erickson, F., 247, 249, 252, 253, 259
Estabrooks, C. A., 245, 259

Fabrega, H., 193, 206
Fawcett, J., 215, 222
Fetterman, D. M., 70, 71, 79, 91, 193, 206
Field, P. A., 26, 37, 42, 273, 277, 282, 296, 366, 373
Fine, G. A., 373
Fine, M., see Kidder, L. H.

Finn, J., 107, 113
Fischer, W., see Giorgi, A.
Fisher, J. A., 254, 259
Fiske, D. W., see Duncan, S. D.
Fiske, M., see Merton, R.
Flaskerud, J., 226, 240
Forrest, D., 151, 154
Fourcher, L. A., 254, 259
Fowler, M., 340, 354
Frake, C. O., 193, 206
Frankel, M., see Teich, A.
Freidman, L., see Kingry, R.
Frenn, M. D., 71, 91
Friesen, W. V., see Ekman, P.
Frost, P., 373
Frye, B., 202, 206

Gadamer, H. G., 118, 121, 124, 127, 129, 132, 273, 277
Geertz, C., 32, 42, 47, 48, 62, 188, 192, 193, 194, 204, 206, 207
Gelles, R., see Larossa, R.
Germain, C., 169, 172, 172, 183, 192, 198, 207, 282, 296, 303, 313
Gift, A., 366, 373
Gilbert, S., see Beldecos, A.
Giorgi, A., 126, 132, 139, 150, 154
Glaser, B. G., 33, 42, 69, 70, 91, 114, 197, 207, 212, 212, 213, 216, 220, 221, 222, 240, 265, 277, 366, 373
Glidden, C., 199, 207
Goetz, J. P., 70, 91, 103
Goffman, E., 173, 183, 296
Golander, H., 169, 172, 183
Goodenough, W., 176, 183
Goodman, N., 51, 62
Goodman, R. M., see Steckler, A.
Goodwin, L., 114
Goodwin, W., see Goodwin, L.
Grandstaff, S., 198, 207
Grandstaff, T., see Grandstaff, S.
Green, S. B., see Aral, S. O.
Greenbaum, T., 227, 240
Grimshaw, A. D., 245, 246, 247, 259
Gross, D., 250, 259

Guba, E., 20, 24, 41, 42, 67, 68, 70,
91, 101, 103, 109, 114, 123,
132, 274, 278, 310, 314, 366,
373
Guglietti-Kelly, I., 151, 154
Gusfield, J., 49, 62

Haekel, J., 170, 171, 184
Halliburton, D., 132
Halling, S., 152, 155
Halpern, 24
Ham, J., see Wermuth, L.
Hammersley, M., 40, 42, 181, 184
Hammond, M., 119, 120, 131, 132
Hare, A. P., 49, 62
Harris, B. G., see Sandelowski, M.
Harris, M., 167, 184
Hartman, D. P., 254, 259
Hastie, R., 240
Haugeland, J., see Dreyfus, H.
Hawking, S., 16, 20
Hawley, D., 362, 364, 373
Heidegger, M., 118, 121, 127, 132,
140, 141, 142, 144, 150, 155,
215, 222
Herdt, G., 72, 91
Hill, G., 235, 238, 240
Hinde, R. A., see Bateson, P. P. G
Hinds, P. S., 268, 277
Hitchcock, J. M., 218, 222
Holditch-Davis, D., see Sandelowski,
M.
Hood, L., 253, 259
Hosie, P. 306, 313
Hospers, J., 52, 53, 62
Howard, M. J., see Knafl, K. A.
Howarth, J., see Hammond, M.
Hubbard, R., 52, 62
Huberman, A. M., see Miles, M. B.
Hughes, C. C., 159, 161, 163, 169,
172, 180, 184, 207
Humphreys, L., 345, 350, 354
Hunter, A., 49, 62
Hurtado, E., see Scrimshaw, S., 197,
208
Husserl, E., 118, 119, 120, 127, 132,
137, 138, 142, 155

Hutchinson, S. A., 219, 223, 259,
271, 279, 300, 301, 305, 308,
313
Huttlinger, K., 194, 207, 307, 314

Irwin, J., see Watson, L.
Irwin, K., 226, 240
Iverson, D. C., see Mullen, P. D.

Jamieson, D., see Bekoff, M.
Jeffers, J., see Hawley, D.
Johnson, E., 151, 155
Jones, S. E., 245, 259
Jorgensen, D. L., 244, 259
Joseph, J. G., 72, 90, 91
Judd, C. M., 68, 70, 78, 91
Judson, F. N., see Aral, S. O.

Karshmer, J., 308, 313
Kay, M., 202, 203, 207
Keat, R., see Hammond, M.
Keller, E., 16, 20
Kendll, P., see Merton, R.
Kendon, A., 250, 256, 257, 259
Kepecs, J., 304, 313
Kidder, L. H., 67, 68, 77, 89, 91
Kingry, R., 240, 266
Kirk, J., 275, 278
Kirkpatrick, S., 201, 207
Klotz, I., 358, 373
Knafl, K. A., 7, 271, 275, 276,
278, 357
Koenig, B. A., 57, 62
Kohak, E., 119, 127, 132
Kohn, A., 358, 363, 373
Koller, A., 55, 56, 62
Koltz, I., 358, 373
Kondora, L., 151, 155
Koziey, P. W., see Angus, N. M.
Krall, S., see Lucero, M.
Krauss, B. J., see Siegl, K.
Krieger, S., 47, 49, 52, 53, 55, 56, 62
Krippendorff, K., 214, 222,
Krueger, R., 226, 229, 238, 240
Kvale, S., 142, 155

Lamb, B., 307, 312, 314
Lamb, D., 16, 20, 194, 207
Lambert, W., *see*, Minturn, L.
Landy, D., 40, 42
Langan, T., 140, 146, 148, 155
Langness, L. L., *see* Cohen, R.
Larossa, R., 354
Laughlin, P., 240
LeCompte, M. D., 70, 89, 91, 97,
    103, 114
Lee, H. A., *see* Frenn, M. D.
Leiban, R., 340, 354
Leifer, M., *see* Halling, S.
Leininger, M., 5, 95, 96, 98, 99, 101,
    103, 105, 109, 114, 160, 172,
    184, 198, 207, 282, 296, 366,
    373
Lehner, P. N., 254, 259
Leviton, L. C., *see* Valdiserri, R. O.
Lightman, A., 10, 12, 20
Lincoln, Y., 20, 24, 41, 42, 67, 68,
    70, 91, 96, 101, 103, 105, 107,
    109, 114, 123, 132, 273, 278,
    310, 314, 366, 373
Ling, J., 151, 155
Lipsey, M. W., 92
Lipson, J. G., 7, 172, 184, 202, 207,
    266, 278, 301, 314, 333, 334,
    342, 346, 352, 354, 360
Livingwood, W. C., 71, 91, 93
Llewelyn, J., 140, 141, 143, 155
Lobo, M. L., 264, 278
Lucero., M. 249, 259
Luckmann, T., *see* Berger, P. L.
Luna, L., 107, 114, 202, 207
Lyter, D. W., *see* Valdiserri, R. O.
Lytton, H., 250, 259

Magilvy, J., 198, 207
Malinowski, B., 160, 171, 183
Manners, R., 295, 296
Marcus, G. E., 38, 42
Margenau, H., 51, 62
Marr, J., 151, 155
Martin, E., 49, 62
Martin, P., 254, 259
Marx, L., 60, 62

Maxwell, E. K., 218, 222
May, K. A., 6, 10, 57, 62, 266, 278,
    309, 310, 314
McArt, E. W., 264, 270, 272, 278
McDermott, R., *see* Hood, L.
McDougal, L. W., *see* McArt, E. W.
McFeat, T., 172, 184
McHutchion, E., 260
McKay, S., 247, 259
McLeroy, K. R., *see* Steckler, A.
McMahon, M., *see* Magilvy, J.
Mead, G. H., 215, 222
Mead, M., 294, 296
Medwar, P. B., 253, 260
Meeraneau, L., 11, 20
Meleis, A., 11, 20, 354
Menn, A., *see* Mosher, L. R.
Merleau-Ponty, M., 215, 222
Merton, R., 226, 239, 240, 359, 373
Messick, S., 241
Michalske, S., *see* Watson, L.
Middleton, J., *see* Cohen, R.
Miles, M. B., 273, 278, 328, 331
Miller, M. L., *see* Kirk, J.
Miller, W. L., 271, 278, 319, 331
Mills, C. W., 55, 62
Minnich, E., 16, 20
Minturn, L., 294, 296
Mishler, E. G., 53, 62
Mishkin, B., 365, 373
Moch, S. D., 151, 155
Montgomery, S. B., *see* Joseph, J. G.
Morgan, D., 240
Morgan, G., 55, 62
Morse, J. M., x, xi, 1, 2, 7, 14, 19,23,
    26, 32, 37, 39, 42, 96, 114,
    160, 167, 168, 172, 180, 184,
    188, 198, 203, 207, 218, 252,
    254, 255, 257, 259, 260, 273,
    277, 282, 283, 296, 373
Mosher, L. R., 71, 92
Moxley, P. A., *see* Stern, P. N.
Muecke, M., 7, 202, 203, 204, 207,
    208
Mulcahey, M. J., 151, 155
Mullen, P. D., 68, 69, 73, 76, 89, 92
Munhall, P., 311, 314, 344, 354
Murdaugh, C. L., 71, 92

Muret, C. T., 214, 222
Myerhoff, B., 47, 62

Narroll, R., 295, 296
Natale, J., see Livingwood, W. C.
Nisbet, R., 48, 49, 50, 54, 62
Nobilt, G. W., 194, 208
NOVA Teachers Guide, 359, 373
Nyamathi, A., 241

O'Brien, B., see Morse J. M.
Ogilvy, J., see Schwartz, P.
Oiler, C., 304, 314
Olson, C., 130, 132
Omery, A., 7
Omidian, P., 346, 352, 354
O'Neill, C. A. see Sims, S. L.
Ortiz de Montellano, B., see
    Villarruel, A. M.
Osborne, J. W., see Angus, N. M.,
    151, 155
Ots, T., 151, 155
Outhwaite, W., 124, 125, 133

Paget, M. A., 57, 62
Palmer, R. E., 143, 155
Pandey, U., 351, 355
Panner, M., see Christakis, N.
Parker, B., see Gift, A.
Parse, R., 125, 133
Patton, M. Q., 67, 68, 69, 70, 92,
    278
Pearce, J. C., 50, 62
Pearson, W. see Bechtel, H.
Peat, F., see Briggs, J.
Pelto, G., 206, 290, 296
Pelto, P. J., 290, 296.
Pepler, C., 247, 260
Perkins, D., 15, 18, 20
Peters, J., see Tripp-Reimer, T.
Phenix, P. H., 50, 62
Piantanida, M., see Ammom-Gaber-
    son, K. B.
Pike, K., 176, 184
Polifroni, E. C., see Breault, A. J.

Pollock, C., see Sandelowski, M.
Preiss, J. J., see Adams, R., 205
Price, L., 283, 296
Pyles, S. H., see Stern, P. N.

Radley, A., 151, 155
Ramhoj, P., 300, 307, 314
Ramos, L., see Scrimshaw, S.
Raudonis, B., 308
Ray, M. A., 117, 124, 129, 133, 303,
    304
Read, K. E., 208
Reason, P., 96, 114
Reeb, 203, 208
Reeder, F., 122, 127, 128, 130, 131,
    133, 273, 278
Reichardt, C. S., 92
Reid, J. C., see Whetstone, W. R.
Rennie, D., 365, 373
Rhodes, L. A., 195, 208
Rice, D. L., see Columbus, P. J.
Richards, L., 218, 222
Richards, T., see Richards, L.
Richardson, L., 49, 57, 62
Ricoeur, P., 121, 129, 130, 131, 133,
    273, 278
Ringo, S., 227, 241
Robbins, R. L., see Wermuth, L.
Roberts, J., see McKay, S.
Rose, J. F., 151, 155
Rosenbaum, J., 107, 114, 202, 203,
    208
Rosenblum, L. A., 255, 260
Rowan, J., 96, 114
Ruby, J., see Myerhoff, B.

Sandelowski, M., 42, 49, 60, 62, 151,
    155, 275, 278, 366, 373
Sandstrom, K. L., see Frost, P.
Sanjek, R., 196, 204, 208
Sarnecky, M. T., 71, 92
Sarter, B., see Cohen, M. Z.
Sass, L. A., 150, 156
Sawyer, L., 336, 355
Sayre, R. E., see Duncan, S. D.
Scaife, M., 250, 256, 260

Schatzman, L., 216
Scheff, T. J., 268, 271, 278
Scheflen, A. E., 253, 257, 260
Schensul, J. J., 88, 92
Scherer, K. R., 250, 260
Schmid, G., 92
Schnecky, M. T., 91
Schneider, J. W., 53, 62
Schoepfle, G. M., see Werner, O.
Schultz, P., 11, 20
Schumann, D., see Bentley, M.
Schwartz, P., 111, 114
Scrimshaw, S., 198, 208
Scudder, J., see Bishop, A.
Sechrest, L., 294, 296
Seidel, J. V., 287, 296
Seigl, K., 72, 92
Shaffir, W. B., 319, 331
Shamdsani, P., see Stewart, D.
Shostak, M., 195, 208
Shuler, P., see Nyamathi, A.
Sieber, J., 353, 355
Silva, M., see Chop, R.
Silver, D., see Fabrega, H.
Silverman, D., 40, 42
Simandl, G., see Frenn, M. D.
Sims, S. L., 220, 222
Singe, P., 16, 20
Singer, M., 40, 42
Slater, P. J. B., 260
Smith, C., 151, 156
Smith, H. N., 60, 63
Smith, L., 310, 312, 314
Smith, M. W., see Carey, M. A.
Smith, S. J., 151, 156
Solberg, S., 257, 260
Sontag, S., 62
Sorofman, B., 328, 331
Spence, D., 304, 314
Spiegelberg, H., 119, 133, 137, 139,
    140, 141, 142, 143, 144, 145,
    147, 148, 156
Spindler, G., 190, 192, 208
Spradley, J. P., 38, 42, 167, 168, 176,
    178, 184, 190, 193, 208, 289,
    296, 303, 314
Stablein, R., see Frost, P.
Stapelton, T., 118, 119, 120, 121, 133

Stasiak, D., 107, 115
Stebbins, R. A., see Shaffir, W. B.
Steckler, A., 92
Stern, P. N., 7, 180, 184, 212, 214,
    221, 222
Stewart, D., 226, 241
Stiles, W. B., 214, 222
Straus, W., see Bentley, M.
Strauss, A. L., 24, 42, 69, 70, 91, 114,
    197, 207, 213, 220, 221, 222,
    240, 265, 277, 274, 278, 373
Street, A. F., 208
Sturtevant, W., 176, 184
Sussman, S., 235, 241
Swanson, J., 6, 24, 42, 66, 70, 71,72,
    84, 91, 92, 93, 278, 347
Swenson, M. M., 88, 93
Szent-Gyorgyi, A., 1, 3, 7

Tanner, C., see Benner, P.
Teich, A., 362, 365, 364, 374
Tesch, R., 164, 180, 182, 184, 266,
    273, 278
Thomas, S., 367, 374
Thompson, J., 124, 129, 130, 133,
    202, 208
Thompson, N. L., see Denne, J. M.
Thorne, S. E., 7, 168, 172, 184, 263,
    268, 278
Tiedje, L., see Kingry, R.
Tien, S. S., 150, 156
Tinbergen, N., 254, 260
Titler, M., see Cohen, M. Z.
Tomm, K., 305, 309, 310, 314
Tripp-Reimer, T., 24, 30, 42, 283,
    296, 303, 314, 318, 320, 323,
    328, 331
Tuana, N., 62
Turnbull, C., 192, 208
Turner, V., 194, 208

Valdiserri, R. O., 72, 93
vanKaam, A., 314
van Maanen, J., 47, 57, 62
van Manen, M., 36, 42, 122, 123,
    127, 131, 133, 139, 150, 156

Villarruel, A. M., 174, 184
Von Eckartsberg, R., *see* Giorgi, A.

Walster, E., *see* Dion, K.
Warren, C., 374
Washburn, W. E., 340, 355
Wasserheit, J. N., *see* Aral, S. O.
Waterman, J., *see* Tripp-Reimer, T.
Watson, J., 16, 20, 125, 133
Watson, L., 312, 314
Wax, M., 355
Weber, R. P., 214, 223
Weeks, M., *see* Schensul, J. J.
Wegner, A. F., 107, 115
Weiss, C. H., 68, 77, 86, 88, 93
Weiss, S. J., 245, 260
Wermuth, L., 93
Werner, O., 38, 42, 97, 115, 160,
    161, 165, 167, 170, 171, 172,
    173, 174, 175, 176, 185, 188,
    192, 193, 196, 197, 208, 209,
    277
Westcott, M. R., *see* Guglietti-Kelly, I.
Whetstone, W. R., 151, 156
White, B. F., 172, 185

Whiting, B., 294, 296
Whiting, J., *see* Whiting, B.
Williams, H., 202, 209
Wilson, H. S., 71, 93, 179, 185, 216,
    219, 222, 223, 259, 273, 278,
    301, 355
Wolcott, H. F., 57, 60, 62, 169, 172,
    185, 193, 209, 254, 260, 300,
    305
Wolf, M., 195, 204, 209
Wolf, Z., 303, 314
Wood, D. D., *see* Hartman, D. P.
Woodhouse, L. D., 71, 91, 93
Woods, N. F., 264, 270, 272, 279
Woolf, P., 362, 374
Wrubel, J., *see* Benner, P.
Wuest, J., 214, 221

Yarborough, A. E., *see* Jones, S. E.
Yonge, O., *see* Morse, J. M.

Zimmerman, M., 142, 147, 156
Zinberg, N., 302, 305, 308, 314
Zuckerman, H., 373

Subject Index

Abstract knowing, 20
Abstract knowledge, 11, 13
Academic integrity, 365
Anthropologic ethnography, 189-191
Art:
    distinguished from science, 53-54
    of inquiry, 52-54
Atheoretical research, 19
Audit trail, 24
Authorship, burdens of, 57-58

Bill of rights, 338
Bracketing, 59, 128, 134-135

Classical ethnography, 171, 191-192
Coding, 29
    narrative, 327-328
Cognitive processes, in data analysis,
    25, 26
Collaboration:
    data analysis, 328
    data management, 325
    methodological issues:
        data collection, 322
        field entry, 321-322
        interviewer training, 323-324

    membership roles, 321
    project design, 320-321
    models of, 319-320
    publication issues, 328-329
Compential analysis, 178
Comprehending, 25, 26, 35
    coding, 29
Concepts, 2
Conceptual basis of methods, 35
Confidentiality, 311-312
    in focus groups, 228
Confirmability, 105
Content analysis, 179-180
Covert research. See Deception
Creativity, 13, 16, 218
Credibility, 105
    in secondary analysis, 274-275
    phenomenology, 130-131
Criteria, qualitative, 96-98, 104-107
Critical ethnography, 194-195
Cross-sectional ethnography, 173
Cultural relativism, 340
Cultural theme, 178
Culture, 160

Data analysis:
    cognitive processes, 25

comprehending, 25, 26, 35
ethnography, 37
ethnoscience, 38
inadequate plans for, 287-288
in grounded theory, 39
in phenomenology, 36, 129
interaction with, 273-274
recontextualizing, 25, 34
sifting, 31
synthesizing, 25, 30-32, 35
theorizing, 25, 32-34, 35
Deception, 345-348
Decontextualizing, 31, 182
Deduction, 290

Eidetic reduction, 139
Emic, 158, 166-167, 213, 290
Epistemology, 137-138
Epoche. *See* Phenomenology reduction
Ethical decisions, in interviews, 307-308
Ethical issues:
   culture and ethics, 339-342
   deception, 345, 348
   ethical relativism, 340
   guidelines, 334-336
   informed consent, 343-345
   institutional review boards, 336-339
   principles for research, 336-337
   reciprocity, 350-353
   risks to informants, 348-350
   subjects *Bill of Rights,* 338
Ethnographic analysis, 174-176
Ethnographic evaluation, criteria for, 196-197
Ethnographic text, 180-182
Ethnography:
   analysis, 174-176
   classical ethnography, 171, 191-192
   classification of, 169-170
   critical ethnography, 194-195
   cross-sectional ethnography, 173
   culture, 160
   data analysis in, 37

defined, 161
distinguishing characteristics, 161-165
ethics and culture, 339-342
ethnohistorical ethnography, 173
fieldwork, 162
holistic ethnography, 171
in health sciences, 197-200
   evaluated, 201-204
interpretive ethnography, 193-194
origin, 159-160
participant observation, 162
particularistic ethnography, 171-172
processual, 170-171
product, 167-169
reflexivity, 165-166, 194
systematic, 192-193
thick description, 188, 193, 196
Ethnogram, 254
Ethnohistorical ethnography, 173-174
Ethnoscience, 176
   data analysis in, 38
Ethology, 253
Etic, 158, 166-167, 290
Evaluation, qualitative criteria, 96-98
Evaluation research:
   analysis, 82-83
   assumptions, 73-74
   design, 77-82
   fourth generation evaluation, 70
   funding, 78
   goals, 81-82
   practice, 68-69
   problems, 67-68
   qualitative and quantitative, 75-77
   randomization, 78
   theoretical issues, 73-77
Exemplary research, 367-368
   mentoring in, 370-372
Experience, in qualitative inquiry, 18

Fieldwork, 162, 316-317
Focused ethnography, 188, 198-199
Focus groups:
   advantages over interviewing, 224
   analysis, 232-234

censoring, 236-237
confidentiality, 228
conformity, 236-237
group leader, 230
limitations, 238-240
participation, 238
pitfalls, 236-237
preparation for, 228-231
purpose, 227
recording, 230
selection of participants, 229
session structure, 227
technique, 226-234
Frameworks, methodological, 215-216
Funding, Evaluation research, 78

Gloserian grounded theory, 212-213, 219-221
Grounded theory, 39
schools of, 212-213
Straussian grounded theory 212-213, 219-221
writing, 217-218

Health science ethnographies, evaluated 201-204
Hermeneutic ethnography, 188
Hermeneutic-phenomenology, 120-122
Hermeneutics, Heideggeman, 145-147
Holistic ethnography, 171

Icon, 29
Index, 29
Inductive, 290
Informed consent, 343-345
violating, 25
Insight, 3, 218
reflective, 124
Intentionality, 139
Interpretation, in phenomenology, 134
Interpretive ethnography, 193-194
Interpretive methods, 213-214

Interventions, 298-299
Interviewing versus focus groups, 224
Interview process:
anonymity and confidentiality, 311-312
bracketing, 59, 128
questions, nature of, 309-310
self-dialogue, 309-310
sensitivity, 310
Interviews, therapeutic. See Therapeutic interviews
Intuiting, 138
Intuition, 3, 13

Knowing, 11
Knowledge:
abstract, 11
as a product, 14

Life-world, 139
Literature, use of, 29

Magic, in science, 15, 218
Meaning-in-context, 105
Mentoring, 218-219, 262, 367-372
minus, 216-217
Methodological framework, 215-266
Methods:
modifying, 219
muddling, 101-103, 214-215

Neutrality, 312
Nursing research:
concepts, 2
theoretical foundation, 2

Ontological phenomenology, 140-141
Ontology, 137

Paradigm:
qualitative, 101

quantitative, 101
Participant observation, 162, 242
Partularistic ethnography, 171-172
Pattern acquisition, 19
Patterning, recurrent, 105
Perspective, 110
Phenomenology:
  credibility, 130-131
  data analysis in, 36, 129
  defined, 118
  eidetic, 137-140, 147
  examples, 150-152
  good, 116
  hermeneutics, 120
  intentionality, 139
  intuiting, 138
  life-world, 139
  methodologic concerns, 126
  ontological, 140-141
  philosophic concerns, 123
  presencing, 142-143
  reduction, 138, 148
  research questions, 128
  schools of, 149-150
  temporality, 144
  theoretic concerns, 123-126
Poststructuralism, 302
Processual ethnography, 170-171
Proposal:
  problems:
    excessive use of verbal reports,
      290-293
    inadequate analysis plans, 287-
      288
    inadequate description, 289
    inadequate justification, 293-
      294
    inappropriate triangulation, 284-
      285
  writing, 45

Qualitative criteria:
  principles, 101
  six central, 104-107
Qualitative ethology, 254
Qualitative paradigm, 101
  inappropriate use, 284-287

Qualitative research:
  art of, 52-54
  atheoretical, 19
  "doing," 4
  experience, 18
  generalizability, 24
  learning, 8
  outcomes, 1-2
  soundness of, 4
  stigma about, 3
Quantitative paradigm, 100, 101

Randomization:
  evaluation research, 78
  inappropriate use of, 285
Rapport, 307-308
Readership, burdens of, 58
Reciprocity, 350-353
Recontextualizing, 25, 35, 182
Reflexivity, 165-166, 194, 307
Reliability and validity issues, 5
  in interpretative research, 286
  in interviews, 312
Reporting research, 275-276
Reproducibility of results, 366-367
Research interviews. See also Interview process
  defined, 301-302
  dissimilarities, 302-305
  ethical decisions, 307-308
  interview agendas in, 305-306
  rapport, 308
  reflexivity in, 307-308
  theoretical models, 303-304

Saturation, 59, 105, 285
Science:
  assumption, 359
  norms, 359-360
Scientific misconduct, 360-364
  mechanisms, 364-365
Secondary analysis:
  analytic expansion, 266
  amplified sampling, 267
  armchair induction, 266
  credibility, 274-275

cross validation, 267
fit of data sets, 270-272
hazards in, 267-269
implications, 272
interaction with data, 273-274
issues, 269-270
reporting, 275-276
retrospective interpretation, 266
Sifting, 31
Sloppiness, methodologic, 15
Straussian grounded theory, 212-213,
    219-221
Symbol, 29
Symbolic interactionism, 215-216
Synthesizing, 25, 30-32, 35
Systematic ethnography, 188, 192-
    193

Temporality, 144
Theme, cultural, 178
Theoretical base, of nursing, 2
Theorizing, 25, 32-34, 35
Theory construction, 24

Therapeutic interviews. *See also* In-
    terview process:
defined, 301-302
dissimilarities, 302-305
ethical decisions, 307-308
interview agendas in, 305-306
theoretical models, 304-305
rapport, 308
reflexivity in, 307-308
Therapeutic relationships, 298
Thick description, 188, 193, 196
Tracking procedures, 325
Transferability, 106
Triangulation, 289

Verbal reports, excessive use of, 290-
    293
Videotaped recording:
advantages, 245-247
data analysis, 253-258
ethical considerations, 252-253
limitations, 247-248
optimal data, 248-252

About the Authors

Joan L. Bottorff, RN, PhD, is an Associate Professor at the School of Nursing, University of British Columbia, Vancouver, Canada. A graduate of the College-St. Jean-Edmonton General Hospital School of Nursing, she holds a BEd and MEd from the University of Saskatchewan, Saskatoon, and a BScN, MN, and PhD in Nursing from the University of Alberta, Edmonton. Her research focuses on nurse-patient interaction, using ethological methods, and the evaluation of models of health promotion.

Joyceen S. Boyle, RN, PhD, is Chair of the Department of Community Nursing at the Medical College of Georgia, Augusta. A graduate of Brigham Young University, she holds a master's degree in public health nursing from the University of California, Berkeley, and a PhD in nursing from the University of Utah, Salt Lake City. As a certified transcultural nurse, she has published numerous articles on culture, health, and nursing care. She is co-editor of the text *Transcultural Concepts in Nursing Care.* Her clinical and teaching experiences include community health nursing with diverse cultures, women's health, and qualitative research. She has completed numerous field studies in Guatemala, the People's Republic of China, and in Appalachia in the United States. Her interests are women's health and health promotion in high-risk populations.

Martha Ann Carey, RN, PhD, is a Nurse Consultant for the National Center for Nursing Research at the National Institutes of Health, Bethesda, Maryland. She received her BS in nursing from Loyola University, Chicago, and her PhD in social psychology from the Graduate Center of the City University of New York. She serves on the Board of Directors of the American Evaluation Association and is a reviewer for several journals. Her current research involves personality, neuropsychology performance, and cognition in HIV patients.

Linda Chapman, RN, DNSc, is Associate Professor and MSN Program Graduate Coordinator, Samuel Merritt College, Department of Nursing, Oakland, California. She received her BSN from the University of Utah, Salt Lake City, and her MSN and DNSc from the University of California, San Francisco. She has published articles in her research area of expectant fathers' roles during labor and birth. Her special interest is gender differences in health care experiences and the contribution of qualitative research to understanding that phenomenon.

Marlene Zichi Cohen, RN, PhD, is Assistant Professor and Director, Office of Nursing Research, University of Southern California, Department of Nursing, and Kenneth Norris Jr. Comprehensive Cancer Center, Los Angeles. She obtained her MS in psychiatric-mental health nursing and her PhD in clinical nursing research from the University of Michigan, Ann Arbor. Her research, which uses predominantly phenomenological methods, focuses on the emotional needs of the physically ill and understanding how nurses can provide better care to these persons.

Melanie Dreher, RN, PhD, FAAN, is Dean and Professor of Nursing, University of Massachusetts School of Nursing, Amherst. As a nurse and an anthropologist, her research has focused on women and children in Caribbean cultures and on the developmental, social, and behavioral consequences of substance use, cross-culturally. She also has written extensively on public health nursing delivery models and on research methods. Currently she is conducting an ethnographic study of Jamaican women who use crack/cocaine and the effects on their children.

Sally Hutchinson, RN, PhD, FAAN, is a Professor at the University of Florida, College of Nursing, Gainesville. She teaches master's and doctoral students courses in research methods and is faculty preceptor for psychiatric nursing students. Her research interests lie in diverse areas: nurses and their work, bipolar disorders, and Alzheimer's dementia patients. She is on the editorial boards of *Image: Journal of Nursing Scholarship, Nursing Research, Qualitative Health Research, Western Journal of Nursing Research,* and *Advances in Nursing Science.* She co-authored the book *Applying Nursing Research: A Resource Book* (with Holly Wilson) and has written numerous chapters in books and articles in research journals. She has been a co-leader of Professional Seminar Consultants trips to China, East Africa, Australia/New Zealand, and Scandinavia and has been a research consultant in Brazil.

Kathleen A. Knafl, PhD, is a Professor in the Department of Psychiatric Nursing and Associate Dean for Research in the College of Nursing, University of Illinois, Chicago. Her research focuses on how the family responds to a child's health care problems. She has been interested particularly in issues and strategies associated with triangulation and conceptualizing the family as a unit of analysis and has published extensively. Her experiences as research standards officer for her campus stimulated her interest in exploring issues of scientific integrity and misconduct germane to qualitative research endeavors.

Madeleine Leininger, RN, CTN, PhD, LHD, DS, FAAN, is Professor of Nursing and Anthropology, Colleges of Nursing and Liberal Arts, Wayne State University, Detroit. She is the founder and a leader in transcultural nursing and human care. She developed the theory of culture care and also the ethnonursing research method as the first method specific to advance nursing science. She was an early and persistent leader in the use of qualitative research, beginning with her ethnonursing and ethnographic field study with the Gadsups of Papua, New Guinea. She is the author and editor of 26 books and of 100 published articles and has given more than 500 keynote addresses worldwide. She is known internationally as a theorist, researcher, educator, administrator, consultant, clinician, and change facilitator.

Juliene G. Lipson, RN, PhD, FAAN, is Associate Professor in the Department of Mental Health, Community and Administrative Nursing, and on the Medical Anthropology Program faculty at the University of California, San Francisco. A nurse-anthropologist, she coordinates the international/cross-cultural master's specialty in nursing and co-directs the Mid-East S.I.H.A. Project, a health resource center for Middle Eastern immigrants. She authored *Jews for Jesus: An Anthropological Study,* co-authored *Self-Care Nursing: Theory and Practice* (with Nancy Steiger), and has written numerous journal articles and book chapters. Although she has collaborated with Afaf Meleis on a cross-sectional qualitative/quantitative study of immigration, ethnic identity, and health in five groups of Middle Eastern immigrants, most of her work has been ethnographic in style. She has studied birth-related women's self-help/support groups and the health and adjustment of Iranian immigrants and Afghan refugees.

Katharyn A. May, RN, DNSc, FAAN, is Professor and Associate Dean for Research, School of Nursing, Vanderbilt University, Nashville. She received her doctorate in nursing science from the University of California, San Francisco. She serves as Associate Editor of *Qualitative Health Research* and is on the editorial boards of *Health Care for Women International* and *Journal of Perinatal and Neonatal Nursing.* She has published extensively in the areas of expectant and new fatherhood, the impact of high-risk pregnancy on families, and nursing research methods. Her co-authored maternity nursing texts have twice received the American Journal of Nursing Book of the Year Award.

Janice M. Morse, RN, PhD, is Professor of Nursing and Behavioral Science, School of Nursing, College of Health and Human Development, at the Pennsylvania State University, University Park. With doctorates in both nursing and anthropology, she conducts research into patient care—in particular, patient comfort, patient falls, and patient restraints and into women's health issues, such as menarche, childbirth, and breast-feeding, and cross-cultural health. She has published more than 100 articles, has authored and co-authored several books, including *Qualitative Nursing Research: A Contemporary Dialogue, The Illness Experience: Dimensions of Suffering* (with Joy Johnson), and is the editor of the international multidisciplinary journal *Qualitative Health Research.*

Marjorie A. Muecke, RN, PhD, FAAN, is a program officer at the Ford Foundation, New York, on leave from her position as Professor of Nursing, and Adjunct Professor in the Department of Anthropology and the Department of Health Services at the University of Washington, Seattle. She received a BA in German literature from Mount Holyoke College, South Hadley, Massachusetts; a diploma from the post-bachelor of arts Coordinated Program, Radcliffe College-Massachusetts General Hospital School of Nursing; an MA in child psychiatric nursing from New York University; and an MA and PhD in cultural anthropology from the University of Washington. Her research is based primarily in Thailand and involves a longitudinal study of nonclinical families and the sociocultural construction of gender and health. In the United States her research focuses on resettled refugees. Recently she has consulted to the World Health Organization in community health nursing in Indonesia and to the Ford Foundation in developing applied research in AIDS prevention and women's rights in Thailand.

Anna Omery, RN, DNSc, is currently the Senior Research Coordinator and Clinical Nurse Specialist with the UCLA Liver Transplant Program. She obtained an MS in medical-surgical nursing and a DNSc from Boston University. Her research program includes studies on cardiac output, pain and ethics, and moral reasoning. She has a long-standing interest and expertise in philosophy of science and development of qualitative methods.

Jennifer Peters, RN, MSN, is a doctoral candidate in gerontological nursing at The University of Iowa, Iowa City. Her fields of interest are health promotion and disease prevention in older adults. As a doctoral student, she has collaborated with several research teams, most recently the Health Heritage Study team.

Marilyn A. Ray, RN, PhD, CTN, CNAA, holds the Christine E. Lynn Eminent Scholar Chair in Nursing at Florida Atlantic University, Boca Raton. A graduate of a hospital diploma program in Hamilton, Canada, she holds a BSN and MS degrees from the

University of Colorado School of Nursing. She has an MA in cultural anthropology from McMaster University, Hamilton, Canada, and a PhD in nursing from the University of Utah, Salt Lake City. As a certified transcultural nurse and a certified nursing administrative consultant, she has completed research on caring in organizational cultures. She has an interest in qualitative research methods, with a special focus in the human sciences and phenomenologic/hermeneutic and caring methods inquiry. She teaches transcultural nursing, nursing administration, and advanced qualitative research methods. Her publications reflect interests in organizational culture, caring, ethics, and phenomenologic and caring methods. Her current research focuses on ethical caring in complex cultural organizations using the methodologic process of caring inquiry that has been published in *Caring: The Compassionate Healer*. She is developing and writing new methodologies related to caring inquiry.

Margarete Sandelowski, PhD, RN, FAAN, is Professor in the Department of Women's and Children's Health, School of Nursing, University of North Carolina, Chapel Hill. Her doctoral degree is in American studies, with an emphasis on women's studies, from Case Western Reserve University, Cleveland. She has published many papers in nursing and social science journals and anthologies in the areas of reproductive technology, infertility, and qualitative methodology. She is also the author of three books including, most recently, *With Child in Mind: Studies of the Personal Encounter With Infertility.*

Bernard Sorofman, PhD, is Associate Professor in the College of Pharmacy at The University of Iowa, Iowa City. His doctoral degree is in social and administrative pharmacy. He has participated in several collaborative research teams with scholars in nursing, one continuously since 1984. His research focuses on lay health care and the use of medications.

Phyllis Noerager Stern, DNS, FAAN, is Professor and Chair of the Department of Parent-Child Nursing, Indiana University School of Nursing. She received her advanced degree at the University of California, San Francisco. She is well known for her early (1980) description of the grounded theory method for nursing audiences. She has written articles and book chapters detailing the method. She edited *Women, Health, and Culture; Pregnancy and Parenting; Lesbian Health: What Are the Issues?* and numerous articles describing her research studies on women's health and culture, family survival strategies in crisis situations, including stepfather families and survivors of home fire, and how women do their work. She is editor of the journal *Health Care for Women International* and co-founder and chief executive officer of the International Council on Women's Health Issues.

Janice M. Swanson, RN, PhD, is Director of Clinical Nursing Research, Summit Medical Center, and Professor at Samuel Merritt College, Department of Nursing, Oakland, California. She received her BSN from Wayne State University, Detroit; her MS and PhD from the University of Maryland; and completed a postdoctoral research fellowship at the University of California, San Francisco, in medical sociology and nursing. She has co-edited the books *Men's Reproductive Health* (with Katherine Forrest), *From Practice to Grounded Theory: Qualitative Research in Nursing* (with W. Carole Chenitz), and *Community Health Nursing: Promoting the Health of Aggregates* (with Mary Albrecht). She is a member of the editorial board of *Health and Social Care in the Community* and *Image* and also serves as reviewer for the *Journal of Professional Nursing, Public Health Nursing,* and *Qualitative Health Research.* She has published articles in her research area of community aspects of reproductive health. Her current project, funded by the National Center for Nursing Research, describes the process (qualitative evaluation) and tests the outcomes (quantitative evaluation) of an intervention carried out by nurses in the community to prevent HIV infection in young adults with genital herpes. She serves as a member of the Nursing Research Study Section, Division of Research Grants, National Institutes of Health.

Sally Thorne, RN, PhD, is Associate Professor of Nursing at the University of British Columbia School of Nursing, Vancouver, Canada. Her research in the fields of chronic illness experience and health care relationships has provided her with opportunities to challenge existing qualitative approaches and to optimize the use of the research findings. Her recent book *Negotiating Health Care: The Social Context of Chronic Illness* is illustrative of her interest in making the knowledge constructed through qualitative inquiry accessible to a broad audience, ranging from health care consumers and professionals to health policy makers.

Toni Tripp-Reimer, RN, PhD, FAAN, is Professor and Director of the Office for Nursing Research Development and Utilization, The University of Iowa College of Nursing. She received her MS in nursing and MA and PhD in anthropology from The Ohio State University, Columbus. She has conducted qualitative health research since 1976. Her primary area of research focuses on ethnogerontological nursing. She has authored more than 60 articles, chapters, and books.

James E. Waterman, RN, MSN, is a doctoral student in gerontological nursing at the University of Iowa, Iowa City. His area of interest concerns social support and hospitalized elderly. He has participated in qualitative data analysis on the Health Heritage Project, as well as with a study of Alzheimer's special care units.

Holly Wilson, RN, PhD, FAAN, is a Professor in the Department of Mental Health, Community and Administrative Nursing, the University of California, San Francisco. Her active research and teaching focus is on psychogerontology and decision making with elderly patients who have Alzheimer's dementia. She has published more than 60 scientific and scholarly articles in the professional literature and is the author and co-author of 15 books, foremost among them are her award-winning psychiatric nursing text and her research in nursing text. She is a national and international speaker and consultant and has presented papers and served as visiting lecturer in Japan, the Philippines, the People's Republic of China, Hong Kong, Kenya, Israel, Argentina, New Zealand, Canada, Sweden, Norway, Denmark, as well as throughout the United States.

the evolution of mara dyer

ALSO BY MICHELLE HODKIN

the unbecoming of mara dyer